THE ROLE OF THE ECONOMIST IN GOVERNMENT

THE ROLE OF THE ECONOMIST IN GOVERNMENT

An International Perspective

Edited by
Joseph A. Pechman
The Brookings Institution

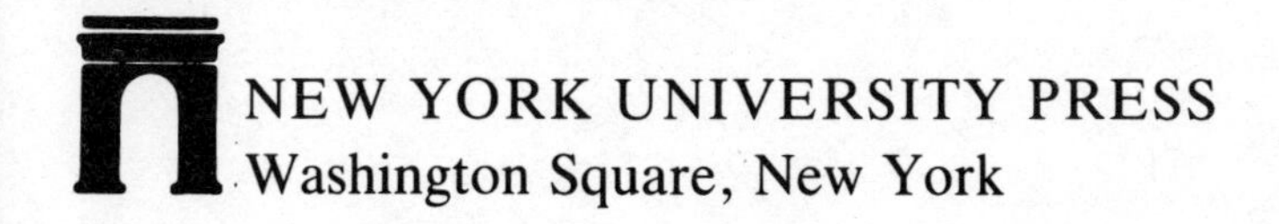

Manufactured in Great Britain

First published in the U.S.A. in 1989 by
NEW YORK UNIVERSITY PRESS
Washington Square
New York, NY 10003

Library of Congress Cataloging-in-Publication Data

The Role of the economist in government: an international perspective
/edited by Joseph A. Pechman.
p. cm.
Includes bibliographies and index.
ISBN 0-8147-6611-0
1. Economic policy. 2. Administrative agencies. 3. Government economists. 4. Comparative economics. I. Pechman, Joseph A., 1916–
HD75.R65 1989
338.9—dc20 89-34199
CIP

CONTENTS

The contributors vii
Preface ix
Joseph A. Pechman

1. Introduction and summary 1
Robert H. Nelson

Europe 23

2. The United Kingdom 25
Alec Cairncross

3. West Germany 47
Norbert Kloten

4. France 73
Michel Albert

5. Austria 89
Hans Seidel

North America 107

6. The United States 109
Joseph A. Pechman

7. Canada 125
Ian Stewart

8. Mexico 147
David Ibarra and José-Luis Alberro

The Far East 171

9. Japan 173
Saburo Okita

South America 193

10. Argentina 195
José Maria Dagnino Pastore

11. Colombia 213
Lauchlin Currie

International organizations 229

12. The International Monetary Fund and the World Bank 231
Richard Goode and Andrew M. Kamarck

13. The Organization for Economic Cooperation and Development 255
J. C. R. Dow

14. The European Economic Community 279
Manfred Wegner

15. The General Agreement on Tariffs and Trade 301
William B. Kelly

Index 319

THE CONTRIBUTORS

José-Luis Alberro is professor of economics, El Colegio de Mexico.

Michel Albert is chairman of Assurance Generales de France and formerly Commissaire du Plan of the French government.

Alec Cairncross was formerly economic adviser to the British government, head of the British Government Economic Service, and master of St Peter's College, Oxford.

Lauchlin Currie was formerly assistant to the President of the United States and later economic adviser to the Government of Colombia.

J. C. R. Dow is visiting fellow at the National Institute of Economic and Social Research in London and formerly Assistant Secretary General, Organization of Economic Cooperation and Development, in charge of the Department of Economics and Statistics.

Richard Goode was formerly director of the Fiscal Affairs Department of the International Monetary Fund and senior fellow at the Brookings Institution.

David Ibarra was formerly Secretary of the Treasury and Director General of the Central Bank of Mexico.

Andrew M. Kamarck was formerly director of the Economics Department and of the Economic Development Institute of the World Bank.

William B. Kelly was formerly deputy director-general of the General Agreement on Tariffs and Trade and Associate US Trade Representative, Executive Office of the President of the United States.

Norbert Kloten is a member of the board of the German Federal Bank (President of the Land Central Bank of Baden–Württemberg) and was formerly chairman of the Council of Economic Experts of West Germany.

Robert H. Nelson is a senior staff member of the Economics Advisory Group, Office of Policy Analysis, the US Department of the Interior.

Saburo Okita is chairman of the Institute for Domestic and International Policy Studies and formerly Director General of the Planning Bureau, Economic Planning Agency, and Minister of Foreign Affairs of Japan.

José Maria Dagnino Pastore is a director of the Institute for International Economics and formerly Minister of Economics of Argentina.

Joseph A. Pechman is senior fellow emeritus and formerly director of economic studies at the Brookings Institution.

Hans Seidel is a director of the Institute for Advanced Studies and formerly a member of the Council of Social and Economic Affairs of Austria.

Ian Stewart is Skelton-Clark Fellow in political studies at Queen's University and formerly Deputy Minister of Finance of Canada.

Manfred Wegner is director of the Institute for Economic Research in Munich and formerly head of the economics department of the Commission of the European Community.

PREFACE

Economists have become influential throughout the world since World War II. This is partly because their ideas and policy prescriptions have become more relevant to real-world problems and partly because governments have assumed a larger role in their economies to promote economic growth and stability and to manage the welfare state. Economists have also greatly improved their techniques of analysis and their ability to process large masses of economic data. With the growth in the complexity of economic problems and the development of powerful tools of analysis, economists have come into their own as diagnosticians, advisers and advocates on a wide range of economic affairs.

The enhanced role of the economist dates from the time when John Maynard Keynes liberated economics from the doctrine that equilibrium at full employment is the natural state of the economy. It is now generally agreed that full employment is not preordained and that governments can and should intervene – through fiscal and monetary policies – to prevent large-scale unemployment, to contain inflation and to promote international economic stability. Macroeconomics has undergone considerable modification and elaboration since Keynes and macroeconomic policies have by no means been uniformly successful, particularly since 1973. In fact, the nature and effectiveness of macroeconomic policies have become very controversial among economists. However, the notion that governments must play an active role to achieve their economic objectives is now widely accepted.

But growth and stability are by no means the only preoccupations of economists. Economists generally favor letting private markets allocate resources or distribute goods and services, rather than appealing to some central agency to make such decisions. Prices set in *competitive* markets are good guides to the relative value of different things when they reflect the preference of a large number of buyers and the costs of a large number of sellers. Given sufficient competition, private markets will allocate resources efficiently. Accordingly, most economists oppose government intervention in private markets through tariffs and import quotas, price supports, interest rate ceilings, high minimum wages, price and wage controls and other methods of intervention. Where markets are not competitive or simply do not exist, the economist tries to prescribe government policies that would most closely correspond to a market solution.

Economists analyze problems with much the same approach and tend to use similar techniques, but there are significant differences among them on micro- as well as macroeconomic policies. Most economists are not non-partisan – there are conservative economists, liberal economists and radical economists. They differ because of differences in values and in their evaluations of the effectiveness of the market mechanism and government solutions to social and economic problems. However, recent tendencies in western countries to deregulate their economies, and in centrally planned countries to introduce market incentives, suggest that the differences among economists – at least with respect to microeconomic policies – are narrowing. In addition, the need to maintain international stability and to promote a free flow of goods among nations is now universally accepted.

This book is designed to show how governments have been using economists to develop economic policies and how their ideas have influenced these policies. To provide an international perspective, former officials of ten countries and five international agencies were asked to describe the organizational structures in which economists have been operating in their countries, to evaluate their effectiveness and to suggest changes in organization that would enhance the role of the economist. The contributors to the volume are not only eminent economists; they have also had first-hand experiences in the development of economic policies as ministers of finance or economic planning, chairmen of economic councils or official economic advisory groups, or top economic advisers to their governments or major international organizations. Except for my contribution, these essays appear for the first time in this volume and I have considerably revised and updated my own contribution since it first appeared.

The organizational structure in which economists operate depends on historical circumstances in each country as well as on the receptivity of economic advice by the heads of government and cabinet officers. In some cases, economists are located in the office of the president or prime minister. In others, special councils or advisory boards have been set up to provide economic analysis and to develop policy options. In still others, economic advice filters up to the top through agency heads, usually the minister of finance or economic planning and the head of the central bank. No one particular organization seems to be more effective than any other. The effectiveness of economists depends more on the quality and relevance of their advice and their ability to communicate with policymakers than on where they happen to be located in the governmental apparatus.

Although there is great diversity among the countries and international organizations represented in this volume, the fortunes of economists have followed roughly the same cycles almost everywhere since the end of World

War II. The influence and prestige of economists increased as the western economies flourished during the 1950s and 1960s. The prosperity of that period was attributed in considerable degree to the macroeconomic policies developed by economists to stimulate economic growth. In the 1970s and 1980s, faith in economists waned as it became clear that they did not have effective methods of combating 'stagflation'. Nevertheless, economists continue to play an important role in the development of economic policies in most countries.

I am grateful to the authors for taking time out of their busy schedules to contribute chapters to this volume. The experiences they describe will be an invaluable source of information for those in and out of public life who are interested in understanding the role of the economist in government and how that role can be enhanced.

Joseph A. Pechman
Washington, DC
1989

1 · INTRODUCTION AND SUMMARY

Robert H. Nelson

As long as there have been governments, they have had to deal with problems that are economic in nature. It is only in the past fifty years or so, however, that governments have widely employed a special class of personnel formally designated as economists (Coats, 1981). Before that, economic tasks were for the most part performed by generalists whose formal study of economics, if any at all, was confined to a smattering of economics as part of a well-rounded education. Government economic issues were widely regarded as mixed with political, administrative, legal and other factors, leaving economists with no unique claims to expertise.

However, as governments gradually assumed greater responsibility for managing economic affairs, the need for economic specialists developed. An active management role demanded that governments collect data to monitor economic performance, requiring the use of analytical methods and skills that most civil-service generalists did not possess. The supervision of an industry in some cases required specialized knowledge that government officials lacked but which economists were prepared to supply. Economic theories and writings were also becoming more technical in character, often expressed in mathematical form, demanding specialized expertise to interpret their meaning. *The General Theory*, for example, was written by John Maynard Keynes (Keynes, 1936) for an audience of economic professionals and could not easily be grasped by those outside the profession. The exercise of macroeconomic control over the economy would become an especially important area where governments found it necessary to seek out economic specialists.

The entry of large numbers of economists into government raised some important new questions. Where would economic offices be placed organizationally within the government? How would economic experts succeed in communicating with political leaders who typically had little or no background in economics and often found economic reasoning difficult to follow? What would happen when an economist reached a conclusion that was politically damaging to current leadership? In general, what would be the nature of the role that economic experts would assume in the process of governing? The answers to such questions belong more to the subject matter of political theory than of economic theory. Yet, for economists in government, some answers had to be given.

The following chapters of this volume survey the historic role of economists in ten nations and five multinational organizations. The subjects examined include the status of economic experts, the nature of the interactions between political leaders and economists, the types of economic arguments that have proven most persuasive, and the general impact and influence of economists in the making of economic policy. The chapters also describe the organizational arrangements for the delivery of economic advice. The many differences among nations in these regards reflect their widely varying political systems and cultures, which range from a military dictatorship to parliamentary regimes to the highly dispersed system of power in the United States.

Economic advisers to governments in some nations are located in special advisory bodies, chartered and funded but still outside of government. In other cases, economic advisory groups are located within the government, but remain in staff positions separate from the agencies directly responsible for administering governmental activities. A third possible arrangement is to place economists within the administrative agencies themselves. A number of nations, for example, put their economic experts responsible for macroeconomic advice in the treasury or finance ministry. Economists may be further dispersed in government, all the way down to isolated individual economists on staffs with diverse backgrounds. All these arrangements may exist within the same government, sometimes varying according to the economic function.

Despite such diversity, however, the contributors to this volume describe a consistency in the fortunes of economists that transcends the individual political and organizational arrangements for government economists. Economists in many nations first began to make significant contributions to government decision making in the 1930s and 1940s. Their inputs and impact typically increased further through the 1950s. The worldwide prestige and influence of government economists reached a high point in the 1960s, reflecting the widespread view that the keys to rapid economic growth had been discovered. National income and product in many countries grew rapidly, seeming to confirm the wisdom of closely following the advice of economic experts.

But the 1970s and 1980s, especially the years following the OPEC (Organization of Petroleum Exporting Countries) price shock of 1973–4, have been a much more troubling period for government economists. Economists throughout the world have faced a changing political environment in which their professional expertise has been more often subject to challenge and in which their professional voices have been less likely to be heard. In some degree, these events have reflected a loss of confidence among economists themselves in their own level of understanding – a development that many of the contributors to this volume note – and a failure to sustain professional agreement on key economic questions. In most countries there were also broader forces at work, such as a new pluralism of social values and new public attitudes turning against the role of experts, and sometimes even science itself, that acted to undercut the status and influence of economic experts. As the social authority of expert elites eroded, government decision making became increasingly subject to interest-group pressures. A consistent theme throughout the chapters in this volume is the politicizing of economic policymaking that occurred throughout the world in response to the events of the 1970s and 1980s.

If economists wish to have a greater policy impact in the new world environment, some significant changes in their educational training and their own professional image may be required. Recognizing the declining social deference to expertise and the overtly political context in which economic policy decisions are made, economists in and out of government may have to make greater efforts to educate and persuade political leaders. Even more important, since politicians are often tightly constrained by public attitudes and opinions, economists may need to become much more effective in reaching out to educate the public at large in economic matters. At present, the skills of economic professionals in public education – including how to write and speak so as to hold popular attention and then to communicate clearly and persuasively – are left almost to chance, receiving little emphasis in the formal training of economists and assigned little importance in the internal priorities of the economics profession itself. As a consequence, many of the most talented economists today do little either to develop or exercise the skills needed to be effective economic advisers.

THE EARLY YEARS

Although the economic crisis of the 1930s brought more economists into government service in a number of countries, a more decisive event was World War II. Suddenly, governments were assuming responsibility for the management of whole national economies. In England, as Alec Cairncross describes in Chapter 2, the first staff of economists (outside agriculture) was established in 1939–40. Soon to be known as the Economic Section, this small group of economists played an important role in the formulation of British wartime policy – part of the period under the leadership of Lionel Robbins. In the United States during the war years, economists streamed into Washington, including Paul Samuelson, Milton Friedman and many other future leaders of the American profession.

As the war ended, the specter of the 1930s depression still haunted many minds. The influence of Keynesian economics was also spreading, causing governments to look to economists for answers to problems of employment and national output. In England in 1944, the White Paper on Employment Policy announced the intention of the government to maintain a permanent central staff of economists. This staff, which retained the name Economic Section, would conduct economic studies, review the overall economic situation, coordinate with other economists in individual departments and submit assessments of economic trends and policies to ministers. Following Robbins, James Meade was the next director of the Economic Section, which was centrally located in the Cabinet Office until 1953, when it was transferred to the Treasury. The Economic Section for many years was the leading voice for economic expertise within the British government.

In the United States, the Employment Act of 1946 created a staff of economists with somewhat similar responsibilities, the Council of Economic Advisers (CEA). Consisting of three members, and an additional small professional staff, the Council was directed to advise the president on the necessary means to promote 'maximum employment, production and purchasing power'. The CEA, which today still operates under essentially the same arrangements, has been especially prominent in macroeconomic policymaking, but has also become involved in government policy decisions in many other areas such as industry regulation, environmental policy and farm policy.

In other nations, it was often the pressures of postwar reconstruction that created the greatest need for the services of economists. In West Germany, the 'Freiburg School' during the war years helped to lay the intellectual groundwork for the postwar creation of a market economy. Significantly influenced by this school, Ludwig Erhardt lifted much of the existing superstructure of economic controls in 1948. In that year a meeting of West German economists and commercial law specialists also set the future framework for a system of expert advisory councils to government agencies. There have since been a large number of councils created for many purposes, but the two most important have been the Economic Advisory Council, serving the Ministry for Economic Affairs, and the Finance Advisory Council, serving the Ministry of Finance.

Although the West German councils are connected to particular government departments, they are independent of the departments and are staffed with distinguished scholars and other nongovernmental experts (some but usually not all of them economists, depending on the subject matter). The councils are not intended to provide direct advice on the substance of government policy decisions – in fact they are strictly instructed to keep out of such political matters – but to conduct scientific studies, identify pressing economic issues and raise policy options for government consideration. In the assessment of Norbert Kloten (Chapter 3 of this volume), the West German system of advisory councils has been an important part of the process of forming economic policy.

In Japan, there were no government economists identified as such before World War II. But in 1947 the first Economic White Paper was issued by the Research Division of the Economic Stabilization Board. This paper and other writings by Japanese economists were influential in government circles, and the board itself was an important contributor in establishing a Japanese market system and directing the Japanese postwar recovery. In general, as Saburo Okita explains in Chapter 9, government economists in Japan have had an unusually large policy influence over the years, compared with most other nations. They have been located in three main agencies, the Economic Planning Agency (with around 500 employees), the Ministry of Finance and the Ministry of International Trade and Industry (MITI).

In 1955, the Japanese government adopted a system of five-year economic plans, whose preparation was placed under the direction of the Economic Planning Agency. These plans take a broad view of social and economic trends and conditions, set overall national goals and describe the basic policy directions and measures that will be required to reach those goals. The plans serve to convey to government officials, businessmen and other Japanese citizens the general directions in which the government seeks to move the Japanese society and economy. The development of the plans also provides a process by which the various social interests can assemble, express their views and work together to form the social consensus necessary for government action in Japan.

In France, economists were less prominent in the postwar years, compared with the nations mentioned thus far. The French government did not – and still does not today – place economic specialists in prominent positions but seeks a civil service of administrative generalists with a wide range of knowledge and skills. The National School of Administration was created in 1945 to serve this purpose. It has attracted many of the most talented products of French schooling, who have provided much of the staffing for the finance and other ministries of the French government. But the training of future government administrators has not emphasized economics and generally less priority has been given to the acquisition of professional skills and expertise of any kind. Over the years, some of the most influential Frenchmen in economic matters have not had any special training in either administrative or economic subjects. Jean Monnet, for example, lacked an economic background, but was a founder of the French postwar system of economic planning and was a central figure in the creation of the European Economic Community. The French economists of greatest international reputation have typically had engineering backgrounds, rather than university training in economics.

France is the exception, however, among the developed western nations examined in this volume. In Canada, economic specialists began entering government in the 1930s, a significant expansion in their numbers occurred during World War II, and then a further rapid growth took place after the war, influenced by a new goal to manage the Canadian economy in order to achieve high output and employment levels. Canadian economists concerned with matters of macroeconomic policy have been located in the Departments of Finance, Trade and Commerce, and External Affairs, as well as the Treasury Board, Bank of Canada and, since the early 1960s, the Economic Council of Canada (similar in many ways to the Council of Economic Advisers in the United States).

In Austria, the US administrators of the Marshall Plan sought economic data and analyses that required the assistance of economic specialists, resulting in the creation in the 1940s of economic sections that still exist today in some ministries. A desire to implement Keynesian theories, combined with demands for better statistics on the part of the social partners in Austria's 'corporatist' system of governance, also spurred greater use of economists. As in some other countries, many Austrian economists in the postwar years did not have formal university training in economics, but were government officials who had acquired and developed economic expertise in the course of their government work.

In the 1940s' retrospective view, the depression of the 1930s was caused not only by the failures of macroeconomic policy, but also by a failure of the world trading systcm. Kcyncs and other leading economists thus pushed strongly for the construction in the postwar era of a new institutional framework for international economic relations. The International Monetary Fund (IMF) was one result, established by the Bretton Woods agreement in 1944 (along with the World Bank). The General Agreement on Tariffs and Trade (GATT) resulted from negotiations completed in Geneva in 1947. The Organization for European Economic Cooperation (OEEC), the predecessor to the current Organization of Economic Cooperation and Development (OECD), was also established in 1947. All of these organizations have been heavily involved in the study of world trading patterns, exchange rates, international capital flows and other matters of international economic concern. Their staffs have included large numbers of economists, many with formal training and some others whose economic expertise was acquired more through practice than experience.

The international organizations have gone beyond trade issues to use their influence to promote sound economic policies within individual countries. As a condition for receiving IMF credits, many nations have been required to curb spending, raise revenues and adopt other measures to control inflationary tendencies. In the postwar years the World Bank helped to persuade Australia, Denmark, Iceland, Finland, Norway and Spain, among other countries, to abandon the tight economic controls that were a legacy of World War II, thereby giving markets a much freer reign. As Richard Goode and Andrew Kamarck comment in Chapter 12, World Bank advice in this regard was especially important in Spain in helping to lay the basis in the 1950s for its subsequent economic success.

In summary, the economic crisis of the 1930s and the events of World War II set the stage for a sharp expansion in the numbers and influence of government economists in the postwar years. Although the degree of acceptance of Keynesian theories varied, nations were determined to do all they could to maintain high levels of national output and employment. The depression was also blamed on protectionist trading policies of the 1930s, leading to a postwar determination to liberalize trading rules and to develop an international framework to prevent any repetition of past mistakes. A further critical task requiring the efforts of economists was the reconstruction of the many national economies that had been decimated by the war itself. To these special factors of the time was added the continuing general growth of government responsibilities in the era of the modern welfare state and the resulting growth in government demands for economic data and analysis.

THE GOLDEN YEARS

By 1960, it was possible to look back and conclude that the major economic goals of the postwar years had been accomplished with remarkable success. If government economists did not deserve all the credit, they certainly had contributed importantly. Building on this success, there would be a further enhancement of the stature and influence of government economists in the 1960s. Economists now sought to boost the rates of growth of national economies, asserting that they possessed the economic knowledge and skills to achieve more precise macroeconomic control. Government economists also began to extend the scope of their concerns to many new microeconomic fields such as health, housing, education and environment.

The most ambitious effort was the 1960 Plan to Double National Income, the most successful of the Japanese economic plans. The plan set a target of 7.2 per cent real growth to be sustained for the next ten years. It proposed measures in five broad areas to encourage this growth: improving social overhead; modernizing Japanese industry; encouraging exports with an emphasis on greater cooperation with developing countries; increasing the resources devoted to scientific and technological research; and achieving greater social stability by addressing the problems of the traditionalist sectors of the Japanese economy. In the event, the goals of the new plan were exceeded, as Japanese real economic growth averaged 10.7 per cent per year during the 1960s.

Okita states in Chapter 9 that the plan contributed importantly to the economic success of Japan in the 1960s, partly because of the realistic economic assessments the plan offered, its carefully developed analysis and its clearly specified national goals. These features helped to build private-sector confidence in the future of the Japanese economy and thus spurred private-sector investment and greater efforts in research and development.

Moreover, Japanese political leadership publicly adopted the plan, committing the nation to take the steps necessary to achieve its goals.

In the United States, the 1960s were also a period of rapid economic growth for which government economists could claim some significant credit. Following the advice of Chairman Walter Heller of the Council of Economic Advisers, President Kennedy in 1963 proposed to Congress a substantial tax reduction, a fiscal stimulus approved by Congress in 1964. The tax cut was soon followed by rapid growth, the federal budget moved into surplus, and US unemployment fell to 4.1 per cent in December 1965, an economic boom that lasted through much of the 1960s.

In the early 1960s, government economists in the United States also began to assume a much greater role in policymaking at the Defense Department. Following this precedent, the Bureau of the Budget later in the decade introduced the Planning, Programming and Budgeting System (PPBS), which sought to apply benefit–cost and other methods of economic analysis in microeconomic fields throughout the federal government. Although the PPBS proved unwieldy, its goals and spirit were carried on less formally through the creation in the 1970s of policy study offices in numerous departments and agencies. These offices did not always hire professionally trained economists, but their way of thinking was that of applied economics, taking close account of the political and institutional setting. Although there is wide variation in the policy influence of these offices, some have had a significant impact in their departments.

In England, a similar sharp expansion in the number of government economists in microeconomic fields began around the same time. Following the election of the Labour government in 1964, a large new department, the Department of Economic Affairs, was created. Departments of the British government such as Environment, Transport, Trade and Industry, Agriculture, and Employment and Energy recruited many new economic specialists for their staffs. The number of government economists rose from only twenty-one in 1964 – most of them in the Economic Section – to a peak of 408 in 1978, falling back slightly to 390 in 1986. British economists advocated measures in the 1960s to stimulate more rapid economic growth, but were less successful in this respect than economists in many other nations.

West German government leaders had long been skeptical of the need for macroeconomic management, believing that the market contained its own internal forces of self-correction to maintain high employment. However, in the international enthusiasm of the 1960s for stimulating growth and high employment, these views were abandoned. The Council of Economic Experts was created in 1963, patterned in some respects after the Council of Economic Advisers in the United States. Like the American council, the West German council conducts studies of employment, income and price trends. It develops forecasts, publishes an annual report assessing the state of the economy and examines various policy options. But the West German council also differs from the American council in key respects. First, it is independent of any government department and its members – drawn from a pool of leading scholars and other recognized economic experts – are not government employees. Second, although encouraged to examine policy options, the West German council is forbidden to propose and recommend specific policy measures. Third, the council is authorized to call any government official, including the chancellor of the West German government, who must then give testimony. The government is further required by law to give its comments on the annual reports of the council.

In Austria, the Council of Social and Economic Affairs was established in 1963, the same year as the West German Council of Economic Experts. Both councils collect economic data, prepare forecasts and study economic issues. But the twelve-member Austrian council is not composed of leading economic experts, as is the West German council. Instead, the Austrian council includes representatives from the main social interest groups of labor, business and agriculture. Hans Seidel (Chapter 5) finds that in the 1960s the Austrian council was a key political instrument – its staff providing expert advice and studies as called upon – in the bargaining process by which the social partners in Austria forged a political agreement on government policy. Many of the most important policy decisions in Austria are not made within the formal structure of the Austrian government, but are reached by the major social-interest groups among themselves and then carried out by the government.

A period of rapid expansion in the number of Canadian government economists occurred in the late 1960s and 1970s, as systems analyses, benefit–cost studies, cost-effectiveness assessments and other such efforts in microeconomic fields spread rapidly throughout the federal government and then the provincial governments – all very similar to the PPBS and its policy office offshoots in the United States. By the late 1970s, there were estimated to be 4,000 Canadian economists in the federal public service and a similar number in the provincial services.

In Mexico, economists began to acquire influence in government policy-making in the 1930s, and carried out important functions in the 1940s and 1950s. In 1962, the Intersecretariat Commission was created, responsible for developing short- and long-range plans for social and economic development. Mexican economic planners followed the worldwide pattern of the 1960s in making economic growth the principal policy objective and adopting Keynesian concepts and tools for fine-tuning the economy. In this and in other ways they were rejecting older and heavy-handed ideological themes of the Mexican past in favor of a new modern pragmatism and rationalism. It was a shift away from the political–economic tradition of Latin culture and closer to the Anglo-Saxon tradition. All this seemed to be working well during the 1960s, as the Mexican economy sustained high rates of growth with low inflation.

Among the nations examined in this volume, England and Argentina experienced some major economic difficulties in the 1960s. For most nations, however, the 1960s were a period of high growth, low inflation and political stability. Government economists helped to lay the basis for this economic golden era in several key ways. They proposed particular policy measures, such as the Kennedy tax cut in the United States, that successfully stimulated growth. They encouraged private-sector investment by promising the support of government and creating a climate of confidence in the future. Businesses could boost employment and production with assurances that economists now had the knowledge and tools to prevent recurrences of the cyclical instabilities that had plagued market economies in earlier eras. The explosive growth of world trade was occurring in the context of an international economic framework designed and successfully managed in significant part by economic experts.

The rise of economists in government was one of a number of signs – or so it seemed to many during the 1960s – that a new and better era in social and political relationships was arriving. National hatreds and ideological clashes as recently as World War II had caused immense destruction of physical property and vast loss of human life. It could be hoped that this terrible waste had finally convinced the world – or at least the western developed world – of the futility of the old political and ideological controversies. Instead, it would be preferable to give a new class of expert managers the responsibility for running government. These managers would be pragmatists, who had learned scientific habits of thought and would apply rational analysis instead of emotion to public affairs.

The ascendancy of economic managers in government was particularly important to this vision. Past social tensions had often been exacerbated by struggles over the distribution of a fixed or even shrinking total supply of goods and services. Now, it could be hoped that these struggles would be rendered unnecessary by the rapid growth of the social pie. This optimistic outlook had a self-reinforcing character. As long as the optimism was widely shared, business and consumer confidence surged, investments and purchases rose, rapid growth occurred, and social tensions were in fact diminished to the point where economists and other professional managers were given a substantial leeway in government to exercise their skills.

HARD TIMES FOR ECONOMISTS

By the end of the 1960s, the organizational arrangements for providing economic advice were largely in place in most nations. There was often a central advisory council, further staffs of macroeconomists were found in the treasury, central bank and other key agencies, and in a number of countries microeconomists were scattered in substantial numbers throughout the individual departments. At the beginning of the 1970s a key question was how all this apparatus of expert economic advice would perform.

If government economists in the 1960s focused on stimulating more rapid economic growth, the critical problem facing economists in the 1970s would be inflation. Indeed, the inflationary problems of the 1970s may have been caused in part by the policies of the 1960s. The application of Keynesian policy instruments could easily turn out to be a one-way street. Governments were happy enough to fire up the engines of growth; but if these efforts threatened to set off inflation, requiring the imposition of fiscal and monetary restraints, the retreat from economic stimulus might well prove to be much more difficult. Indeed, economists were often painfully reminded in the 1970s of a fact that had been less noticeable in the 1960s – that the exercise of economic policy remained ultimately a political act, not a set of decisions that any society would entrust to economic experts alone.

Besides a lack of government restraint, there were other critical causes of inflation, most notably the two OPEC price shocks of 1973–4 and of 1979. Shortages of agricultural outputs and other natural-resource products helped further to spur inflation. In the United States the pressure of sustaining the Vietnam War, especially with many citizens reluctant to make major sacrifices for this purpose, generated another inflationary impetus.

The inflationary forces of the 1970s tended to be most damaging in less developed nations, where social and political institutions were more fragile to begin with. Lauchlin Currie in Chapter 11 describes the recent severe stresses on the social order in Colombia, as a GNP growth rate that had averaged almost 5 per cent for thirty years fell sharply, and growth of per capita income approached zero in the 1980s. The basis for this decline in economic performance was laid in the 1970s and especially in the years following the OPEC price shock of 1973–4. During 1975–8, further spurred by an international coffee boom, monetary expansion in Colombia ranged from 24 per cent to 37 per cent and inflation from 17 per cent to 29 per cent. As in many other countries, Colombian political leadership responded with measures more often harmful than beneficial. The government sought to offset the impact of inflation on important social interests, keeping the currency overvalued, maintaining spending by entering into excessive foreign borrowing, dampening consumer prices and encouraging or tolerating excessive wage increases.

Currie concludes that the modest influence of Colombian economists has been partly attributable to their tendency to disagree among themselves – at least on matters of macroeconomic policy. However, the fundamental factor that limits the influence of economists is the resistance found in the Colombian social and political culture to the general way of thinking and the types of policy proposals typically offered by economists. In Colombian politics arguments for equity almost always win out over arguments for efficiency and there is a long tradition of hostility to government actions that are seen as resulting in the accumulation of any large private gains.

In Argentina as well, as José Pastore describes in Chapter 10, the political culture has been inhospitable to economic policymaking. Indeed, reflecting the extreme volatility of Argentinian politics, the average tenure for the thirty-one ministers in charge of the Ministry of the Economy between 1958 and 1985 was eleven months. In an environment of such great instability, it has proven impossible to meet even basic requirements for economic policymaking. Economic data, for instance, are very poor, leaving Argentina without any consistent set of annual GNP estimates over the past twenty years, and requiring economists to use calculations for income distribution made twenty years ago or more. The persistent political instability of Argentina encouraged high inflation and low growth in the 1960s, a forewarning of problems that would occur much more widely in the 1970s.

Mexico followed the more typical pattern with high growth and low inflation in the 1960s, but then followed by a period of rapid inflation from 1970 to 1976 during which the external debt quadrupled. The Mexican government – much like the Colombian government – aggravated matters by refusing to devalue the peso, increasing domestic wages and subsidies, and controlling consumer good prices. As social tensions escalated, and the economy fared poorly, Mexican political leaders became still more reluctant to heed the policy advice of economic experts, and moved in many cases to improvise their own economic prescriptions.

As a major oil exporter, Mexico benefited greatly from the rise in world oil prices from 1974 on. However, Mexico used its infusion of oil income more as a boon to Mexican consumers and businesses, instead of building long-run productive capacity. The government sector expanded sharply, as public expenditures rose from 33 per cent of gross product in 1976 to 51 per cent in 1984, and foreign indebtedness rose correspondingly. When oil prices fell in the 1980s, the consequences for Mexico were dire, as some indicators suggested a decline in real wages of more than 20 per cent from 1980 to 1986.

David Ibarra and José Alberro (Chapter 8) do not exempt Mexican government economists from blame for the economic policy failures of the past two decades, especially when there was almost always some economist to support the various predilections of political leadership. They suggest that, if Mexican economists are to achieve greater influence, the future work of economists should involve a closer linking of political and economic arguments. This blending is required both in the development of realistic economic proposals and in greater efforts that should be made to build support among the Mexican public for sensible economic policies. Based on the Mexican experience, economics is best seen not as a science with its own well-defined subject matter, but as a value-laden field of inquiry that is often difficult to separate from other elements in the process of social decision making. Moreover, this process does not work by means of rational long-range planning as much as by a series of incremental steps that in many cases are aptly described as a form of 'muddling through'.

Although the more developed nations suffered less severe damage, they tended to experience much the same problems in the 1970s. Japanese economists have had to work in a new political environment in which growth slowed significantly following the first oil crisis. Tax revenues grew more slowly, yet spending for social welfare and public works continued to rise. By 1979, the Japanese government was obtaining 40 per cent of its funding through borrowing. Seeking a solution to the budget deficit, Japanese economic planners called for a broad-based consumption tax that would both cut domestic consumer spending and raise government revenues. But this plan proved to be much less politically acceptable than previous proposals of Japanese economists designed to achieve higher economic growth and production. Failing to obtain greater revenues through taxation, the Japanese government in the 1980s gradually reduced the deficit by curbing government expenditure, but here as well the government was not closely guided by the advice of economic experts.

Okita generally finds a significant decline in Japan since the 1960s in the policy impact and influence of government economists. Four factors appear to have contributed most significantly to this development. First, the political environment in Japan has been altered to reflect a wider range of social values and policy goals, complicating the development of social agreement around particular economic policies. Second, economic theory itself has lost some of its scientific credibility, encouraging Japanese politicians to assume a greater role in deciding economic questions. Third, because economists were forced in the 1970s and the 1980s to prescribe means of dealing with slower growth and a greater scarcity of social resources, expert economic advice became politically painful and was therefore more likely to be rejected by Japanese politicians. Fourth, economic planning became more complicated as international economic forces assumed greater and greater significance.

Like almost every contributor to this volume, Cairncross finds that since the 1970s the formulation of economic policy in the United Kingdom has been further politicized. Governments have sought to choose their own economic advisers from among economists who were regarded as politically trustworthy, a trend most apparent following the election of the Conservative government in 1979. In the 1980s many key government economists have held views outside the mainstream professional outlook that had characterized government economists until then. Cairncross finds that mainstream British economists themselves bear considerable blame for a loss of public prestige, partly owing to the mistake that he sees as the greatest failure of postwar British economic policy advice – a willingness to engage in a persistent overstimulation of the economy in response to popular pressures for higher rates of growth.

Cairncross finds a sharp decline in the participation and effectiveness of university economists in government policymaking – especially in comparison with Keynes, William Beveridge and other economic stars of an earlier era. The degree of interaction between university economists and government economists has generally declined sharply. Most university economists in England today no longer regard the education of the public in economic policy matters as part of their social responsibility, a development that Cairncross regrets.

The United States was another country in which the failure to deal successfully with inflation was both a major policy failure in the 1970s and also a key factor in a loss of public esteem of economists. As in other nations, American political leaders preferred to attack the symptoms rather than the causes of inflation. Comprehensive wage and price controls were imposed in 1973 and oil prices remained controlled until 1981. Following the OPEC price shock of 1973–4, an average reduction in real income of about 2 per cent was suddenly imposed throughout the developed nations of the world. In the United States, labor unions through wage increases, retirees through cost-of-living adjustments, businessmen through price increases, and other social interests all sought to pass the burden of a reduction in real income to someone else. Government policy did not resist but more often abetted or encouraged this destructive tendency.

Although inflation in the United States declined sharply in the 1980s, the basic structural problem of total social demand well in excess of total social outputs remained as unresolved as it had been in the 1970s. In the 1980s, however, this problem was transformed to take on a new form, huge federal budget and trade deficits, as the United States engaged in massive foreign borrowing. Unless the US budget deficit is brought under control, it could at some point leave the United States facing the circumstances that many Latin American nations face today – excessive foreign debt, a depreciating currency, a resurgence of inflationary pressures and eventually downward pressure on real income.

As Joseph Pechman observes in Chapter 6, there has been no lack of criticism by US government and other economists of US budget deficits. However, the US public and political leadership find it easier today to ignore economic experts because at least some economists can be found on almost every side of the debates on deficit and other policy issues. Moreover, the members of the economics profession in the United States have often done poorly in communicating their concerns to the general public. For example, the public dialogue is still not well informed concerning the close links of the trade deficit to the budget deficit, despite the long period in which these deficits have persisted and the great policy importance of the subject.

In Canada, continuing inflation throughout the 1970s and bitter battles over energy policy created major social strains. It became much more difficult to obtain agreement within government on all kinds of policy matters, or to build a consensus among affected social interests. Economic policy debate has been characterized by a cross-current of professional advice. Ian Stewart describes in Chapter 7, for example, how Keynesians, monetarists, rational expectationists and neo-Keynesians all were found within the ranks of the macroeconomic advisers to the Canadian government.

The Canadian public and politicians came to see economists as offering not only technical advice, but also advice that contained major distributional and thus socially divisive consequences. In the 1960s, when the total national output was expanding steadily, it was easy enough to leave economic policy to economic experts, but the 1970s and 1980s offered much more challenging circumstances for Canadian economic advisers. As a result, if they wanted to have significant policy influence, Stewart finds that Canadian government economists had to show a new sophistication concerning political factors and to be much better versed in the legislative, legal and other institutional implications of their advice. The Canadian public has generally shown a growing skepticism towards the claims of economists to possess a special expertise in matters of public policy. Economics instead has come often to be seen as one perspective – one might even call it an 'ideology' – that may find itself in conflict with environmental, religious and other basic outlooks. All these outlooks have varying roots in political, philosophical, legal and other schools of thought, as well as varying ideas concerning economic issues.

THE INTERNATIONAL ORGANIZATIONS

The trends of the 1970s affected not only economists in individual nations but also in international economic organizations. William Kelly (Chapter 15) finds that political pressures within and among nations are increasing the danger of a renewal of the 'beggar-thy-neighbor' trading policies of the 1930s. Using quotas, internal purchasing requirements and in other ways, many nations have effectively subverted the spirit, if not the letter, of the General Agreement on Tariffs and Trade (GATT). Indeed, in Kelly's view GATT and the world trading system based on its trading rules may today be in jeopardy.

The policy influence of World Bank economists on member countries, according to Goode and Kamarck (Chapter 12), was considerable for the Bank's first quarter-century, but then fell to an all-time low during the 1970s, recovering somewhat in the 1980s. The major loss of influence in the 1970s was attributable to three main factors. First, the availability of large OPEC surpluses that demanded recycling diminished the pressure on developing countries to look to the World Bank for project financing. Second, the Bank itself sought aggressively to expand its own loan activities, thus undercutting the credibility of any threats that it might withhold loans until Bank terms and conditions were met. Third, the interdepartmental Economic Committee of the Bank was abolished, a victim partly of internal Bank resistance from area and sector departments whose autonomy was challenged. This committee had effectively coordinated the Bank's approach to country macroeconomic policies, often pushing the Bank to demand macroeconomic improvements of borrower nations.

J. C. R. Dow describes in Chapter 13 a similar low point during the 1970s in the fortunes of the IMF and the international supporting role played by the OECD. As the international economic climate became more turbulent in the late 1960s and early 1970s, the need for larger and more frequent adjustments strained the political capacity of the international system to agree on appropriate exchange rates. Nations had conflicting priorities with respect to preventing inflation and preventing unemployment, and in general became less willing to accommodate their own national policies to serve exchange-rate stability. Growing macroeconomic differences of opinion among economists around the world also complicated the task of reaching international agreements. The postwar Bretton Woods system finally broke down in 1973, replaced by a system of floating exchange rates, and undercutting the traditional role of the IMF.

In the years following the OPEC shock of 1973–4, further powerful forces arose whose consequences for national economies and exchange rates were difficult to predict. In these 1970s circumstances of economic instability and national policy disagreements, floating rates offered an impersonal market mechanism that responded quickly to changing economic developments, did not require nations to reconcile their political disagreements in an overt way, and was indifferent to the policy disputes of economists around the world. Offsetting these advantages, the market created a high degree of instability, one that greatly exceeded any changes in the underlying fundamental economics. In the 1980s, therefore, the leading trading nations have been able to agree sufficiently to move gingerly to reassert some measure of international coordination of exchange rates.

Manfred Wegner explains in Chapter 14 that the European Economic Community (EEC) had high hopes on entering the 1970s for establishing a monetary union. These hopes were dashed, however, by much the same factors that complicated exchange-rate coordination. A monetary union required individual nations to subordinate their own economic policies to overall EEC goals. Yet, Germany and France, among other EEC countries, differed on the relative dangers of inflation and unemployment, on the proper role of EEC economic planning and on other key policy questions. The rapid pace of economic events of the 1970s, and the poor understanding of these events, made disagreements among EEC countries all the more difficult to reconcile. During the 1980s, partly motivated by an EEC-wide acceptance of an urgent need to control inflation, some tentative steps towards a monetary union have been achieved.

The experiences of economists in international economic organizations in the 1970s and 1980s further demonstrated the highly political character of economic policymaking today. Exchange-rate stability or a monetary union require that diverse nations agree to coordinate closely their fiscal, monetary and other policies, policies all having major social consequences that inevitably are matters of intense political concern within each nation. The achievement of effective international economic measures thus becomes a matter of finding not only sound economic answers but also answers that will facilitate agreement among the nations involved. Economists within international organizations, like government economists elsewhere, have been forced to pay more attention and to develop greater sophistication in blending economic and political factors in their formulation of economic policy advice.

THE ENVIRONMENT FOR ECONOMIC ADVISING TODAY

In national and international organizations alike, economic advisers have confronted a similar set of problems throughout the world in the 1970s and 1980s. Alternative economic policies could differ greatly in their consequences for particular social groups and nations. In a period of social tensions due to inflation and other stresses, the attempts of governments to develop economic policies frequently set off political squabbling, as social interests and nations sought to pass the buck to someone else. The results sometimes appeared to be a virtual political gridlock, as each major party seemingly possessed the power to veto any economic or other policy proposal detrimental to its interests.

In seeking to defend proposed economic policies, politicians now were forced to confront difficult questions of social justice – why this group and not that group should be forced to suffer the burdens of economic adjustments necessary to deal with inflationary pressures or other problems of national or international scope. Political dialogue took on a more ideological character, partly because adversely affected groups often sought to head off government actions by making appeals to abstract social ideals. Such factors tended to undermine the coherence of economic policy, further shrinking the available social pie, and aggravating the economic problems. The favorable 1960s cycle of economic growth, greater social optimism and confidence, and further economic growth now tended to work in reverse – in the 1970s yielding inflation, greater social tensions and policy confusion, and then less output and further inflation.

Economists by and large have not reacted well to the domestic and international challenges of the 1970s and 1980s. The leading theories and writings have seldom taken much explicit account of political factors, instead exploring the consequences of economic policymaking in an abstract world where economic technicians execute policies as prescribed. Many economists have not regarded themselves as having the responsibility to go directly to the public to educate citizens on the necessity of certain policies. Economists have almost always disavowed any responsibility for defending the social justice of the policy measures they proposed, even when such a defense might be a vital part of gaining their public acceptance. Then, as economic policymaking became more disjointed, and economic forecasts performed poorly, members of the profession have advanced new concepts and theories, confronting the public with a welter of conflicting economic explanations.

Economic policymaking was being politicized for other reasons as well. Environmental and other new values were being asserted in politics, yet benefit–cost and other economic tests found it difficult to give these values a full accounting. The theories and policy prescriptions of economists were based on assumptions of the self-interested behavior of rational man – and such behavior was at least implicitly endorsed by economists. Yet, some religious and other leaders, as well as many ordinary citizens, found this vision of impersonal human rationality to be lacking and perceived a challenge to their own religious and ethical beliefs (US Catholic Bishops, 1984). Despite the 1960s optimism concerning the arrival of a new pragmatic and managerial era, fierce political partisanship, divisive ideological controversy and other age-old habits of mankind showed in the 1970s and 1980s that they had not lost all of their former punch, and that matters of economic policymaking were not exempt.

Having said all this, it is important to add a major qualification. Although mentioned only in passing by most contributors to this volume, there were some economists who fared better in the new circumstances and who in fact have had substantial policy successes in the past two decades. When achieving fiscal and monetary restraint proved an exceedingly difficult chore, some economists turned from demand to the production side of the inflation problem. Supply-side aspects had not received the same attention in mainstream economics over the years, but there had nevertheless been a steady stream of writings on the detrimental impacts of government regulatory policies, the distorting effects of national tax systems, the mismanagement of government enterprises, and other inefficiencies caused by government actions. Significantly influenced by economic arguments, and with prominent economists often playing an important advocacy role, many governments in the 1970s and 1980s turned to address these problems. In the United States, government and other economists played a key role in two of the most important policy developments of the past fifteen years, the deregulation movement and federal income tax rate reduction and simplification.

In other countries, transportation, communication and other key industries were more likely to be nationalized outright, rather than regulated as in the United States. Thus, instead of deregulation, much the same policy thrust took the form in other nations of privatization (Goodman, 1985; Roth, 1987; Harding, 1987). Tax rate reduction has also proved to be a worldwide trend of the 1980s. The economic advocates of these policies in a number of cases adopted a more ideological tone and also made a greater effort to reach out to persuade the public of the merits of the policies. Like macroeconomic policy advice in the 1960s, the supply-side arguments also had the great advantage of a much rosier message to offer – how to expand the total amount of goods and services to be made available to everyone.

Indeed, a case might be made that the past decade has not been so much a period of declining influence for economists as one of a shift of influence from one group of economists to another. Nations all over the world have been taking steps to reduce the role of central planning, to loosen the grip of government commands and controls over the private sector, and to rely more heavily on the market mechanism. The changes of this kind in China and the Soviet Union – due in significant part to the arguments made by the economists of these nations – have received worldwide attention and may represent events of deep historic significance. Such worldwide trends reflect a much greater acceptance by the political leaders of the world of the core message of economics for much of its history, that self-interested behavior and the institutional framework of competitive markets is the most effective way of organizing an economic system.

In the postwar years, however, economists had moved beyond their traditional advocacy of competitive markets to argue that economic knowledge and skills now allowed governments to manage a national economic system as a whole. In the macroeconomic field, economists thus could fine-tune the economy to curb its instabilities. Many economists also believed that benefit–cost studies, systems analysis and other tools would enable substantially greater economic rationality to be achieved in the day-to-day decisions throughout the departments of government. This vision in the United States can be traced historically to the scientific management aims and outlook of the American progressive movement (Nelson, 1987). It is this particular vision of the economist as expert manager of a social system (along with other social scientists), more than the overall influence of economists, that has suffered during the past fifteen years. Indeed, these years have caused many people to wonder how far the role of governments as expert managers of economic systems can in fact be carried, when management decisions must be made through pluralist practices of democratic politics in the West.

CONCLUSION

The contributors to this volume do not identify any single best way of organizing the economic advisory function. The organizational options include the locating of economic advisory groups outside of government; expert advisory groups within government but outside the operating agencies; and staff advisers within the treasury, central bank and other government economic agencies with operating responsibilities. Some nations have created large economic planning agencies, whereas others scatter their economists among many departments, and still others rely much less on economic specialists in any formal capacity.

Nevertheless, if forced to speculate, based on the evidence of recent trends, it may be that those organizational arrangements that attempt to insulate economic specialists from close participation in politics or from day-to-day involvement in government decision making will prove to be the less effective in the long run. Success in persuading political leaders is likely to depend on the frequent access of economic advisers to these leaders. Involvement of advisers in the implementation of economic policy is likely both to improve the quality of the advice given and to allow economists to make decision inputs at the times and places with the best chance of having an impact.

The chapters in this volume suggest that a world intellectual and policy community may be emerging – much as a world economic system is emerging – in which the fate of government economic advisers is less dependent on organizational and other developments in individual nations and more on overall worldwide trends. Despite wide differences among nations in the organizational and other arrangements for giving expert economic advice, and wide differences in national political systems and cultures, a common thread has run through the experiences of government economic advisers all around the world. Government and other economists in most nations had much success in the years immediately following World War II and rose to a height of influence in the 1960s, but saw their impact and public prestige decline sharply in the 1970s and 1980s.

As long as the prescription was faster economic growth, and government economists delivered successfully enough on this prescription, an expanding social pie alleviated social tensions, dissolved political obstacles and smoothed the way for the technical advice of economists to be readily accepted. But in less happy circumstances, where economic prescriptions could adversely affect important social interests, the expertise of economists has faced much tougher political sledding. If government economists had maintained a professional consensus, made accurate forecasts and passed other tests of scientific legitimacy, it is possible that political leaders would have been willing to accept even very stern medicine prescribed to combat inflation and resolve other problems. But the conditions of scientific credibility were not met. As the public prestige of economists has slipped, politicians have felt much freer to interject their own pet economic theories in place of those offered by economic experts.

It is unlikely that these developments will soon or easily be reversed. Hence, if economists have found economic advice to give, and want to see this advice followed, it will be incumbent on economists – both government and university – to improve their powers of persuasion. They will have to acquire greater facility at reaching out to politicians and, perhaps even more importantly, to the constituencies and other groups to whom politicians listen. Government and other economists will also have to accept a greater responsibility to defend the full consequences of their policy proposals, including distributional, legal and administrative, as well as efficiency consequences. Most significant economic policies cannot readily be separated into sets of economic and noneconomic social consequences, the former to be analyzed by economists and the latter by other specialists. Rather, in the political arena, policies typically have to be taken as a whole and compared with other policy alternatives in this light.

The changes required to achieve greater influence of economists may demand some rethinking of the character of economic education and of the content of professional obligations and responsibilities. Greater emphasis on learning economic and other history, the institutional arrangements of the economy, political schools of thought, legal practices and theory, and even ethics and other aspects of philosophy may be needed. Following the enormously productive precedent of physical science, economists have emphasized skills in reducing economic problems to very well defined and narrow components – partly to facilitate a quantitative formulation. The time may have come to shift the balance back towards big-picture skills – the ability to integrate diverse materials into a successful explanation of events, or a persuasive 'story'. Historically, the one greatest contribution of economics has been its vision of the competitive market, an integrative vision that gives a meaning and sets a framework for understanding diverse events that otherwise might seem purposeless or even harmful. This overarching vision of the market also emerged from a tradition of thought that wove together economic, political, legal, philosophical and other social considerations that were deemed to be relevant.

Perhaps being an economic professional should also be considered to involve duties that go beyond the generation of economic knowledge and encompass the ability to make this knowledge useful to society. It is also possible that, in seeking to apply economic knowledge more successfully, the quality of economic theory itself will be improved. It is often said that one of the most important parts of research is the framing of the questions. If research economists are not familiar with the world in which economic policies are applied, they may lack a perspective and an understanding necessary to ask the right questions. Indeed, many observers today fear that too many economists are applying highly refined reasoning to draw sophisticated conclusions to questions that are not worth the effort.

The marketplace of political and economic ideas is much like an ordinary market for goods and services in that a strong sales force and good advertising may be helpful but long-run success largely depends on the quality of the product. It may be that the diminished influence of economic experts in recent years is sending a message, one that calls for economists – like many currently struggling firms and industries – to review past practices and to make necessary internal changes to improve the quality of the product. In the last analysis, it will be the merits of economic ideas, and the quality of economic thinking, that determine the influence and impact of government economists. The place of economists in organizational charts, the channels for transmitting economic advice, the total numbers of government economists and other arrangements will make a difference but will most likely be the lesser factor.

BIBLIOGRAPHY

Coats, A. W. (ed.), *Economists in Government* (Durham, NC: Duke University Press, 1981).

Goodman, John C. (ed.), *Privatization* (Dallas: National Center for Policy Analysis, 1985).

Harding, Harry, *China's Second Revolution: Reform after Mao* (Washington, DC: Brookings, 1987).

Keynes, John Maynard, *The General Theory of Employment, Interest and Money* (New York: Harcourt Brace, 1936).

Nelson, Robert H., 'The economics profession and the making of public policy', *Journal of Economic Literature* (March 1987).

Roth, Gabriel, *The Private Provision of Public Services in Developing Countries* (New York: Oxford University Press for the World Bank, 1987).

US Catholic Bishops, *First Draft–Bishops Pastoral: Catholic Social Thinking and the US Economy*, printed in *Origins* (5 November 1984).

EUROPE

2 · THE UNITED KINGDOM*

Alec Cairncross

BEGINNINGS: THE ECONOMIC SECTION

In the United Kingdom economic policy is dealt with by ministers either at their discretion or after approval in Cabinet or in committees of the Cabinet. The key figure is normally the Chancellor of the Exchequer – the Prime Minister as a rule having other things to think about – by virtue of the wide range of responsibilities falling on the Treasury. These include at least five distinct functions, each of which might be (and in some countries is) entrusted to a separate agency. It acts as a Ministry of Economic Affairs in charge of economic policy, a Ministry of Finance in charge of taxation, a Ministry of the Public Sector controlling public expenditure and the nationalized industries, a ministry in control of monetary policy and a ministry responsible for the civil service, including pay, control of manpower, etc. Foreign economic policy, which might be thought to be a matter for the Foreign Office or the old Board of Trade (now the Department of Trade and Industry) is more likely to take shape in the Treasury. The Chancellor of the Exchequer is consequently in a dominant position in relation to other economic departments; and, not surprisingly, the Treasury is the largest employer of economists in Whitehall.

It was not in the Treasury, however, but in the Cabinet Secretariat that a staff of economists was first established in 1939–40. Until then there had been no regular arrangements for the appointment of economists to any department of government except the Ministry of Agriculture. Members of the highest grade in the civil service, the Administrative Class, were recruited by competitive examination with a wide choice of papers from which candidates were free to select in accordance with their university training. These might include one or more papers in economics but this would be unlikely to have any influence on the duties and department to

* I am grateful for assistance and criticism from Dr Ian Byatt (Deputy Chief Economic Adviser, HM Treasury), Mr Hans Liesner (Chief Economic Adviser to the Department of Trade and Industry) and Sir F. J. Atkinson (formerly Chief Economic Adviser).

which they were assigned, their place in the examination being the critical factor. Keynes and Hawtrey, for example, were examined mainly in mathematics, and were then assigned, one to the India Office, the other initially to the Admiralty. Neither had taken a university examination in economics. Once appointed, at ages between twenty-one and twenty-four, recruits were expected to be capable of advising, or procuring advice, on any matters referred to them and to acquire on the job such expertise as their duties required.

On two occasions before 1939, however, recruitment was on a different basis. The first was in the war of 1914–18 when it was necessary to find temporary staff for the much enlarged duties that the government assumed. This staff included some who are now thought of as economists and statisticians such as William Beveridge (Ministry of Food), Hubert Henderson (Cotton Control Board), Walter Layton (Ministry of Munitions) and Arthur Salter (Ministry of Shipping). Keynes, too, rejoined the Civil Service, becoming head of a division dealing with external finance in the Treasury. But whether they thought of themselves as economists, and separated by such a label from other Treasury figures like Sir Basil Blackett and Sir Otto Niemeyer, is doubtful.

The second occasion on which economists were brought in was in 1930 with the setting up of the Economic Advisory Council. This followed agitation for the creation of an Economic General Staff, a proposal made by Beveridge in 1923 and revived by Keynes and Layton in 1928. The Council, which had twenty members of whom only three were economists, fell far short of this proposal. Its total cost, including clerical staff, was £6,500 per annum and did not stretch to the purchase of an adding machine for Colin Clark. It lasted little more than a year but was survived by a Committee on Economic Information which met regularly until the outbreak of war and prepared a series of surveys of the economic situation. The Committee included among its members Keynes, Stamp, Henderson and (from 1936) Robertson, and provided a channel along which advice on economic policy could flow to the Treasury.

Throughout the interwar years there was also a Chief Economic Adviser whose main duties were to represent the government at international meetings on economic issues and to undertake on its behalf commercial and financial negotiations with other countries. The first to hold the title was Sir Hubert Llewellyn Smith on his retirement as Permanent Secretary to the Board of Trade. He was succeeded by Sir Sydney Chapman who had taken over from Sir Hubert as Permanent Secretary. Neither seems to have had a professional staff or to have been consulted on domestic issues of financial or macroeconomic policy. They represented the government on imperial and international committees and at international conferences, but the matters under discussion were nearly all of interest to the Board of Trade rather than to the Treasury.

Chapman was succeeded in 1932 by Sir Frederick Leith-Ross who held office until his retiral in 1946 to become Governor of the National Bank of Egypt. Leith-Ross, a Treasury official, was an expert on finance rather than trade matters and was much involved in negotiations on intergovernmental debts in the 1930s. He, too, had little to do with domestic economic policy and not a great deal more with the formative stages of international economic policy. Like his predecessors he was an experienced civil servant acting largely on his own on an international stage.

What marks the period before 1939 is the absence of a full-time staff of economists at the center of the government machine. No such group existed anywhere within the government to advise the prime minister, the chancellor or any other minister charged with responsibility for economic policy (with the possible exception of the Minister of Agriculture). Ministers in need of expert advice had either to rely on such expertise as was available from administrators within their own department, or to seek advice elsewhere from business and financial circles or from some academic economist, or turn to the Bank of England, which acted as the government's financial adviser but was equally lacking in professionally trained economists.

That such a situation should persist may seem odd. But the government at that time was much less deeply involved than now in managing the economy. Macroeconomics, indeed, was in its infancy; microeconomics was regarded as nearly all first-year stuff for an economics student. A civil servant like Hawtrey could acquire a familiarity with economic analysis comparable with that of any professional economist. Above all, economic policy was dominated by the institutional setting in which problems arose and required a more intimate knowledge of the setting than economists usually possessed.

What changed things was the upheaval of World War II. The government was slow to appreciate that a wartime economy has to be planned and that planning raises technical economic issues. It was not until July 1939 that it arranged for a review of its economic and financial plans by Lord Stamp, aided by 'one or two economists and perhaps a prominent industrialist'. The 'one or two economists' turned out to be Henry Clay and Hubert Henderson who soon felt the need for a staff to provide and sift economic information. It was proposed that the staff should consist of a few economists or statisticians – 'say two or three at the outset' – who would have to be recruited from the universities or elsewhere because no civil servants 'possessing the necessary qualifications' could be spared by their departments.

The first appointments to the staff, christened the Central Economic Information Service, were made at the end of 1939. Like the Stamp Survey it was located in the War Cabinet Office, not the Treasury, and remained there when, at the end of 1940, the Stamp Survey was wound up and its staff split into the Economic Section under John Jewkes and the Central Statistical Office under, first, Francis Hemming, then Harry Campion.

In the course of its brief existence in 1939–40, the Stamp Survey submitted scores of papers to ministers on almost every aspect of the war economy. Stamp himself was offered and declined the post of Chancellor of the Exchequer in January 1940 and was a member of the Ministerial Committee on Economic Policy. Henry Clay was economic adviser to the Bank of England and, like Sydney Chapman, had held the economics chair at the University of Manchester. Hubert Henderson was the author of the best-known introductory textbook in economics, *Supply and Demand* (Henderson, 1922), and had been don, editor and ally of Keynes before becoming secretary of the Committee on Economic Information. Stamp, Clay and Henderson formed a highly productive trio but they did not work under the direction of any single minister, and during the first critical year of their existence exercised their influence on policy largely through the circulation of papers. Some of these went to the Economic Policy Committee under the Chancellor, Sir John Simon, but this was not as it proved a very effective body.

Until officially reborn as the Economic Section, the Central Economic Information Service was in much the same position. At the change of government in May 1940, the total staff did not exceed about half a dozen economists, of whom John Jewkes and Austin Robinson were the most senior, and the work at first consisted largely in the preparation of documents analyzing the prospects for four limiting elements in the war effort: shipping, foreign exchange, raw materials and manpower. With the arrival of Ely Devons in March 1940 a more determined effort was made to assemble and circulate the secret statistics necessary for the conduct of the war (there being then no Central Statistical Office). A kind of manifesto entitled 'Urgent economic problems', a comprehensive review of current issues of policy complete with recommendations, was circulated at the beginning of June. In addition, the members of the group built up their own sources of information within Whitehall mainly through contact with economists who had joined other economic departments.

After a difficult period in the second half of 1940 when the staff doubled but there was no satisfactory ministerial outlet for its work, responsibility for economic policy was entrusted to the Lord President's Committee, of which the chairman after the death of Neville Chamberlain in November was Sir John Anderson. The Economic Section, as it had begun to be called, became established as Anderson's staff, preparing briefs, bringing up issues for decision and monitoring the implementation of policy. Anderson was a highly competent chairman who enjoyed the confidence of the prime minister and of departments generally and he was left to get on with the job of economic coordination. By the time Anderson moved to the Treasury and was succeeded by Attlee in 1943, the Lord President's Committee was firmly established in this role and the Economic Section, now under Lionel Robbins, had become an indispensable instrument in the formulation of policy.

In 1943, for the first and only time in British history, an official committee prepared a report on 'The role of the economist in the machinery of government'.[1] This addressed itself to the need under postwar conditions for a central organization along the lines of the Economic Section. The conclusions of the committee found expression in the White Paper on Employment Policy issued in 1944, which announced the government's intention 'to establish on a permanent basis a small central staff' qualified to study economic trends and submit appreciations of them to ministers.

In the Committee's view, the function of the Section would be to receive, supplement and appraise economic intelligence; to make or arrange for studies on subjects not covered by any one department; and to present 'coordinated and objective pictures of the economic situation as a whole, and the economic aspects of projected government policies'. It should be able to commission special studies by universities or other institutions. It should stand ready to supply economic advice on request to departments and work closely with them, sharing frequently in the formulation of departmental policy in advance of submission to the departmental minister. Constant informal exchanges of view among all economists in the government service would be encouraged by the existence of the Section which should maintain particularly close contacts with economists employed in departments.

After the appearance of the White Paper, James Meade, who was to succeed Lionel Robbins as Director, wrote to Edward Bridges, the Cabinet Secretary and about to become head of the Treasury, to enquire about future working relationships. Since 'financial policy is bound finally to become the central instrument of economic policy', advising on the decisive aspects of economic policy would be advising on the economic aspects of Treasury policy. So would the Treasury retain its own advisers – at that time it had Keynes, Henderson, Catto (who succeeded Montagu Norman as Governor of the Bank of England) and, at least nominally, Leith-Ross – or would it turn to the Economic Section for advice and admit the Director to budgetary and other confidential discussions? On all of his questions Meade received reassuring answers. The Section was to have 'an increasingly close and intimate connection with the Treasury', which would rely on it alone for technical advice.

For the first eight years after the war the Economic Section remained in the Cabinet Office. It was not until 1953 that it was absorbed by the Treasury where it has remained ever since. Initially the influence of the Section was limited because it continued to serve the Lord President (Herbert Morrison) in his capacity as economic coordinator, when in fact, as Meade had predicted, the main instruments of economic coordination in peacetime were in the Treasury and the responsibility of the Chancellor of the Exchequer, Hugh Dalton. Dalton, being himself a professor of economics and the author of a textbook on public finance, felt in no great need of economic advice and tended to pooh-pooh Meade's suggestions. The split between the economic and financial aspects of policy contributed to the succession of crises in 1947 while Dalton's attitude to advice from the Section hastened Meade's resignation in that year. Although members of the Section had been able to brief Morrison and (on occasion) Prime Minister Attlee, and Meade had been a member of the Treasury's Budget Committee, the arrangements for the organization of economic advice in the first two postwar years were, as a member of the Section later confessed, 'a complete flop'.

A fresh start was made with the arrival of Robert Hall as Director in 1947 and the replacement of Dalton by Stafford Cripps as Chancellor of the Exchequer. Hall came to have great influence on policy largely because he had the ear of the Chief Planning Officer, Sir Edwin Plowden, who in turn had great influence on Cripps. The Hall–Plowden team did not always get its ideas accepted easily and was regarded with some distrust and hostility in parts of Whitehall; but it played a critical part in economic policymaking after 1947, notably in the devaluation of 1949, rearmament in 1950 and the rejection in 1952 of the Robot scheme to float the pound, block sterling balances and make the pound convertible on external account.

The last of these involved a long and bitter fight with the Treasury and disposed Hall to contemplate a return to academic life in 1953 when Plowden left for another appointment. This produced an immediate response from the Treasury of which the most important part was the transfer to it of the Economic Section from the Cabinet Office and the designation of Hall as the government's economic adviser. These changes made for a more intimate association with the Chancellor. Hall was, however, virtually a member of the Treasury team already.

Under Hall and for many years thereafter the main concern of the Section was employment policy. The Director was a member of the Budget Committee and he more than anyone helped to shape the budget judgement, i.e. the decision how far the budget should seek to restrict or expand the pressure on available manpower and capacity. For this purpose the Section needed to form a view, in quantitative terms, of the impact on the economy of changes in taxation and expenditure, in monetary policy, and in the use of other instruments of demand management such as restrictions on consumer credit. Administrators and chancellors, however, continued to be guided by less sophisticated indications of the effects of policy changes, such as the budget surplus or, in later years, the PSBR (public sector borrowing requirement).

In its efforts to keep track of changes in the economy the Section became involved, on the one hand, in pressing for improvements in economic statistics, and on the other, in preparing short-term forecasts on the basis of those statistics. Once quarterly national accounts became available after 1955 the forecasting work expanded side by side with research into the underlying relationships governing the behavior of the economy. This absorbed a high proportion of the time of the staff. In later years, a computable model of increasing complexity was introduced and this continues to occupy a substantial number of the economists in the Treasury.

Apart from employment policy, and with it economic stabilization and growth, many other aspects of policy were investigated by the Section. It advised on investment policy and was responsible for the introduction of the investment allowance in 1953 and the test rate of discount in the 1960s. It produced theoretical papers on inflation and disinflation, on pricing in the nationalized industries, on wage behavior, on the relation between employment and output, and a long list of other subjects. It battled for an incomes policy as early as 1942. It worked on the future demand for steel, on agricultural subsidies, on the effects of hire purchase restrictions. In addition it was and is deeply involved in all aspects of international economic policy, starting with James Meade's wartime proposals for an international trade organization. Much of the time of the Director, from Meade until the present day, is occupied in attending meetings abroad – in Paris, Brussels, Washington and elsewhere – of economic experts from other countries. Much of the time of the staff goes to assessing economic developments abroad, offering advice on balance-of-payments prospects and recommending measures appropriate to those prospects.

Given the limited size of the staff in the 1940s and 1950s, large areas of policy had to be neglected. For example, comparatively little work was done on public expenditure or on industrial and regional policy. It was only in the 1960s that the practice began of posting members of the Section to work within the expenditure divisions of the Treasury. At the same time some members were assigned temporarily to other departments, e.g. the Foreign Office and the Ministry of Overseas Development. Neither practice could go very far so long as the Section remained a small group of carefully selected economists, at first numbering no more than a dozen and even in the early 1960s rarely exceeding fifteen.

Apart from members of the Economic Section, a number of agricultural economists and a few specialists working on economic intelligence in the Ministry of Defence, there were virtually no economists in Whitehall up to 1964 except those who acted as research officers or had joined as administrators after studying economics at university or subsequently. In the latter group there were over 300 in the 1960s, including at least twenty-five with postgraduate degrees; but their previous field of study in no way ensured that their administrative responsibilities would have any material economic content.

If departments outside the Treasury suffered from a shortage of economists, this was partly because of difficulties in recruitment, difficulties shared by the Economic Section itself. Entry was to junior posts as economic assistants or economic advisers, with little chance of early promotion or of promotion on a par with what an able administrator might expect. Apart from the Director and Deputy Director there were in 1961 no posts above the level of Economic Adviser (a grade to which promotion was not uncommon at 28). It required considerable dedication to contemplate a career in the Economic Section under these circumstances. Even to recruit a university economist for two years raised difficulties when it might involve moving house for that limited period, was not always acceptable to university employers, and could mean some sacrifice of income.

ORGANIZATION: THE GOVERNMENT ECONOMIC SERVICE

The first big expansion in the number of government economists began in 1964 with the return of the Labour Party to office. A large new department, the Department of Economic Affairs, was created and charged with the coordination of economic policy. It was staffed largely with economists recruited from outside the civil service, many of them from the National Economic Development Organization – the planning body created by the Conservative government in 1961. At the same time, the Labour government created new departments such as the Ministries of Technology and Overseas Development with important economic responsibilities and these also recruited staffs which included economic advisers. Some existing departments, notably the Ministry of Transport, took occasion to bring in professional economists and appointed them to new senior posts. Within a year or two the number of economists in Whitehall increased greatly and the number of departments employing economists also expanded.

The Department of Economic Affairs was not a success. It renewed the split that had proved so disastrous in 1945–7 between financial policy and economic policy. The new department enjoyed none of the powers over the economy – over the budget, monetary policy and the exchange rate, for example – that were the prime instruments of economic policy: these remained with the Treasury. Nor did it absorb the Economic Section or its responsibilities for economic forecasting. Instead, it was obliged to concentrate on prices and incomes policy at the height of a boom and on long-term planning in the face of acute uncertainty over the future of the exchange rate.

If the government's purpose was to trim the wings of the Treasury, which carried too heavy a burden of responsibility in relation to the rest of Whitehall, it would have been wiser to have established a separate department to control public expenditure, especially as the divisions of the Treasury responsible for such control already came under a Treasury minister, the Chief Secretary, who shared with the Chancellor membership of the Cabinet. It would have made more sense to break up the Treasury along functional lines rather than try to pit the long term against the short.

Another consequence of the change of government in 1964 was the arrival in Whitehall of a number of politically committed economic advisers including Thomas Balogh (adviser to the Cabinet), Nicholas Kaldor and Robert Neild. Each of these operated on his own or with a single assistant while the Economic Section carried on under its Director. The multiplication of senior economists advising the prime minister, the chancellor, the Cabinet and various ministers created a much more lively atmosphere of debate throughout Whitehall. Many new and radical proposals were put forward and economic policy took a more adventurous form. At the center, however, there were more economic advisers than matters requiring advice; and although there were important departures in policy, especially tax and incomes policy, there was much unnecessary friction and a lack of coherence in the policies adopted.

The influx of economists made it necessary to reconsider the position of the Economic Section. The title of 'Economic Adviser to HMG', held by the Director since 1953, was dropped. At the same time his duties as a kind of informal labor exchange for economists were recognized by his designation as Head of the Government Economic Service. The new title, however, was at first something of a misnomer since ministers continued to make appointments without consulting or even informing him. The Government Economic Service amounted at that stage to little more than a collection of private armies of economists but became more of a reality once recruitment followed a more uniform procedure.

The establishment of the Government Economic Service led to a prolonged expansion in the number of government economists and in the number of departments employing them. This is illustrated in Table 2.1. The expansion of the Service was very rapid after 1964. It grew from a score or so excluding the agricultural departments and some research economists to nearly 400, scattered over some twenty different departments, by 1986. This was still quite a small number in comparison with the 2,500 or so members of the Administrative Class.

The big expansion was in the application of microeconomics, few economists outside the Treasury being concerned with macroeconomic issues except as a background to their work. Departments like Environment, Transport, Trade and Industry, Agriculture, Employment and Energy, recruited transport economists, industrial economists, labor economists and so on, who usually advised on particular sectors of the economy or specific projects, applying price theory and cost–benefit analysis or engaging in project appraisal. Apart from agriculture, these departments had either no career economists or only one from time to time until the mid-1960s, while now they account for roughly half the total.

It is difficult to resist the impression that there are now too many young economists in relatively junior posts. Out of the 390 economists employed in 1986, only fifty-six were at the level of Senior Economic Adviser (equivalent

Table 2.1 Government Economic Service staff in post, 1964–86

Department	1964	1969	1974	1976 (Dec.)	1984 (1 April)	1986 (1 Jan.)	Peak
HM Treasury	17½	28	53	62	69	78	78 (1986)
Depts of the Environment and Transport	—	38½	74	74	55	58	75 (1977)
Dept of Trade and Industry	—	31	43	51	35	36	
Office of Fair Trading	—	—	—	8	10	11	
Monopolies and Mergers Commission	—	—	—	4	8	8	65 (1978)
OFTEL	—	—	—	—	—	2	
Total	17½	97½	170	199	177	193	199 (1976)
Overseas Development Administration	—	22	32	37	32	38	40 (1977–8)
Ministry of Agriculture	x[1]	—[1]	21	27	22	23	27 (1976)
Dept of Employment	—	4	21	22	19	23	
Manpower Services Commission	—	—	—	6	17	17	40 (1986)
Dept of Health and Social Security	—	3½	14	20	21	22	22 (1986)
Scottish Office	1	3	18	21	22	20	28 (1977)
Dept of Energy	—	—	11	21	15	17	21 (1976)
Dept of Economic Affairs / Prices and Incomes Board	—	44½[2]	—	—	—	—	44½ (1969)
Other departments[3]	3	17½	38	47	31	37	47 (1976)
Total	21½	192	325	400	356	390	408 (1978)

Notes:
1. Economists in the Ministry of Agriculture were not members of the Government Economic Service until 1974.
2. Most of the economists in the Department of Economic Affairs were absorbed into the Treasury in 1970.
3. These include (figures for 1986 in brackets): Foreign and Commonwealth Office (9); Education and Science (7); Civil Service College (5); Defence (4); Inland Revenue (4); Customs & Excise (2); and Cabinet Office, National Audit Office, ECGD, Forestry Commission, Home Office and Welsh Office (1 each).

to Assistant Secretary) and seventeen at a more senior level, seven of them in the Treasury. This meant that for non-Treasury staff there were only ten really senior posts for 312 economists. Half the members of the Service are Economic Advisers, a grade to which able economists would expect to be promoted by the age of thirty or earlier. A further 117 are at lower grades and presumably in their twenties. Given that most entrants are in their early or middle twenties and that retirement at sixty is compulsory, these figures imply a predominantly young service in which the vast majority are in relatively junior posts and the chances of promotion beyond the level of Senior Economic Adviser are decidedly limited and shrinking. At present, for example, there are only three posts at the level of Deputy Secretary – and two of the three also carry wide administrative responsibilities – whereas a dozen years ago there were seven. About five economists annually are promoted to be Senior Economic Advisers and there is only about one appointment a year above that level.

The promotion block has been accompanied by a cessation of recruitment to the more senior posts and an increasing segregation of university economists from government. For many years from the mid-1950s senior staff were recruited to the Economic Section on a two-year basis with excellent results. Many of the best-known members of the academic profession served in government in this or some other way. Now this kind of link no longer exists. Departments do, however, maintain links with academic economists and have tried to encourage their interest in policy-related issues: for example, by using them to prepare reports, which are usually published. In addition, about twenty government economists a year are released or seconded for service in other capacities – in the City or with a commercial or industrial undertaking. This may widen their experience; but it does nothing to bring together the thinking of those in government and those who are educating the next generation of economists.

Economists who served in government from the 1920s to the 1960s were unanimous in testifying to the inadequacy of the average administrator's grasp of economics and to his frequent inability to see the bearing of economic considerations on the matters under discussion. Since then the general level of understanding of economic issues has improved, thanks in part to the great infusion of economists working alongside the administrators.

Modern government undoubtedly needs the services of trained economists. But is it wise to organize them in a separate economic service as few other countries do? The answer depends on how strict the separation is, the degree and kind of economic expertise required, and the best way of combining economic and administrative expertise. There will always be some posts which it would be difficult for administrators to fill, just as there are administrative posts for which economists are not particularly suited. National income forecasting is an obvious example of work best left to highly trained economists. Other work requires expert economic advice of a kind administrators can rarely supply: for example, cost–benefit studies, investment appraisal, and the formulation of tax policy, monetary policy, prices and incomes policy, and so on. In all of these, and in the detailed forecasting that goes on all over Whitehall, it is unwise to dispense with the services of an economist. It is also difficult, as a rule, to dispense with the services of an administrator. The fundamental problem is therefore how to organize collaboration between general administrators and economists, whether they are in separate services or one.

In such collaboration members of a specialist service are liable to be at a disadvantage if, as often happens, it is the administrator who stands closer to the minister and incorporates the economic advice in a general brief. There is a danger that the economist's contribution will be kept within the limits of his specialized discipline instead of overflowing on to wider aspects of policy. Specialist advice may then be subordinated to advice formulated in more comprehensive terms by an administrator and the specialist service in turn be rated as inferior to the general administrative service. One way of avoiding such a situation used increasingly by departments is to combine economists and administrators in units that divide the labor of analyzing problems, identify and examine the policy options and produce recommendations in quantitative terms. This enables decision taking to be based on a more adequate analysis and at the same time to be more decentralized than in the past.

Another method is to allow economists to compete for the posts in which the more complex issues are handled. It may be more desirable to put in such a post someone who is primarily an economist rather than an administrator, in order to make sure that the policy is on the right lines even at some risk to the administrative aspects of the policy. From this point of view, the split between an administrative and an economic service can be carried too far. Economists need to be given an opportunity of acting in an administrative capacity and administrators in economic departments need to be given an opportunity of acquiring some familiarity with economics. There should be no bar to the movement of staff between posts in one service and the other.

Unified grading is now being introduced, extending downwards to Grade 7 (Principal/Economic Adviser), and movement between the two services should be greatly eased. Economists recruited as specialists will be able to go on to become administrators, if so minded and sufficiently competent, much as specialists entering a business as chemists or engineers may move over to managerial posts as they become more experienced. Such arrangements could also help to improve the career prospects for young economists, especially if, with a shortage of Principals, some gravitate towards general administration and leave more room for the promotion of their colleagues. Whatever the effect of unified grading, quite a number of economists have already moved to senior administrative posts. Within the Treasury, for example, the posts held by former members of the Government Economic Service include one at Deputy Secretary level, three at Under Secretary level and three secretarial posts in the Chancellor's office including that of Principal Private Secretary.

However, the movement should not be all in one direction. Administrators may wish to serve for a time in the Economic Service and should have an opportunity to do so. It is also desirable that an effort should be made to raise the general level of economic understanding among administrators even if it is higher today than it was thirty years ago. In 1962 the government created for this purpose a Centre for Administrative Studies (CAS) with a view to giving young Principals (aged about 28) a more adequate grounding for their job including a course in economics extending over six months and conducted initially by Kit Macmahon, now Chairman of the Midland Bank. Unfortunately the experiment was abandoned when the CAS was merged with the Civil Service College. The occasional short course on which administrators are now sent is no adequate substitute.

If the experience of the Treasury is anything to go by, however, the infiltration of economists into more and more departments should enable some of their expertise to rub off on their colleagues in administrative posts. How far this has gone is difficult to judge from outside. Whereas in the past, ex-government economists wrote a stream of articles about their experience, now a great silence has descended and very little appears in print reflecting on the interaction between economists and administrators.

EVALUATION: SUCCESSES AND FAILURES

If one seeks to evaluate the existing machinery by which economic advice is tendered to government in the United Kingdom, one has to start from the fact that all except the formal arrangements is secret. We know there is a Cabinet but little of what goes on in Cabinet discussions or in the ministerial committees that do the work that never reaches Cabinet. We know that there is a Chief Economic Adviser but not what he does, what advice he tenders, what advice is accepted, what his relationship is with other officials. We are dependent on chance statements by ministers, what emerges in evidence to select committees, what is ferreted out by the press, personal contacts, etc. As to other economists, they are even more out of the public eye and difficult even to identify in a departmental list of staff, now that they are no longer herded together in a single unit like the Economic Section.

We must also bear in mind the many sources of advice pressed on ministers from every side: by the press, by other ministers, by friends and correspondents, over lunch or dinner, in representations from pressure groups of all kinds. The Chancellor in particular is offered much advice outside his department, notably from the Governor of the Bank of England, the CBI (Confederation of British Industry), the TUC (Trade Union Congress) and the City. It is rarely possible to say whose advice was decisive on any issue. The minister himself may be unable to say; he may not be the final authority, and may not know what tipped the balance in Cabinet or in public acceptance.

There is a similar abundance of advice *within* departments, most of it from administrators who would rarely claim to be economists. Since the Permanent Secretary is the minister's Principal official adviser, the Chief Economic Adviser will usually work in close association with him and may, indeed, see himself as advising the Permanent Secretary quite as much as the minister or ministers. He may minute the minister directly on matters recognized to be within his province but he usually takes the precaution of discussing important matters first with the Permanent Secretary or at least keeping him posted. The minister may, of course, bring in his own advisers and seek their personal advice. But they, too, usually find it best to work with the machine without, of course, surrendering their independence of judgement or refraining from making their judgement known to the minister. Ministers have limited time and cannot afford to consult all their advisers individually on every issue. Economic advisers are listened to in proportion as the minister finds their advice acceptable, well-informed, sensible and constructive.

All this makes it difficult to assess the influence of government economists on policy. However, instances can be cited with confidence of interventions that were of critical importance. There can be no doubt at all of the enormous influence in the special circumstances of wartime of the economists who entered Whitehall at that time. This was true not only of the Economic Section as advisers to the Lord President on all the issues of economic policy and coordination that he handled, but of economists scattered over other departments as well. It was in part through their contacts with fellow economists elsewhere in Whitehall that the Economic Section was so effective in contributing to economic coordination. Other examples can be drawn from the postwar years for which the records are now available under the thirty-year rule. In 1949, for example, the decision to devalue the pound goes back to efforts by Robert Hall, the Director of the Economic Section, to convince his Treasury colleagues from April 1949 onwards of the wisdom of this step. It is true that it was Hugh Gaitskell who was the key figure among the ministers and that he was persuaded by Nicholas Kaldor and Paul Rosenstein-Rodan, neither of whom was a government economist at the time. But it is by no means certain that Gaitskell, who was not a member of the Cabinet, would have carried the prime minister and the Cabinet with him, had not the official Treasury been brought round to support the operation largely by Robert Hall's arguments.

It would be possible to pick other illustrations of a less dramatic kind. The Budget Committee of (mainly Treasury) officials relied on the Economic Section for almost the whole of the fourteen years of Hall's directorship for an assessment of the economic outlook and for guidance on the action required to maintain the pressure of demand within acceptable limits. Hall normally advised on the specific amount that should be added to or deducted from the tax receipts; the Budget Committee usually endorsed his judgement; and the Chancellor, while he might not accept the advice in full, accepted it as a measure of what he ought to aim for. If a package of measures had to be devised to give effect to the budget judgement, that too would reflect, in part at least, the advice of the Economic Section.

When we turn to more recent times, there have been examples of both success and failure. None of the government's economic advisers had much influence on its decision not to devalue in 1964 or to devalue in 1967. These were decisions taken, in the one case, on political grounds and in the other, for lack of the means to prevent it. Nor did any of the economists have much to do with the various attempts by the government to join the European Economic Community or with their ultimate success.

One area of policy in which the government's economic advisers – mainly Lord Kaldor – did have some influence was tax policy. The Selective Employment Tax was originally proposed by Lord Kaldor in 1966 and was accepted on grounds rather different from those used by him to justify it: whatever it might do to efficiency, or to manufacturing, it was primarily a tax on distributive services introduced at a time when some new source of revenue was thought necessary. Like the Regional Employment Premium, another of Lord Kaldor's brainchildren, it did not long survive.

It is more difficult to speak with confidence on the role of economists in the 1970s and 1980s. Treasury economists would seem to have played an important part over the past ten years in the development of monetary policy: in particular in articulating and operating the medium-term financial strategy; and, at a later stage, in the shift away from broad money targets to reliance on narrow money and to the increased importance now attached to movements in the exchange rate. Another important change in policy to which Treasury economists made a major contribution was the revision in the structure of business taxation in 1984. At the personal level Sir Alan Walters at No. 10 Downing Street has taken public credit for some loosening of monetary policy after the débâcle of 1980 when the pound went to $2.45. He has also been largely responsible for Mrs Thatcher's opposition to Britain's joining the European Monetary System.

All these are matters of macroeconomic policy when the vast majority of members of the Government Economic Service now deal with microeconomic issues. It is these issues that have come to the forefront under a government that has abandoned demand management. They are not the issues of high policy on which the Economic Section once advised but are usually entangled in institutional detail requiring careful study. It is hard to assess how successful economists have been in dealing with them. One can, however, point to the work done on investment appraisal in the public sector from the mid-1960s onwards, with the introduction of the test rate of discount and present-value calculations; the Byatt report on export credit, questioning the high subsidies to exports concealed in the offer of credit at noncommercial rates of interest; and the review of competition policy by the Department of Trade and Industry in the late 1970s when two Green Papers were published.

These are only a few of the wide variety of jobs on which government economists have worked. Others include work on energy modeling and on long-range assessments of world energy markets as an element in domestic energy policy; on transport, including cost–benefit studies of various

Channel Tunnel projects, and a new system of investment appraisal for road schemes; on employment, where proposals for selective employment measures have been analyzed and results monitored; and social security, involving comprehensive reviews of existing arrangements. In all this work much of the influence of economists has been on the climate of thought and the way business is transacted, notably in the spread of quantitative methods of analysis.

An increasing amount of work done by government economists is published. Much of it appears in Government Economic Service Working Papers, of which there are now over 100. Other work is embodied in Green Papers floating policy proposals or in departmental publications (for example, *Regional Industrial Policy: Some Economic Issues* and *A Study of Business Finance under the Small Business Loan Guarantee Scheme*, both issued by the Department of Trade and Industry).

What of the failures? Given the state of the British economy it cannot be pretended that economic policy was always a resounding success. But there is little agreement as to what went wrong and how it might have been avoided: still less on the share of the blame that should fall on government economists. Even if it is accepted that the biggest failure was inflation, that tells us little unless there is agreement on the cure, which there most certainly is not.

The main error for which economists were to blame was in overstimulating the economy in response to the popular clamor for growth. It is clear in retrospect that on the occasions when economic activity eased, the fiscal stimulus was nearly always late and excessive and underestimated the recuperative power of the economy. A second error, accompanying the first, was to use too short a time horizon. This was not true of the immediate postwar years when it was possible to foresee and measure the scale of the adjustments needed (e.g. in the balance of payments). Thereafter, policy was shaped against a horizon that was usually one or at most two years except in the case of public expenditure. The planning of investment was correspondingly circumscribed. Efforts to link government planning and industrial planning, as in the National Plan of 1966, turned out to be built on sand and did not survive the devaluation of 1967. The fundamental difficulty was that there was little or no margin for error so that it was not possible to take corrective action gradually while holding to a steady course. Instead, even small departures from trend had to be made the occasion for decisive action of a kind that made it difficult to stick to a long-term view.

But perhaps the biggest failure of all was the instability of policy: the reversals with a change of government on incomes policy, nationalization and other issues; the imposition of one kind of tax by one government and its removal by the next; the uncertainties as to the life expectation of any new instrument or institution of the government's creation. Few of these uncertainties were attributable to government economists.

CONCLUSION: LESSONS FROM BRITISH EXPERIENCE

There is no unique solution to the problem of tendering economic advice. The arrangements made have to conform to the forces of supply and demand, which vary from country to country. In the United Kingdom much depends on the personality of ministers, especially the prime minister and the Chancellor of the Exchequer. Much depends also on the ability of individual advisers and their rapport with ministers. Arrangements will also vary with the state of professional opinion and whether there is a consensus of any kind or deep and open disagreement.

From time to time proposals have been made for changes in current arrangements for the formulation of policy: either in the distribution between departments of responsibility for economic policy or in the distribution of economists between departments. These are large issues that cannot be pursued very far here. There is, for example, the question of how centralized in a single department economic policy should be. Should power to make key economic decisions be so highly concentrated in the Treasury? If so, is there not a danger that these decisions will go unchallenged when a wider dispersion of authority and economic advice would run less risk of serious error? As argued earlier, there is a case for detaching from the Treasury at least those divisions that control public expenditure so as to form a separate department. The Treasury would, however, retain responsibility for the budget (which in Britain relates only to revenue proposals), monetary policy and the rate of exchange. There should be no attempt to revive a Department of Economic Affairs when the Treasury already answers to this description, and is as capable of drawing up long-term plans as short-term ones if the government so desires.

Changes have also been suggested in the organization of economic advice: for example, a build-up of economists in the Cabinet Office or in No. 10 Downing Street that might offer advice to the Cabinet or to the prime minister. The first of these alternatives might seem to echo the creation of the Economic Section in the Cabinet Office in 1940. But in wartime economic policy was coordinated by the Lord President, not the Treasury, and the Economic Section acted as the staff of the Lord President, not of the Cabinet. There can be no escape from the conclusion that it is the minister who is in charge of economic policy, now the Chancellor, who most needs a staff of economic advisers. It would be a mistake to create a rival staff of any size attached to some other minister or to the prime minister.

This does not mean that there is no place for a group of economists, or a mixed group of experts, who could investigate long-term interdepartmental issues such as the future of the motor-car industry or the adequacy of industrial research and development and prepare reports for ministers to study at their leisure. Such a body was created by Edward Heath in 1970 in the form of the Central Policy Review Staff under Lord Rothschild. It survived for a decade or so but was abandoned by Mrs Thatcher. A 'think-tank' of this kind may be preferable to a series of interdepartmental committees as a means of reviewing certain topics. But it is liable to excite the suspicion, if not hostility, of the departments on whose work it encroaches, and has to tread delicately in order to carry them with it. It is also likely to have a hard struggle to find a market for its output unless it is under the direction of a minister or can count on the continuing interest of a busy prime minister.

A staff attached directly to the prime minister is another matter. It has always been necessary for the prime minister to receive briefs on the wide variety of subjects coming before the Cabinet and these are supplied by the Cabinet Secretary or by the various private secretaries loaned to No. 10 Downing Street by other Whitehall departments (including the Treasury). In addition prime ministers have on occasion had personal advisers, some of them economists or holding strong views on economic policy: Lord Cherwell, Lord Balogh and Sir Alan Walters are examples. The intervention of these advisers has had its successes; but the record is erratic and not very reassuring.

Prime ministers have also felt the need for more systematic briefing by politically committed advisers who can propound alternative policies to those coming from the Treasury. Such a need has been met since 1974 by a policy unit housed within No. 10 Downing Street and including a few professional economists although the head of the unit, until the appointment of Brian Griffiths, could hardly be so described. The members of the unit, like policy advisers in other departments but unlike members of the Government Economic Service, give up their posts on a change of government. Apart from offering a second opinion to the prime minister, the unit serves essentially as a device for supplementing civil service machinery with advice in which the political element is given fuller consideration.

The prime minister is, of course, entitled to decide what arrangements should be made in No. 10 for the tendering of economic advice: whether to trust the Chancellor and his staff and offer him full backing if he can make a convincing case or to take an active and independent interest in economic policy assisted by a personal adviser or policy unit so as to be able to query Treasury advice. The first alternative runs the risk of allowing major decisions to be taken without an adequate check; the second, if carried too far, undermines the freedom and morale of the main economic policy-making department and may end by obliging the prime minister to take over responsibility when he is fully occupied in other directions. It seems best to rely primarily on the Treasury to formulate policy, leaving it to the Chancellor to discuss it with the prime minister, however advised, and see it through Cabinet with his support.

Since the party in power changes from time to time there is a question whether economic advisers may not have to be changed too. However, no one seems to ask this question about administrators who are in established posts and are expected to advise whatever government comes to power. During the war and for many years afterwards it proved possible for economists to offer advice on a nonpolitical footing. From 1964, however, governments began to recruit as advisers within the main economic departments economists wearing the political colors of the party in office. For a time it seemed as if this was a temporary aberration. But it happened again, less markedly, when the Labour Party took office in 1974. Broadly speaking, the advice offered on demand management on those occasions (although not on all other aspects of policy) remained within a common tradition of thought. The government advisers who entered the Treasury in 1964 and in the 1970s expressed views that might almost equally readily have been advanced by members of the Economic Section. The party label in practice meant very little and by no means secured preferential treatment for the advice offered.

From about 1976 policy underwent a sea-change. A few years later, the incoming Conservative government took a leaf from the Labour Party's book and installed economists of its own persuasion in a number of key posts: Sir Alan Walters, Sir Douglas Hague and then Professor Brian Griffiths at No. 10 to advise the prime minister; Sir Terence Burns in the Treasury as Head of the Government Economic Service. In the same spirit a new Governor of the Bank of England was appointed whose views were congenial to the government. In this case the appointment was strongly criticized by the opposition, which, contrary to past custom, was not consulted before it was made.

All of these economists held views on economic policy very different from those characteristic of government economists over the previous generation. The economics profession was no longer united on objectives of policy or on the theory underpinning the main objectives; and, as Henderson had predicted in 1943, the issues on which economists differed became the subject of acute party controversy. The danger of an alternation of economists from one administration to the next, such as is typical of the US Council of Economic Advisers, has come visibly nearer. Key appointments both within the civil service and elsewhere (e.g. to the governorship of the Bank of England) have become increasingly politicized. It would appear that whereas the party system by itself is quite compatible with continuity of service, once the economics profession falls apart on major issues, economic advisory services are bound to become discontinuous. Perhaps this will prove to be true only of macroeconomic policy and hence affect only a limited part of the Government Economic Service; but once discontinuity sets in, there is a risk that it may spread, and the appeal of a *career* as a government economist will be correspondingly diminished.

At the end of the war, academic economists were in demand and their stock (though not their pay) was high. What they had to say commanded attention and respect. In the United Kingdom this is no longer true. The standing that Keynes, Beveridge and others won for the entire profession is a thing of the past. Few British economists are known to the public; fewer still are listened to. One hardly ever sees in the British press a quotation, an article or even a letter from an academic economist. If the media want to give space to comments on the current economic situation, or to news bearing on it, they hardly ever approach an economist in academic life but are more likely to print what they are told by an economist in touch with financial markets working in the City, usually with a firm of stockbrokers. There is always a danger that economists in government may suffer similar neglect and that ministers may revert to what David Henderson has called 'Do-it-yourself-economics'.

Another danger is of a sharp division between the two groups of economists: those in the universities and those in government. The circulation of economists between the two, once an important, if limited, feature of the profession, has virtually ceased. As has been not uncommon in the past, the Government Economic Service recruits more young economists than can hope to be promoted to top positions. The oversupply of young economists then produces a high rate of turnover and a reluctance to draw in still more economists from academic life. Very few economists in academic life under the age of forty have served in government. This inevitably colors their interests and their approach to economic problems.

In a democracy it is the voter who decides who is to rule him and who has in the end to approve or disapprove the economic policies of the government in office: their priorities, their success, depend on how the public reacts. It may be true, as Ely Devons used to argue, that the voter is asked to pronounce only on issues incapable of rational demonstration. He may have only a limited understanding of the issues. But if there is no debate, his chances of understanding are diminished. One of the jobs of economists is to promote debate and improve public understanding. Those who advise ministers may contribute by writing ministers' speeches or drafting White Papers. But they need also to embark on the process of public education and debate more deliberately and consciously. Too little is published in the form of a detailed review of economic performance and prospects such as the *Economic Survey* used to provide. By comparison the *Red Book* issued at the time of the Budget is too slight, the monthly *Economic Progress Report* too short-term, and the Government Economic Service's Working Papers too technical for the general public. It would also assist informed debate if there were more economists in public life with government experience. There needs to be a process of renewal, of movement into government and back so that the debate can be invigorated, both in and out, by the new arrivals.

There is a need for circulation of another kind. Economists in government need to be familiar with the scene in other countries. In the 1960s hardly any of the members of the Economic Section had ever set foot in the United

States or lived in Europe. Now government economists are seconded to the IMF (International Monetary Fund), OECD (Organization for Economic Cooperation and Development) and the European Economic Commission or go on visits to other governments. As the world economy draws closer together, nothing is more necessary in a government economist than some first-hand knowledge of how foreign economies operate and some contact with the thinking and personalities of other countries.

NOTE

1. The report has never been published but is available in the Public Records Office in PRO CAB 87/373. The extensive evidence given to the Committee by Keynes, Robbins, Henderson, Meade and others is reviewed in Cairncross and Watts (forthcoming).

BIBLIOGRAPHY

There is a full bibliography in:

Coats, A. W. (ed.), *Economists in Government* (Duke University Press, 1981).

Articles by former members of the Economic Section (1939–64)

Cairncross, Alec, 'On being an economic adviser', in *Factors in Economic Development* (London: Allen and Unwin, 1962).

Cairncross, Alec, 'The Work of an Economic Adviser' and 'Economists in Government', in *Essays in Economic Management* (London: Allen and Unwin, 1971).

Chester, D. N., 'The role of economic advisers in government', in Thirlwall (ed.), *Keynes as a Policy Adviser* (London: Macmillan, 1981).

Hall, Sir Robert, 'The place of the economist in government', *Oxford Economic Papers* (June 1955).

Hall, Sir Robert, 'Reflections on the practical application of economics', *Economic Journal* (December 1959).

Henderson, P. D., 'The use of economists in British administration', *Oxford Economic Papers* (February 1961).

Little, I. M. D., 'The economist in Whitehall', *Lloyds Bank Review* (April 1957).

Marris, Robin, 'The position of economics and economists in the government machine: A comparative critique of the United Kingdom and the Netherlands', *Economic Journal* (December 1954).

Other articles

Brittan, Samuel, 'The irregulars', in Richard Rose (ed.), *Policy-Making in Britain: a Reader in Government* (London: Macmillan, 1969).

Coddington, Alan, 'Economists and policy', *National Westminster Bank Quarterly Review* (February 1973).

Hallett, Graham, 'The role of economists as government advisers', *Westminster Bank Review* (May 1967).
HM Treasury, 'The Government Economic Service', *Economic Progress Report*, No. 99 (June 1978).
MacDougall, G. D. A., 'The machinery of economic government (some personal reflections)', in D. Butler and A. Halsey (eds), *Policy and Politics: Essays in Honour of Norman Chester* (London: Macmillan, 1978).
Mitchell, Joan, 'Special advisers: a personal view', *Public Administration* (1978).
Opie, Roger, 'The making of economic policy', in H. Thomas (ed.), *Crisis in the Civil Service* (London: Blond, 1968).
Peacock, Alan, 'Giving economic advice in difficult times', *The Three Banks Review* (March 1977).
Postan, M. M., 'A plague of economists', in *Fact and Relevance: Essays on Historical Method* (Cambridge: Cambridge University Press, 1971).
Shanks, Michael, 'The irregular in Whitehall', in P. Streeten (ed.), *Unfashionable Economics: Essays in Honour of Lord Balogh* (London: Weidenfeld and Nicolson, 1970).

Books

Brittan, Samuel, *Steering the Economy: the Role of the Treasury* (Harmondsworth, Penguin Books, 1971).
Cairncross, Alec, and Watts, Nita, *The Economic Section 1939–61* (London: Unwin Hyman, 1989).
Chester, D. N. (ed.), *Lessons of the British War Economy* (Cambridge: Cambridge University Press, 1951).
Coats, A. W. (ed.), *Economists in Government* (Duke University Press, 1981).
Devons, Ely, *Papers on Planning and Economic Management* (Manchester: Manchester University Press, 1970).
Donoghue, Bernard, *Prime Minister: the Conduct of Policy under Harold Wilson and James Callaghan* (London: Jonathan Cape 1987).
Heclo, Hugh, and Wildavsky, Aaron, *The Private Government of Public Money* (London: Macmillan, 1974).
Henderson, Hubert D. *Supply and Demand* (New York: Harcourt Brace, 1922).
Howson, Susan, and Winch, Donald, *The Economic Advisory Council 1930–1939: A Study in Economic Advice During Depression and Recovery* (Cambridge: Cambridge University Press, 1977).
Hutchison, T. W., *Economics and Economic Policy in Britain* (London: Allen and Unwin, 1968).
MacDougall, Sir Donald, *Don and Mandarin* (London: John Murray, 1987).
Meade, James, *Diary, 1944–47* (London: Unwin Hyman, 1989).
Peacock, Alan, *The Economic Analysis of Government and Related Themes* (Oxford: Martin Robertson, 1979).
Plowden, Lord, *Industrialist in the Treasury: the Post-War Years* (London: André Deutsch, 1989).
Plowden, William (ed.), *Advising the Rulers* (Oxford: Blackwell, 1987).

3 · WEST GERMANY

Norbert Kloten

INTRODUCTION

The role of the economist in West Germany's political decision-making process today reflects the conditions that prevailed when a new order of government and a new economic order were created after World War II. In both cases these orders did not evolve from a previous state of affairs, but were the intended consequences of a deliberately created framework. This does not rule out a considerable element of historical coincidence. The structure of the new state was in many respects predetermined in part by pragmatic and in part by preventive actions of the British, French, and above all American military governments in their zones of occupation. In the final analysis the new order of government was an expression of the Germans' bitter experiences during the Weimar Republic and the years that followed. It also reflected the contending ideas that arose in West Germany after Germany's collapse at the end of the war. The Basic Law of 23 May 1949 created a federal state with three levels of government – the federal government, the Länder, and the local authorities – and with strict separation between the powers of the federal government and the Länder, as well as between the legislative, executive and judicial authorities at both levels.

Within the federal government, the Chancellor decides the policy line to be adopted. Each minister runs his department independently and on his own responsibility within the framework of the Chancellor's guidelines. Differences between the ministers are settled by the cabinet (not by the Chancellor). There is a close relationship and close cooperation between the government and the ruling parliamentary party (or parties), the two frequently joining together to respond to the opposition in parliament.

The economic order developed step by step in a process that continued until well into the 1950s. The real moment of its birth, however, can be readily identified – this was when, a few days after the Allies' currency reform of 20 June 1948, Ludwig Erhard lifted most of the economic controls, many of which dated back to the war years. The success of this act of insubordination against the British–American authority prompted the Christian Democratic Union and the Christian Social Union – which had opposed the idea – to accept Erhard's market-economy approach. Thus, neoliberal tendencies, developed from a variety of sources, prevailed and with them a way of thinking about regulatory concepts in which suborders must be consistent with the overall order comprising the state, the economy and society. Achievement of such an order is the task of the state. A strong state is presupposed, but the state's power is circumscribed by rules of law and action that are compatible with the order.

The early conceptual work on this type of economy had essentially been developed by economists during the war years, partly in exile. Many of them were related to the 'Freiburg School' which supported the idea of a free market economy. The key work was Walter Eucken's *Grundlagen der Nationalökonomie* (The Foundations of Economics), published in 1940. The decisive influence acquired by neoliberals can be especially attributed to Ludwig Erhard, Franz Böhm, Wilhelm Röpke, Alexander Rüstow, Alfred Müller-Armack, backed by other university and public figures such as former members of the Erwin von Beckerath 'working group' – one of the Freiburg groups opposing National Socialism – which sought already during the war years to formulate the design of a new economic order after the collapse of the regime.

On 23 January 1948, at the invitation of the bizonal economic authority, seventeen German economists and commercial-law experts met in Königstein-Taunus for the purpose of establishing an advisory council to express scientific opinions on questions of economic policy. At this meeting it was decided that an economic advisory council not subject to political directive should be established. This council would itself take the final decisions regarding the choice of topics and their content; its independence would include the right to co-opt additional members; its members would not receive either direct or indirect remuneration for their work; and its reports would be published as quickly as possible. These features were accepted when the council was attached to the Federal Ministry for Economic Affairs following the establishment of the new state (September 1949). They also applied to all similar advisory councils set up later by ministries and federal authorities.

The standards for drawing upon the knowledge of independent consultative bodies reflect the outstanding contribution made by the neoliberals to the new economic-policy maxims and to a way of thinking in categories of a symbiotic division of labor between government authorities and outside experts. In this respect, politics needs a permanent challenge from the academic world, for only the latter can evaluate the consequences of alternative courses of action in a disinterested manner. By fulfilling this function, scholarship promotes the objectivization of political discussion without jeopardizing the primacy and decision-making freedom of the political authorities. The persuasiveness of the evaluation is derived from the scholar's authority, which is established by expert knowledge and objective analysis. This in turn requires external and internal independence for the adviser, as well as institutional arrangements to guarantee it. To insure independence, the results of the consultation must be published without delay. The general public thus becomes the last recipient of the advice provided and is at the same time a *forum externum* where the insights gained by scientific means are debated.

If scholarship fulfills its role, it proves itself as the intellectual conscience of politics. It limits the politician's desire for power by imposing upon him the burden of proof for his action. Seen in these terms, scholarship performs a social function and becomes a constitutive element of a political system based on the principle of freedom. But scholarship can complement politics only if the two are oriented toward the same goals. In the early days of the Federal Republic of Germany, this appeared to be guaranteed, at least in economic policy.

DEVELOPMENT OF THE ECONOMIC ADVISORY SYSTEM

In March 1950, a scientific advisory council was set up at the Federal Ministry of Finance as the successor to the Tax Advisory Council (which had come into being on 13 May 1948) and the subsequent Fiscal Policy Advisory Council of the bizonal finance authority. From the outset, the Finance Advisory Council cooperated closely with its counterpart council – the Economic Advisory Council – at the Federal Ministry for Economic Affairs. These were followed by other advisory councils, all of them based on the same model and all of them including economists. However, the real center of economic policy consultation remained the Economic Advisory Council and, in the field of public finance, the Finance Advisory Council. (See the synoptic table in the Appendix for details of the advisory bodies discussed in this chapter.)

Very soon, however, the Economic Advisory Council freed itself of a specific reporting obligation. In the beginning, it had produced one or two reports each year on the economic outlook. In view of the ever-growing volume of statistical data and the lack of research staff, but above all on account of its tendency to concentrate on the imminent basic decisions in the field of regulatory policy, it handed over the task of reporting on the economic situation to the economic research institutes in 1950. Since then, a 'joint diagnosis' has been produced twice a year by the German Institute for Economic Research (DIW), the HWWA-Institute for Economic Research, the IFO-Institute for Economic Research, the Institute of World Economics at the University of Kiel (IfW) and the Rhine-Westphalia Institute for

Economic Research (RWI). All these institutions engage in empirical economic research, supported on a contractual basis by the federal government and the Länder. Since 1963 this 'joint diagnosis' has included a forecast of overall economic developments (quantitative forecasts had previously been disapproved of). An emotional debate in the early 1970s concerning the question of administrative direction of private investments led in 1971 to the establishment of a Commission on Economic and Social Change ('Structural Commission'), which produced vast quantities of paper without being able to answer the key questions. In 1978 the economic research institutes got a mandate from the Federal Ministry for Economic Affairs to submit – every three years – a 'structural report', comprising a basic report and coverage of institute-specific topics.

There were already signs in the mid-1950s of a trend towards the establishment of advisory bodies with specifically defined mandates. These bodies are integrated into the process of preparing political options, but not into the decision-making process in the narrower sense of the term. The first body of this nature was the Agricultural Advisory Council, which was set up in 1955. The results of its consultations are incorporated in the *Report on the Agricultural Situation*, which is presented to the Bundestag and Bundesrat by the federal government on 15 February each year. The second council with a specific mandate is the Social Security Advisory Council, established in 1957 in conjunction with the introduction of wage-linked retirement pensions. Three of the Council's twelve members are economists and social scientists, with the chairman having to date always been an economist. The major task of the Social Security Advisory Council is to examine whether and to what extent the present and future financial position of the pension system (seen in terms of fifteen years) will bring pensions into line with the gross earnings of current members of the labor force. Its report, which since 1985 has been submitted by 15 December each year, must be passed on by the federal government to the Bundestag and Bundesrat.

Perhaps the most important step towards institutionalizing the knowledge of economic experts in the political decision-making process was the establishment of the Council of Economic Experts (Sachverständigenrat zur Begutachtung der gesamtwirtschaftlichen Entwicklung) by a Federal Act of 14 August 1963. As far back as 1954, the Economic Advisory Council had advocated the establishment of national accounts and in 1956 it proposed the creation of a special authority staffed by experts to develop these accounts. In the report *Instruments of Cyclical Policy and their Institutionalization in Law*, it also discussed the implications of conflicts of aims and the conditions for simultaneous achievement of several macroeconomic goals. At that time, an active counter-cyclical policy was regarded in West Germany as incompatible with a market economy. According to this view, the state's objectives could be fulfilled through the establishment of basic conditions for economic growth and a guarantee of price stability. Erhard too shared this opinion and it was not until 1962 that he agreed to set up a separate cyclical policy department within his ministry. Influenced not least by the efforts of the Commission of the European Communities to establish medium-term forecasts and programs along the lines of the French planning system at the Community level, Erhard hoped that a special German consultative body – the Council of Economic Experts – would provide him with backing for his policies in his dealings with other countries, as well as with support on the domestic scene to counteract the ever-increasing demands on the state by special interest groups.

The statutory mandate of the Council of Economic Experts is to submit a report on the current economic situation and its foreseeable development on 15 November of each year in order to 'facilitate opinion-forming within all agencies responsible for economic policy and among the general public'. The Council is directed to examine how 'price stability, high employment, and balance-of-payments equilibrium, accompanied by a continuous and appropriate rate of growth, can be achieved simultaneously within the framework of the market economy order'. It is required in particular to 'indicate undesirable trends and possible ways of preventing or eliminating them'. It must include an analysis of 'the formation and distribution of income and wealth'. The annual reports must be submitted to the federal government, which passes them on to the legislative bodies (Bundestag and Bundesrat) without delay and publishes them simultaneously.

The law gives the Council of Economic Experts independent status. To avoid conflicts of interest, the five members – each appointed for a period of five years by the federal president, with reappointment permissible – must not belong to the government or any legislative body at the federal or Länder levels; nor may they otherwise be employed in the public service, except as university teachers or as staff members of an economic research institute. They cannot be representatives or staff members of a business association or of an employers' or employees' organization (ultimately, the Council consisted of professors or heads of research institutes). The Council, which elects its own chairman, must be consulted before any new member is nominated by the federal government. The functions of a general office for the Council, which is aided in its work by a research staff, are performed by the Federal Statistical Office. In addition, the Council also has the legal right to call upon the relevant federal ministers and the President of the Deutsche Bundesbank to give their views. The authorities at federal and Länder levels must provide the necessary administrative assistance and the federal government is required to give the legislative bodies its comments on the annual report within eight weeks of its submission.

All this means that the Council of Economic Experts has an immensely strong position. To ensure that the Council does in fact confine itself to giving advice and does not intervene in the political process, it is forbidden – as a counterpart to the provisions for ensuring that politicians do not exert undue influence on the Council – to recommend specific economic and social policy measures. It is required to provide alternative courses of action on the basis of assumptions about economic development. It is the task of the federal government to draw policy conclusions from the reports.

From the institutional point of view the Council was strengthened by the Act of 8 June 1967 to Promote Economic Stability and Growth (Stability and Growth Act). This Act, which was unanimously passed by all the parties in the Bundestag and is geared to an identical set of macroeconomic goals, was seen as the 'basic law of the market economy in process-steering terms' and as a 'synthesis of the Keynesian message and the Freiburg imperative' (Karl Schiller). It allocated to the Council's reports a key role in the opinion-forming process in the field of counter-cyclical policy. It also created new institutions such as the 'concerted action' of management, labor and the government (originally intended to be a forum for the joint discussion of how far the incomes policy was in line with the overall economic situation), the Public Authorities' Business Cyclical Council, and, by means of a subsequent Act, the Financial Planning Council, whose meetings the Council was invited to attend when appropriate.

Despite the careful balancing of rights, obligations and prohibitions, the design of the Council of Economic Experts contains inherent conflicts which soon became apparent. The special position of the Council and the experiences in the meantime provoked opposition, particularly in connection with the question as to whether the Council's authority – including its autonomy within the parliamentary decision-making process – was justifiable. Already in the early 1970s it was a common opinion that a similar status should not and would not be granted again to any consultative body. This became apparent when the Council of Experts for Environmental Issues was set up at the end of 1971 in order to introduce greater objectivity into the increasingly heated discussion of environmental questions. This Council too is independent, has conflict-of-interest regulations governing membership, takes its own decisions on the topics to be covered, and so on, but it does not have the authority comparable to that of the Council of Economic Experts. The same applies to the Commission on Monopolies set up in 1973. The task of this Commission is to assess trends in industrial concentration, to appraise merger control and the control of abusive practices with regard to market-dominating enterprises, and to suggest amendments to the law. The establishment of the Monopoly Commission represents the last major step in the institutionalization of expert knowledge, particularly that of economists, in the policy-formation process.

FEATURES OF THE ECONOMIC ADVISORY SYSTEM

In 1977, the federal government alone maintained over 350 advisory councils. A considerable number of these advisory councils are the almost exclusive preserve of economists; even when they are in the minority, they have considerable influence. The common feature of these councils is that they represent a form of 'external consultation'; in other words, they are not incorporated into government agencies. The consultative bodies operate on a contractual basis (permanent contracts as in the case of economic research institutes), or are set up by administrative acts (as in the case of the scientific advisory councils at the federal ministries), ministerial decrees (as in the case of the Council of Environmental Experts), or legislative acts by the Bundestag (as in the case of the Council of Economic Experts or the Monopoly Commission). The decisive organizational features are that each body is granted independence from governmental directives and the results of their deliberations are directed towards the general public as well as government agencies.

The German consultation system reflects the view that, although politicians have the power to shape events, they need expert advisers (possessing verifiable specialized knowledge) to make appropriate decisions. However, the economist does not see himself as a mere supplier of factual information, with goals laid down by the politicians. While respecting Max Weber's postulate of value-free scientific assertions in the sense of 'objectivity' and 'neutrality', all economists working in an advisory capacity have in fact committed themselves to the basic norms of a social and economic order founded on the concept of freedom. This gives the consultation a policy consistency and establishes priorities for targets and the use of appropriate economic policy instruments. The German consultative bodies regard themselves as institutions removing the ideological aspect from political issues and paving the way for progress in the efficiency of political action. It is thus appropriate that the expert advisers are not intended to be and do not wish to be either 'clearing houses' operating prior to decisions (formulation of compromises between representatives of different views or interests) or 'arbitration bodies' (determination of the right course in the event of conflicting opinions). Internal consultation, as in the case of the US Council of Economic Advisers, would blur the dividing lines.

Although external consultation has dominated the scene, there have nevertheless been attempts to create advisory bodies within the government to assist the Federal Chancellor in forming his opinions. The principal recipients of the advice of external bodies are *de facto* the government departments; as the responsible government agencies in each case, they are in contact with the consultative bodies at an early stage and evaluate the results. Despite having the authority to lay down policy guidelines, the Chancellor is dependent on the information submitted by the departments and the views of the officials at the Chancellery – unless, like Helmut Schmidt, he is able to form an opinion of his own through *ad hoc* discussions with experts. The disadvantage of not having a specific institutionalized consultative body for the Chancellor was recognized early on, but only two attempts were made to remedy the situation.

One attempt, which was little more than rudimentary, was made by Erhard in 1964. The intention was to set up a political planning section within the newly established political department of the Chancellery. This section was supposed to devote itself to long-term planning, working in close contact with independent outside experts, but it was actually confined to a small group of advisers known as the 'special group'. This group, made up of professors and journalists, was intended to submit alternative recommendations to the Federal Chancellor in the course of periodic discussions. However, they met rarely, and the group was dissolved after the fall of Erhard in the late autumn of 1966 and has been totally forgotten.

A far more ambitious move was the attempt made during the subsequent 'grand coalition' between the Christian Democratic Union/Christian Social Union (CDU/CSU) and the Social Democratic Party (SPD) to establish a planning staff at the Federal Chancellery, which was designed primarily to act as an aid for the new Chancellor, Kurt Georg Kiesinger, in guideline planning and in monitoring its implementation. Within the Chancellery's organizational setup, this unit ranked alongside three specialized departments and was divided into five groups to be led by highly qualified experts from outside the public service. A panel of seven independent experts, mainly from the fields of economics and social sciences, was established in 1967 to advise the head of the planning staff on a permanent basis and the Chancellor on specific issues. Cooperation between the planning staff and the panel of experts was good and their jointly formulated analyses repeatedly influenced the Chancellor's opinion. However, the Chancellor's interest in the planning staff and its work subsequently flagged. The specialized departments at the Chancellery attempted to prevent the planning staff from gaining access to essential information from the ministries. The panel of independent experts was dissolved following the end of the 'grand coalition' in October 1969.

Under Chancellor Willi Brandt, the planning staff and the subsequently created Chancellery planning section were advised by an interdisciplinary team of external experts (until 1972), but the political advantage of this arrangement was small. The planning department itself went through a number of stages as an instrument of long-term planning and early coordination of the plans of the individual government departments, but its efforts were repeatedly frustrated by the resistance of the ministries.[1]

The Bundestag and Bundesrat have no advisory bodies of their own. They must form their opinions with the aid of the official reports and generally available information, unless the Bundestag decides to conduct a hearing (which is rarely the case in the field of economic policy) or a commission of inquiry is set up at the request of one-quarter of the members of the Bundestag. This has been done repeatedly, generally with some success.

RELATIONSHIP BETWEEN GOVERNMENT AGENCIES AND ADVISORY BODIES

The features of the advisory bodies reflect a basic consensus regarding the contribution of the world of scholarship to political decision making. Despite all the criticism which has been directed at it in the meantime, this basic consensus essentially exists today. It would otherwise not be possible to explain the fact that the consultative bodies created since 1948 have many essential features in common. Continuity in their work would also be inconceivable given the inherent potential for conflict with the government, the legislature, the administration and the social groups. There have of course been instances of friction and indeed conflicts which have attracted a great deal of attention.

It was above all the group surrounding Erhard which advocated the introduction of a more scientific approach, based on scholarship, in politics. In contrast, the independent expert adviser was regarded with suspicion by politicians who did not wish to see their political actions subjected to constraints. The latent tensions emerged when the Council of Economic Experts was set up. Konrad Adenauer, together with sections of the parliamentary CDU, opposed the creation of such an organization. They were afraid that it could become a kind of 'fourth power' which would unnecessarily restrict the room for political maneuver. Erhard was able to achieve his objective only with the aid of a collective motion by the parliamentary CDU/CSU (backed especially by the CSU members).

Among all West German Chancellors, Helmut Schmidt put up the most vigorous opposition to the Council as an independent body of experts. During his time as a minister, he was annoyed by its power to solicit the views of government officials and the fact that the government was required to comment on its reports: 'I'm the one who's going to ask the questions here,' he said. The fact that he, like other responsible ministers and the President of the Bundesbank, had the right to express their views to the Council apparently counted for little by comparison with the Council's right to call upon him to give his views. In the end, Schmidt abided by the provisions of the law and the Council proved to be a fair and useful partner for him as well.

Other causes of disputes between the Council and members of the government were the Council's own interpretation of the role assigned to it and the positions which it adopted with regard to both analysis and possible remedies. Erhard, who had envisaged the Council as a moderate group that would help to justify his policies, found himself confronted with a body which, above all under the influence of Herbert Giersch, was ambitious in its analysis and its political conclusions and was even regarded as militant. Instead of taking the line that the essential risk to overall economic stability lay solely or at least primarily in the demands made by social groups (particularly the trade unions), the Council adopted the view that it lay in the undermining of monetary policy by external influences. The result was a clear-cut plea in favor of more flexible exchange rates. This provoked a sharp reaction on the part of those who opposed revaluation of the Deutsche Mark; their political spearhead was Franz-Josef Strauss, the then Federal Minister of Finance. The topic became a political issue in the late autumn of 1968, with the solution taking the form of a 'substitute revaluation' through tax measures which did practically nothing to improve the situation.

Schiller, who as Federal Minister for Economic Affairs sided with the Council, was increasingly drawn into a confrontation with Strauss. Many people believed that it was the greater credibility of Schiller's position that finally decided the outcome of the general election in the autumn of 1969. Strauss sought to place the blame not least on the Council of Economic Experts, which he had accused of manipulating opinions and of influencing others by means of 'terrorism'. The repercussions of this dispute were felt for a long time afterwards. However, the Council never again found itself in such fierce conflict with members of the government, although differences did occur from time to time. When it complained in a special report in May 1973 that the federal government was not fulfilling its leadership role in the field of fiscal policy, it was attacked by Schmidt with considerable severity. There was also a confrontation beginning in 1976 when the Council advocated a 'supply-oriented policy'. Again, individual members of the Bundestag raised the question as to whether bodies like the Council of Economic Experts should perhaps be made responsible to the legislature in some way.

For the German Trade Union Federation (DGB) and the majority of industrial trade unions, a distrust of independent expert advisers is almost traditional. To them, independent advisory bodies are out of place in a democratic society; they are suspect because they tend to emphasize the responsibility of the unions to maintain stability in the economy as a whole (that according to the advisory bodies the employers have the same responsibility, does not matter to the unions). Disagreements regarding interpretation of the macroeconomic goals and the political priorities to be established are also common. Even the SPD's Godesberg Program of 1959, which endorsed the market economy, was unable to bridge the traditional differences between labor and the government over macroeconomic policies. (The SPD and probably also the majority of the industrial trade unions have in the meantime come to regard this program as outdated.) The unions nevertheless initially agreed to participate in Schiller's 'concerted action', not least on account of the persuasiveness of the Council's arguments.

In the aftermath of the superboom in 1969 the unions, which as well as employers' organizations had been legally granted autonomy in negotiating wage rates (1949), refused to enter into agreements of any kind. Nor were they (and sometimes the employers as well) too happy about the fact that the

Council of Economic Experts, which has always favored a balanced view of the issues, was represented in the 'concerted action'. The pressure exerted by the industrial trade unions alone meant that the DGB would refuse to allow itself to be restricted in determining wage adjustments. After having hesitantly been prepared to cooperate, the DGB in the end refused to yield in the early 1970s to the Council's efforts to get both unions and employers' organizations to participate in quantitative determination of the scope for wage increases on the basis of medium-term target projections. The meetings of the 'concerted action' became fewer and fewer under Chancellor Schmidt, who during his time as a minister had already shown little interest in such action. They were finally discontinued in favor of direct *ad hoc* discussions between the Chancellor and the DGB, sometimes also with the employers. The strained relationship between the DGB and the Council worsened yet again (from 1976 onwards) as a result of the uncompromising advocacy of a supply-oriented stabilization policy by the majority of the Council's members. The Council was accused of having violated its statutory mandate by 'dogmatically upholding one-sided doctrines in the guise of independence'.

The system of consultation between the administration and the independent advisers offers opportunities for mutual understanding and at the same time minimizes the potential for friction. The officials responsible for preparation of the strategic positions and tactical action of the government departments must have an interest in both the fundamental insights and specific argumentation provided by the advisory bodies. However qualified the staff may be, they are overburdened with day-to-day questions, and repeatedly lose touch with the front line of academic research. Effective cooperation with the advisory bodies allows them to put forward their own ideas at an early stage and in a convincing form. The expert advisers are for their part dependent on information from the government departments; they view the ministerial officials who do the direct preliminary work for the minister as the natural recipients of their advice. If the advisers can convince these officials, they have already gone a long way towards influencing the political decisions. The result is frequently a marked degree of trust between the administration and the advisory body, particularly if policy conceptions running along the same lines prevail and teacher–pupil relationships continue to be effective.

Expert know-how has naturally also accumulated within the ministries in the course of time; participation in decision-making processes has created self-confidence and independence. Many ministerial officials in the basic policy departments have long since come to regard themselves as discussion partners of equal standing, but at the same time as the 'spearhead' of scholarship in the political sphere. The same applies to the economics department of the Deutsche Bundesbank. Of course, conflicts are frequently in evidence. Every bureaucracy attempts to withhold information from the advisory bodies and to outmaneuver them when disagreements regarding appropriate courses of action become apparent. The administration then regards itself as the entity responsible for preparing political positions or protecting group interests. Backing from expert opinion based on scholarship is sought wherever such knowledge is convenient and inexpensive.

The relationship between the two most important government economic departments – the Federal Ministry for Economic Affairs and the Federal Ministry of Finance – and their advisory councils has generally been cooperative, even during periods when there were considerable differences of opinion. It goes without saying that the ministries try to avoid restrictions that may be created by the existence of the expert bodies. The Stability and Growth Act stipulates, for example, that the government must comment on the annual report of the Council of Economic Experts in its own annual economic report. This requirement was fulfilled at first by integrating the comments into the annual economic report as an introductory section, which gave the Council's views a special status, but made it difficult for the government to justify its preferred program. The burden of proof – not always easy to bear – for deviations was eliminated when the coordinating Federal Ministry for Economic Affairs decided in 1973 to use the Council's report primarily as a source of arguments to justify the government's own political intentions and merely to 'tack on' a brief appraisal in the final section.

EFFECTIVENESS OF THE ADVISORY COUNCILS

It is difficult to measure the success or failure of consultation. If anything can be measured at all, it is the extent to which proposed measures are transformed into political action. However, this test cannot be applied when the advisers are forbidden to make recommendations, as is the case with the Council of Economic Experts; furthermore, the results of consultation are very rarely implemented unchanged by the politicians. In many cases, moreover, the purpose of the consultation is to ward off political demands, for example from social groups or from abroad; it is 'non-action' rather than action which is the criterion of success in such cases.

Above all, it is clear that the acceptance by the politicians of measures which have been suggested or recommended *expressis verbis* cannot represent an adequate yardstick for the quality of the consultative work. In cases where such measures are not accepted, it is necessary to determine why the politicians have denied themselves the advice of the advisers. The consultative mandate itself must therefore be taken as the initial starting point. Given the assignment of a role to consultation involving independent experts which – as is the case in West Germany – is intended to provide objective judgements, the question to be asked is whether it fulfilled this function. As it is basically aimed at the general public, its influence on the opinion-forming process among the public is an important criterion of success. It goes without saying that opinion among the relevant academic circles is also of interest.

All consultative bodies made up of independent experts in West Germany have viewed the role assigned to them as a significant mandate. The awareness of a responsibility to society, the economy and the state reflects both the reconstruction efforts after World War II and the specifically German way of thinking regarding data-setting regulation ('order policy'). The latter characterizes especially the work of the scientific advisory councils. However, the Council of Economic Experts, which is committed to evaluating macroeconomic policies, views itself as a body which aims to tackle these tasks from the viewpoint of both regulatory policy and process steering.

It is almost impossible today to conceive just how effective the basic positions of the advisory councils had been since the June 1948 currency reform. Sustained by the success of Erhard's liberalization policy and the shaping of the economic order, the model of the market economy came to play a key role in West Germany. The Economic Advisory Council, often in close cooperation with its counterpart council at the Federal Ministry of Finance, made a greater contribution to this development than present-day economists are generally aware. There was no important economic-policy topic on which it did not express an opinion; it produced twenty reports between the beginning of 1948 and the end of 1950 alone and a total of fifty-one by the end of the 1950s. Its first report provided Erhard with highly appreciated backing for his lone course. Other trail-blazing contributions concerned the phases of internal and external liberalization, the role of monetary and currency policy, the creation of a system for regulating competition, the economic integration of Europe, the forms to be taken by cyclical policy, international trade and monetary order, aspects of a rule-bound economic policy or of price indexing, and many other topics. The Economic Advisory Council's influence was strengthened by the fact that Erhard was personally advised by some of its members, such as Böhm and Fritz W. Meyer.

The Finance Advisory Council matched the effectiveness of the Economic Advisory Council in its own field. It expressed its views on the important fiscal policy questions of the day and among other things paved the way for the replacement of the turnover tax by the value-added tax. Its cooperation with the Economic Advisory Council yielded useful reports on tax reform, cyclical policy, the capital markets, and numerous other subjects.

Since the mid-1960s the Council of Economic Experts has been the key advisory body on economic affairs. Although the scientific advisory councils lost some of their importance, no rivalry developed among them because a number of the members of the Council of Economic Experts belong to the

Economic Advisory Council or Finance Advisory Council. The work of both advisory councils continued almost unchanged in the subsequent decades. They produced important expert reports, which were highly regarded by the responsible departments. However, there was increasingly little response on the part of the public to these reports. While continuing to have influence within the administration, the scientific advisory councils had less discernible effect on political decisions.

The Council of Economic Experts caused considerable stir with its first few reports. It accepted the constraint that it should suggest options, founded on scholarship, for a rational economic policy and promoted the idea that the stabilization problem can be appropriately tackled only with the aid of consistent policies. It was also prepared to ally itself with political and social groups and the media in order to give emphasis to its views *vis-à-vis* hesitant government agencies. The key factor in the Council's stabilization policy is production potential. It defines cyclical movements as fluctuations in the degree to which the production potential is utilized. The essential task is to place the utilization of the production potential on a steady footing such that the result is balanced growth accompanied by price stability and full employment. The Council's views of what appears to be feasible for the next year are presented in the form of target projections – based on status quo forecasts – along with an assessment of the scope and opportunities for action. The forecast figures are thus not identical with the political targets (a source of continual misunderstanding when judgement is being passed on the accuracy of the Council's forecasts). The Council sets out alternative courses of action (since it is prohibited from making recommendations) indicating how the targets can be realized. As all the alternatives are generally not given equal weight, the Council's priorities virtually always become apparent.

The Council surprised both the government and the public with its interpretation of creeping inflation as an international phenomenon in the system of fixed exchange rates. It urged coordinated stabilization policies on the part of all political decisionmakers (government agencies as well as unions and employers' organizations). These included safeguards for the economy against external disturbances (mainly greater flexibility in the exchange rate), a wage policy not affecting the cost level (which was based on distribution neutrality) and the concept of the cyclically neutral budget (based on a budget calculated to eliminate the effects of the business cycle).

The Council's ideas usually gave rise to heated debates. Every new report was eagerly anticipated and even special reports were political events. The Council's analyses soon came to be regarded as first-rate sources of information. Opinions differed, however, as regards the forecasts, target projections, and the proposed policies. There were complaints about the length of the reports, but the language in which they were formulated won general approval. After a brief period, the Council's analytical position and measurement concepts had become established elements of the stabilization policy debate.

The Council attracted a great deal of attention in the early 1970s with its attempt to develop an overall indicator of cyclical trends. As might be expected, this attempt did not prove successful. The same applies to the 'arithmetical credit maximum', a measure based on the banks' free liquid reserves, which was intended as an indicator of relative ease or tightness of monetary policy. Most important, only meager success was achieved in stabilization policy despite the impressive programs for action contained in the Council's reports and the government's annual economic reports. The hopes which had been pinned on the Stability and Growth Act were not fulfilled. Overall economic development was not steady, the monetary authorities lost control over the monetary sector, the distribution struggle became more intense, and both the government and the Bundestag developed a preference for 'tailor-made' measures rather than the actions envisaged in the Act.

The Council of Economic Experts reacted by redefining the role to be assigned to each policy sector in its 1974–5 report. It allotted the leading role to the monetary authorities, who were required to establish and publish its basic guideline annually in advance in the form of a monetary target. From as early as 1972 onwards, the Council had developed a measurement concept for the money supply geared to the monetary base as an intermediate target variable. Fiscal policy was committed to the financing of public expenditure and relieved of anticyclical tasks. Incomes policy was expected to minimize conflicts between stabilization policy and employment. All in all, the Council moved away from counter-cyclical policies in the sense of gearing action to the phase of the business cycle and favored instead medium-term policies based on the growth of production potential. The Deutsche Bundesbank, which had come to conclusions similar to those arrived at by the Council, pursued under the conditions of flexible exchange rates a tight monetary policy and has been publishing monetary targets since December 1974. This policy has on the whole been successful.

Following a series of somewhat unproductive stabilization programs in the second half of the 1970s, the government since 1982–3 has been pursuing a 'budget consolidation course' which is highly controversial in political circles and among public finance experts, but which was on the whole unavoidable. This course involves reducing the accumulated structural deficits and cutting the ratio of public expenditure to the GNP. The labor-market participants have learned from experience, particularly from the events of 1974. Although wage agreements have not strictly speaking conformed to the stabilization requirements, they have still been moderate on the whole.

Up to the mid-1970s, the government and the Council of Economic Experts did not expect that either potential growth or full employment would give rise to medium-term stabilization problems. In the years that followed, however, unsatisfactory trends in potential growth (a declining propensity to invest) and employment (rapidly increasing unemployment which also reflected demographic factors) caused the Council to emphasize supply-oriented measures to promote growth and create jobs. Its theory that expansion-oriented demand management could not solve the nation's economic problems led to fierce disputes with politicians and trade union officials as well as economists. On the whole, however, the Council proved to be a trendsetter once again. Views along these lines have at any rate been influential within the government and the public for some years now. The line adopted by the Council of Economic Experts has also been supported by the great majority of German economists.

Nevertheless, the Council's reports no longer meet with the same response as they did in the past; nor is the feeling of anticipation before the submission of a report as strong as it once was. The Council of Economic Experts seems to have lost some of its influence; the work of consultation is continuing, but it has developed into more of a routine and seems to have less determining force than in the past. The specialized advisory councils have been playing an even more marginal role in political decisions for years; in fact, they are frequently found in opposition to the government's programs in their fields. For example, the Monopoly Commission disagrees with the Federal Cartels Office in Berlin which may well influence a forthcoming revision of the Act Prohibiting Restraints of Competition. The Council of Environmental Experts is today faced with environmental activists of every conceivable type. The Social Advisory Council continues its efforts in a field that has for years been due for extensive reforms, but action is nevertheless repeatedly postponed because of the delicacy of the issues.

The economic research institutes continue to perform useful work. The joint diagnoses, which the institutes regard as competitive with the reports of the Council of Economic Experts (which they are not) are generally not free of compromises and, in most cases, the related economic-policy recommendations are somewhat meager. The purpose of the structural reports is more to ward off demands for political actions which are questionable from the regulatory-policy viewpoint.

The loss of importance of the advisory councils can be ascribed to a number of factors:

1. West Germany's reconstruction after the war and the country's return to the international (and above all European) community of states was essentially completed by the end of the 1950s. The major system-determining decisions had thus been taken. Macroeconomic policy had its greatest fascination in the late 1960s and early 1970s. Since then its reputation has declined because of the unsatisfactory performance of the stabilization policy.

2. From the beginning of the 1970s, concern for the poor and disadvantaged led to an increase in the ratio of public expenditure to the GNP to around 50 per cent and the levies ratio to roughly 40 per cent (particularly as a result of the increase in social security taxes). Fiscal and social policy were left to deal with the consequences, but the results achieved have not been convincing.
3. Now that the basic data-setting and macroeconomic policies have lost some of their original *raison d'être*, regulatory policy in particular has entered a stage of diffusion. This is the result of diverging political interests, the appearance of competing models, and ideological differences regarding the equity and efficiency of the market economy.
4. The increasing heterogeneity of values and indeed the lack of a consistent system of values, together with the breaking up of political responsibilities (including regionalization of economic policy), have led to a pluralism of judgements, a fragmentation of competence and in part to an economic policy of 'muddling through'.
5. The level of prosperity achieved, the tendency to make demands on the state, and the adherence to 'established' rights have hardened political views. As a result, the political climate is geared more to the status quo than to reform.

Thus, the present environment offers less scope for the development of new and conceptually comprehensive ideas by independent experts than in earlier years. Consultation is often used as an alibi for failure to face problems and as a means of justifying politically opportune action. Political challenges from independent experts are not exactly sought after in such a situation and reference to disagreements among the professional economists becomes a popular defense. Other factors that have played a role in the declining influence of the advisory councils include static membership, a certain sterility of topics, and repetitive policy recommendations. Continuity is not necessarily an advantage; it may also stand in the way of new ideas and impulses.

WHAT CAN BE IMPROVED?

There are still good reasons for a system of external consultation of the type developed in West Germany, especially if – as is indeed the case – the traditional ideas regarding the relationship between politics and scholarship prevail. However, the present system has its weaknesses. Anyone aiming to improve it should bear the following points in mind:

1. Any form of consultation, above all consultation involving independent experts, will be successful only if society wishes to place politics on a scientific footing. The influence of consultative work will also reflect

the standing and authority of the advisers, as well as their powers of judgement and persuasion.

2. The results of high-quality consultation will be more readily accepted, the more the basic policy views of the politicians coincide with those of the independent experts and the greater the extent to which the recommended action is in line with actual political intentions.
3. External consultation is particularly capable of yielding recommendations which are well founded in analytical terms, free of partial considerations and with horizons extending far into the future. By contrast, internal consultation has a better chance of exerting a permanent and suggestive influence on the political decision-making process.
4. Independent status and minimal areas of friction with the government machinery are essential prerequisites for effective advisory work during and beyond legislative periods.

Although there are features within the given structure of independent expert consultation which should be improved in West Germany, change will be difficult. For example, there is a good deal to be said for broadening the spectrum of views represented by the members of the consultative bodies; this could lead to greater variety in the topics and a more radical approach to the issues covered by consultation and to the alternative courses of political action discussed. The best way to achieve this might not be by establishing new consultative bodies or merely by expanding the membership of the given advisory councils, but rather by creating improved forms of cooperation between the existing consultative bodies and the government agencies responsible for them. In any case the rules of consultation should be modified in such a way that 'fossilization' is avoided, greater variation is achieved in terms of the make-up of the consultative bodies and more efficient methods are used in the preparation and presentation of reports.

In West Germany, it has so far been impossible to solve the problem of how the Federal Chancellor can make use of the knowledge of independent experts in an institutionalized form. Unless he is competent in specific fields himself, he is dependent on the government departments for information and proposals for political action. Anything supplied to him passes through a system of narrowing pipes, as it were, and often reaches him in diluted form. When forming an opinion, he is much too heavily dependent on the advice of the staff closest to him or on the suggestions of individuals (bankers and industrialists) with whom he is familiar. Although this system functions, aspects of day-to-day politics and a certain orientation towards specific interests will always be involved.

Nowadays, almost no one advocates setting up a special consultative body responsible to the Chancellor exclusively. Nevertheless, it might be worthy of consideration. If a 'Chancellor's Advisory Council' should become a reality, it would have to operate solely within the Chancellery, the principal task of its members being to identify fundamental issues, to sharpen the Chancellor's eye for systematic considerations and conceptual conformity and to make him conscious of politically feasible options. In other words, the members would have to confine themselves to a role of furnishing the Chancellor with basic elements he needs to form his own opinion. The Council might also be required to evaluate for the Chancellor important recommendations made by other advisory councils or by the government departments. An advisory council as outlined for the Chancellor would conform to the institutional framework of the German governmental system. There also would be clear distinction between such a council and the American Council of Economic Advisers.

A Chancellor's Advisory Council might consist of five or six highly qualified experts from a variety of disciplines (confining it to economists alone would be too restrictive). The members would have to exhibit a high degree of loyalty to the Chancellor and of respect for the competence of governmental agencies and legislative bodies. As the element of trust is a key factor, it should be possible to withdraw membership of the Council at any time. It is a difficult question whether and to what extent the Council should be integrated into the Chancellor's office. Nevertheless, it must at least have its own small secretariat, preferably attached to the Minister of State at the Chancellery; it might cause conflicts if the Council were assigned to one of the government departments with its own particular interests.

Consultative bodies have to prove themselves in a changing environment. It must therefore be their goal to improve this environment as far as their capabilities reach.

NOTE

1. Another attempt to introduce the knowledge of the independent expert on an internal basis was equally unsuccessful. To prepare the basic concept for a comprehensive reform of the German tax system envisaged by Alex Möller, then the Federal Minister of Finance, Professor Heinz Haller, a member of both the Finance Advisory Council and the Economic Advisory Council, was appointed Undersecretary of State – with civil service status – at the Federal Ministry of Finance. Haller performed his work in virtual isolation and returned to his chair at the Swiss Institute of Technology in Zurich when the enthusiasm for reforms wore off after Möller's resignation in 1971.

BIBLIOGRAPHY

v. Beckerath, E. and Giersch, H. (eds), *Probleme der normativen Ökonomik und der wirtschaftspolitischen Beratung* (Problems of Normative Economics and Economic Consultation), Publications of the Association for Social Policy, new series (Berlin, 1963). With contributions by (among others) Rau, W., Wolf, E. and

Tuchtfeldt, E. on 'Der Wirtschaftswissenschaftler als ständiger Mitarbeiter bei staatlichen und nichtstaatlichen Instanzen der Wirtschaftspolitik' ('The economist in a permanent capacity with governmental and non-governmental economic-policy bodies'); and by Koch, W. and Meinhold, H. on 'Der Wirtschaftswissenschaftler als Berater wirtschaftspolitischer Instanzen' ('The economist as an adviser to economic-policy bodies').

Bolte, K. M., 'Die Arbeit der Kommission für wirtschaftlichen und sozialen Wandel' ('The work of the Commission for Economic and Social Change'), in *Hamburg Yearbook for Economic and Social Policy*, vol. 23 (1978), pp. 264 ff.

Borner, S., *Wissenschaftliche Ökonomik und politische Aktion – Eine politische Ökonomie der professionellen Beratung der Wirtschaftspolitik* ('Scientifically Founded Economics and Political Action – Political Economics for Professional Economic-Policy Consultation') (Berne and Stuttgart, 1975).

Eucken, W., *Grundlagen der Nationalökonomie* (The Foundations of Economics) (Jena: Gustav Fischer, 1940).

Gäfgen, G., 'Formen und Erfolgsbedingungen wissenschaftlicher Beratung der Wirtschaftspolitik' ('Forms and conditions for success of economic-policy consultation by expert advisers'), *Discussion Papers of the Faculty of Economics and Statistics of the University of Konstanz*, Series I, no. 232 (1987).

Gutowski, A., 'Zur Theorie und Praxis der unabhängigen wirtschaftswissenschaftlichen Politikberatung' ('On the theory and practice of economic-policy consultation by independent experts'), in *Hamburg Yearbook for Economic and Social Policy*, vol. 28 (1983), pp. 9–24.

Habermas, J., 'Wissenschaft und Politik' ('Scholarship and politics'), *Open World, Journal for Economics, Politics and Society*, no. 86 (1964), pp. 413–23.

Härtel, H.-H., 'Entwicklung und Leistungsfähigkeit der wirtschaftspolitischen Beratung am Beispiel des Sachverständigenrates' ('Development and efficiency of economic consultation based on the example of the German Council of Economic Experts'), in *Controversies in Economic Policy*. Edited and introduced by D. B. Simmert. Publications of the Federal Political Education Centre, no. 146 (Bonn, 1980), pp. 91–108.

Jantz, K., 'Zur Struktur und Wirkungsweise des Sozialbeirats' ('On the structure and operation of the Social Advisory Council'), in K. Schenke and W. Schmähl (eds), *Alterssicherung als Aufgabe für Wissenschaft und Politik* (Provision for Old Age as a Task for the Fields of Scholarship and Politics). On the Occasion of the 65th Birthday of Helmut Meinhold (Stuttgart/Berlin/Cologne/Mainz: Kohlhammer, 1980), pp. 285–98.

Jöhr, W. A., and Singer, H. W., *Die Nationalökonomie im Dienste der Wirtschaftspolitik* ('National Economics in the Service of Economic Policy') (2nd edition, Göttingen: Vandenhoeck & Ruprecht, 1964).

Kantzenbach, E., 'Zehn Jahre Monopolkommission' ('Ten years of the Monopoly Commission'), *Economy and Competition, Journal for Cartel Law, Competition Law and Market Organization*, vol. 34 (1984), pp. 5–15.

Kloten, N., 'Wissenschaftliche Erkenntnis – Politische Entscheidung' ('Scientifically based findings – political decisions'), in E. Helmstaedter (ed.), *Neuere Entwicklungen in den Wirtschaftswissenschaften* (Recent Developments in Economics), Publications of the Association for Social Policy, new series, vol. 98 (Berlin, 1978), pp. 883–901.

Kloten, N., *Der Staat in der Sozialen Marktwirtschaft* ('The State in the Social Market Economy'), Walter Eucken Institute (pub.), Papers and Essays no. 108 (Tübingen, 1986).

Leman, Ch. K., and Nelson, R. H., 'Ten commandments for policy economists',

Journal of Policy Analysis and Management, vol. 1 (1981), pp. 97–117.
Lindblom, Ch. E., *The Policy-Making Process* (Englewood Cliffs: Prentice Hall, 1968).
Lompe, K., *Wissenschaftliche Beratung der Politik* ('Policy Consultation Involving Expert Advisers') (Göttingen: Otto Schwartz, 1966).
Meißner, W., *Die Lehre der Fünf Weisen. Eine Auseinandersetzung mit den Jahresgutachten des Sachverständigenrats zur Begutachtung der gesamtwirtschaftlichen Entwicklung* ('The Doctrine of the Five Wise Men. An Examination of the Annual Report of the German Council of Economic Experts') (Cologne: Bund, 1980).
Molitor, R. (ed.), 'Zehn Jahre Sachverständigenrat zur Begutachtung der gesamtwirtschaftlichen Entwicklung. Eine kritische Bestandsaufnahme' ('Ten years of the German Council of Economic Experts. A critical assessment'). Miscellany in the series *Economics Today* with contributions by (among others) Gäfgen, G., Engelhardt, G. and Neumark, F. (Frankfurt/M: Athenäum, 1973).
Nelson, R. H., 'The economics profession and the making of public policy', *Journal of Economic Literature*, vol. 25, no. 1 (1987), pp. 49–91.
Richter, R. (ed.), 'Der Sachverständigenrat zur Begutachtung der gesamtwirtschaftlichen Entwicklung' ('The German Council of Economic Experts'). Essays on the occasion of the twentieth anniversary of its establishment by (among others) Krelle, W. and Wallich, H. C., *Journal of Institutional and Theoretical Economics*, vol. 140 (1984), pp. 330–86.
Schmidt, K., 'Der Sachverständigenrat zur Begutachtung der gesamtwirtschaftlichen Entwicklung: Institution, Meßkonzepte und wirtschaftspolitische Leitlinien' ('The German Council of Economic Experts: the institution, its assessment concepts and economic guidelines'), *Proceedings of the Scientific Society of the Johann Wolfgang Goethe University Frankfurt am Main*, vol. 21, no. 4 (Stuttgart, 1985).
Schlecht, O., 'Was soll und kann der Sachverständigenrat leisten? Die Aufgabe des Sachverständigenrats zur Begutachtung der gesamtwirtschaftlichen Entwicklung' ('What should and can the Council of Economic Experts achieve? The task of the Council of Economic Experts'), *Bulletin of the Press and Information Office of the Federal German Government*, no. 125 (1963), pp. 1113 ff.
Sievert, O., 'Die wirtschaftspolitische Beratung in der Bundesrepublik' ('Economic consultation in the Federal Republic of Germany'), in H. K. Schneider, (ed.), *Grundsatzprobleme wirtschaftspolitischer Beratung. Das Beispiel der Stabilisierungspolitik* (Fundamental Problems of Economic Consultation. The Example of Stabilization Policy), Publications of the Association for Social Policy, new series, vol. 49 (Berlin, 1968), pp. 27–67.
Tietmeyer, H., 'Angewandte Wirtschaftsforschung im Dienste der Politikberatung – mehr als nur ein Alibi für die Wirtschaftspolitik?' ('Applied economic research in the service of policy consultation – more than just an alibi for economic policy?'), in B. Keller and A. E. Ott (eds), *Angewandte Wirtschaftsforschung im Spannungsfeld zwischen Wirtschaftstheorie und Wirtschaftspolitik* (Applied Economic Research Caught in the Tensions between Economic Theory and Economic Policy), Publications of the Tübingen Institute for Applied Economic Research, vol. 41 (Tübingen, 1983), pp. 165–88.
Wallich, H. C., 'The American Council of Economic Advisers and the German Sachverständigenrat: a study in the economics of advice', *Quarterly Journal of Economics*, vol. 82 (1969), pp. 349–79.
Weigelt, K. (ed.), 'Die Bedeutung wirtschaftswissenschaftlicher Gutachten für die Politik' ('The importance of expert economic reports in the political sphere').

Working publication No. 4 of the Political Academy of the Konrad Adenauer Foundation, Wesseling Eichholz, with contributions by (among others) Lamberts, W., Tietmeyer, H. and Watrin, C.

Wilhelm, W., *Wissenschaftliche Beratung der Politik in der Bundesrepublik Deutschland* ('Policy Consultation Involving Expert Advisers in the Federal Republic of Germany') (Berlin: Beuth, 1968).

Zimmermann, H., 'Wirtschaftspolitische Beratung unter Wertabstinenz ('Economic consultation without values'), *Journal for National Economics*, vol. 28 (1968), pp. 305–40.

APPENDIX: Economic consultation bodies and institutions in West Germany

	Governmental consultative bodies			
	Scientific advisory councils		Special-purpose consultative bodies	
	Scientific Advisory Council at the Federal Ministry for Economic Affairs	Scientific Advisory Council at the Federal Ministry of Finance	Council of Economic Experts	Council of Experts for Environmental Issues
Institutional data:				
Established on	23 January 1948	13 May 1948	14 August 1963	28 December 1971
by	Simple act of establishment by the bizonal economic authority	Simple act of establishment by the bizonal finance authority	Federal Act	Decree
Attached to/set up by	Federal Ministry for Economic Affairs	Federal Ministry of Finance	Federal Government (with Federal Statistical Office as general office)	Federal Ministry for Environmental Protection (formerly Federal Ministry of the Interior) (with Federal Statistical Office as general office)
Legal form	Without legal capacity	Without legal capacity	Without legal capacity	Without legal capacity
Legal basis for consultative work	Statutes of 28 February 1958 (amended on 13 May 1971) in conjunction with Section 62 of the Joint Rules and Regulations of the Federal Ministries (GGO)	Statutes of 10 April 1968 in conjunction with Section 62 of the Joint Rules and Regulations of the Federal Ministries	Act concerning the establishment of a Council of Economic Experts of 14 August 1963 (as amended on 8 June 1967); Standing Orders of the Council of Economic Experts	Decree concerning the establishment of a Council of Environmental Experts at the Federal Ministry of the Interior of 28 December 1971; Standing Orders of the Council of Experts for Environmental Issues
Relationship with government authorities	Independent	Independent	Independent	Independent
Financing	Federal Government	Federal Government	Federal Government	Federal Government
Organizational structure:				
Membership	University teachers from the fields of economics and jurisprudence, coopted members (appointed by the Federal Ministry for Economic Affairs at the suggestion of the Advisory Council)	University teachers from the fields of economics and jurisprudence, coopted members (appointed by the Federal Ministry of Finance at the suggestion of the Advisory Council)	The members are appointed by the Federal President for a period of five years at the suggestion of the Federal Government (after consultation with the Council of Economic Experts); re-appointment is permissible; two members proposed by the employers' and employees' organizations respectively; there are conflict-of-interest regulations governing membership	The members are appointed for a period of three years by the Federal Minister for Environmental Protection in agreement with the Federal Government; members may be reappointed twice; there are conflict-of-interest regulations governing membership
Number of members	Up to 25	Up to 25	5 (plus research staff)	12 (plus research staff)
Chairmanship/ administration	Chairman and deputy chairman elected for two years from among the council's members; re-election permissible	Chairman and deputy chairman elected for two years from among the council's members; re-election permissible	Chairman elected for three years from among the Council's members; re-election permissible	Chairman elected from among the Council's members; may be re-elected once
Remuneration for consultative work	Honorary	Honorary	Lump-sum remuneration	Lump-sum remuneration
Consultative mandate	Advisory Council itself determines the subjects of its consultative work; expert opinions on current and fundamental aspects of economic policy. The wishes of the Federal Ministry for Economic Affairs regarding consultation on specific topics are taken into account	Advisory Council itself determines the subjects of its consultative work; expert opinions on current and fundamental aspects of fiscal policy. The wishes of the Federal Ministry of Finance regarding consultation on specific topics are taken into account	Periodic appraisal of the overall economic situation and its foreseeable development; indication of undesirable trends and possible ways of eliminating/preventing them; investigation of how the goals of price stability, high employment, balance-of-payments equilibrium and continuous and appropriate growth can be achieved simultaneously within the market economy; Federal Government can commission the Council to produce special reports; Council has the right to consult relevant individuals; must not make recommendations	Appraisal of the environmental situation and related trends as well as analysis of undesirable developments and indicating of possible ways of preventing or eliminating them. The Council determines the topics itself; it deals with questions at the Minister's request only if the topic appears suitable and the project is compatible with other work
Special features			Federal Government must comment on annual reports	
Intended recipients of advice	Official recipient: Federal Ministry for Economic Affairs; through publication of expert reports, general public also reached. Federal Ministry for Economic Affairs determines when reports are to be published	Official recipient: Federal Ministry of Finance; through publication of expert reports, general public also reached. Federal Ministry of Finance determines when reports are to be published	Official recipients: Federal Government and general public	Official recipients: government agencies responsible for environmental policy and general public

APPENDIX: Economic consultation bodies and institutions in West Germany (contd)

	Governmental consultative bodies (contd)		
	Special-purpose consultative bodies (contd)		Auxiliary bodies
	Social Security Advisory Council	Commission on Monopolies	Within the legislature: Commissions of Enquiry
Institutional data:			
Established on	23 February 1957 (expanded on 30 April 1963)	3 August 1973	Set up as required in individual cases
by	Federal Act	Federal Act	Resolution by the German Bundestag upon a motion in accordance with Section 56 of the Standing Orders of the Bundestag (if the motion is tabled by one quarter of the members of the Bundestag, a commission must be set up)
Attached to/set up by	Federal Ministry of Labour (also acting as general office)	Federal Government	German Bundestag
Legal form	Without legal capacity	Without legal capacity	Without legal capacity, 'not committees' of the Bundestag; within the meaning of Section 54 ff.; Standing Orders of the Bundestag
Legal basis for consultative work	Section 1273 ff. of Reich Insurance Code (RVO); Section 50 ff. of Salaried Employees' Insurance Act (AVG); Standing Orders of Social Advisory Council	Section 24b in conjunction with Section 22 ff. of Act Prohibiting Restraints of Competition (GWB); Standing Orders of Monopoly Commission	Section 56 of Standing Orders of the Bundestag and mandate as stated in Bundestag resolution; Standing Orders of Bundestag applied by analogy in all other respects
Relationship with government authorities	Independent	Independent	Independent
Financing	Federal Government	Federal Government	Federal Government
Organizational structure:			
Membership	Council consists of 4 representatives of the insured, 4 employer representatives, 1 representative of the Deutsche Bundesbank and 3 representatives from the fields of social science and economics; they are appointed by the Federal Government for four years (representatives of the insured and employers appointed at the suggestion of the managing boards of the social insurance institutions or their associations, representatives from the academic sphere appointed following consultation of the West German University Vice-Chancellors' Conference)	The members are appointed for a period of 4 years by the Federal President (at the suggestion of the Federal Government following consultation of the Commission); re-appointment is permissible; there are conflict-of-interest regulations governing membership	The members are appointed by the Speaker of the Bundestag with the agreement of the parliamentary parties (in cases of doubt, in proportion to the size of the individual parties); the parliamentary parties may each delegate one additional member (or in exceptional cases, several members)
Number of members	12 (plus research staff)	5 (plus own offices)	Generally 9 (plus additional members delegated by the parliamentary parties)
Chairmanship/ administration	Chairman and two deputies elected from among the Council's members; re-election is permissible	Chairman elected from among the Commission's members	The rules regarding the election of committee chairmen applied by analogy to the appointment of the chairmen and their deputies
Remuneration for consultative work	Honorary	Lump-sum remuneration	
Consultative mandate	Assessment of the likely financial position of the pension insurance system and the question of the adjustment of existing pensions, to be examined each year and covered by means of special legislation; special reports on individual problems	Assessment of the company concentration situation and its likely development, appraisal of the control of abusive practices with regard to market-dominating enterprises and appraisal of merger control, indication of amendments to the law considered necessary, Federal Government can request the Commission to produce additional reports; the Commission must be brought in for cases requiring ministerial authorization	According to mandate and Bundestag resolution
Special features	Reports form a separate component of the legislative procedure and are mandatory in law	The Federal Government passes on its comments on the reports to the legislative bodies; the Commission has no right to information from authorities or trade and industry	Sections 56 IV of the Standing Orders of the Bundestag stipulates that the commissions must submit their report by the end of the legislative period. If this is not possible, an interim report is to be submitted, on the basis of which the Bundestag will decide whether or not the commission is to continue its work
Intended recipients of advice	Official recipients: Federal Ministry of Labour and Federal Government; through publication of reports, general public also reached	Official recipients: Federal Government and Federal Ministry for Economic Affairs; through publication of reports, general public also reached	Official recipient: German Bundestag

APPENDIX: Economic consultation bodies and institutions in West Germany (contd)

	Governmental consultative bodies (contd)	Nongovernmental consultative bodies		
	Auxiliary bodies (cont) Within the executive: Institute for Labour Market and Occupational Research (IAB), Nuremberg	German Institute for Economic Research (DIW), Berlin	Independent economic research institutes HWWA-Institute for Economic Research, Hamburg	Institute of World Economics at the University of Kiel (IfW), Kiel
Institutional Data:				
Established on	2 May 1967	July 1925	1908	1914 (Kaiser Wilhelm Foundation)
by	Simple act of establishment by self-governing bodies of the Federal Employment Office (Bundesanstalt für Arbeit); confirmed by Federal Act on 1 July 1969	Setting-up of association	Simple act of establishment by the administration of the Free and Hanseatic City of Hamburg, subsequently as a subsidiary agency on the basis of Hamburg's 1952 Act concerning Administrative Authorities	Act of foundation
Attached to/set up by	Federal Employment Office		Subsidiary agency of the Authority for Science and Research – Higher Education Office – of the Free and Hanseatic City of Hamburg	Classified as an institute of the Christian Albrechts University, Kiel (but not part of the University of Kiel in law)
Legal form	Department of Federal Employment Office, without legal capacity	Registered association	Without legal capacity	Research institute of the Land of Schleswig-Holstein, without legal capacity
Legal basis for consultative work	Sections 3 II and 6 I of Employment Promotion Act (AFG) in conjunction with 'medium-term point-of-main-effort programmes' (five-year period 1983–7 covered by programme of 21 September 1982)	Statutes	1947 resolution of the Senate of the Free and Hanseatic City of Hamburg and internal administrative directives	Statutes
Relationship with government authorities	Medium-term point-of-main-effort programmes laid down in agreement with Federal Employment Office and Federal Ministry of Labour; independent with regard to research work	Independent	Independent	Independent
Financing	Federal Employment Office	50% Federal Government, 50% Land of Berlin, funds from outside sources, members' subscription, Association of the Patrons of the DIW	50% Federal Government, 50% Free and Hanseatic City of Hamburg, funds from outside sources, Society of the Friends and Patrons of the HWWA	50% Federal Government, 50% Land of Schleswig-Holstein, funds from outside sources
Organisational structure:				
Membership	Staff of Federal Employment Office (civil service career possible)	Federal Government, Land of Berlin, political parties, trade unions, associations, companies, etc.; the organs are the board of trustees (members) and the managing board (director and up to 5 other members)	The organs are the institute management and the advisory board (20 members, in particular Senators of the Free and Hanseatic City of Hamburg, Federal Ministers, representatives of Hamburg University, chambers, trade unions and the patrons' society)	The organs are the committee (all research staff), the assembly (all nonresearch staff) and the institute council (director, heads of department and an appropriate number of elected members from the other two organs)
Number of staff	Approx. 90 permanent posts	Approx. 190	Approx. 250	Approx. 170
Chairmanship/ administration	The head of Department VII at the Federal Employment Office is the Director of the IAB	Director and board comprising heads of department	Director (professor of economics at University of Hamburg) and permanent deputy	Director (professor of economics University of Kiel) and deputy (appointed by the Schleswig-Holstein Minister of Education on the proposal of the Director)
Remuneration for consultative work		Remuneration for joint reports, project fees	Remuneration for joint reports, project fees	Remuneration for joint reports, project fees
Consultative mandate	Collection and evaluation of material on labour market and occupational research; structural analyses on the development and status of technical progress according to sectors of economic activity; periodic assessment of the employment situation and its development, particularly as a result of the structural changes within enterprises: surveys among workers regarding profession and labour market; studies on changes in professions, requirements in terms of young personnel, etc. The research results must be evaluated for the purpose of assisting the Federal Employment Office in its work and submitted to the Federal Ministry of Labour	Joint diagnosis, structural report, also analysis of the economic circulation system and its cyclical fluctuations, answering of current questions relating to economic policy and monitoring of long-term structural changes, partly in form of commissioned reports.	Joint diagnosis, structural report, also analysis of international economic problems as well as of economic development in West Germany and its international economic integration, partly in the form of commissioned reports	Joint diagnosis, structural report, also analysis of world economic trends and structural changes in industrialized countries, regional studies, examination of growth and industrialization processes in developing countries, partly in the form of commissioned reports
Special features		Production/further development of econometric models		Library acts as a central library for the field of economics in West Germany
Intended recipients of advice	Official recipients: Federal Employment Office, Federal Ministry of Labour; through publication of results, general public also reached	General public and government agencies responsible for economic policy	General public and government agencies responsible for economic policy	General public and government agencies responsible for economic policy
Research staff		98	89	66

APPENDIX: Economic consultation bodies and institutions in West Germany (contd)

	Nongovernmental consultative bodies (contd)			
	Independent economic research institutes (contd)		Research institutes run by the labour market participants	
	Ifo-Institute for Economic Research, Munich	Rhine–Westphalia Institute for Economic Research (RWI), Essen	Economic and Social Science Institute of the German Trade Union Federation (WSI) Düsseldorf	Institute of German Trade and Industry (IW), Cologne
Institutional data:				
Established on	1949	1943	1946	1951
by	Setting up of association	Setting up of association	Resolution on establishment by the German Trade Union Federation	Setting up of association
Attached to/set up by			German Trade Union Federation (DGB)	
Legal form	Registered association	Registered association	Company with limited liability (since 1954)	Registered association
Legal basis for consultative work	Statutes	Statutes	Articles of association	Statutes
Relationship with government authorities	Independent	Independent	Independent, tied to interests of DGB, not bound by directions as regards research work	Independent, tied to interests of companies and company associations
Financing	50% Federal Government, 50% Land of Bavaria, funds from outside sources, members' subscriptions	50% Federal Government, 50% Land of North Rhine–Westphalia, funds from outside sources, members' subscriptions, Society of Patrons and Friends of the RWI	DGB grants, donations	Members' subscriptions
Organizational structure:	Businessmen from industry, commerce, banks, insurance companies, company associations, trade unions, etc. (approx. 1,000 members); the organs are the members' meeting, the board of trustees (107 members from trade and industry, the academic world, trade unions and public administration), the board (18 members from board of trustees, heads of department and Institute's staff council) and the managing board (director and 4 other members, elected for five years; re-election permissible)	Companies, business associations and public entities; the organs are the members' meeting, the board of administration (28 members from trade and industry, the academic world and public administration) and the management board (executive director and 2 research directors)	The 4 members are the DGB's investment management and trust company, the Bank für Gemeinwirtschaft, the Neue Heimat Städtebau company and the Volksfürsorge insurance company; the organs are the boad of trustees (members of the DGB national managing body and 4 representatives of the shareholders) and the institute management (2 managing directors)	40 business and social-policy oriented associations as ordinary members, 60 companies and associations as extraordinary members; the organs are the members' meeting, the managing board (42 entrepreneurs), the presiding board (president and 4 vice-presidents), the advisory board (500 representatives of trade and industry) and the management
Number of staff	Approx. 210	Approx. 90	Approx. 70	Aprox. 200
Chairmanship/ administration	Director of institute and managing board	Management board (on the basis of Rules and Regulations with the approval of the board of administration)	2 managing directors	Presiding board and management
Remuneration for consultative work	Remuneration for joint reports, project fees	Remuneration for joint reports, project fees	Project fees	Project fees
Consultative mandate	Joint diagnosis, structural report, also analysis of short-term and medium-term economic trends, sector-specific structural and competition studies; monitoring of economic trends abroad, partly in the form of commissioned reports	Joint diagnosis, structural report, also business-cycle and structural research, regional economic studies, analysis of public finances, reporting on craft industries and commerce, partly in the form of commissioned reports	No governmental consultative mandate, own business-cycle and structural research, distribution research, social policy with the aim of providing the DGB and its individual trade unions with scientifically based consultation services	No governmental consultative mandate, analysis of current questions relating to economic and social policy, theoretical and empirical analysis of relevant regulatory and fundamental problems, representing of trade and industry's views and goals *vis-à-vis* the general public
Special features	Entrepreneur surveys developed and conducted by the Institute (Ifo tests)	Own quarterly national accounts	Its wage archive represents the most comprehensive set of documentation in this field	
Intended recipients of advice	General public and government agencies responsible for economic policy	General public and government agencies responsible for economic policy	DGB, individual trade unions; through publication of research work and analyses in individual cases, general public also reached	General public
Research staff	110	40	30	70

4 · FRANCE*

Michel Albert

Translated by Sean Daley

Influence is not something that can be measured easily. A given decision is most often the result of a complex interplay of influences, among which it is difficult to isolate the influence of the economist. Furthermore, although few of those who take part in decision making would claim to be professional economists, many are convinced that they have some knowledge in this area. Professor Henderson, better than anyone, has shown how widespread, in France and elsewhere, is this kind of 'do-it-yourself economy' (DIYE) (Henderson, 1986). The first section of this chapter will try to answer the following question as clearly as possible: who are – and who are not – those economists capable of influencing economic decisions?

Much like the analysis of influence, the description of power centers necessarily involves a certain oversimplification, given the complexity and interdependence of the phenomenon being described. The second section, then, tries to show how a balance of power among the different ministerial departments is established, to identify the tensions which remain, and to show the main weak points in the decision making process.

Finally, in a more concrete perspective, the third and final section gives a description which shows both the positive and negative aspects of three cases in which the work of economists was used as a basis for decision making or for orienting economic policy.

THE ECONOMISTS

In France, the profession of economist is not clear cut, and to obtain a more concrete picture of the role of economists in government, one must first understand which economists are actually called upon to work with and advise those in positions of political power. In the United States, for example, the president relies on the Council of Economic Advisers, and chooses its members primarily from the vast reserves of academics in the

* This article was elaborated and discussed in a seminar, chaired by Michel Albert; participants had considerable experience in advising government policymakers.

universities. Naturally, there are exceptions to this rule – Beryl Sprinkel is one – when banking or corporate economists are selected, but in most cases the university system is able to provide the political authorities with well-trained economists who are respected by their peers and who often have prior experience as advisers in government or in the private sector.

Similarly, in the United Kingdom, there is a tradition of small groups of advisers to the ministers or to the major government departments; these positions are invariably staffed by eminent academics who feel perfectly at home, even within the highest levels of government. It is hard to imagine, for example, that the French Treasury would accept an adviser with the rank and status of A. Burns within the British Treasury. In both these cases, the status of the economist as 'adviser' is clear; he is a true 'professional', recognized as such by his colleagues (even if they do not share all of his ideas), in a society in which it is possible to rely on a strong university tradition.

The situation in France is unquestionably more complex, and it cannot be understood without keeping in mind the dual nature of our higher education system, which is divided into the universities and the *grandes écoles*. It is not easy to give an unbiased picture of the state of economics departments in French universities, especially since this is a sector of our educational system which is rapidly changing. Nevertheless, several points can be safely made.

In France, once a professor of economics has passed the competitive examination known as the *agrégation* his academic advancement no longer really depends on his producing research work. A recent and somewhat controversial report brought out that over half of university professors were doing no research work whatsoever. The fact is that those professors of economics in universities who can point to serious publications in major international journals are all too rare.

A second difficulty is that the content of university programs for too long focused exclusively upon institutional and social subjects, and it was only towards the end of the 1950s that the teaching of economics became fully autonomous from the law departments. Thus, several generations of students suffered from an inadequate training in economic analysis, not to speak of the lack of quantitative studies, which only really began to develop in the early 1960s, primarily under the impetus of Professor H. Guitton. These efforts have been fruitful, and today there is a generation of young economists who are more open to the quantitative disciplines.

Finally, in part at least, economic thought in French universities was long dominated by approaches that are ideological in nature (Marxism, 'Third-Worldism', historical criticism), in preference to the humble and tenacious observation of mechanisms and facts. Consequently, many academics seem to be locked into certain frames of mind which, although well structured and highly organized, do not necessarily provide the most useful intellectual basis for answering the questions faced by political decisionmakers.

Nevertheless, several eminent individuals have stepped out of this academic world and have played an important advisory role in government, before finally coming to take up high-level political responsibilities themselves (Robert Marjolin, Jean-Marcel Jeanneney, Raymond Barre). On the other hand, it has been rare to find teachers from university economics departments who play a serious advisory role for national economic policy; this is especially true for macroeconomic policy. At the very most, such individuals could be counted on the fingers of both hands.

The second division of the French higher education system is made up of a set of typically French institutions known as *grandes écoles*. This tradition is a long-standing one, as a number of French *grandes écoles* were founded in the eighteenth century (the School of Bridges and Roads – l'Ecole des Ponts et Chaussées – was established in 1747). These 'great schools', primarily scientific in nature, have concentrated over the years on training engineers and teachers (for example l'Ecole Normale Supérieure); by the nineteenth century certain of their graduates turned to economics and contributed to the advance of knowledge (e.g. J. Dupuit at the Ecole des Ponts et Chaussées, and A. Cournot at the Ecole Normale Supérieure). It would be interesting to describe in greater detail this French tradition of 'engineer economists', but for the sake of brevity I will only mention several names well known outside of France: Pierre Masse, former General Commissioner of Planning and former chairman of the national electricity company (Electricité de France); Maurice Allais, professor at the Paris School of Mines (l'Ecole des Mines de Paris), who did not hold a position directly involving him in economic policy, but who was the teacher of such well-known economists as Marcel Boiteux, Edmond Malinvaud, and Jacques Lesourne.

Two important new institutions were created immediately after World War II: the National School of Administration (l'Ecole Nationale d'Administration – ENA) and the National Institute of Statistics and Economic Studies (l'Institut National de la Statistique et des Etudes Economiques – INSEE). The National School of Administration is designed to train 'general' high-level government administrators (as opposed to the technical corps of the government administration or the teachers trained in the other *grandes écoles*). Since 1945, the School has trained for all sectors of the government administration exceptionally highly qualified candidates who generally go on to hold positions of responsibility, normally within the framework of a major 'corps' of the state: the Inspection of Finances (Inspection des Finances), the Council for Administrative Appeals (Conseil d'Etat), the Court of Auditors (Cour des Comptes), the regional administration as prefects or in the central government administration.

However, the training given at the ENA places little emphasis on economics. An economics 'major' set up in the 1960s has recently been eliminated; this attempt at specialization did not, in fact, provide a real in-depth training in the economist's profession, either because the School's curriculum did not supply the necessary basics, or because the dominant attitude in the School tends to view true professional expertise as being of secondary value. Several remarkable ENA graduates have acquired a solid knowledge of economics and have gained recognition as excellent economists, but the merit for this is largely their own, the result of an open mind and of years of hard work. Such being the case, the influence which ENA graduates have on decisionmakers as economic advisers is uneven at best. In the major central administrations, and particularly in the Ministry of the Economy and Finances, the main directors, often ENA graduates, traditionally act as advisers to ministers either through direct contacts or through memoranda in which they outline their views.

Another specifically French element of political and administrative organization should be mentioned here – an important role is played by 'ministerial cabinets', small groups mostly made up of government officials, which work directly for the minister and help him carry out his duties and act as a liaison between the ministers and the various ministerial departments and agencies. Even so, the real influence of the members of these ministerial cabinets should not be overestimated. Naturally, certain members of the president's hand-picked staff (equivalent to the White House staff in Washington) and some advisers to the prime minister have occasionally had a major impact on policy decisions. Similarly, the Director of the Cabinet of the Ministry of the Economy and Finances – who is most often chosen from among the members of the 'corps' of the Inspection of Finances – can contribute to the formulation and implementation of new orientations in macro- and microeconomic policy. However, we should have no illusions about the meaning of the more modest title of 'technical adviser'; in most cases, such technical advisers primarily play the admittedly useful role of liaison between the ministers and the departments or agencies of the ministry.

Yet another quite typically French institution, and one of special importance, is the National Institute of Statistics and Economic Studies. Established in its present form in 1945, the INSEE is somewhat unusual, in comparison with many foreign statistical agencies, in that it is not only responsible for producing national statistics and for coordinating a partially decentralized statistical network, but it also carries out its own economic studies. The Institute also runs a school, the National School of Statistics and Economic Administration (l'Ecole Nationale de la Statistique et de l'Administration Economique – ENSAE), which trains statistical economists for both the government (and particularly for the INSEE) and for the private sector. Under the leadership of Edmond Malinvaud, the curriculum of the ENSAE developed a solid general education in statistics and economic analysis, coupled with additional training in the main applied fields. In the government administration, the graduates of the ENSAE either hold what are essentially professional and technical positions in the fields of data collection and processing; or they can occupy posts of responsibility in government economic departments or ministerial cabinets. The INSEE today is a major source of intellectual talents and abilities, though its image is often that of an embattled fortress, proud and independent. A general director of the INSEE must, in fact, maintain a delicate balance, for the Institute is directly under the supervision of the Minister of the Economy and Finances, but it must still preserve the tradition of independence, objectivity and scientific rigor which have been its main strengths since its inception.

This discussion of the various meanings of the term 'economist' in France may be confusing to a reader who is unfamiliar with the idiosyncracies of the land of Descartes. To reassure such readers, I shall close this first section with the observation that, most fortunately, eminent individuals have had a major influence as 'economic advisers' without having gone through any of the channels I have just described. Two names should suffice: Jean Monnet, who was the first Commissioner of Planning and who played a key role in the birth of the European community; and Jacques Delors, who was one of the chief assistants of Pierre Masse in the Planning Commission before becoming one of the most important advisers of Prime Minister Jacques Chaban-Delmas. Nevertheless, it must be admitted that, in the way it produces economists as in other areas, France suffers from a certain rigidity of structure that may be diminishing, but which is still very real and which suggests that an optimum has not yet been reached.

THE INSTITUTIONS

Before describing the distribution of powers and influences within the government, I would like to make several points regarding the role of the two legislative houses. Firstly, in France the legislative houses have only limited resources for carrying out independent studies. The Senate, however, through the efforts of several dynamic individuals, did set up roughly ten years ago a small group which, on the basis of its own hypotheses, carries out middle-term macroeconomic projection studies; technically, however, these studies are completed using the forecasting departments of the government administration (the INSEE and the Directorate of Forecasting of the Ministry of the Economy and Finances). This initial experiment, though quite modest in scope, has unquestionably been a success. As for the National Assembly, it currently has no corresponding body. Thus, the analyses of the government (developed by the various government agencies), especially with respect to the macroeconomic studies involved in preparing the budget, are not confronted with a direct counter-appraisal by the legislature.

Yet another specifically French institution is an advisory body, the Economic and Social Council (le Conseil Economique et Social – CES), which is made up of representatives of management and labor, and 'distinguished specialists' appointed by the government, and whose task is to submit 'opinions' to the government. It must be admitted that, since it was created, the CES has made only a very minor contribution to the formulating of economic and social policies. The opinions given by each of these groups, which supposedly represent the vital forces of the country, often merely express the concerns of interest groups, and the non-binding nature of these consultations has led successive governments often to consider them as little more than an unavoidable formality.

In France, as in most western democracies, the powers within the government can be categorized under a few simple headings, which are necessarily interdependent, but which make it possible to understand the context in which decisions are made. The following breakdown can be made:

1. The financial power, which encompasses the formulating and implementing of the budget, the domestic and foreign management of the public treasury, and, more generally, a basic responsibility for maintaining the main financial equilibria; it constitutes a firm and relatively well-defined core.
2. The economic power, whose make-up is far less clear, since this will be a function of the extent to which the government, whether deliberately or unwillingly, is involved in the economy. Until the turning point in economic policy of 1982–3, the various ministries, and in particular the Ministry of the Economy and Finances, traditionally worked within the framework of a planned economy through policies which have today lost much of their importance. Such was the case, for example, of the varying interest rates practiced from one sector to the next, as well as the administered price policy which only disappeared entirely in 1987. However, the competition policies, which have grown in importance, have not been eliminated, nor have foreign trade policies.
3. The social power, which is responsible for labor, employment and social welfare. The fact that the social security system is managed jointly by labor and management gives the Ministry of Social Affairs a supervisory, rather than a truly administrative status.
4. The sectoral-technical power, in which are mixed together agriculture, equipment (roads, infrastructure), transportation, housing, etc. The appropriate ministries have a supervisory role, especially as regards the nationally owned corporations in the specific sectors (a supervision which is at times uncomfortably shared with the 'financial' power); however, they sometimes try to be the defenders of a 'sectoral outlook', a position which is not without ambiguity if it entails an excessive dependence on the sectors in question.

To understand the interplay of influences among these different political spheres, one must be able to appraise accurately the importance of the administrative bodies through which these powers are exercised. The administration of the Ministry of Finances is characterized first of all by a strong tradition of competence and adaptability to highly diverse problems; the administration is fully at the service of the Ministry; and its strength lies in the coherence with which it proposes and develops a single 'finances viewpoint', which is always considered to be important in interministerial deliberations. It is largely staffed by young administrators who are often the best of ENA graduates. However, it is not without certain faults which are the counterparts of its qualities – many questions are approached in isolation from other problems, and they are sometimes settled hastily on the basis of short-term considerations and financial constraints. Furthermore, young administrators tend to change duties frequently, and, in spite of their great adaptability, they often acquire only superficial competence. Lastly, as an indirect result of their ENA training, in certain cases they lack a clear conceptual frame of reference that would make it possible to articulate better the economic and financial spheres.

The Bank of France, which Napoleon wished to be controlled by the state, but not excessively so, is far from being an institution as independent as the West German Bundesbank, for example. More or less dependent, according to the personality of the Minister of the Economy and Finances, the Bank represents a relatively closed world, protected by its statutes and its recruitment procedures. In defining domestic and foreign monetary policies, the Bank only has partial responsibility, as it is under the supervision of the Minister, a supervision which is firmly exercised by the Directorate of the Treasury. It must be said that, compared with issuing institutions in other industrialized countries, the Bank of France, in spite of the sheer size of its staff, has insufficiently developed its capacities for carrying out studies.

In the economic sphere, a certain imbalance between the emphasis placed on legal and regulatory questions to the detriment of economic concerns is very unfortunate. An examination of the way in which pricing policies have been conducted in France bears this out conclusively. Another example is the newly created Commission on Competition, which includes few professional economists, in spite of the rapid changes in the analytical foundations on which a competition policy should be based. And in the field of bilateral and multilateral trade relations, it would be easy to show that the policies chosen occasionally favor the short term, the first reflex often being a purely defensive one.

The social ministries are – and this is most unfortunate – the poor relations within the administration as a whole. Within the values system of most ENA students, these ministries have little prestige since they do not lead to the swift advancement which awaits the brightest students who normally choose to work in the Budget or Treasury. A sizeable segment of the administration in this sector view themselves more as the defenders of the underprivileged categories under their supervision, rather than as serving government policies and the citizenry as a whole.

The technical ministries, lastly, are staffed by graduates of the ENA and by members of the major technical corps of the state (Mines, Bridges and Roads, Armaments, etc.). The coexistence with them of administrators of different backgrounds and training can be a source of rivalry if poorly handled; but it can also be a source of enrichment if a true spirit of collaboration is established. The French tradition of 'engineer economists' contributes to this decompartmentalization; even though technical progress requires continual adaptation, it is to be hoped that this tradition, which seems to be losing momentum in the newest generation, will endure.

This description would be incomplete if it failed to mention the ongoing debate over the role of the Commission of Planning (le Commissariat du Plan). Within the administration as a whole, it is only the financial sphere – if only through its preparation of the budget – that has an overview, and the Commission of Planning has unquestionably played an important role by introducing new concepts, confronting different ideas, and ensuring that a plethora of micro-decisions remains oriented in the same overall direction. At the high points of its history, the Commission of Planning has had the merit of providing the authorities in the economic, social and technical spheres with an overall viewpoint which was not entirely dominated by the imperatives of the short term. Naturally, such a role can easily lead to rivalries and serious potential conflict with the financial sphere. As long as high expansion created considerable macroeconomic room for maneuver, the Commission of Planning, as a government department where a spirit of openmindedness reigned, was able to function as an irreplaceable forum for new ideas and as a mechanism for providing general overviews. The main error of the staff of the Commission was that they did not see early enough that times had changed and that, for a medium-sized country such as France, the constraints of the short term had now become insurmountable obstacles (the Seventh Plan, formulated immediately after the first oil crisis, was characterized by this shortsightedness). This error was made because the government itself was far from aware of the gravity of the situation at the time, and was far from ready to listen to the rare individuals who raised their voice in warning. Finally, it was a convenient way of reassuring the public – and themselves – by avoiding bleak prospects and emphasizing a bright and unthreatening future.

In spite of several attempts to include the concept of alternate choices under constraint more effectively in the Planning Commission's studies, the role of the Planning Commission in formulating economic policies is today very slight. Paradoxically, it is at the very moment when the need for economic policies based on duration, credibility and tenacity is most clearly perceived, that the influence of the Planning Commission is at its ebb.

THREE CASES

Three examples will be presented to illustrate the ways in which political authorities can react to economists' studies.

The macroeconomic studies linked to the preparation of the budget

In France, as in most countries, the studies for preparing the budget are based on macroeconomic projections developed by government agencies. An original aspect of French institutions, though, is the fact that these projections are debated by the Commission of Accounts and Economic Budgets of the Nation (Commission des Comptes et Budgets Economiques de la Nation – CCBEN) before they are submitted to the Parliament when the Finance Bill is tabled.

The CCBEN was created in 1952. Its first chairman was Pierre Mendes-France. Since 1960, it has been chaired by the Minister of the Economy and Finances. Its membership has varied over time, but the original principle of including three categories of members remains: there are the representatives of labor and management (union and managerial representatives), appointed by the Chairman of the Economic and Social Council; several members are senior administrators involved in the formulating of economic policies (Directors of the Budget, the Treasury, Tax Law, Forecasting, the Commissioner of Planning, the Governor of the Bank of France) as well as the chairman or secretaries of the Finance Committee of the National Assembly and the Senate; and, lastly, there are 'distinguished specialists' appointed by the Minister of the Economy and Finances. These can be academics, directors of private forecasting agencies, journalists, and the like. In all, the Commission is comprised of some thirty members.

The CCBEN reviews past accounts and projected macroeconomic accounts (called economic budgets) formulated during the preparation of the budget; these macroeconomic accounts, covering the current year and the following year, are presented to the CCBEN in March and October, that is, at the beginning and end of the budget preparation process.

Created at a time when faith in the virtues of a 'concerted economy' was at its greatest, the CCBEN has, in spite of several momentary difficulties, withstood the test of time relatively well. This merits further explanation. One possible reason may be found in the fact that the work of the Commission is well coordinated with government administration as a whole. It is true that, for the Director of the Budget, who each year must carry out a delicate task in which he is subject to strong political pressure, macroeconomic studies are a constraint, especially if they reveal a modest growth of the tax base that will reduce the increase in projected resources. However, a macroeconomic study, if it is carefully done and if it is sufficiently explicit, can allow him to evaluate certain dangers and consequently to avoid certain risks – for example, it is very likely that a serious and persistent disequilibrium in the social security programs in France will ultimately affect the budget of the state. Coherent and well-documented economic forecasts in this area can make it possible to implement the necessary corrective measures at a sufficiently early stage. Similarly, the work of the CCBEN contributes to a certain ministerial decompartmentalization, since many of its studies are compared with the research carried out by other ministerial departments (for example, it would be impossible to construct a detailed and credible projection of the social security accounts without cooperating closely with the appropriate divisions of the Ministry of Social Affairs).

A second consideration is that, since the Commission is chaired by the Minister, both he and his cabinet must necessarily become involved in the preparation of the budget items. This includes defining possible economic policy options, ranking government priorities for each budget item, and taking into account the various political, economic and social constraints involved. Working together this way allows political decisionmakers, especially in the preparatory stage, to become aware of certain time limits (themselves constraints on policy *implementation*). It also brings home to policymakers, by highlighting strong interdependencies that only macroeconomic analysis can bring out, the fact that everything cannot be done at once. Thus, when in 1984 the government made public its intention to reduce mandatory levies, macroeconomic studies soon showed that merely attempting to stabilize the increase of the percentage of levies in the GDP would already be a major task, given the tax measures that had been decided on elsewhere and the constraints affecting the budget. In the final phase, the macroeconomic studies carried out during the summer are tabled in Parliament and form an appendix to the Finance Bill, and will provide a basis of reference for certain parliamentary questions or debates.

Paradoxically, though, it is primarily because the government administration has lost its monopoly of macroeconomic forecasting studies that government decisionmakers have been led to use them more frequently. Until the late 1970s, the government administration did, in fact, have a near monopoly in this area. Several organizations have been created since then, and they have developed with the support and encouragement of the government authorities. These organizations have their own financing and intellectual resources, and carry out macroeconomic forecasting studies on a regular basis. Thus, outside the government administration, there now exists in France a series of research and forecasting institutes, within universities, in the National Council of French Management, in trade unions, and in other institutions, and they have gained solid experience. These various institutes regularly compare their research, and the meeting of the Commission of Accounts (Commission des Comptes) is itself preceded by a meeting of a 'technical working party' in which professional economists review and compare the hypotheses and the conclusions of their studies. The results of this comparison are then reported to the Minister in the Commission of Accounts, which helps to define major concerns and, in certain cases, to relativize the government's own studies.

These developments are very positive. They reduce the tendency of any government, whatever its political allegiances, to give in to the temptation of espousing overly optimistic prospects or of adopting an overly legalistic line. In addition to the macroeconomic studies which aid in the preparation of the budget, plans are currently under way to extend this mechanism to other areas of economic policy.

Changing concepts and policies regarding income distribution

In France, more so than in the rest of Europe, it has taken time for the public and for politicians to realize the magnitude of the changes imposed by the two successive oil crises. Unlike our partners, and, especially, our main partner, West Germany, we were slow to adapt primarily in two areas. First, we let the purchasing power of wages grow beyond the capacity of our productivity, which, although it did continue to rise, was nevertheless hard hit by the unfavorable trends in the terms of trade. Second, social security spending continued to grow (through 1984), which caused an increase in the contributions burdening firms. It is likely that these two elements, in the long run, combined to worsen the impact of the economic crisis in France.

Paradoxically, the ideas of economists in the 1970s were tending towards a better understanding of the importance of the relationship between the primary distribution of income and employment. It was in this period that the theory of disequilibrium was developed in the research of economists of the CEPREMAP (Centre d'Etudes Prospectives d'Economie Mathématique Appliquées à la Planification – Center for Mathematical Economics Applied to Planning) such as J. P. Benassy and Y. Younés and in the syntheses of E. Malinvaud (1977). These studies brought out clearly that it was possible for there to be situations of lasting disequilibria on labor markets which might be due, depending on the configuration of parameters, either to insufficient aggregate demand (Keynesian unemployment), or to an excessive level of real wages (classical unemployment).

In 1979–80, with the preparation of the Eighth Plan, the problem of the rise in the purchasing power of wages was, for the first time, given a central position in the socioeconomic debate (this Plan was to cover the period of 1981–5; however, it was never presented to Parliament for approval). A majority of both labor and management accepted – and this was something quite new in France – to consider policies which focused on the need for reestablishing the profit margins for firms. This meant studying the consequences of lower growth of the purchasing power of wages, of a stricter control of the increase in social spending, and, if necessary, of a rebalancing of the accounts of the social security system by levies on households rather than on firms, all of which would be beneficial to employment in the middle term. In return, there was to be a reappraisal of the organization of working time and working conditions, which will be discussed later.

It is no exaggeration to state that, just before the change of government of May 1981, a significant number of economists and socioeconomic officials – including those on the left – were aware of the fact that France was faced with a serious problem of primary distribution of wages and that corrective measures were called for. It is difficult to determine the exact causes behind this awareness; no doubt it was the combined effect of a favorable sociopolitical context, a shifting of the left-leaning CFDT (Confédération Française et Democratique du Travail) trade union federation towards the center in 1978, and the birth in France of an as yet tiny Social-Democratic left. And then there was the personality of the former Prime Minister, Raymond Barre, who had been influenced by his term in Brussels as European Commissioner and had been impressed by West German economic policies. Finally, ideas were changing in the field of economic analysis, although they were often highly theoretical in nature and would have been difficult to apply to concrete situations. In all, it was an exceptional period, and will probably be recognized as such one day, in which a real dialogue, short lived it is true, came into being within the Planning Commission.

In 1981–2, however, the Socialist government of Mr Mauroy had to keep the election promises it had made regarding income distribution and which ran counter to the awareness just mentioned. From this there followed a 'lax' policy characterized primarily by the reduction in the legal working week (to be discussed later), the raising of the legal minimum wage (SMIC), and a significant upgrading of family benefits. The alliance with the Communist Party forced the government to continue a policy of stimulating public consumption. At this time, France maintained a policy of expansion, while, in the wake of the second oil crisis and the recession in America, most of our partners had tried to lower domestic demand. In 1982, the French economy was growing at a rate of 2.5 per cent, while the German economy showed a negative growth of −1 per cent. This short-term gap had a dramatic impact on our foreign trade, which had a deficit of 2.8 per cent of the GDP in 1982.

In mid-1982 and early 1983 there was a major reappraisal of income policies. The Finance Minister J. Delors proposed to stop the strong indexing of wages by setting *ex ante* a standard of price increases to which wage increases would be aligned. Prime Minister P. Mauroy committed the government, on a multiannual basis, to a policy of not increasing the costs of firms either through raising taxes or social contributions, a promise it was to keep. Looked at four years later, this policy, maintained by the Chirac government, has achieved results: in 1987, the profit margin rate of firms (the ratio of the gross operating profits to the value added) has returned to a level comparable to that of the period before the first oil crisis.

These policies, essential for the recovery of the French economy, illustrate well the gradual filtering through of ideas which originated in the work done by economists in the late 1970s. The major shift in the economic policies of the left in 1982–3 was only accepted because of the persuasive efforts of a few advisers to both the President and the Prime Minister, certain of whom had participated in this earlier work and had thoroughly understood its importance in the middle term. The decisive role played by certain directors of the central government administration, such as M. Camdessus, then Director of the Treasury, should also be mentioned. Finally, within trade union organizations, certain individuals gave convincing advice; they were no doubt in a position to do so because they had worked in the Planning Commission earlier and had participated in the research mentioned above.

This episode illustrates that economic policies are not formulated in a vacuum, and shows that the complex filtering through of ideas is a gradual process.

A mistaken economic policy: the reduction of working time in 1982

In 1982, the Mauroy government decreed two measures which, in hindsight, can be seen as clear economic policy mistakes: the lowering of the legal work week from forty to thirty-nine hours (without a corresponding wage reduction) and the introduction of a fifth week of paid vacation. This mistake was the outcome of four erroneous viewpoints.

First, there was an outdated view of what real 'social progress' should consist of. The fact is that, thanks to the economic expansion of the 'thirty glorious years' (an expression used by J. Fourastié designating the thirty years of high growth during 1945–75), France has made major strides in social progress since the Popular Front (the Socialist government of 1936–7 which passed the 'law of forty hours' and introduced mandatory paid vacations for all wage-earners). To announce the lowering of the working week to thirty-five hours (fortunately this plan was never carried out) and, out of nostalgia for 1936, to give an extra week of paid vacation is, in the France of the 1980s, an orientation of dubious relevance.

Next, this policy revealed a serious lack of understanding of the constraint represented by France's need to be competitive internationally. To share labor without sharing income is an illusion, for, in a world of fierce competition, it will lead to a loss of foreign markets and, consequently, to a further decline in overall employment.

A third error was the belief that the government should regulate, in a centralized and uniform manner, the main working conditions of the workforce. Naturally, government should fully exercise its responsibility to prevent and eliminate abuses. But within these limits, it is dangerous to try to regulate working conditions in a centralized and uniform way, 'with the policeman's whistle', as it has been described.

Finally, without falling into naive 'productivism', we should emphasize the effect of the false signals which such measures sent to the public. At a time when France faced major challenges, was it not misguided to lead the public into believing that the French could work less while earning the same amount? This mistake is all the more difficult to understand given the fact that the macroeconomic studies, in spite of their limitations, had made it possible, as early as the late 1970s, to focus on three basic problems regarding the organization of working time.

Firstly, these studies showed the dangers of considering a reduction in working time in isolation from income trends. A reduction in the average working time could not improve aggregate employment unless the wage-earners concerned simultaneously accepted a reduction in wages. The second problem which the studies had only incompletely analyzed was that of a possible increase in the hourly productivity of labor. Few studies provided any serious basis for evaluation, and thus a certain prudence in this area was called for. Finally, it was apparent that, when the working week was reduced in this way, it would be impossible to ignore the problem of the lessened use of installed capital equipment, and that, unless care was exercised, firms would be unable to remain competitive either nationally or internationally.

To understand how an error of this kind could be made, we must look for the causes in the influence of simplistic ideologies upon the thinking of a segment of the French left, in the pressure brought to bear on the government by the hard-line left CGT (Confédération Général du Travail) trade union federation, and, lastly, in the desire of certain political advisers to pull off a 'coup'. Meanwhile, the highest authorities of the state were unaware of the seriousness of these steps, which surprised, and even outraged, the economists who were acting as advisers at the time, and who were faced with a *fait accompli*. An overall appraisal of these two measures *ex post* leads to a simple conclusion: in terms of creating jobs, their impact was negligible. Furthermore, it is likely that they accelerated the decrease in the apparent productivity of capital based in France and that they contributed to the structural decline of our competitiveness.

If nothing else, at least one good thing has come from this unfortunate experiment: today, a segment of the public has become aware of the need for allowing greater freedom in these areas to decentralized negotiation. France still faces major problems related to the use of capital goods, part-time labor, and the need for certain sectors to adapt to fluctuations in demand. The solutions, we can be sure, will not be found in uniform policies dictated from Paris. These are a series of basic problems that must be faced by the majority that will come to power after the presidential elections of 1988.

CONCLUSION

In the light of the French experience, we can see three ways of enhancing the usefulness of economists to political decisionmakers: by integrating them better at the different levels of government, by ensuring that they be fully qualified professionally, and, lastly, by reminding them on occasion that a certain humility is necessary.

Nothing is more dangerous than an economist who is out of touch with reality. If he is to be of value to political decisionmakers, he must first be a good listener so that he can grasp the full implications of the questions which he must try to answer. This ability to listen should not exclude an ability to evaluate, and, especially, to distinguish what is essential from what is secondary. It is also important that he be well integrated within traditional government departments. These sometimes have incomplete or short-term views that the economist may tend to judge as being simplistic. Nevertheless, these departments are capable of showing the constraints – especially those concerning implementation – which any attempt at change will invariably come up against. A failure to take such constraints into account might well mean that the economist himself will fall into the trap of oversimplification. Even when middle-term policies are involved, this requirement holds true. As early as 1975, Jacques Delors stated:

> The Commission of Planning should not lose interest in current affairs, for its credibility in the eyes of any government is a function of its ability to come up with solid arguments based on a good background file when a problem must be solved.
>
> (Delors, 1975)

Being professional is first of all a matter of being fully competent. Naturally, this means understanding and mastering the skills and techniques which are at the economist's disposal, but it also implies that the economist will use them carefully to give a faithful interpretation of information to the decisionmaker, without distorting his analyses. This requires a capacity for detachment in two areas. Firstly, he must be skeptical of simplistic ideological currents, whether they be on the left or the right. Secondly, he must keep a distance from a direct involvement in politics. Jean Monnet, the founding father of French planning, understood this well when he observed in his *Mémoires*:

> I have no desire at all to remain in the background, but if self-effacement is what it takes to get things done most effectively, then I choose to stay in the background.
>
> (Monnet, 1976)

Finally, the need for a certain humility should be emphasized. Pierre Masse, in a recently published work, gave economists a serious warning:

> Economists are much criticized. Certain of them have, it is true, been almost arrogant, and have led others to believe that their science could provide solutions to all problems. Their science? Is it not instead a quest? In recent years, it has been less than a scientific quest. It has rather degenerated into an attempt to uphold, if necessary through sophistry, doctrines formulated in other contexts and based on other observations.
>
> (Masse, 1984)

Humility consists in having the courage to admit that there are questions which economic 'science' cannot answer, and to make this clear to decisionmakers. It also means not forgetting, and not letting others forget, that any evaluation is subject to sizeable margins of error. Finally, it means being aware that the filtering through of ideas is complex and takes time. Thus, when an economist sees that his advice goes unheeded in the present, he should patiently carry on his work, in the hope that it will bear fruit in the future.

BIBLIOGRAPHY

Delors, Jacques, *Changer* (Paris: Editions Stock, 1974).

Henderson, David, *Innocence and Design: The Influence of Economic Ideas on Policy* (Oxford: Basil Blackwell, 1986).

Malinvaud, E., *The Theory of Unemployment Reconsidered* (Oxford: Basil Blackwell, 1977).

Masse, Pierre, 'Aléas et progrès, entre Candide et Cassandre', *Economica* (Paris, 1984).

Monnet, Jean, *Mémoires* (Paris: Editions Fayard, 1976).

5 · AUSTRIA

Hans Seidel

In order to understand what economists are doing in and for the government, the institutional framework and the intellectual environment have to be taken into account. In Austria both differ from those in other industrialized countries in important respects.

This chapter is organized as follows: it begins with an overview of the Austrian economic policy and its institutions. The next section deals with the market for economists. The third and longest section describes the role of economists in different roles related to the political decision-making process. As reference, the period since World War II was selected, which shows a remarkable continuity as well as gradual changes in institutions and ideas.

THE INSTITUTIONAL FRAMEWORK

Austria is a federal republic. Economic policy both at the federal and the local level has been and to a certain degree still is characterized by neocorporatist features, which in Austria, according to political scientists, are more dominant than in any other industrialized country of the West. The large social groups are represented by highly centralized interest organizations with compulsory membership: the Chambers (Kammern) of Labor, of Business and of Agriculture (which in national accounts terms are part of 'general government'). These three chambers and the Federation of Trade Unions constitute the core of the 'social partners'. They are integrated into the bureaucratic and political decision-making process both individually and collectively. The chambers are entitled to written comments on bills before they are passed on to parliament; in many cases the chambers participate in the drafting of bills from the very beginning. All interest organizations have links to the two large political parties. Labor is primarily linked to the Socialist Party (SPÖ), business and agriculture are mainly represented by the People's Party (ÖVP). The two large parties set up a coalition government from 1946 to 1966 and again since 1987.

The large interest organizations in Austria do not only act individually in the governmental and parliamentary arena; they also cooperate as social partners outside the constitutionally defined decision-making process, mainly in the field of prices and wages policy (income policy) but also in other areas of common interest. Since 1957 this cooperation is institutionalized in the Parity Commission on Prices and Wages (Paritätische Kommission für Preis- und Lohnfragen).

Social partnership is based on the idea that the big interest groups can reach consensus on important questions of economic policy. Their willingness to compromise is widely regarded as a consequence of the negative experiences of the First Republic (1918–38). The Austrian political parties and social groups have learned their lesson from the civil war of the 1930s and the German reign between 1938 and 1945. They found out that cooperative games are more rewarding for all participants than non-cooperative games.

Although no formal *social contract* has been formulated. a common understanding exists regarding basic economic principles and structures. The Austrian economy is considered a mixed economy with reliance on market forces but with strong public-sector ownership not only in the utilities but also in the manufacturing industry. Some authors even claim that nationalization, at least for the postwar period, has been a prerequisite for labor to identify itself with the Second Republic. Government interventions in the market process are frequent, and an ingenious variety of techniques has been developed to promote investments.

Until the beginning of the 1980s, a clear vision of macroeconomic strategies prevailed. Again as a result of the sad experiences of the 1930s, full employment had top priority among the usual macroeconomic goals. In order to achieve these goals, instruments were assigned to goals in a simplistic way and responsibilities distributed accordingly. Roughly speaking, the government (including the National Bank) was assumed to be responsible for the level of employment, using as instruments mainly fiscal and monetary policies. The social partners were expected to moderate the rise of prices and wages by an appropriate income policy (based on constant factor shares in national income). This concept could not be realized all the time: in 1952/53, in order to end the postwar inflation, a restrictive fiscal and monetary policy was introduced which plunged the economy into a classical stabilization crisis. Nevertheless, the above-mentioned assignment of instrument to goals guided economic policy most of the time. Austria appears to be one of the few countries where an institutionalized income policy has been pursued with demonstrably good results over a long period.

The notion of the modern welfare state and Keynesian macroeconomic policy prevailed in many industrialized countries until the 1970s. In Austria, however, these ideas were so strongly rooted in the mind of policymakers and their experts that after the first oil crisis a special mix of macroeconomic policies labelled 'Austrian Keynesianism' was developed, at a time when demand management in a growing number of industrialized countries was increasingly considered inappropriate or even destructive. The concept of Austrian Keynesianism is somewhat ambiguous. Essentially, it combines measures designed to moderate cost pressures (income policy, hard currency policy) with measures designed to stimulate demand (expansionary fiscal policy). In the short run, this policy mix proved to be successful. The Austrian economy absorbed the real and nominal shocks resulting from the oil price rise without endangering full employment. In the 1980s, however, this concept had to be abandoned. Economic policy, as in other countries, shifted gradually from macroeconomic Keynesianism to microeconomic structural adjustment strategies when it became clear that the world economy would not return to its previous growth path and, by adhering to a full-employment concept, rigidities of all kinds were bound to develop.

The political strength of the social partners and their capacity to solve outstanding economic problems has changed somewhat over time. In the 1960s the compromise of the presidents of the interest organizations in many cases dominated the administrative and political decision-making process in government and in parliament. Concerns about a tendency towards an unconstitutional regime of chambers (Kammerstaat) were expressed. In the last fifteen years, however, the social partners have lost some of their previous strengths in shaping economic policy. In the 1970s the one-party socialist government had taken the lead, although it stressed the importance of consensus strategies, but indicated that it had to make decisions if the social partners could not agree on a certain course of action. In the 1980s the decay of Austrian Keynesianism restricted the spectrum of activities of the social partners further. Nevertheless, they still have many possibilities to give expert advice to the government and to influence administrative and political decisions individually or collectively. They are still engaged in the implementation of price and wage policy, and are capable of compromising on important questions of labour relations. To mention just one example: the Austrian trade unions did not have to strike in order to obtain shorter working hours.

From a broader view the withdrawal of the social partners from general economic policy matters and the return to their original tasks, as well as the accompanying tendency towards a more *pluralistic society* have been a byproduct of general socioeconomic developments: the increased openness of the economy strengthened international competition and left little room for national macroeconomic strategies. Changes in the social composition of the labor force (the sharp decline in the numbers of self-employed, both in agriculture and elsewhere) as well as unavoidable structural adjustment strategies, weakened the assignment of interest organizations to political parties. The trade unions may reluctantly accept the closing down of unprofitable firms which deteriorate employment prospects in the short run, but they cannot be held responsible for such actions. Last but not least, increased concerns over environmental damages shifted the focus of political activities from economic to environmental problems.

THE MARKET FOR ECONOMISTS

During the long period of prosperity following World War II, the government proper, the social partners and government-related agencies (especially research institutions) developed a growing demand for economists. Experts were needed to collect data and to organize these in a meaningful way. Experts had to analyze and to forecast macroeconomic developments and to clarify microeconomic issues. Last but not least, they were asked to advise policymakers on matters of economic policy strategies and on their implementation.

Several factors contributed to the growing demand for economic experts with professional skills in the bureaucratic and political decision-making process. A major stimulus came from outside. In order to implement the European Recovery Programme (ERP) at the end of the 1940s, the US authorities were asking for programs and forecasts which required economic expertise. The Austrian government, for example, had to develop consistent investment plans for individual industries. It had to forecast foreign-exchange requirements and to estimate the difference between the expected and the desirable growth of money supply as a prerequisite for the release of counterpart funds. Moreover, membership in international economic organizations such as the Organization for European Economic Cooperation (OEEC – later transformed into OECD) or the IMF, had a durable stimulating effect on economic thinking and analysis. OECD examinations and IMF consultations forced the government agencies involved to assess the current development of the Austrian economy, to take stock of outstanding problems and to defend the measures taken in a convincing way. In order to participate actively in working groups and committees, delegates had to be familiar with the language of economists. Some of the economic sections in ministries now in existence were developed out of the ERP Bureau established at the end of the 1940s.

The second impetus came from the diffusion of Keynesianism. The idea that government had to play an active role in order to keep the economy on a full-employment path was widely accepted both among politicians and bureaucrats. Demand management, as time passed by, appeared to be a task of economic engineering based on generally accepted ideas concerning macroeconomic behaviour and the reactions of the economic system to government interventions, especially to monetary and fiscal stimuli. Forecasting, assessing the forecast, simulation of the effects of possible government interventions and formulating packages of economic measures in order to stabilize the economy became an essential assignment for economic experts in and outside the civil service. Especially in the Ministry of Finance it was recognized that the relation between the budget and the economy goes both ways and that consequently fiscal policy has to play an important role in any stabilization strategy.

The third stimulus came from the social partners, especially from the Council of Social and Economic Affairs, to be described later on. The compromises of the social partners were based on a realistic assessment of the relative power of each group as well as on the belief that the room for maneuver is limited by economic laws or necessities. The social partners took great pains at improving statistics. They employed many economists and they did much to enhance economic knowledge among larger circles.

With increasing demands for economic information and advice the question arose as to how neutral economists can and should be *vis-à-vis* political parties and ideologies. Although no definite answer has been found, a typical pattern has emerged. In Austria the political parties strongly influence appointments and promotions in the public sector including publicly owned enterprises. One would expect, therefore, that economic policymakers would select advisers belonging to the same political party and sharing the same ideology. The social partners, especially, rely heavily on their experts with intimate knowledge of their respective organizations.

Nevertheless, there always has been a demand for the nonpartisan expert. One reason was that, until the middle of the 1970s, it was widely believed that trained economists know how the economy is working and on the basis of this knowledge were able to predict with sufficient accuracy what would happen in future given a set of values for the exogenous variables. Perhaps more important was that cabinet ministers felt that they were mainly confronted with practical problems and that ideology did not help very much to solve them in an efficient way. They therefore looked for competent assistance wherever available. But even in those cases, not just technical skill and practical experience were required but also reliability and responsibility. The neutral experts had to accept the rules of cooperative games, they had to consider possible negative psychological effects of forecasts and they had to have an intuitive feeling as to which measures might be acceptable to the political parties and interest groups.

One of the intellectual drawbacks of this system is that it reduces the spectrum of unprejudiced discussions of economic problems. Since most experts belong to a political party, to an interest organization or to the group of neutral experts in advisory functions, public discussions of controversial economic issues are limited. Economic structures and strategies upon which social partners or the large political partners have agreed, are unimpeachable. A lengthy public discussion on the subject of a major tax reform in which a wide range of professional experts participate, as recently happened in the United States, is hardly possible.

Switching from demand to supply, in the first two decades after World War II the rising demand for economists could hardly be met. Most members of the Austrian school of economics (in the wider sense) had left Austria in the 1930s and did not (or were not asked to) return after World War II. The professors of economics teaching at the universities had practically no contacts with the international scientific community and could not meet the rising demand for macroeconomics of the postwar era. The age of Keynes was introduced by economists outside the universities, mainly at the Austrian Institute of Economic Research, where Kurt Rothschild and Josef Steindl were staff members after their return from emigration.

Until the middle of the 1960s economics was taught mainly as a subsidiary subject at the faculties of law and business administration. (The renowned members of the Austrian school of economics before World War II had a degree in law, which may explain their dislike of mathematics.) Therefore, with the exception of the scientific community at the universities no clear-cut distinction between economists and non-economists was possible. Skills acquired during professional life had to be taken as a criterion rather than education and university degrees.

It was not until the 1960s (approximately at the same time as in Germany) that Austria made great efforts to catch up with the development in social sciences in Britain and the United States. The professors Theodor Pütz and Wilhelm Weber at the University of Vienna educated a generation of young economists who could meet international standards. Furthermore and most important, at the Austrian universities, faculties of social science were established, where students could take a degree in economics. At the same time the standard of the courses in economics generally was improved (also at the law faculty). Last but not least, in 1963 the Institute of Advanced Studies (IHS) was founded with the financial support of the Ford Foundation at the initiative of two former Austrian professors, Paul Lazarsfeld and Oskar Morgenstern. The Institute offers a two-year postgraduate course in the social sciences, and applies advanced formal techniques in empirical research projects. Approximately fifty full professors in different social sciences started their career at the IHS. As a result of these efforts the supply of economists who by any standard can be regarded as highly qualified, was enhanced considerably.

For the reasons mentioned it is difficult to estimate how many economists are working in Austria. Roughly speaking, there are about 100 scholars with knowledge corresponding to PhD level in the United States, and about 1,000 economists with a graduate education at Masters level. The rising supply of qualified economists, unfortunately, did not, as was generally expected, make the economists more respected and more influential in bureaucracy and politics. On the contrary, the idea widely held in the 1960s and even in the 1970s that economics would become an established profession like medicine, law and engineering has turned out to be too optimistic. The economist as an adviser has been met with increasing suspicion. As in other countries the reasons are two-fold.

First it had to be acknowledged that the socioeconomic system is more complex than macroeconomic models assume. Already during the 1970s it became obvious that economists have only a limited capacity to forecast (even on a conditional basis and with advanced techniques) and that the old Keynesian consensus on macroeconomics cannot be maintained. The progressive view, that the economic profession equipped with advanced techniques will be able to solve economic problems in a satisfactory way, suffered a setback. In Austria the reputation of economic advisers was especially damaged by the loss of competence in the field of macroeconomic policy because, up to now, they have not been very successful in shifting their activities to other more promising microeconomic issues such as deregulation in the United States or reprivatization in the United Kingdom.

Second, the gap between applied economics and academic economics, between the simple verbal arguments of advisers and the sophisticated mathematical methods modern theories use, has widened. It may be that the use of mathematics is the only way to learn what scholars in economic theory really mean. But advanced techniques for practical purposes are only useful if robust results can be obtained. They are quite useless if they just demonstrate the complexity of socioeconomic systems, in which almost anything is liable to happen.

The majority of young economists with a command of economics above graduate level started an academic career or joined the staff of research institutions. Only a few accepted a job in government or in other policy-orientated agencies. Since the demand for scholars at the universities is now largely satisfied, most economists will have to accept nonacademic jobs. Whether they succeed will crucially depend on their ability to acquire, in addition to their formal education, a working knowledge of legal and institutional facts, as well as the entrepreneurial talent to sell what they are able to produce. Hopefully the young economists will be able to fulfill the requirements of practical jobs. Given the low level of economic knowledge and the lack of economic thinking among a large part of the Austrian bureaucracy, an integration of highly trained economists in the decision-making process could produce sizeable benefits for the society as a whole.

ECONOMISTS IN DIFFERENT CAPACITIES

Economists serve the government in different capacities:

1. As politicians.
2. As civil servants.
3. As members of advisory boards.
4. As informal advisers.

The following survey indicates how frequent and influential economists have been in these functions in Austria.

Politicians

It does happen, although not very frequently, that professors of economics make a political career and are appointed cabinet ministers. The most outstanding examples, although not the only ones, before World War II, were Eugen von Böhm-Bawerk and Joseph Schumpeter. Both were Ministers of Finance, the former at the turn of the century, the latter in 1922 when inflation started to gallop. In the postwar period two men holding a chair in economics were Ministers of Finance (and as such members of the Cabinet) and later became Governors of the Austrian National Bank: Reinhardt Kamitz and Stephan Koren. Kamitz was responsible for the stabilization program which ended the postwar inflation in 1952. Koren launched a budget consolidation program at the end of the 1960s. In his position as Governor of the central bank he was responsible for the so-called hard-currency option (tying the Austrian schilling to the Deutsche Mark). Both were staff members of the Austrian Institute of Economic Research (Österreichisches Institut für Wirtschaftsforschung – WIFO) or its predecessor. Their active university career was relatively short. They regarded economics as a tool box to solve practical problems rather than as an intellectual exercise. Being economists themselves they did not need much advice from other experts. Their main problem seemed to be to achieve at a political level what they regarded as sound economic policies.

In addition, Professor Wilhelm Taucher has to be mentioned: he had been Minister of Trade before World War II and was head of the Austrian ERP Bureau during the era of the Marshall Plan. Two other examples of lesser importance could be added: Adolf Nußbaumer and Hans Seidel (the author of this paper) served as independent experts in the Kreisky government as state secretaries. The former was professor of applied economics at the University of Vienna, the latter director of the Institute of Economic Research. Given the limited jurisdiction of state secretaries and the obstacles non-party members have to face in the political arena, they could only marginally influence economic policy.

In parliament there have always been members with a thorough knowledge of economics. This is especially true for the speakers who are in charge of representing the views of their parties on economic matters in parliament and in their committees. Some of them are professors of economics or have acquired professional experience in research institutions or in economic sections of the chambers.

Civil servants

The different government agencies employ only a limited number of economists. Judged by university degrees, in 1971 nearly half of all employees with higher education in government (central and local government, social security agencies, chambers) had studied law.

As has been mentioned before, law students have to take courses and pass examinations in economics approximately at the undergraduate level. But especially the older generation of civil servants forgot most of it. Many of them complained that they found it difficult or even impossible to apply in practice what they had learned in economics at university (when the lectures given in economics still were of poor quality). They concentrated on the legal aspects rather than on the economic and social aspects of given problems. The 'monopoly' of lawyers has been critized by many social scientists who argue that the civil service needs more economists, sociologists and scholars in political science, capable of analyzing complex socio-economic phenomena and of exploring the options available for government action.

Actually the educational background of high-level officials has changed very little. Until 1981 the share of lawyers declined somewhat, but they still have better chances to attain top positions than graduates from other faculties. Most of the civil servants with a law degree are regarded as generalists and not just as legal advisers. Since 1971 the percentage of graduates in the social sciences has increased slightly, but did not exceed 8 per cent by 1981. It is not known how many of them had a degree in economics. From the yearly statistics of graduations one can infer that probably no more than 3 per cent of all high civil servants are trained economists.

The detailed description here focuses on the following institutions: economic ministries of the federal government, the National Bank, the chambers and the Institute of Economic Research; the latter acts in many respects as a government agency.

Federal government

In the federal government economists may be employed in a broad range of positions within the bureaucratic structure. But by and large they tend to be concentrated in the economic ministries (Ministry of Finance, Chancellery, Ministry of Economic Affairs, Ministry of Social Affairs), either in the bureau of the cabinet minister or in special economic or economic policy sections.

In Austria most of the civil servants, at least in the higher ranks, are career officials with tenure. Problems are likely to arise if the minister does not have confidence in the division heads, either because they do not belong to the same political party, or for purely personal reasons. One solution was to enlarge the minister's bureau, which originally had purely administrative functions, by adding personal aides, who were selected and appointed by the minister himself. These political secretaries usually were promising young men and women with experience in relevant jobs outside the bureaucracy. They had to screen reports presented by the career officials, they had to write memos on different subjects, they were asked to prepare speeches for the minister and to keep the minister informed as to what was going on in and outside the ministry. Most of them had some knowledge in economics; some were economists at a graduate level.

For some time, the Ministry of Finance employed between five and ten personal secretaries, mostly on a temporary basis. They left the ministry at the latest when the minister resigned, using their acquired knowledge for a personal career outside the bureaucracy. (The present chancellor Vranitzky had served some years as personal secretary in the Ministry of Finance before moving up the ladder as a bank manager and finally was appointed Chancellor of the Federal Republic.)

For a minister to work with many personal aides is obviously only the secondbest solution, because it disturbs the cooperation between him and the career officers. Moreover, personal aides are usually very busy with routine tasks and have no time for more analytical studies. In some ministries, therefore, economic sections or strategic planning sections were established, instead of or in addition to personal secretaries.

These sections are normally fairly small; they employ around four career officers with a university degree. They have to write reports on general economic matters (e.g. contributions to the yearly economic report presented by the government to parliament), they represent their ministry on different committees, they act as delegates to working parties or committees of international organizations, they gather information on foreign countries prior to official visits from abroad, etc. According to the special tasks of a ministry, additional assignments are added. The staff members usually have to perform some analytical work and to monitor research projects, carried out by specialized institutes at the request of the ministry.

Perhaps the most ambitious attempt at introducing economic analysis into the bureaucratic process was made in the 1970s in the Ministry of Finance. Already in the 1960s an economic section was set up. It merged with a group called the Fiscal Policy Section, which at its height occupied more than ten highly skilled civil servants. Some of them had taken a postgraduate course in the IHS (Institute for Advanced Studies) and therefore were familiar with advanced techniques of empirical analysis. They developed a computer-supported database and a macroeconomic model designed to simulate the effects of fiscal policy measures. The results were used as background information for fiscal policy decisions, e.g. whether a contingency budget should be released and what quantitative efforts were to be expected. Some of the staff members published reports on different subjects of fiscal policy.

In the meantime the staff of the Budgetary Policy Section was split into three different sections; one of them is again called the Economic Section.

A characteristic feature of nearly all economic or strategic policy sections in the federal government is that their 'production functions' are inherently unstable. Their size, functions and importance, if not their existence, depend on the minister's confidence in the personal attributes and capabilities of his economic staff, or the ability of the staff members to convince other sections or divisions that they can make valuable contributions to common problems.

The Austrian Central Office of Statistics, unlike that in some other countries, concentrates its activity on collecting and publishing data. It does not analyze data and is not engaged in model building.

The Austrian National Bank

The National Bank is somewhat better equipped with economists than is the federal government. Quite a few economists work in departments engaged in the banking business. The economic department proper has fifteen staff members including the head of the department; the majority of them have a degree or have taken a postgraduate course in economics. The economic department produces both the bank's monthly and annual reports as well as the internal reports concerning general economic questions.

The quantity and quality of information which the staff provides for the Governor or the directors of the National Bank are clearly superior to those which are made available to the Minister of Finance by his staff in similar situations and for the same purpose. Although the bank with its ample financial resources could well afford to employ a few scholars engaged in basic research (which may not pay off in the short run), economic analysis with advanced techniques is not regarded as an important task of the economic department. An attempt to build an econometric monetary model for the Austrian economy was abandoned. The influence of the economic section of the National Bank on bank policy depends very much on the personal relationship between the Governor and the head of the department (who normally is not a member of the board of directors). Part of the tasks which in other countries economists perform in the civil service has been and to certain degree still is carried out by two other organizations: the Austrian Institute for Economic Research and the large-interest organizations (the chambers and the Trade Union Federation).

The chambers

The Chamber of Labor in Vienna (which represents labor at the federal level) and the Federal Chamber of Business have organized their economic staff along similar lines. Both chambers have an economic policy department, an economic (scientific) department and a statistical department.

Most of these departments are equipped with ten to fifteen staff members. Furthermore, economists are employed by various other departments, some of which were set up by separating special assignments from the economic departments. The representation of agriculture at the federal level (Präsidentenkonferenz der Landwirtschaftskammern) also has an economic policy department, although on a smaller scale, and most of the staff members are specialists in agricultural problems.

In principle, the division of labor in the Chambers of Labor and Business between the economic, the economic policy and the statistics departments is the following: the economic (scientific) department is mainly engaged in analytical and empirical studies and edits journals published by the chambers; the economic policy department does practical business, negotiating with other chambers or government agencies on various acute problems; and the statistics department provides the whole organization with statistical information and may even collect primary statistical data. Which (if any) of these departments perform the role of a 'think tank' investigating strategic problems, depends on the capabilities of the staff in these departments, their relation to the presidents and the priorities of the chamber's policy.

It is worth noting that some staff members of either chambers chose a university career. Especially the Chamber of Business, at least in the first decades after World War II, encouraged young scholars to start a university career although most of them chose statistics and law rather than economics.

Both chambers publish an economic journal: the Chamber of Labor, *Wirtschaft und Gesellschaft*, the Chamber of Business, *Wirtschaftspolitische Blätter*. Many of the papers published are of high quality, and some internationally renowned economists have made contributions. Furthermore, the scientific department of the Chamber of Business organizes, at regular intervals, symposia on matters of general interest (e.g. 'International Trade under Uncertainty'), mainly with German-speaking economists.

According to a long-standing tradition (which in the case of the Chamber of Business goes back to the middle of the nineteenth century), long before the idea of social partnership had emerged, the chambers had acquired a reputation for knowing more about the realities of economic life than the government *per se*. Therefore, it is not surprising that the experts of the chambers advise the political parties and the heads of ministries. Quite frequently they are nominated for top positions in government and other official institutions. During the thirteen years of the SPÖ government a whole team of experts left the Chamber of Labor and the Federation of Trade Unions, and became heads of ministries, top civil servants, top managers in the nationalized industries or directors of the National Bank. On the other hand, in many cases top officials in the government relied on the advice of experts from the chambers rather than from their own divisions. This was especially true when the minister belonged to a different political party than that of his top officials.

The Austrian Institute of Economic Research

All institutions mentioned so far (government proper, chambers, National Bank) employ only a limited number of highly trained economists who are familiar with advanced techniques. The experts they need (or at least believe they need) should have a broad education, an adequate knowledge of institutions and of legal issues, and some management qualities. Monitoring highly trained economists appears to be too difficult. If these institutions believe that advanced techniques can shed some light on specific problems, they ask research institutes to deliver the required expertise.

The Austrian Institute of Economic Research (WIFO) is the successor of the Austrian Institute for Business Cycle Research (Österreichisches Institut für Konjunkturforschung) which was founded in 1926 by Ludwig von Mises; Friedrich v. Hayek and later Oskar Morgenstern were directors. The old institute not only engaged in empirical research but became famous for its intellectual atmosphere and for the publishing of important contributions to economic theory written by staff members or scholars attached to the Institute.

This tradition was discontinued after World War II, although some capable economists were working at the institute. From the very beginning the WIFO was policy oriented; its main aim was to provide policymakers with the information and analysis they needed to solve practical problems. (The shift of emphasis probably was one of the reasons why Oskar Morgenstern, who was not on very good terms with the successor of his old institute, promoted the foundation of the Institute for Advanced Studies.) The WIFO, although legally a private nonprofit organization, did much of the work which in other countries was and is performed by economists in government agencies or in the central bank. Economists of the WIFO participated in official delegations to the OECD, they made contributions to official documents, they provided, on request, written and oral information to top civil servants and heads of ministries. They participated in various internal ministerial meetings. In many cases where major economic decisions had to be made, the institute was asked to prepare detailed studies.

The amount of information and advice requested from the WIFO varied according to the persons in leading positions, especially in the Ministry of Finance. Generally speaking, the need was greatest in the postwar era, when the number of civil servants was relatively small and economists were almost nonexistent in the bureaucracy. For example, in 1949 when the ERP Bureau was set up in order to administer the Marshall Plan a special economic section was established in the Bureau, headed by the director of WIFO, Franz Nemschak, who assigned his staff for this purpose. With the increase in the supply of economists and the establishment of economic sections in ministries and chambers, the WIFO lost its 'monopolistic' position. But even now it is not just a research institute which occasionally writes lengthy papers for the government, but it is also involved in many stages of the decision-making process.

As an insider the WIFO has access to classified information, but at the same time it has to accept the rules for insiders. Of course, there is no censorship and all parties concerned affirm the objectiveness of the Institute. But the WIFO is not supposed to make policy recommendations in its reports and it has to weigh very carefully the evidence presented in case of controversial issues. Drafting its monthly reports is a highly qualified job, which requires not only intimate knowledge of facts and solid economics, but also diplomatic skill.

A good example of the cooperation of WIFO, social partners and government proper is the forecasting procedure. Since 1964 the WIFO at the request of the Council of Social and Economic Affairs (Beirat für Wirtschafts- und Sozialfragen) makes quantitative short-term forecasts to be revised quarterly. (Some years later the Institute for Advanced Studies entered the forecasting business by running a large-scale econometric model; but it has remained a junior partner.) Before publication the WIFO presents its forecast to a working group of the Beirat, in which experts of the social partners, the Austrian National Bank and different ministeries participate. At this meeting the experts of the different institutions learn about the details and the critical assumptions of the forecasts. They can make their own judgement and advise their presidents. That same afternoon, an Economic Policy Debate (Wirtschaftspolitische Aussprache) is scheduled with the members of the Parity Commission under the chairmanship of the Chancellor of the Federal Government. In this debate the Minister of Finance, the governor of the National Bank and the director of WIFO make short statements. Then during a general discussion the head of the ministries and of the large-interest organizations express their views about urgent problems and possible solutions.

This procedure was very useful as long as the Austrian government subscribed to an 'activist' fiscal and monetary policy in order to keep the economy on a steady path. Since the beginning of the 1980s when the increasing openness of the economy reduced the scope for demand management, and supply-side problems became predominant, more flexible procedures were introduced. The working group meets only twice a year and high-level economic policy debates are fixed at irregular intervals and not necessarily restricted to short-term stabilization policies.

Advisory boards

The most important advisory board is the Council of Social and Economic

Affairs. The Beirat was established in 1963, the same year as the German Advisory Council (Deutscher Sachverständigenrat). The motives for establishing advisory boards were similar: after the immediate postwar period when reconstruction of the devastated and disordered economy by and large had been completed, economic policymakers had to cope with the problems of normal peacetime economies. At that time the predominant view of macroeconomics was Keynesian. Governments were expected to pursue an activist macroeconomic policy designed to achieve important goals like full employment, internal and external stability, economic growth and fair income distribution. In order to live up to expectations governments needed the advice of experts, conveniently organized in a council, as had been demonstrated in the United States by the establishment of the Council of Economic Advisers.

Although both the Austrian and the German councils were set up at approximately the same time and with a common understanding as to how the economy works and what roles governments should play, their concepts and their framework were fundamentally different. The German Sachverständigenrat is a body of independent experts from the scientific community with legally defined tasks. Its reports are brilliantly written and exhibit an intimate knowledge of modern economic theory. But the Sachverständigenrat has no direct access to policymakers. It influences economic policy only indirectly by publishing competent views. In contrast to the German model the Austrian Beirat is part of the institutionalized system of social partnership and as such has no legal foundation. The Beirat consists of twelve members and two secretaries, all of them staff members of one of the big four organizations representing labor, business and agriculture. The presidents of these organizations determine the subjects to be investigated, which results are acceptable and therefore eligible for publication.

The advantages and disadvantages of this setup are evident. The experts of the interest groups have an intimate knowledge of their organizations, they have a feeling as to what results seem to be acceptable, and they make sure at 'in-house' discussions that their views will be supported by their presidents. If the Beirat makes a recommendation, therefore, it incorporates a political compromise among powerful interest groups. Naturally, a compromise can only partly be explained by referring to facts and general economic reasoning: it also has to reflect political and tactical considerations that are usually not explicitly stated. The papers of the Beirat, therefore, are intellectually less stimulating and show less scholarship than those of the Sachverständigenrat, but if the Beirat agrees on certain issues they cannot be easily put aside by the government. The members of the Beirat are mostly senior economists in their respective organizations and their activities in the Beirat are viewed as being important in furthering their careers. Some members of the Beirat eventually become high-ranking officials or even ministers.

The influence of the Beirat on economic policy was surprisingly high in the 1960s, especially in the first years of its existence, when the social partnership dominated the democratic institutions (government, parliament) and were able to agree on programs prepared by experts. In those days a chairman of the Beirat explained the political decision-making process as follows: 'the governmental bureaucracy is quite efficient, but it has to be told what to do. It is up to the social partners backed by the counsel of the Beirat to elaborate appropriate guidelines.' Although somewhat exaggerated, this statement was not far from the truth. One of the first studies published by the Beirat was a stabilization program containing a number of recommendations designed mainly to reduce the structural component of inflation. Some months after the program had been presented, the government was asked to 'report' why the reactions were rather slow, and which recommendations were taken up.

The 'heroic' period of the Beirat, however, did not last very long. Some large-interest organizations felt that their internal decision-making process was unduly prejudiced by their own experts, and restricted their room for maneuver. The turning point of the power of the Beirat appears to have been reached at the end of the 1960s when the labor members of the Beirat recommended the introduction of the French system of 'planification'; a proposal which was met with strong opposition on behalf of the entrepreneurs. At the beginning of the 1970s, the socialist government, although stressing the importance of social partnership, was eager to demonstrate leadership, while the ÖVP did not use the Beirat to get information or to influence the course of economic policy of the government, something the socialists did when they were in opposition.

Although the Beirat has lost advisory competence and political influence, it has established many working groups comprising external experts, and has published a series of useful empirical studies. The work of the Beirat was especially valuable when the presidents of the social partners had already agreed in principle on a specific subject (e.g. in a reduction of working hours), and the issue needed additional expertise to work out the details.

The Beirat, at regular intervals, produced medium-term forecasts of the federal budget, made valuable suggestions to improve statistics, took up the question of environmental protection, evaluated industrial, energy and balance-of-payment policies. But strangely enough, the Beirat did not discuss principles of macroeconomic policies, especially the rise and decline of 'Austrian Keynesianism'. A very cautious critique of the decision by the National Bank to tie the Austrian schilling to the Deutsche Mark was contained in a report on balance-of-payments problems published at the end of the 1970s.

The Beirat is by far the most important advisory body. There are other advisory councils, attached to ministries, some of which are mandated by law. But these councils are specialized in certain subjects (e.g. in regional policies or in labor market policies). Experts of the social partners (not necessarily economists) are the usual members and sometimes control the work of these councils.

One exception has to be mentioned. In 1983 Herbert Salcher, then Minister of Finance, set up a Scientific Council to the Ministry similar to the advisory bodies to various ministries existing in Germany. Rules and regulations were set up. Approximately one-half of the professors of economics in Austria were members of that council. A study on stabilization policy was finalized but never published. The council, although not dissolved formally, no longer convened after Salcher had left the office. The present Minister, Ferdinand Lacina, invites some professors of economics at irregular intervals to participate in a round-table discussion. These discussions, based on working papers presented by members of the group, are intellectually stimulating.

Informal advisers

Ludwig von Mises claimed that all important economic policy decisions in the interwar period were strongly influenced by his informal recommendations to policymakers or their advisers. This probably was an exaggeration, but fairly frequently, informal exchange of views occurred between politicians and economic experts both during the First and the Second Republic. Clearly, informal talks provide only incomplete information, especially as keeping diaries and writing memoirs have become unfashionable.

The political parties occasionally organized talks with academic economists who were either party members or who sympathized with their ideologies. The ÖVP in the 1960s established a group working on long-term problems (Aktion 20). At present, politicians and economists of the ÖVP meet at an Economic Council (Wirtschaftsrat), where current problems are discussed. The SPÖ in its 1970 election campaign published a program with the assistance of more than 1,000 experts of different kinds. Although it is difficult to judge from outside, the general impression is that few academic economists have the knack for becoming think-tanks for their political parties.

At least as important were informal consultations, whose members were selected according to their assumed advisory capacity irrespective of their political party affiliation. I shall mention a few of these informal consultation groups, in which I personally participated:

1. Reinhardt Kamitz, late in 1951 before he became Minister of Finance, developed a program for economic reform. His drafts were discussed in a small group which met regularly at the 'Rennverein', a fashionable club in the center of Vienna, at the invitation of industrialists interested in economic policy. Two participants were economists of the

Institute for Economic Research (WIFO). To use all available expertise informal hearings were arranged with outstanding personalities.

2. In 1963 when Josef Klaus became Minister of Finance, a monthly meeting was held with three bank executives, the director of WIFO and his deputy, and a well-known economic journalist. The minister appeared with a list of questions and the group was invited to provide answers and to make suggestions. The 'Klaus-Runde' was dissolved a year later, when the minister resigned.
3. In his long tenure of office during the 1970s, Minister of Finance Hannes Andrösch discussed economic policy problems intensively with people from whom he expected to get useful advice. I wrote a few papers for him (e.g. on the state of the federal budget). I was also invited to participate in a small discussion group whenever problems of monetary and fiscal policy had to be evaluated. In quite a few cases I had the satisfaction that some of my proposals were incorporated into economic policy measures.
4. The above mentioned informal advisory groups were policy oriented. They were small, the discussion was confidential and focused on policy measures. Tangible results were expected. The meetings of professors of economics whom Chancellor Kreisky occasionally invited in his home had a somewhat different character. The group was fairly large: it usually comprised about twenty persons. The principal purpose of these meetings was to exchange general information concerning the state of the economy and to present personal views as to how outstanding problems might be resolved, rather than working out details for specific actions. The chancellor did not mind when the experts could not reach an agreement on specific points.

The different roles which economists play in the bureaucratic and political decision-making process are to a large degree complementary. Economists are needed within the bureaucracy, as members of official advisory boards and in their capacity as informal advisers. Compared to other industrialized countries, Austria has less economists in civil service; politicians seem to prefer informal and confidential meetings, in order to communicate with economists and to learn their views.

NORTH AMERICA

6 · THE UNITED STATES*

Joseph A. Pechman

The economist has played an important role in the development and implementation of economic policy in the United States since the end of World War II. Although economic ideas have always influenced business and government policies (frequently, but not always, in a constructive way), it is only in recent years that economists have occupied key positions in government, and have entered actively into the formulation of economic policies.

Government interest in the advice of economists was officially declared in the Employment Act of 1946. Under this Act, Congress stated that it was the responsibility of the federal government to use all its powers to promote 'maximum employment, production and purchasing power'. The Act set up a three-man Council of Economic Advisers (CEA) to assist and advise the president on economic matters, and a congressional Joint Economic Committee (originally called the Joint Committee on the Economic Report) to review and evaluate the president's annual economic report, to be submitted each year shortly after Congress convenes. The machinery set up by the Act has remained virtually unchanged since the Act's inception.

The first chairman of the Council of Economic Advisers, Edwin Nourse, was a strict constructionist in his interpretation of the Employment Act; he believed the council should give economic advice to the president, but argued strongly against participation by the council in the legislative process or in partisan debate. His successors disagreed with this view. Each had a particular style, but each was ready not only to develop policy options but also to persuade the president and Congress to adopt the policies they advocated. Although the influence of the council changes as administrations change, the council usually has an important voice in economic policy decisions.

The economist has also become influential in other agencies of government as his role as presidential adviser has become more secure. The major

*Adapted from Pechman (1975). I am grateful to Richard Goode, Robert W. Hartman and Robert H. Nelson for their helpful comments and suggestions.

departments and independent agencies have always enlisted economists at the operating level, but few economists ever participated in policymaking. This tradition was decisively broken beginning with President Kennedy's administration. Since 1961, four of the eight directors of the Office of Management and Budget (formerly the Bureau of the Budget) have been professional economists, three chairmen and most members of the Board of Governors of the Federal Reserve System have been economists, and economists have served as cabinet and subcabinet officers, and as presidential appointees in many other departments and agencies.

In recent years, economists have become influential in the legislative as well as the executive branch of the US government. Although the Joint Economic Committee does not have power to initiate legislation, it does influence congressional and public attitudes on economic policy. Its professional staff is usually small (often consisting of only four or five economists, and never more than a dozen), but they carry weight with committee members. The annual hearings on the president's economic report are the occasion for the presentation of views on current economic policies by academic economists, as well as economists of business, labor and agriculture. The committee's report was given considerable prominence in the press in its early years, but it has received less attention recently because the committee has become more partisan with the passage of time.

The Congressional Budget Office (CBO), which was established in 1975 to provide expert staff support for Congress in preparing the budget, is another legislative agency that influences economic legislation. It has a staff of about 175 professionals, most of whom are economists. All the directors and all the deputy directors of CBO have been economists. Aside from making economic and budget projections, the CBO prepares budget options which are seriously considered by Congress. Congress also receives reports and advice on economic issues from the Congressional Research Service, which employs about fifty economists, the General Accounting Office, which employs about eighty economists, and the staffs of numerous congressional committees.

This chapter reviews and evaluates the role of the economist in economic policy in the United States. The first section describes how economic policy is made. The division of responsibilities between the executive and the legislative branches of the federal government have a profound effect on the decision-making process and the execution of economic policy. The performance of economists in the post-World War II period is discussed in the second section. The record, it will be found, contains embarrassing failures as well as some successes. Finally, methods of improving the administration of economic policy are suggested. These suggestions are neither novel nor revolutionary, but they continue to provoke disagreement and debate.

ORGANIZATION

The decision-making process in economic policy is led by the president, who has the advice and assistance of his cabinet, the Council of Economic Advisers, and the Office of Management and Budget (OMB). The decisions reflect the economic and social philosophy of the administration, modified to satisfy or appease prevailing views in Congress and among the voters. Presidents are not trained in economics when they are elected and few become economic sophisticates even by the time they leave office. Therefore, the decision-making process is structured to educate the president in economic issues and the implications of the options that are open to him.

Before the Employment Act was enacted in 1946 there was no govermental machinery with a presidential perspective for systematic analysis and review of economic policies. Because the Treasury Department had control of fiscal policy, the Treasury staff was the federal government's main economic secretariat. When the OMB (originally the Bureau of the Budget) was split off from the Treasury in 1939 and made a separate agency in the Executive Office of the President, the bureau's staff became independently influential in the process. After the enactment of the Employment Act, the Council of Economic Advisers took a major role in preparing the president for making economic policy (although the Treasury Department, Budget Bureau and other agencies continue to be in the picture on policies related to matters of concern to them). In most administrations, a group of high officials of the major economic agencies of the government coordinates the economic policy options that are transmitted to the president. The Secretary of the Treasury or a senior White House aide usually chairs this group, but the CEA takes a leading role in its deliberations. The Board of Governors of the Federal Reserve System, established in 1913 as an independent agency to manage the nation's banking system and to control money and credit, is also consulted by the president and is often represented in the coordinating group or one of its subcommittees.

The 1974 change in congressional budget procedures enhanced the role of economists in government, this time at the legislative level. The Congressional Budget Act of 1974 requires Congress to approve a concurrent resolution that provides the basis for congressional consideration of taxes in relation to expenditures. The resolution, ordinarily passed in the spring of each year, specifies levels of budget outlays and budget authority for the next fiscal year, the recommended level of taxation, the surplus or deficit that is 'appropriate in the light of economic conditions', and the debt limit. An attempt is made to reconcile the differences between the amounts specified in the resolution and the actions of the appropriations and tax committees, but the final budget totals rarely meet the targets.

The Congressional Budget Office, which is the congressional counterpart of the Office of Management and Budget in the executive branch, makes independent five-year economic and budget projections, estimates the cost of all bills reported out by congressional committees, and prepares a report that re-estimates the president's budget on the basis of its own economic assumptions. These reports have become the basis on which congressional budget decisions are made. The CBO also issues useful reports on specific budget issues, the state of the economy and the relation of the budget and economic developments.

Although the president controls his own administration, he cannot control the legislative process, even when he is a member of the majority party in Congress. Budget and tax policies, two of the major instruments of general economic policy, must be approved by Congress; with the American system of weak party discipline, this severely restricts the flexibility and timeliness of economic decisions. Economic mistakes are often made because the division of political power between Congress and the president makes it difficult to agree on fiscal actions and to time them appropriately.

Since the economic issues are varied and complex, there is no single channel through which all economic decisions are made in the United States. *Macroeconomic* policies – those that are concerned with the determination of national aggregates such as employment, income and production, and with the general price level – generally involve the Treasury Department, the Office of Management and Budget, and the Council of Economic Advisers. Even though monetary policy is one of the major instruments of macroeconomic policy, a separate channel through the independent Federal Reserve Board was established by legislation for the conduct of monetary policy. *Microeconomic* policies – those that are concerned with the economic behavior of individuals and businesses – are usually initiated in the department or agency directly responsible for the area in question. There are a number of networks through which these proposals are then channeled to the president.

Macroeconomic policy

Whether he likes it or not, the president is almost continuously involved with macroeconomic policy. Hardly a year goes by without one or more economic crises or disturbances that require presidential attention. At a minimum, the president must be in touch with congressional actions that will have a significant influence on his budget program. Presidents must also deal with tax policy, trade issues, exchange rates, regulatory issues and a host of other economic matters, and most of them have considered it important enough to be familiar with the latest economic statistics to comment intelligently on them.

To inform the president on these matters, the CEA maintains a steady flow of memoranda to the president (sometimes the flow becomes a flood) commenting on economic developments, presenting alternative methods of dealing with emerging problems and suggesting new economic initiatives on the part of the president. Some presidents see the council frequently, usually only the chairman, while others prefer to deal with the council through memoranda and White House intermediaries. During these contacts, the council members are acting not only as advisers but also as tutors of the president on economic policy. Some chairmen are more effective in this role than others.

Major decisions on stabilization policies usually evolve during preparations toward the end of each year for the president's opening messages to the new session of Congress which convenes early in January. The CEA, the Treasury, and the OMB jointly prepare the official economic projections for the coming year. Obviously, many of the economic decisions made during the year depend on the administration's expectations of the year's economic profile.

Members of the CEA and their staff participate actively in the development of macroeconomic policies. For example, President Kennedy's 1963 deficit was hammered out in numerous meetings of the Council and other agencies. Similarly, President Johnson's council was heavily involved in the decision to raise taxes to finance the Vietnam War; President Nixon's council took a leading role in the decision to improve wage and price controls and float the dollar in 1971; President Ford's council played a major role in the administration's 1975 tax-cut recommendations; President Carter's council helped develop a tough anti-inflation program, including consumer credit controls and tight money in 1980; and President Reagan's council openly supported tax increases to reduce his deficits, to the chagrin of the White House staff and the president himself.

Because of their substantive responsibilities, the Secretary of the Treasury and the director of the OMB are also key figures in the development of macroeconomic policy. As the nation's chief fiscal officer, the Secretary of the Treasury carries the most weight in government councils on economic matters and is usually the administration's economic spokesperson. He is also expected to 'sell' the administration's tax program to the Congress. The director of the OMB has the central role in the budget process and has easy access to the president. Members of the White House staff are also important in making economic policy decisions.

Consideration of economic policy usually begins with the State of the Union Message, delivered in early January every year. Originally a political instrument, this address has increasingly taken on economic significance. More often than not, the president announces his overall budget and tax plans in this message, the details of which are spelled out soon after in the *Budget Message* and the *Economic Report*. These messages are transmitted to the Congress in late January or early February, usually within two days of one another. *The Budget*, which is the nation's fiscal planning document, presents the administration's expenditure requests, estimates the tax revenues, and any tax changes that may be proposed. The *Economic Report* reviews the economic developments of the prior year, defends the administration's economic projections, provides the economic rationale for the major economic proposals made by the president, and analyzes selected economic issues judged to be of particular current importance.

Shortly after the *Economic Report* and the *Budget* are sent to Congress, the Congressional Budget Office prepares a detailed analysis of the president's proposals and estimates the budget impact of his program. The House and Senate Budget Committees and the Joint Economic Committee then hold hearings on the state of the economy and on the president's program. The Secretary of the Treasury is grilled by committee members to expose weak points in the administration's economic plans and to develop alternative strategies. The same treatment is accorded to the chairman of the CEA, the director of the OMB and other administration officials. The director of the CBO also appears before the committees to explain his projections and differences with the administration's analysis. Private experts representing labor, business and agriculture, and professional economists from academic and business life also testify. From this broad spectrum of opinion, the Budget Committees and the Joint Economic Committee have little trouble in identifying where the administration is vulnerable. Their reports, which are completed in the spring, set the stage for the economic debates of the year and for the legislative review and action on the president's budget.

The economists in both the executive and legislative branches of government are closely involved with Congress as the legislative program makes it way through the legislative mill. They testify to congressional committees on the economic implications of the program and are consulted when changes or compromises need to be made to expedite a particular bill. They are also called upon frequently to explain economic and budget issues in speeches, radio and television appearances, and press conferences. Congress and the president have had trouble agreeing on how to eliminate the budget deficits in recent years, but this reflects the difficulty of the issues rather than any particular weakness in the procedures or bad economic advice.

Monetary policy

Monetary policy is made by an independent authority – the Board of Governors of the Federal Reserve System – because Congress believes that control of the monetary system should be insulated from the political process. The board consists of seven members who are appointed by the president and approved by the Senate for fourteen-year terms. (Each member may serve only one full term, but may also finish an uncompleted term of a predecessor.) The functions of the Federal Reserve System are carried out through twelve regional Federal Reserve Banks which have operational responsibilities but little substantive control over monetary policy.

The major policy unit of the Federal Reserve System is the Federal Open Market Committee, which consists of the members of the Board of Governors, the President of the New York Federal Reserve Bank, and four presidents of other federal reserve banks who serve on a rotating basis. The Open Market Committee meets every three or four weeks to decide on the policies to be pursued until the next meeting in the government securities market. The meetings are full-scale seminars on current economic developments. Divergent views are thoroughly aired and frequently the policies are adopted over the objection of a substantial minority.

During the early days of the Federal Reserve, the strongest influence was exerted by the president of the New York Federal Reserve Bank, which manages the domestic and foreign financial transactions of the Federal Reserve System (under instructions of the Open Market Committee). As the role of the federal government in economic affairs became more important, the center of power shifted to Washington. In recent years, the chairman of the Board of Governors (the board's spokesman before Congress and the president) has often exercised a decisive personal influence over the conduct of monetary policy.

There is no formal apparatus for coordinating monetary policy with other economic policies of the federal government. There is, of course, continuous communication among the officials and staffs of the Federal Reserve, the Treasury Department, and the CEA. As already noted, the chairman of the Federal Reserve Board meets periodically with the president. Major differences of opinion occasionally develop between the president and the chairman of the Federal Reserve Board, and in instances when the disagreement has come to a public showdown, the chairman generally has been able to stand his ground. For this reason, presidents usually exercise great caution in making appointments to the chairmanship of the board.

Aside from the Federal Reserve Board, Congress has created a large number of independent agencies to supervise financial institutions and to insure adequate flows of credit to particular markets. Among the most important of these agencies are the Federal Home Loan Bank Board, which regulates and makes credit available to the savings and loan associations; the Federal National Mortgage Association, which purchases and sells home mortgages; and the Farm Credit Administration, which provides credit to farmers. These and other agencies pursue policies to help their constituencies, policies which are sometimes inconsistent with those of the president or the Federal Reserve Board. Usually, the differences are reconciled through interagency discussion; on occasion, the president is called on by his advisers to do some armtwisting. Although the situation is unsatisfactory, there is little inclination in Congress to change it.

Microeconomic policies

Although much attention is lavished by the press, radio and television on macroeconomic policies, government at all levels is concerned mainly with microeconomic policies. Large offices and bureaus have been created to deal with the poor, the aged, farmers, Indians, other minorities, consumers, labor, business, and many other groups. In many cases, several agencies are concerned with a single problem, each with its own legislative mandate and its own constituency. Agencies are sometimes more loyal to their constituencies than they are to their cabinet officers or to the president. To protect the interests of their constituencies they have their own lines of communication to Congress through influential members of legislative or appropriations committees.

Given the complexities of modern government, it is impossible to coordinate all governmental policies from the center. Most presidents attempt to cope with the situation by organizing interagency committees or task forces, assigning the coordination responsibility to trusted members of the White House staff, or setting up a separate coordinating unit in the White House. Such approaches succeed to some extent, especially when the president is actively concerned with the particular problem which the arrangement is designed to solve. More often than not, as soon as the attention of the president and his staff is diverted elsewhere, the agencies revert to their old routines. This is not to say that changes are never made or that the agencies always drag their feet, but is meant to emphasize that the forces arrayed against innovation are formidable.

Much of the coordination of microeconomic policies is exercised by the staff of the Office of Management and Budget. The budget examiner assigned to an agency is usually at least as knowledgeable as, and in some cases more knowledgeable than, the agency head and many of his subordinates. The examiner usually knows the history of past attempts to alter the terms of reference for that agency, the strengths of the interest groups involved, the legislative alignments for and against any particular change, and the political price that may have to be paid to push a bill through Congress. Because of their long experience, some of the examiners tend to be cynical and conservative about new legislative initiatives. However, the examiners and other staff members of the OMB are dedicated to supporting the president and make extraordinary efforts to help him achieve his objectives.

The role of the economist in the development of microeconomic policies varies from issue to issue. Most government departments have staffs of economists to assist them in developing economic policies. More often than not, political considerations temper the advice of economists, but economic considerations are no longer disregarded either in the executive or legislative branches of government. The staff of the CEA is too small to be involved in more than a handful of microeconomic issues at one time, and these issues tend to be those that the president is interested in at the moment. The small (and generally youthful) staff of the council influences interagency discussions because of its competence and knowledge of economics. But the council rarely prevails when disagreements with the operating agencies occur unless the chairman is persuaded to take the issue to the president. Even then, the chances of success are not great. However, economists both inside and outside the government have had considerable influence in the movements to deregulate major industries (in particular, airlines, transportation and finance) and to reform the US tax system.

PERFORMANCE

The performance of the US economy since the end of World War II has been quite good in comparison with earlier periods, but far short of the standards set by the Employment Act of 1946. Economic growth has been punctuated by eight recessions, but there has not been an economic crisis remotely resembling the depression of the 1930s. The greatest success of the entire period was the enactment of a large federal income-tax reduction in 1964 when the federal budget was running a substantial deficit. This tax cut helped restore full employment for a short time and also generated enough revenues to eliminate the budget deficit. The greatest disappointment has been the difficulties in coping with inflation in a satisfactory manner. As a result, the twin goals of full employment and price stability have not been achieved simultaneously for more than brief periods. In the 1980s, the greatest economic success has been the curbing of inflationary pressures that grew to menacing levels in the late 1970s. However, increases in defense spending and large tax cuts generated large deficits, which reduced national saving, weakened the competitiveness of US goods in world markets, brought on large balance-of-payments deficits and turned the United States into a large external debtor.

Performance with respect to other economic objectives must also be rated disappointing. Energy policy has been vacillating and has failed to put the country in a position to withstand a prolonged interruption in the supply of oil from abroad. Economic growth has reduced poverty in the United States, but the number of poor persons is still about 14 per cent of the population. Although incomes have risen, those in the lower end of the income scale have not kept pace with those at the upper end, so that the relative distribution of income before and after taxes has become more unequal. State and local governments have not coped satisfactorily with urgent needs for public services and facilities in an increasingly urban nation. These are only examples of a large number of failures which have plagued the nation in recent years, failures which are attributable to basic political and social cleavages in society, rather than to economic ignorance or mismanagement. Indeed, economists have offered imaginative solutions to many of these problems, but few of these solutions have been politically acceptable. The following discussion of successes and failures in economic policy is confined to macroeconomic policies.

The new economics

The year 1960 marked a transition between what was then called the 'old' and the 'new' economics. The new developments were stimulated in part by the hearings and staff report of the Douglas Subcommittee on Employment, Growth, and Price Levels; in part by the continued influence of the stabilizing budget policy of the Committee for Economic Development (a private group of businessmen); and in part by the recognition that the federal government had been restraining the growth of the economy in the late 1950s through unnecessarily tight fiscal and monetary policies. Although the full employment budget concept had been originated in a document prepared by the Committee for Economic Development more than ten years earlier, and the basic theory had been developed still another decade earlier, it was not part of the language of the economist or the layman until 1960. An interesting reflection of the tenor of the times is that the fact that the federal government was running a large full employment surplus did not become generally known until it was highlighted in testimony before the Joint Economic Committee six weeks after the 1960 election.

A new era in domestic economic policy was ushered in with the inauguration of John F. Kennedy. Beginning in early 1961, economists inside and outside the federal government have generally been ahead of the administration in proposing remedies. Their attention first focused on the problem of unemployment, and later on means to combat inflation. President Kennedy was converted fairly quickly by Walter W. Heller, the chairman of his Council of Economic Advisers, to the need for a massive tax cut even in the face of a budget that was already in deficit. Nevertheless, the new president deemed it necessary to proceed cautiously in the interest of keeping down this deficit, even though he was persuaded by his Council of Economic Advisers that the true test of a good budget is the condition of the economy and not whether the budget is in balance.

The new economics was at the peak of its popularity during the eighteen months prior to escalation of the Vietnam War in mid-1965. An ambitious package of domestic social programs was enacted in that year on President Johnson's recommendation and excise taxes were also slashed. Meanwhile, as business conditions improved, the budget rapidly moved into balance. In fact, the federal surplus in the national income accounts reached $4.3 billion in the first half of calendar year 1965 and unemployment dropped to 4.1 per cent in December of that year. All of this was according to the script, and the active use of fiscal and monetary policies achieved an unprecedented degree of support both inside and outside the economics profession.

Another innovation of the new economics was the development and implementation of wage–price 'guideposts'. In 1962, the CEA proposed that the rate of growth of productivity for industry as a whole should serve as a benchmark for wage and price behavior. Although no specific figure was even formally advocated, the Council repeatedly called attention to statistical data that showed gains in long-term productivity growth in the neighborhood of 3 to 3.5 per cent a year. Presidents Kennedy and Johnson actively supported the guideposts, even to the extent of publicly berating industries and firms that violated them. Perhaps the most celebrated case was the public demand by President Kennedy in 1962 that the steel industry should withdraw an announced price increase, on the ground that the prior wage settlement had been well within the guideposts. The steel companies acceded to the president's demand after some grumbling. The president and the CEA continued to cajole, twist arms, and jawbone in public and private in the effort to win compliance with the guideposts. This policy seems to have had some effect in restraining wage and price increases between 1962 and 1965. While a number of professional economists believe it reduced the rate of growth of wages by about 0.5 per cent a year, others dispute this judgement. The guideposts became ineffective when the strong rise in military expenditure for the Vietnam War upset the balance between demand and supply.

Inflation

The need for restraint of aggregate demand became evident early in 1966, and economists began calling for a tax increase long before the administration was ready to move. The president's economic advisers agreed with this diagnosis, but were overruled on political grounds. Recognition of the need for higher taxes came rather late, since the rate of growth of the economy had accelerated after mid-1965 and slowed down markedly after the first quarter of 1966. However, even within government, the degree to which military expenditure would escalate was not known during the last half of 1965. In any event, a tax increase early in 1966 (when the magnitude of the military effort became clear to the economists in the administration) would have exercised a desirable restraint on prices and helped to prevent the monetary crunch in the summer of 1966. It might even have succeeded in salvaging the wage–price guideposts which became ineffective as soon as excess demand was allowed to develop.

Following a pause in the economy's growth in the first half of 1967, brought about largely by the extremely tight monetary policy, the administration finally urged Congress to enact a 10 per cent increase in personal and corporation income taxes. In this effort, it had the strong support of the president's own economic advisers and many of the nation's outstanding economists. Congress accepted the 10 per cent surcharge, but the legislation was not approved until the spring of 1968, long after inflation had resumed. During the first half of 1967, prices rose at an annual rate of 2.6 per cent per year and accelerated to an annual rate of 4.2 per cent in the second half of 1968.

The worst of both worlds: inflation and unemployment

To the surprise of most observers, the enactment of the surtax did not cool down the inflation. There is evidence that the tax increase cut into the growth of consumer expenditure on goods and services other than automobiles, but spending on automobiles was apparently unaffected. Furthermore, the surcharge on corporate income taxes did not bring about a reduction in business spending for plant and equipment; in fact, the investment boom which had begun in 1964 and paused only briefly in early 1967 continued unabated.

Thus, when the Nixon administration took office in January 1969, it was faced with the problem of cooling down an overheated economy. During the last quarter of 1968, real gross national product rose at an annual rate of 2.8 per cent, prices rose at an annual rate of 4.4 per cent, and real business fixed investment rose at an annual rate of 13.5 per cent. Unemployment was down to an average of 3.8 per cent, close to the lowest level in ten years.

President Nixon's economic advisers came into office with the firm belief that the inflation could be brought under control by gradually reducing the rate of growth in demand through fiscal and monetary policies. At an early stage, the president announced his opposition to the former guideposts and pledged a hands-off policy with respect to private wage and price decisions. Since the federal budget was already running a large surplus (2.2 per cent of the gross national product in the first half of 1969, on the national income basis), the only major change in policy during 1969 was a drastic tightening of monetary policy. Credit in all markets became extraordinarily tight, and some interest rates rose to levels which had not been experienced for as long as a century.

The monetary squeeze soon had its effects. The investment boom reached its peak in the second quarter of 1969, industrial production began declining in the fall, and real growth of the economy was halted in the fourth quarter. As the recession wore on, the Nixon administration recognized the need for switching from restraint to demand stimulation as a brake on rising unemployment. The president submitted a deficit budget for fiscal year 1972, but emphasized that his program was consistent with a balanced budget at full employment. Thus, after more than two decades of education by economists, a Republican as well as a Democratic administration embraced the full-employment budget concept as the basic tool of fiscal policy planning.

In August 1971, President Nixon abandoned his policy of gradualism and announced a new economic policy which included fiscal stimulation, devaluation of the dollar, and direct controls over prices and wages. His economic advisers both in the Treasury and in the CEA helped develop this program (although most of them had publicly opposed controls before joining the administration). The new policy generated a substantial boom in 1972 and 1973 which lowered the unemployment rate to 4.5 per cent.

The price and wage controls moderated the rate of growth of prices to about 3.5 per cent and wages to about 6 per cent in 1972. Nevertheless, price controls were eased in early 1973 and were abandoned entirely on 30 April 1974. The general price level surged upward, mainly because of a large rise in world agricultural prices (resulting from poor harvests in 1972 and 1973) and in energy prices (resulting from the higher prices charged for oil by Arabian producers beginning in the fall of 1973). Wholesale and consumer prices rose at rates exceeding 10 per cent a year in 1974, and wages moved up rapidly in an effort to catch up. But there was no policy – other than general fiscal and monetary restraint – to moderate the pace of inflation. The result was that 1974 and 1975 were years of recession.

The cycle had already turned by the time the Carter administration took office in early 1977. A five-year recovery and expansion ensued, during which output and employment increased rapidly. Fiscal and monetary policies were somewhat restrained, yet inflation accelerated and then erupted in 1979 to double-digit rates as a result of the second oil shock. The administration's economists developed a set of voluntary pay and price standards during the oil-price explosion. To curb the inflation fever, the administration and the Federal Reserve took strong steps to reduce the growth of demand, including a program of selective credit controls. The restraining actions produced a short and sharp recession early in 1980, but the economy rebounded in the second half. When Ronald Reagan took office in January 1981, the economy was exhibiting surprising strength, inflation was again running at double-digit rates, and interest rates were at or close to historic peaks.

Supply-side economics

The Reagan administration's budget priority was to reduce income tax rates. The 'supply-side' economists, who had been outside the professional mainstream, persuaded the president that reductions in marginal tax rates would greatly stimulate work and saving incentives, increase the growth of output, and thus pay for themselves. Congress responded by cutting individual income tax rates by 23 per cent across the board over a period of three years, increasing depreciation allowances, and gutting the estate and gift taxes. The 1981 tax reductions for individuals and businesses cut the revenue potential of the federal tax system by about 20 per cent.

Had expenditures been cut at the same time, the policy might have been successful. But at the request of President Reagan, Congress raised defense outlays sharply and, despite reductions in the growth of non-defense outlays, the budget deficit soared. In the meantime, the Federal Reserve Board tightened monetary policy to curb inflation, and a severe recession developed in the latter half of 1981. This policy was relaxed in the summer of 1982, after it became clear that inflationary pressures had subsided.

Since 1982, the US economy has been expanding, unemployment has been reduced from the recession level, and prices have been rising only moderately. But the legacy of the large tax cuts enacted in 1981 remains. The deficits are still high to the chagrin and embarrassment of the supply-siders and the balance of trade has deteriorated badly. The value of the dollar rose during the period of high interest rates, but it has been declining sharply since early 1985.

Economists are agreed that continuation of these policies will culminate in one of two scenarios, either of which would retard growth. If the Federal Reserve accommodates the large deficits by a policy of monetary ease, the rise in aggregate demand will soon generate accelerating inflation, which could be brought under control only by bringing the economic expansion to a halt. If the monetary authorities restrain the growth of money and credit, interest rates will rise and the economy will grow slowly, if at all. Opinion is now almost universal – including economists who served in the Reagan administration – that the budget should be brought under control even if it involves increased taxes, but the president and Congress have not been able to agree on a plan of action.

PROCEDURAL IMPROVEMENTS

The institutional arrangements in which the economists now operate in the US government place them in strategic positions to influence economic policy. In the executive branch, the Council of Economic Advisers is firmly entrenched in the office of the president and is consulted by most presidents on important economic issues. Economists are also influential in the major federal economic agencies, such as the Treasury Department and the Federal Reserve, and in the independent regulatory commissions, such as the Federal Trade Commission, the International Trade Commission and the Home Loan Bank Board. Economists are less influential in the legislative branch of the government, but their influence has been increasing. The Congressional Budget Office plays a key role in the congressional budget process and the staff of the Joint Economic Committee helps set the economic agenda for Congress. These institutional arrangements are now widely accepted and it is doubtful that other arrangements would make economists any more effective than they have been in recent years.

The key problem is the political resistance in both the executive and legislative branches of the federal government to make the hard choices.

Part of the problem is the continued disagreement among economists about major issues, which confuses those who are receiving their advice. Another part is the lack of economic understanding by public officials and legislators and the difficulty economists have in communicating with them about economic matters. But the major reason is that political considerations often outweigh economic considerations in the development of economic policies. For example, federal deficits have remained large even though economists agree that political considerations should be set aside in seeking an appropriate compromise solution. Changes in procedures alone will not resolve such issues, but something would be gained by creating conditions for more responsible and less partisan consideration of economic policies. The following suggestions, which are neither new nor original, are offered to promote this objective.

First, economists should always make clear to those they are advising when they are speaking as economists and when they are expressing personal political judgements. They should put more emphasis on their areas of agreement and explain the reasons for their differences when there is disagreement. They should also make an effort to explain difficult economic problems in nontechnical language, so that the public and political leaders will better understand the issues and the alternative solutions. For the most part, economists should accept the political decisions of the president and Congress even when they disagree with them. In some (rare) instances, however, when a crucial matter is at stake, they should consider resigning their posts when the decisions made are clearly detrimental to the national interest.

Second, in 1985, Congress adopted a procedure which mandates reductions in spending if certain deficit targets are not met. The procedure has failed to produce agreement largely because President Reagan refused to accept a tax increase as an element in a deficit-reducing program. Unless some such mechanism for reaching agreement between the president and Congress is adopted, the budget deficit will remain unacceptably large and future presidents will find no room in the budget for new spending initiatives and will be unable to use fiscal policy to help stabilize the economy.

Third, there is still a major difference of opinion among economists about methods of restraining inflation. Some believe that inflation cannot be prevented unless the power of big business and big labor unions over price and wage decisions is curbed. Others argue that controls distort management decisions, operate unfairly in different industries and occupations, and are generally ineffective. This disagreement is not confined to economists, but extends to businessmen, labor union officials and political leaders. Few people now regard price and wage controls as a viable option because of the difficulties of achieving agreement on the details of the program and of implementation once it is adopted. In my opinion, a mechanism needs to be created to develop an incomes policy if recurrence of inflation is to be prevented. Any incomes policy will need the support of labor and management, but these groups will not reach agreement without leadership and vigorous support by the president.

It may be noted, in conclusion, that these and other procedural changes can make only marginal improvements in the nation's economic policies, so long as the country remains divided on major national issues. The budget deficit will not be eliminated if Congress cannot agree with the president on a program of spending cuts and tax increases. Inflation will not be overcome if major groups in society refuse to accept the restraints that are necessary to prevent it. Even if they are part of the decision-making process, economists cannot force the public, the president and Congress to face up to the difficult choices required to achieve the nation's economic objectives.

BIBLIOGRAPHY

Ackley, Gardner, 'Providing economic advice to government', in Joseph A. Pechman and N. J. Simler (eds), *Economics in the Public Service* (Norton, 1982).

Bailey, Stephen K., *Congress Makes a Law* (New York: Columbia University Press, 1950).

Flash, Edward S., Jr., *Economic Advice and Presidential Leadership: The Council of Economic Advisers* (New York: Columbia University Press, 1965).

Hargrave, Erwin C., and Morley, Samuel A. (eds), *The President and the Council of Economic Advisers: Interviews with CEA Chairmen* (Boulder, CO: Westview Press, 1984).

Heller, Walter W., *New Dimensions in Political Economy* (Cambridge, MA: Harvard University Press, 1966).

Nelson, Robert H., 'The economics profession and the making of public policy', *Journal of Economic Literature*, vol. 25, no. 1 (March 1987), pp. 49–91.

Nourse, Edwin G., *Economics in the Public Service: Administrative Aspects of the Employment Act* (New York: Harcourt Brace, 1953).

Okun, Arthur M., *The Political Economy of Prosperity* (Washington, DC: Brookings Institution, 1970).

Okun, Arthur M., 'The formulation of national economic policy', *Perspectives in Defense Management*, vol. 2 (December 1968), pp. 9–12. Reprinted in *Selected Essays of Arthur M. Okun*, edited by Joseph A. Pechman (Cambridge, MA: The MIT Press, 1983), pp. 584–94.

Pechman, Joseph A., 'Making economic policy: the role of the economist', *Handbook of Political Science*, vol. 6 (Addison-Wesley, 1975).

Rivlin, Alice M., 'Economics and the political process', *American Economic Review*, vol. 77, no. 2 (March 1987), pp. 1–10.

Stein, Herbert, *Presidential Economics: The Making of Economic Policy from Roosevelt to Reagan and Beyond* (New York: Simon & Schuster, 1985).

7 · CANADA

Ian Stewart

It is an uneasy time to write about the role of the economist as an adviser to government. Fifteen to twenty years ago, approaching the last crest of the post-World War II growth era, an ebullient optimism infused both economics and economists. The macroeconomic system seemed to respond to Keynesian prescription. Econometric model building proceeded apace to lend policymakers an even greater capacity to fine-tune aggregate performance. The final building blocks of the welfare state fashioned from 'fiscal dividends' were being put in place. Tariff barriers to world trade were tumbling and an emerging tier of Third World countries was beginning to display growth rates that held hope of eventually defying the exponential arithmetic of widening disparities. The hard efficiency core of the economic discipline was made more palatable by the promise of continuing growth, full employment and the resources to attend to the more equitable distribution of incomes, wealth and opportunity. In Canada this ebullience and assurance extended beyond matters of interpersonal welfare to a broad-based attack on interregional disparities in growth and economic wellbeing.

North American graduate schools of that era turned out professional economists with a broadening range of quantitative skills. Applied economic analysis was as creditable a route to professional advancement and standing as were more theoretical attempts to extend the reach of the discipline. Though well understood, the distinction between the positive and normative applications of economic analysis acted as no great constraint upon the issues with which economists concerned themselves. It would not be an error to describe the dominant ethos of the profession as activist and left of center. In Canada the literary apotheosis of this temper is to be found in the second volume (written by the economics staff) of the Royal Commission on Taxation (the Carter Commission) which reported in 1967 recommending full subscription to a radical reform of the Canadian tax system in what has become known as the Haig–Simons tradition of equity and neutrality.

These years represented the culmination of both a broadening and a deepening of the direct and indirect flow of economic policy advice to governments in Canada – a broadening in the sense of the range of institutions in which policy-directed research could be found, and a deepening in the sense both of the professional qualifications of the researcher/adviser and of the sophistication of the analyses. The direct and by far the most dominant activity took place, as it takes place today, through the departments and agencies of the professional public services at both the federal and provincial levels.

STRUCTURES AND ORGANIZATION

The public service

With only modest historical inaccuracy one can say that the birth of the modern professional service and the emergence of a small coterie of professionally trained economists in the central economic departments and agencies of the federal government coincided in the early 1930s. This number grew slowly through the 1930s, was significantly expanded through the years of World War II, and began to grow rapidly in the early postwar years, influenced by Keynesian-inspired commitments to macroeconomic management. In particular, the rapid expansion in the gathering and dissemination of economic data, with the new national accounts at their core, attracted both full-time statisticians and economists and part-time academic researchers and advisers into the Dominion Bureau of Statistics (now Statistics Canada).

As in all industrial countries at the time, the federal public service continued to grow steadily through the 1950s and 1960s under the influence of the expanding programs and services of government. Variously named economic intelligence, research and advisory functions expanded not only in the central economic departments and agencies (the Departments of Finance, Trade and Commerce, External Affairs, Treasury Board, the Bank of Canada) but also in those departments less concerned with macroeconomic management but involved with an expanding array of social programs, transfers and employment policies (the Departments of Labor, Health and Welfare, Manpower). These functions also expanded in those departments more concerned with traditional microeconomic management (the Departments of Transport, Energy Mines and Resources, Northern Development, Agriculture and, later, Regional Economic Expansion). The latter part of this period and on into the 1970s also saw the very rapid expansion of provincial administrations and the growing employment of those with economic training in functions very similar to their federal counterparts.

The Privy Council Office, which under parliamentary government acts as the secretariat to the prime minister and cabinet and is part of the professional public service, expanded to provide briefing and advisory services to the prime minister and to the chairpersons of committees of cabinet. In particular, the capacity to provide the prime minister with independent advice on contemporary economic developments and on proposals with economic consequence coming forward from ministers grew with the recruitment of professional economists into the Secretariat. More recently, the prime minister's political office has acquired a capacity to provide the prime minister independent economic advice and a more political reflection upon the economic proposals of cabinet ministers.

This whole movement may be said to have reached its crest in the late 1960s and early 1970s as growing government preoccupation with internal structures, management and control combined with an exuberant social science preaching the virtues of cost–benefit analysis and planning, programming and budgeting systems. A new breed of graduate entered the public service schooled in graduate schools of economics or business and equipped with modern quantitative tools. Almost overnight the departments of government reorganized to incorporate planning branches and prepared to use the new tools and the new people in a quest for effectiveness, efficiency and a new rationalism in government.

It should be noted here that, in this essay, an 'economist' is taken to be anyone who occupies a position in economic information gathering and dissemination, research or advice giving whether or not their formal economics training extended much beyond an undergraduate degree. It is the case, however, that as these two decades proceeded they were associated with a rising level of professional accreditation among those holding economics positions and among those holding management and senior advice-giving responsibilities in economic departments. By the end of the 1970s it has been estimated that there were approximately 4,000 economists, broadly defined, in the employ of a federal public service of close to 300,000 employees, and probably a similar number in the service of the ten provinces which comprise the Canadian federation. Of these perhaps 5 per cent would be involved in advice giving as opposed to research and information functions, and a similar proportion but not necessarily the same people would hold graduate degrees. Given the restraint that has dominated governments and fiscal affairs in Canada since the mid-1970s one could take these numbers as reflecting today's situation.

In the parliamentary system, departments and agencies of government serve a minister and play a more or less continuous role of responding to the needs of the minister, whether in advice giving, research functions or information gathering and communication. Of course, in departments with large statutory and program obligations the preponderance of public servants is engaged in operational responsibilities. The close relationship which must obtain between a minister and his department and the virtual monopoly which the department exercises on the minister's time and energies dictates that the direct economic advisory function is dominated by the permanent public service. But the two and a half decades succeeding World War II also saw the growth of institutions offering a less direct role for the economist who would offer public policy advice in Canada.

Nongovernmental organizations and Royal Commissions

Given the dominance of the public service, Canada, perhaps peculiarly even among the parliamentary democracies, has not spawned a wide array of quasi-public institutions nor enjoyed the invigorating effects of a good deal of traffic between the private sector or academia and public service. It is of course the case that the quality and quantity of economic advice flowing from private interests and organizations grew markedly through the period. It is also true that a few small private but primarily public-interested economic research organizations competed for the ear of governments.

Royal Commissions on economic issues have been the principal means by which academic economists have played an indirect and independent advisory function. In the parliamentary tradition, Royal Commissions are appointed with broad inquiry powers to report on issues which seem to demand a deep and reflective look – cynics would say to report on issues that a government is unwilling to confront or on which some time and airing is required for a political consensus to emerge. Since the early 1950s there have been a number of commissions concerned primarily with economic matters, including two on Canada's economic prospects (Gordon and Macdonald); one on the Canadian banking and financial system (Porter); one on the tax system (Carter); one on Canadian oil policy (Borden); and two examining matters of government structure and organization with direct relevance to the advisory process on economic policy (Glassco and Lambert). On all of these commissions, but particularly on those directed to economic issues, professional academic economists have dominated the research staffs and compiled a body of applied research on Canadian economic policy matters. The direct influence of this research and the commission reports on the policies of governments has, perhaps, been less important or at least less easy to identify than has been the contribution to a broad public and professional understanding of Canadian economic issues and how economists address them.

The Economic Council of Canada

An institutional development particularly worth noting was the creation, by the government of the day, of the Economic Council of Canada in the early 1960s. Formally answerable to the prime minister, the Council is selected by the government to be representative, though not formally, of a wide array of public and private interests outside government. The chairperson presides over the Council as well as directing the economic research staff serving the Council. The intention was to create an institution better able to address medium- and longer-term issues and less concerned with those of the near term, and with a capacity to seek consensus among the research economists on the staff of the Council and the interests and views represented on the

Council. It was also able to be a vehicle to which governments could address references on broad economic issues not quite of the moment to demand a Royal Commission.

The Council's publications have consisted of a regular *Annual Report* and occasional studies and recommendations on major economic issues, supplemented by a considerable list of supporting research studies in the name of the research staff. Until the arrival of more turbulent economic events in the 1970s the Council enjoyed considerable notice and success. The *Annual Reports* established growth, employment and productivity targets against which to measure medium-term performance which probably had influence both upon the conduct of policy but perhaps more importantly on economic literacy more generally. Similarly, the occasional major studies and the responses to questions referred by governments attracted a wide audience and helped to shape government response. In the atmosphere of the 1960s the Council was respected and listened to, there was considerable collaboration with advisers and researchers within government, and tension with the responsible government departments and agencies was broadly productive.

In this atmosphere the Council flourished. One particular structural difficulty, however, was to contribute to diminishing Council influence in the more contentious times to come. Under the parliamentary system the Council's reports and advice are delivered to the government but the cabinet is under no obligation to act or respond. Parliament, itself, can hear the Council through a parliamentary committee but no regular practice evolved that ensured that the Council's work received particular notice or response. As policy issues became more difficult the Council tended to become one among a welter of conflicting voices with no constituted right to command the stage despite its government auspices.

ENTERING THE 1970s

By the end of the 1960s most of the structures of the Canadian version of the welfare state were in place. A public contributory pension plan and an old-age security system with added benefits for the poor comprised the system for the elderly; an elaborate child-benefit system operating both through direct payments and the tax system served the family; expenditures under a comprehensive national hospitalization and medicare scheme, a national welfare program and assistance to post-secondary education shared jointly by the federal government and the provinces provided universal access; and a national unemployment insurance program protected the unemployed. Equalization, a program by which transfers from the federal government are intended to insure that all ten Canadian provinces are capable of offering the same level of services, continued to mature towards later constitutional sanctity. A new department of the federal government, the Department of

Regional Economic Expansion, had latterly been created to address regional disparities in rates of growth, employment and incomes. And the Bank of Canada and the Department of Finance, after a shallow disturbance in the early 1960s, seemed to have managed monetary, exchange rate and fiscal policies to the maximum advantage of a small but very open economy.

In all of these developments economic advisers within government had played a part, particularly of course in the conduct of macro policy through the principal economic agencies of the Bank of Canada and the Department of Finance. Though there was unease at times between the advisers on macro management, with their responsibilities for the overall efficiency and capacity of the economy, and their colleagues in program departments, acting as advocates for the social and industrial distribution aims of the government, the times seemed to permit the joint pursuit of equity and efficiency. Conflict among economic advisers, between advisers and government political ambitions, or between the efficiency imperatives of the economics discipline and the dominantly distributional aims of government were muted. Nor were there marked tensions between economists and advisers drawn from other disciplines. Political struggles over individual and collective rights in many forms, environmentalist and conservationist challenges, technological concerns, and struggles within the economics discipline itself, were forming but did not yet command a central place.

Had one been writing this essay fifteen years ago, therefore, one might have penned a very exuberant essay on both the economic prospects for Canada and the growing influence of professional economics and economists in the counsels of government. One might have worried a little about the gulf between the academic profession, private-sector advisers and public-servant practitioners and the lack of adequate cross-fertilization – but not made a good deal of it. One might have worried, a little arrogantly, about the capacity and the inclination of ministers to receive and absorb the increasing sophistication of the advice laid before them. But the events of the last fifteen years have diminished both the self-assurance of economists and the assurance of the political authority in the advice they have to offer. The gulf between the academic economist and his public-service counterpart has widened as the academic profession has reverted to a narrower neoclassicism and been more disposed to avoid direct involvement in normative issues. Broad publics display a deep distrust of governments and their advisers, and the economics profession more generally, with the apparent differences of view within it, has become increasingly the focus of public unease. To these developments we now turn.

ADVISORY STRUCTURES UNDER STRESS – THE 1970s AND 1980s

It is necessary, if only sketchily, to describe the impact of the economic shocks of the 1970s and 1980s on the Canadian economy and polity in order to understand the increasing strains among advisers, between advisers and the political authority, and, not least of all, between professional governmental advisers and their academic counterparts as the discipline reverted to a consuming preoccupation with efficiency issues and the market economy.

A listing of worldwide structural economic shocks would be composed of at least the following. Dominant, of course, were the two energy shocks which in their real effect seemed fundamentally to alter the structure of input prices upon which postwar economic growth had been based. But in addition one would include the emergence of new technologies based upon microelectronics and microbiology and the acceleration of technological change more generally; the emergence of new, competitive sources for many of the world's raw materials; the emergence of a group of newly industrializing countries able to import the technologies of the industrial world and combine them with relatively skilled but lower-cost labor; and the rapid emergence of a large group of sovereign principalities whose interests conflicted with the tidy Bretton Woods arrangements. Together with the strains on these arrangements emerging among industrial countries, the difficulties of world economic cooperation and management were escalating rapidly.

The management of these shocks was gravely complicated by the need to attend to another disease, accelerating inflation. A source of growing concern by the end of the 1960s, inflation was greatly exacerbated both by the coincident world boom of the early 1970s as it pressed against capacity constraints and by the structural shocks themselves, particularly the energy shocks. The existence of inflation and the restraint required for its control made the task of adjustment to structural change in an environment of less than adequate aggregate demand a daunting challenge to governments and advisers alike.

As economic performance entered a decade of stagflation and expectations were disappointed, there was a precipitate fall in public esteem for governments and their advisers and an increasing questioning of the size and interventionism of government and of the structures of the welfare state. The economics profession, both within and without government, turned inevitably to reassess the efficiency costs of the structures of policy and the role which perhaps over-exuberant monetary and fiscal policies played in the Canadian inflation experience.

Reappraisal in Canada was stimulated by some further consequences of contemporary economic experience. Worldwide structural forces had some singular impacts on Canada. The *rentier* benefits of a resource-rich nation were eroded both by a steep decline in the terms of trade and by a steady reduction of monopoly advantages across the whole range of Canada's resource exports. Large portions of Canadian manufacturing seemed vulnerable to the steady incursions of imports. Evidence was emerging that Canadian industry lagged in both indigenous research and development effort and in its pace of adaptation to changing technologies. And the energy impacts were to be peculiarly strongly felt in Canada, of which more in a moment.

Domestically, as well, economic developments were calling into question the effectiveness of somc structures of economic policy. Efforts to measure the effects of expenditures on regional development revealed that, apart from the development of infrastructure, the effort had been successful in narrowing income differentials but had had little impact on permanently embedding employment opportunities and growth. Through a fairly substantial fiscal and monetary stimulus in 1974 Canada, alone among industrial nations, had avoided the recession of 1974–5 but had paid a heavy inflationary price which culminated in late 1975 in the application of wage and price controls. In the face of a rapidly growing domestic labor force, neither continuing growth nor rather rapid employment creation prevented the slow ascent of unemployment. Finally these developments, together with increasing attention to the apparent collapse in productivity around 1974, stimulated a broad re-emphasis within the professional economic community on the virtues of privatization, deregulation and a renewed concern for efficiency and government expenditure restraint. A return to a much greater emphasis on the market economy became the creed of a revived economic and political liberalism.

The consequences of all of these developments for the economic advising profession within government can be revealed by closer examination of three policy areas and by a further short note on the evolution of the Economic Council. Energy policies, particularly those relating to oil and natural gas, became both contentious and divisive for the Canadian federation. Similarly, the conduct of macroeconomic policies evolved as economic doctrine developed to reveal tensions both within the economics profession and between the profession and governments. The structures of decision making changed, too, under the impress of restraint with particular consequences for budgeting and allocative decisions.

POLICY ISSUES

Energy policy

Nowhere is the regional diversity of Canada and the political complexity of economic policymaking in an economically and politically decentralized federal state better exemplified than in the field of energy policy. When the OPEC revolution struck in the fall of 1973, the state of affairs in Canada can best be understood as a microcosm of the world situation. Production and reserves of oil and gas were wholly located in the three most westerly provinces and dominantly in one of them, Alberta. Statistically self-sufficient in both, Canada imported oil into the eastern half of the country for logistic and cost-of-transport reasons and exported from the west a quantity of oil about equal to eastern imports. Natural gas, produced in the west, flowed only as far east as the city of Montreal. The discovery of new reserves of conventional oil and gas had seemed to reach a plateau in the west and the exploration of potential reserves in the north and east was just beginning. The huge tar sands deposits, also in Alberta, were still on the technological and cost frontier. Production of both oil and gas in the west and the import of oil in the east were largely in the hands of the multinational oil companies, as was the pace of Canadian exploration and development.

Several other facts are relevant. Under the Canadian constitution the ownership and management of resources is vested in the provincial authority but interprovincial and external trade is under the authority of the federal government. The Canadian energy regulatory authority, the National Energy Board, is charged with licensing exports only in volumes surplus to Canadian long-term requirements and at prices that are 'just and reasonable'. At the outset of the period, royalties imposed by the provinces were expensible by corporations for federal income tax purposes so that as provincial royalties rose against a given level of profits, federal tax collections declined. Finally, the federal obligation to provide equalization payments to less well-to-do provinces rises as the revenues of better-off provinces rise.

Out of this complex blend of elements an array of intersecting issues for dispute and analysis can be distinguished. The first concerned domestic Canadian pricing policy in the face of the quadrupling of international oil prices. Those who believed either in the impermanence of the price rise or who believed that some industrial advantage might lie in Canada's indigenous supplies of relatively low-priced oil and gas opposed those who argued for a rapid adjustment to international price levels in order to induce both additional resource development and structural adjustment on the demand side. If Canadian internal prices were to be kept below international prices, mechanisms for the pricing of exports needed to be distinguished. The measurement, methods of taxation and the appropriate distribution of resource rents between governments and industry, between governments themselves, and whether to use constrained prices as an implicit mechanism of rent distribution to consumers, excited economic and political contention.

Very early on in the unfolding drama Canadians learned that the resource base was not as vast as they had been led to believe. The role of multinationals in providing reserve estimates, in resource exploration and development, and in supplying imports to the dependent east came under scrutiny. Methods and mechanisms for inducing both greater Canadian participation in the oil industry and greater Canadian control of the pace of exploration and development, particularly in the riskier and higher-cost tar sands and offshore regions, demanded examination. Conservation mechanisms as an alternative to high-cost and environmentally questionable development, particularly if price was not to be fully employed as an inducement, spawned a whole new field for analysis and potential policy development. And of course Canada participated in the development of the International Energy Agency and Canadian ministers and officials played a significant role in international energy deliberations.

All of these issues occupied center stage in Canada for over a decade. The political attractiveness of a lower-than-international pricing policy to consumers generally and particularly to import-dependent regions of the country, and the incapacity to contrive a rent-sharing agreement between the federal government and the producing provinces, should international pricing be adopted, led to a series of negotiated intergovernmental agreements. Through the 1970s, the Canadian domestic price was held below international levels (and thus rents were transferred implicitly) and export taxes (and later consumption taxes) were employed to subsidize imports in order to unify the Canadian price. Pipelines were constructed to expand the flow of western oil and gas further east in Canada. Tax and expenditure programs were employed to induce substitution against oil in both industrial and household consumption. A national oil company was formed to be a vehicle for public participation in high-cost exploration and development.

Just as Canadian prices were, in steps, approaching international levels, and the unwinding of these elaborate interventions was in prospect, the second oil shock of 1979 provoked further rounds of contentious internal negotiations and bargaining. Out of a political commitment to continue to shelter Canadians from the full international price, out of a determination to establish a more permanent set of principles for rent sharing among the contending governments and industry, out of a growing recognition of the accumulating costs of forgone industrial and consumer adjustment, the National Energy Program was announced by the federal government in the fall of 1980.

The National Energy Program was a very elaborate attempt to construct an internally coherent – if politically and economically controversial – package of programs and policies. In part the design was shaped by the need to employ expenditure and taxation policies to induce appropriate investment, allocation and substitution responses under a political determination to constrain the use of price and markets for these purposes. In part the Program sought a long-term settlement of the principles of rent distribution among contending governments and industry and between segments of the industry. In further part the Program sought to advantage, relatively, both Canadian-owned components of the industry and Canadian participation in future development as well as to provide significant inducements for the repatriation of foreign-controlled firms and resources. The entire structure was built on the presumption, then almost universally held, that the real and relative international price of oil would continue to advance through the 1980s and beyond. This assumption provided the forecast expansion of rents which could simultaneously appease an intemperate quarrel over shares, finance adjustment policies, and make a net contribution to future energy development, Canadianization and the long-term reduction of the growing federal government deficit.

As difficult federal/provincial/industry negotiations proceeded to put the Program in place it was becoming evident that the underlying price projection was fundamentally flawed. Almost from the outset of an agreement concluded in the fall of 1981 with the major producing province, Alberta, it was necessary to begin backing away from some taxing provisions and to renegotiate a more balanced package. As international prices continued to weaken, industry distemper grew and the fiscal strains of the broad new range of government expenditure commitments worsened. By 1984, a new federal government with a deeper ideological commitment to the market economy proceeded to negotiate the abandonment of the National Energy Program and a return to market pricing.

What reflections on the role of economist as adviser can be drawn from this extended and complex episode? The first OPEC shock caught Canadian governments relatively unarmed to reason about its broad implications. Economic advisory and research teams grew rapidly within the federal government and in the provinces, recruited from within and without government and often without any particular energy specialization. The quantity and quality of energy research and modeling advanced rapidly. After a period of digestion and growth of understanding, it is probably fair to state that the dominant disposition was to advise governments in favor of a more rather than less rapid adjustment to international pricing and associated market demand and supply adjustment. This advice had to repose, however, within the confines of a dominating political concern for the distributional consequences within the federation – among governments, between governments and the industry, and between producers and consumers more generally. The need to be concerned with foreign domination of Canadian resources, the major role of foreign capital in non-renewable resource developments, and hence the vulnerability of Canadian exploration and development to multinational investment strategies added a further layer of economic complication and political imperative.

Interregional, interpersonal and intergovernmental distributional issues have always been a critical concern of the Canadian federal authority. The structure of the Canadian federation with manufacturing and financial service activity concentrated in the central provinces and with the eastern and western provinces subject to varying economic fortune has been a source of almost continuous political tension and has compelled attention to the distributional consequences of market forces and policy structures. Sensitivities to constitutional divisions of authority and responsibility between the federal government and the provinces play a further critical role in the construction of major policy initiatives. Senior economic advisers in Canada have never enjoyed the positivist role of arraying efficiency alternatives while leaving the normative task of prescribing distributional rearrangements among efficient outcomes to political choice.

As criticism mounted through the 1970s that the structures of distributional and redistributional policies and programs were instrumental in causing inadequate economic performance, political authorities became even more reluctant to accept such formalized compartments of ecomomic advice and political choice. What was demanded, if they were to be considered, were integrated packages in which efficiency costs and benefits were arrayed along with their distributional consequences. This does not imply a rejection of efficiency considerations. Indeed as the decade advanced, the recognition that the use of a constrained price invited increasing efficiency and lagged adjustment costs led to a readiness to accept a broadening array of incentive and regulatory programs to offset the damage, to which the National Energy Program gave fullest expression.

Economic advisers were compelled, therefore, if they were to be relevant, to be versed in the political, constitutional, legislative and legal implications of their advice as well as the narrowly economic. As many academic professionals, under the influence of both a resurgent neoclassicism and a preoccupation with inflation and the causes of declining real rates of growth, turned increasingly to a more single-minded advocacy of efficiency considerations, tensions, within the profession, between insiders and outsiders, increased.

Macroeconomic policy

The broad economic advance from World War II until the early 1970s created the illusion of some modest degrees of freedom for the pursuit of an independent structure of macro policies in Canada. The encroaching structural pressures and competitiveness of the 1970s, the integration of world financial markets, the Canadian susceptibility to a rather more virulent form of the inflation disease than its industrial competitors, and the considerable advance in understanding of the consequences of fiscal and monetary initiatives in a small, open economy revealed just how modest and constrained this independence was.

Between a quarter and a third of Canadian gross national product is generated from the export of goods and services. About 80 per cent of these flow to the American market. In a typical year a favorable balance on goods trade fails to offset a deficit in services and the resulting current-account deficit must be offset by inward flows of portfolio and direct investment. Portfolio flows, both short and long term, are highly sensitive to interest-rate differentials and relative rates of inflation with the rest of the world. Direct flows are more closely related to fundamental Canadian economic prospects. With the growing sophistication and integration of international financial markets the exchange rate is sensitive to internal economic management and foreign judgements of it.

Canada entered the 1970s having created its first formal commission seeking to both comprehend and create consensual resistance to growing inflation. In response to a rapid increase in unemployment rates over the growth pause of 1969–70, both monetary and fiscal policy turned expansionary and continued so in resistance to the recessionary force of the first OPEC shock. In response to a very rapid rise in inflation rates through 1975, monetary policy under the direction of the Bank of Canada turned to a formal commitment to monetarist restraint. The government committed itself to a gradualist program of fiscal restraint and launched a formal program of wage and price controls. Modest growth and inflation continued into the 1980s until ascending interest rates, in step with US policies, led to deep recession. Once again a lagging inflation response led to formal wage and price restraint, this time confined to the government sector. After five years of sustained recovery, unemployment rates remain historically high and large federal government deficits firmly imbedded.

Turbulence in the economy was matched by a similar turbulence within the economics discipline. Keynesians, monetarists, rational expectationists and neo-Keynesians competed within the advisory ranks and less certain prescriptions were laid before ministers of finance, and through them to cabinets. As the logic of fiscal and monetary restraint and the demands for more efficient use of available resources became more compelling, the relationship between the Governor of the Bank of Canada and the government, and between the President of the Treasury Board and the Minister of Finance and their cabinet colleagues, was marked by increasing uneasiness and strain. Similarly, the passage of a time when fiscal dividends could easily accommodate the ambitions of spending ministers brought bureaucratic advisers with responsibilities in program departments into increasing conflict with their central economic agency colleagues. Though the logic of positive economic adjustment was broadly accepted, deep conflict surrounded the question of whether particular initiatives would have the effect of accelerating adjustment or simply prop up declining firms and industries. To the degree that advice became dominated by efficiency and adjustment concerns there was a less comfortable relationship generally between advisers and cabinet ministers. Nor was the economic 'ideology' in much less conflict with advancing ecological disciplines on the one hand, and those who urged technological advance and growth through directed industrial strategies on the other.

Advice within the Bank of Canada could afford to be and was more single-minded. The Bank moved from a 'credit conditions' doctrine in the early

1970s to an increasing acceptance of a money-supply doctrine based upon a stable and revealed demand for money and a determination, after a substantial depreciation of the exchange rate, to prevent the exchange rate from being an important transmitter of price shocks to an inflation-sensitive economy. As instabilities appeared in money demand functions in the early 1980s, the Bank gave up targeted increases in money supply but continued to permit credit conditions to be the outcome of a determined anti-inflationary posture. Not surprisingly, the resulting volatility in interest rates particularly through the dramatic escalations of the early 1980s and the sustained high real rates thereafter provoked political animosity. But no minister of finance has been in strong enough disagreement to precipitate the crisis that attempting to direct a governor in the conduct of monetary policy would have entailed.

The two exercises in direct wage and price restraint probably excited stronger differences of opinion within the economics community than any other specific pieces of policy. By and large professionals external to government had concluded that wage and price controls invited inefficiency costs and were either ineffective or were ineffective unless associated with strong fiscal and monetary medicine – in which case they were unnecessary. To the adviser within government, perhaps more sensitive to the political pace at which greater restraint could be applied, they represented a means of accelerating reductions in inflation for any given degree of restraint and hence reducing aggregate restraint and adjustment costs. Since both were conducted against an inflation rate that was, or was about to be, in decline, subsequent analysis has left the matter of effectiveness in dispute. Left open as well is the question of whether the continuous restraint necessary to keep unemployment above the NAIRU (the non-accelerating inflation rate of unemployment, estimated to have increased from just over 3 to over 7 per cent over the past two decades) will not lead to further contention in the future as advisers within government lend their support to experiments in incomes policies.

Under the pressures of continuing restraint and retrenchment the budgets of the minister of finance, annually or semi-annually, have become increasingly the central statement of government economic philosophy, establishing not only the overall fiscal stance of the government but the more particular menu of planned government initiatives and restraints. Though necessarily sensitive to the political needs and directions of the government, the responsibility for advising on the means of achieving maximum aggregate performance brings the economic advisory role in the Department of Finance closer to the mainstream views of the profession (as it frequently does for the minister whatever may have been his previous experience and disposition). The Minister of Finance must employ the force of position and reason to carry his cabinet colleagues with him. In the last analysis the minister must be sustained by the prime minister if the minister's recommendations are to have force and cabinet solidarity is to be maintained. Decision-making structures came under greater strain by the late 1970s, inviting a radical reformation of the process of program, spending and budgeting decisions. The role of the economic adviser at each step of the process can most easily be seen in these new arrangements.

The program and expenditure management system

By the mid-1970s the heady rationalism of planning, programming and budgeting systems had largely foundered under the weight of the divergence of their promise from their capacity to perform, from conflicts within departments between line branches with program obligations and staff planners and evaluators, and from the diversion of political and public-service energy to the struggle with restraint. Most planning branches had vanished or been restructured with less ambitious aims. At the same time, as restraint tightened, the need for structured flows of advice which could enable ministers to meet new contingencies through reallocating resources among existing programs, rather than by planning net additions to government activity, ascended sharply.

The answer was sought in the restructuring and redesign of the cabinet decision-making system. Canadian cabinets have traditionally been large (growing to over forty members at present) and have been composed of co-equals with no distinctions drawn between senior and junior ministers as in some other parliamentary democracies. They have functioned by assigning ministers to functional committees of cabinet according to portfolio; e.g. economic, social and cultural, foreign affairs and defense, government operations, and a Treasury Board committee overseeing the financial management function with a large permanent secretariat. Until the late 1970s, ministers seeking authorization to pursue a new initiative or program brought the proposal and supporting documentation before their colleagues in committee and sought agreement in principle. If agreed to in committee, proposals moved to full cabinet for approval, and where there were expenditure and person/year implications, to the Treasury Board for final funding approval. Of course the prime minister and his senior (by portfolio) economic ministers could, but not without acrimony, effectively stand in the way of any proposal which seriously threatened the fiscal capacity of the government. Nevertheless, through the period of expanding fiscal dividends the system provided considerable accommodation of ministerial ambitions, or of proposals urged upon ministers by their public servant advisers.

As restraint pinched through the late 1970s, however, frustrations grew as the possible availability of new funding fell far short of potential claims and it became evident that some system of priority setting would be required for entitlement to such funds as were available. Some additional incentives were also required in the system to encourage the critical examination of existing programming for potential reallocations. The planning and priorities committee of cabinet which had been the prime minister's committee for considering the longer-run priorities of the government became the executive committee of cabinet. Ministries of state with substantial permanent secretariats were established to preside over the three major functional committees: economic policy, social policy, and external affairs and defense. Functionally the revised system was to operate as follows. Some six months in advance of a budget and the hardening of the government's plans for the next fiscal year, each minister was to bring forward a planning document for his/her ministry evaluating existing commitments and potential new initiatives. In committee, and with the assistance of the secretariat, these documents were to be discussed and consolidated into a document which established priorities among ministers and plans for the committee as a whole. Planning documents from each committee were then to proceed to a consolidated discussion in the planning and priorities committee.

About three months before a scheduled budget the Minister of Finance, having observed and taken part in these discussions and having conferred with the prime minister and the President of the Treasury Board, would be responsible for bringing forward a document which examined the economic situation, the fiscal situation of the government and the respective claims of the committees. In this document the Finance Minister, having considered the priority claims of the committees, advanced a first reconciliation of the government's priorities and advanced a first allocation of funds to committees (or 'envelopes' as they came to be called). These allocations, when agreed to and confirmed in the minister's budget, established the financial sums available to the committees for the next fiscal year and brought the process of program approval and fund allocation together in committee.

This system was launched in 1979 and practiced more or less as described for four years. Designed by economists among others, it had its rationalist strengths but developed its own set of strains which led to subsequent modification. Its primary strengths lay in the formalization of the process of program review and structured argument for new initiatives department by department and committee by committee, and ultimately in the budget presentation of the Finance Minister. For the first time approval in principle of new proposals and their financing was brought together as a single decision within the committees of cabinet. The establishment of ministries of state and their secretariats represented a first attempt to integrate government allocation decisions across the frontier of competing claims. Fiscal control was placed firmly in the hands of the Finance Minister and the ultimate macroeconomic decisions on taxing and spending were integrated with the microeconomic directions of the budget. At each of the steps of document preparation, teams of departmental and secretariat advisers, prominent among which were economists, sought to lay out structured economic argument for ministerial review and decision making.

In part the top-heaviness of the system, however, proved one of its central sources of strain. Ministers grew uneasy as initiatives were forced along a lengthy structured path of bureaucratic and ministerial review. The new ministries of state and secretariats were criticized for opposing reasons. The Ministry of State for Economic and Regional Development became immersed in a lengthy agenda of competing ministerial claims without ever developing a very successful or accepted model for arbitrating among them. The Ministry of State for Social Development, on the other hand, attempted to provide ministers with too-developed a model and became accused of usurping ministerial authority.

By 1983, the recession had effectively stripped the committees of any reserves of new funds and hence of any capacity for initiative. In 1984 the ministries of state were abolished. Nor did the attempt to produce departmental planning documents ever contribute a great deal to the review and evaluation of existing programs and the freeing of resources for reallocation or deficit reduction. Not surprisingly, ministers and ministries proved unwilling to yield pieces of an existing mandate except in circumstances where all were compelled to do so. The entire system came under continuous criticism for excessive hierarchy and excessive demands for collegiality among ministers with a consequent diminishment of individual ministerial authority.

Despite its failures, the concept of envelopes and the linking of program and expenditure decisions survives today. Indeed, given the dramatic shift from an expanding government to restraint and downsizing, it is doubtful whether it would have been possible to manage under the former cabinet decision-making structures. A good deal of the criticism was a reflection of the influence of restraint itself, a situation in which all institutions behave more or less badly.

A FURTHER NOTE ON THE ECONOMIC COUNCIL

Aside from the uncertain institutional channels for Economic Council influence noted earlier, the events of the 1970s reduced the force of the Council's deliberations in further ways. As the medium-term targets which the Council had established in the 1960s became more unlikely to be achieved, and the Council itself was drawn into comment upon shorter-term issues of policy management, tensions with the advisory structures within government and with the government itself rose. To some degree the readiness to receive and consider Council advice diminished as political uncertainties increased. Further, as events tumbled over one another the Council and its staff found it more difficult to anticipate developments and to sustain timeliness in presenting views on major emerging issues.

Particularly damaging was the decision of Canada's major labour organization to withdraw its members from participation in government structures in response to the imposition of wage and price controls in 1975. The Council lost its labor representation and with it the consensual force of its publications. While considerable attention was devoted through the late 1970s to the need to build consensual capacities in the Canadian system, particularly to facilitate the management of inflation and restraint, there was little success. When the government again resorted to wage and price restraints in the government sector in 1982, the labor movement was again estranged. The lack of establishment labor representation on the Economic Council continues to this day and remains a criticial disability.

Attempts by the Council to foster consensus and participation through the sponsoring of national conferences on Canada's economic dilemmas were also unsuccessful as communities of interest chose other vehicles to represent their views to government. Despite these setbacks the Council and its staff remains the major disinterested center of policy research and advice in the country and has sustained an impressive record of policy research and advice, even though that advice now has less influence upon the counsels of government.

CONCLUSIONS

Three dominating issues of recent governmental history have been used to illustrate economic advice-giving structures and processes within the federal government. Many others could have been chosen from the post-World War II period. It has been an impressive period in the increasing influence of the economics discipline, economic research and economic advice. But at its close, tensions in the economic advice-giving process are much more apparent than earlier in the period.

There can be no surprise in this. The reaction that has been provoked by a prolonged period of structural strain and less-than-robust economic performance has brought not only governments and their bureaucracies into disesteem but has revealed cracks and uncertainties among streams of economic advice. Broad publics seem to have accepted, at least implicitly, the fundamental tenet of public-choice theory that a narrower self-interest shapes the motives of advisers and politicians rather than a commitment to serve the public interest. And clearly, consensus about what composes the public interest and the directions which governments ought to pursue is much less sturdy than it appeared to be in the 1950s and 1960s.

In one sense increasing economic strain, the preoccupation with economic fortune and the shift of both the polity and the profession to a renewed liberalism have increased attention paid to efficiency and growth concerns and enhanced the role of economic expertise. On the other, however, the uneven distributional consequences of cyclical and structural forces over the past fifteen years, particularly as these have meaning in Canada in interregional as well as interpersonal terms, have also led to a sustained political preoccupation with the distributional consequences of economic policies. Indeed, intense criticism of the inefficiency consequences of distributional policies has led, if anything, to a rejection by politicians of the notion that distributional choices along some efficiency frontier can be exercised once efficient choices and policies have led to the frontier. As particularly noted in the case of energy policy, ministers prefer to have the choices which they must confront fully articulated in efficiency and distributional terms. In this fundamental sense then, the role of the internal economic adviser, if he or she is to have influence, is much more in an older tradition of political economy than in the modern separation of the disciplines.

This political fact of life, more than any other issue, has been central to the strains which have developed both between politicians and advisers and between advisers and their professional academic colleagues. Conflicts between advisers and the political authority most frequently involve an alleged lack of sensitivity of each to the dominant concern of the other. And as the academic economics profession has become centrally focused upon a renewed neoclassicism, the communications gulf between academic and practicing professionals has widened correspondingly. Nor, aside from placing increased reliance in the market, has there been any single-mindedness about prescriptions to deal with structural change and dislocation either among economists or between economists and governments.

Many of these tensions are illustrated by the current debate within Canada on trade issues. Until recently, Canadian policy has been firmly committed to, and Canada's self-interest seen to be served by, the pursuit of multilateral reductions in world trade barriers. Growing US protectionism, the theoretical and research-supported case for the efficiency and hence real growth gains to be derived from a free-trade arrangement with the United States, the support of this case by the most recent Royal Commission examining Canada's economic prospects (the Macdonald Commission), and the political disposition of Canada's current government have led to the pursuit of such an arrangement as a principal focus of government policy. Whether such an arrangement can be concluded and with what degree of comprehensiveness remains to be seen. In the meantime, the efficiency case appears to be supported by a majority of, though not all, professional economists. Arrayed against the counsels of these economists is a coalition of opposing views whose most common fundamental concern may be said to be an aversion to the harmonizing consequences of a world driven dominantly by efficiency and growth concerns.

Canada has often been said to be a country created against the logic of economic imperative and dedicated to the paying of some inefficiency costs in order to sustain a distinctive and independent nation state. Whether independence and cultural difference is purchased from the fruits of efficient growth or by tampering along the way with the logic of efficiency has once again become central to national debate. And, of course, whether compensation need only theoretically be available to bribe the losers not to oppose such an arrangement or whether compensation must be paid and in what directions and forms revives a debate both from the heart of an older welfare economics and from the modern debate over the most efficient construction of adjustment and distributional expenditures.

This chapter may have given the impression that economic advisers, largely alone, contend for the ear of political authority. This, of course, has never been so. But in matters that might traditionally have been seen as the province of the economic adviser, contention increases. Scientists, engineers and business advisers, fixed upon technological change and advance, urge a new interventionism that contends with a more liberal economic rationale. From quite an opposite direction, ecological professionals with a contending imperative dispute both the application of the economic method to environmental issues, and the logical dominance of the economic imperative itself. Human rights and equal-opportunity movements contest the logic of a reliance on market forces. The neoclassical revival within the economics profession seems only to have sharpened the edges of these disputes.

A number of other developments have consequence for the advice-giving role of economists. In general, restraint has imposed a preoccupation with managerial and administrative efficiency within the public service. In this climate, the relationship between 'staff' advisers and 'line' administrators of departments and agencies, always imperfectly structured, is now even less easy. One has a feeling that imaginative advice no longer flows as freely from teams of researchers/advisers through senior ranks of administrators to as ready a ministerial and cabinet audience. Two further related gulfs in communication, peculiar to the economics profession, seem to be growing. One is between the career public servant and the discipline itself. Except perhaps for major research and theoretical developments in macroeconomics, there is no longer a very easy way for the career professional to stay in touch with the preoccupations of his academic colleagues. With exceptions, economic journals move quickly beyond reach.

Within the academy, the growing specialization between and within the social sciences has made it less likely that the government adviser will have the renaissance qualities which the task seems to demand. Traditional Canadian faculties of political economy have split into separate disciplines and it is now not uncommon for the graduate student in economics or politics to have had virtually no training in the other discipline, let alone any grounding in the competing methodologies of the other social sciences or the natural sciences.

Specialization makes exchange more difficult in the market for knowledge and advice, even within disciplines. Increasingly, it seems, the ranks of governmental adviser will be drawn from schools of public administration or public policy where attempts to sustain an interdisciplinary approach to public policy issues are more common. It seems that in the future the question of who is and who is not an economist, and who offers and who does not offer professional economic advice, may be even less clear than it has been in the less professional past.

As far as institutional developments are concerned, a restless shuffling of the structures of government continues in the search for the most appropriate and effective means of addressing issues and controlling events. This chapter has given some attention to the evolution of the Economic Council, a notable initiative in a country which is not very fertile in surrounding government with public-purposed institutions. As has been observed, the experience with the Council has been mixed, reflecting both the more contentious times and, as with Royal Commissions, the lack of a mechanism which compels government response and which can thereby sustain productive public attention to its work.

There is one final troublesome issue. Fashions in political and economic temper, and the changing structure of economic challenges, cause economic policies to give a greater appearance of cycling than of evolving. For the Canadian public service, sustaining historical and institutional memory through cycles of 'shifting involvements' (Hirschman, 1981) in public and private purpose emerges as a critical issue. It seems likely, for instance, that the next energy shock will propel Canadian policy through a cycle very much like the last, no lasting principle having emerged from the last experience which could inform a succeeding generation of advisers. Just as accelerating technological change seems to demand a growing commitment to reschooling and retraining, so career economic advisers and the public policies they put forward would benefit from a continuous re-immersion in both the discipline and the historical and institutional determinants of political and economic action in Canada.

BIBLIOGRAPHY

The following few references provide trails for the enquiring mind who would pursue these issues.

Doern, G. Bruce, and Toner, Glen, *The Politics of Energy* (Toronto: Methuen, 1985). Discussion on Canadian energy policy and politics.

Hirschman, Albert, *Shifting Involvements* (Princeton, NJ: Princeton University Press, 1981). Has much to say on the cycling fashions in economic advice and advice giving.

Macdonald Commission, *The Royal Commission on the Economic Union and Development Prospects for Canada* (Ottawa: The Queen's Printer, 1985). This and supporting research volumes provide the most recent comprehensive survey of Canadian economic issues and the contributions of economic advice.

Smith, David C. (ed.), *Economic Policy Advising in Canada, Essays in Honour of John Deutsch* (Montreal: C. D. Howe Institute, 1981). On the general matter of the role of the economist in government.

8 · MEXICO

*David Ibarra and José-Luis Alberro**

Mexico's experience, as well as that of many other countries, leads to the conclusion that the design of economic policy and its implementation involve a complex interplay of interests that departs in important aspects from conventional academic wisdom. The process of setting social goals entails the appearance of value-related problems that can only be resolved using noneconomic rationality. Furthermore, governments can rarely press forward with economic strategies that ignore political limitations or fail to take administrative and institutional capacity into account. These topics are discussed in the first section of this chapter, as a prelude to an examination of the difficulties that have arisen as a result of three factors: the erosion of current economic paradigms; problems derived from attempts to stabilize while introducing structural change; and the determination of objectives that must be satisfied, yet are increasingly divorced from the aspirations of the polity.

The third section briefly describes the institutional structure of economic advising in Mexico from the 1930s to the present. The fourth considers the economic and political context of Mexico's economic policy in the postwar period. Up to the 1970s, the influence of economists and economic thought was increasingly felt in the management of public affairs but, in later years, the dissonance between the changes in the international economy and the prevalent development pattern brought about serious complications in the administration of the economy that lowered the prestige and popularity of economic arguments. The fifth section is devoted to a succinct examination of Mexico's longest period of growth, which was associated with an import-substitution strategy, and to a discussion of the problems of productive inefficiency and external strangulation that arose from it to illustrate the effectiveness of economic advice in Mexico. This section also reviews the advances and setbacks in efforts to alter the traditional pattern of development through external openness and other structural changes.

The final section offers some conclusions that assign to economists a role with fewer scientific pretensions, directing them, instead, to the task of

* We are grateful to Ignacio Navarro for diligent research assistantship.

opinion making and integrating economic criteria in a political order.

ECONOMIC REALITIES, PERCEPTIONS AND PARADIGMS

Perhaps with an historical lag, since it occurred in the 1970s and early 1980s, economics began to free itself of the positivism and volunteerism that had permeated the social sciences since Auguste Compte. Little by little, the concepts of economics as a natural science and of economists as scientists, insulated from politics and reluctant to allow their professional work to be tainted by value judgements, began to fall into disrepute.

Today, it is recognized not only that the value judgements of policymakers influence the setting of social goals, but also that governments and large private institutions can alter the formation of the popular preferences that constitute the backdrop for political decisions. On the other hand, since the choice of policy instruments depends on the economic theory used, it is clear that value judgements are always present and that both benefits and burdens are assigned unevenly across the population.[1]

The traditional scheme, which conceives of the formulation implementation and monitoring of economic policy as a sequential process, neatly divided into stages and functions, has come into question. According to the old view, it is strictly up to democratically elected representatives to select the main economic objectives and specify the trade-offs among them in accordance with popular aspirations. Once these parameters are set, it devolves upon a group of public officials to determine the intermediate goals and the instruments to be employed on the basis of value-neutral technical options prepared by professional economists. Finally, the execution of the chosen measures is handed over to a second group of technicians within the public sector.

In practice, however, from its initial inception to its concrete application, economic policy is subject to a process of change in which the original concept is continuously reformulated. Economists rarely limit themselves to exploring the best ways to satisfy given objectives; they often present policymakers with goals that had not been contemplated before, forcing them to choose on the basis of criteria that usually go beyond economic considerations. Pressure groups, political parties and assorted bureaucratic factions must be reconciled at different stages of the economic policy-implementation process. The institutional framework as well as the channels through which these interactions occur affect the form and the viability of proposed economic policy measures and may hinder or facilitate change.[2]

Furthermore, history has tended to debunk the hypothesis of intrinsic harmony between economic goals and social objectives like liberty, equality, justice and democratization. In particular, the notion that social variables have an impact on individuals and collective welfare, whereas economic events affect neither sociopolitical behavior nor structures, appears to have finally lost its validity. Indeed, if it is acknowledged that opposition can exist among economic, social and political goals, then it must be accepted that social phenomena cannot be reduced to predominantly economic categories. Instead of harmonious institutions, democracy and the marketplace have to be viewed as mechanisms that sometimes move in different directions and therefore require periodic adjustments to reconcile dissimilar goals, like rewarding efficiency while pursuing equality (Ibarra, 1987).

Clearly, these considerations underline the futility of current efforts to simplify social goals by trying to institute full employment and growth as the focal point of government action and postulating that the achievement of these ends will, by itself, lead to greater liberty and equality. If this were not true – if, for example, greater economic freedom implied having to make concessions in equality or having to sacrifice economic welfare – then government and society would face unsolvable axiological dilemmas when setting priorities (Berlin, 1969).

In Mexico and in Latin America too, popular support for economic policy is of singular importance. Economic growth and public policies aimed at improving the living conditions of the largest segments of the population play a central role in determining the social balance and, consequently, are an important source of government legitimacy. In a strict sense, the fruits of democracy cannot be enjoyed by simply implanting processes that guarantee political participation and civil liberties; market forces have to be molded to minimize economic inequality.

This fact tempers the common assumption that governments always have the political and administrative wherewithal to carry out the recommendations of economists. Indeed, the management of extra-economic problems may often explain the coexistence of different types of rationality in government decision-making processes. Without necessarily being conservative, politicians prefer to follow established orthodoxies and lines of economic action because, by being easily identifiable and hence predictable, they provoke the least resistance among the groups adversely affected. Incremental progress rather than abrupt reform is more the tendency of politicians than economists (Lindblom, 1977).

In the light of the conceptual separation between politics and economics, to integrate these two domains history has forced governments to develop syntheses that, in some sense, nearly always violate economic or political ideology but seem to limit the immediate costs of any action: needed budgetary belt-tightening is avoided because it can jeopardize the consolidation of fledgling democratic regimes in Latin America; inefficient political cycles of public spending are common in many countries, as is repugnance at correcting government deficits through tax increases; for twelve years (1965–76) Mexican governments were unwilling to devalue the peso even though it was clearly overvalued, because its stability seemed to be one of the pillars of the existing social pact.

In sum, the conventional description of the way in which economic policy is formulated and implemented oversimplifies – particularly in the Third World – an extremely complex process of reciprocal accommodation between politics and economics. Axiological problems that are unsolvable in theory can only be resolved pragmatically through the use of democratic decision making. Thus, governments are frequently unable to pursue a stable set of economic objectives and stipulate their trade-offs with political goals. Even so, economics provides criteria that are indispensable to optimize resource use and explore the complex network of interactions found in productive systems. There is little hope, however, of making economic rationality the ultimate arbiter of political and societal policies.

THE IDEOLOGICAL DEBATE

The loss of faith in positivist rationalism and economic volunteerism has brought about a resurgence of trends that, in opposing statism, assign greater importance to market forces in economic matters.

Inflation and the persistent rise in the share of public expenditures in the total product, combined with the rebirth of competition and interdependence on an international scale, have provoked an ideological backlash that is causing the downfall of the Keynesian paradigm. There is a consensus to limit governmental intervention in the economy and to halt the expansion of the welfare state. There has also been an erosion of the scientific legitimacy of economics that reinforces its limitations in making successful predictions. In the 1980s economic freedom has tended to be more highly valued than social equality, and price stability more than growth.

These new economic models have caused consternation in the Third World. Indeed, the assertion that economic policies can deliberately bridge the development gap is now in dispute; it is said they are incapable of reducing the 'natural rate of unemployment' or of shoring up the process of democratization. On the other hand, market imperfections and renewed protectionism call into question the possibility of catching up simply by inaugurating a new phase of commercial liberalization. In Mexico, and Latin America as well, politicians know that the legitimacy of their governments hinges on their capacity to improve the population's standard of living. Yet the imperative of economic adjustment keeps forcing the postponement of the promise of growth to facilitate price stabilization and the dismantling of protectionism. The political costs are high.

This trend towards the separation of economic policy from popular aspirations substituted social and democratic goals with economic growth first, and with price stability later. Faced with crises in their balance of payments, several countries have had to accept the elevation of policy instruments such as credit, public expenditure levels, or the exchange-rate parity to the status of goals after having had to resort to the International Monetary Fund (Spraos, 1986). This process of degradation of social objectives contrasts vividly with the manifest decision of the people to accept economic sacrifices to achieve political modernization, as demonstrated by the widespread support for the current restoration of democratic regimes in several Latin American countries.

Changing the development model while simultaneously stabilizing the economy constitutes a task that must no longer be postponed. Nevertheless, to persist in the use of traditional recessive measures could be counterproductive. If this route is not feasible, an alternative option is to merge political with economic solutions by organizing cooperative reconstruction efforts based on social consensus. Instead of imposing solutions, agreements on incomes policy schemes can be reached to combat inflation without dampening the rate of growth. In the same way it would be possible to redefine priorities and the limits of state participation in the economy, creating a new, acceptable distribution of income that would assign the burdens of economic adjustment with greater equity.[3] The fundamental challenge of the 1990s remains to grow while transforming the economic structure and recovering stability. Failure to satisfy these objectives would, in the long run, impose excessive burdens on the modernization of the political system.

Whether orthodox or unorthodox solutions are subscribed to, it should be recognized that economists, as advisers to Third World governments, are in a serious bind. They must take into account the long-term trajectory of the economy while recognizing political overlapping and the value judgements implicit in their recommendations. They must acknowledge the influence of the prevailing economic models, often developed in other countries, and labor without clear specifications regarding the trade-offs between social goals. Yet economic criteria – though not the only guide in decision making – constitute an indispensable ingredient in the formulation of government strategies.

Thus, apart from their narrowly defined professional work, economists must also assume an unequivocal political role in order to be effective as active participants in the design of government policies: that of persuading the authorities of the validity of economic concepts, taking into account the interests at play, the institutional organization of the country and the presence of problems beyond the scope of their specialty.

THE INSTITUTIONAL STRUCTURE OF ECONOMIC ADVISING IN MEXICO

After the Revolution, the administrative structure of the Mexican government was relatively simple. Most economists worked at the Secretariat of the Treasury whose main function was to collect taxes and distribute the revenues to three main spending agencies: the Secretariats of Education, Defense and Transportation. The only way to finance a budget deficit was with foreign borrowing, which limited the possibilities of macroeconomic mismanagement.

Economists started being influential during the great depression. Indeed, his outspoken opposition to the iron-clad rule of a balanced budget took Alberto J. Pani, a financial expert, to the Secretariat of the Treasury in 1932. The following year, the bylaws of the Bank of Mexico, which had been created in 1925, were amended to transform it in a modern central bank with the power to emit paper money; the active monetary policy that ensued greatly facilitated the process of recuperation. The Secretariat of the Economy was created that same year to oversee the government's participation in industry and commerce; in 1947 the National Patrimony Secretariat was formed to administer the nation's resources and the growing number of public enterprises: the railroads had been nationalized in 1937 and the oil industry in 1938, while the electricity and telephone systems would follow suit in 1963 and 1972; by 1982 the government managed over 1,000 para-state companies and entities.

In 1954 the Investment Commission was constituted as a direct dependency of the president, with virtually the sole purpose of studying, evaluating and determining priorities among public investment projects. In 1959 planning activities were concentrated in the recently created Secretariat of the Presidency but in 1977 the new Secretariat of Programming and the Budget would formally take them over and wrest budgetary matters away from the Secretariat of the Treasury. Finally, in 1983, the industrial promotion section of the then Secretariat of Patrimony and Industrial Promotion was merged into the Secretariat of Commerce to form the Secretariat of Commerce and Industrial Promotion; the remainder became the Secretariat of Energy, Mines and Parastate Industry.

Hence, while their names and exact responsibilities have changed over the 1933–83 period, there are now five main institutions that participate in shaping macroeconomic policy: the Secretariat of the Treasury (SHCP), the Secretariat of Programming and the Budget (SPP), the Secretariat of Commerce and Industrial Promotion (SECOFI), the Secretariat of Energy, Mines and Parastate Industry (SEMIP) and the Bank of Mexico.

Each entity is responsible for a different block of economic policymaking: revenues collection and debt management go to the Treasury, spending to Programming and Budget, monetary policy (including interest and exchange-rate policy) to the central bank, commercial and industrial policy to Commerce and the management of para-state industry (including investment and subsidization of production through pricing of state produced goods) to SEMIP.

While this organization may seem to reflect an optimal division of labor, in fact the relationships among the five have been far from harmonious. There have been several attempts to alleviate the tensions between the major players through a number of bureaucratic coordination mechanisms; the first attempt was the creation, in 1962, of the Intersecretariat Commission, charged with the preparation of short- and long-term plans for economic and social development; the Spending and Finance Commission was established in 1968; and the president's Council of Economic Advisers in 1985 to advise the president on five matters:

1. The establishment of long-term economic goals.
2. The instrumentation of economic policies to attain those long-term goals.
3. The analysis of the domestic economy and the behavior of the main economic variables.
4. Economic events in other countries and their impact on the Mexican economy.
5. To serve as liaison to economic advising bodies of other countries.

The Council is composed of three economists named by the president, one of whom acts as the chairman; it has a technical staff of fifteen professional economists who work in different areas: fiscal affairs, foreign trade, monetary matters, etc. Having been in existence for less than three years, its main role has been advisory, mostly reviewing and sometimes coordinating policy proposals emanating from different secretariats. Its main role so far has been in macroeconomic management, reflecting current economic events as much as its members' expertise.

Four cabinets, in agricultural affairs, economics, foreign trade and health, were created in 1983 to coordinate the work of different agencies in those areas. They are formally part of the Secretariat of the Presidency and their technical departments serve as communication channels to share both statistical information and position papers. They are chaired by the president himself and are the fora in which alternative policies are discussed and major options chosen. It is often the case, however, that participants have a unified position which is simply ratified.

The frequency with which each cabinet is convoked depends on the importance of the problem in hand: the Economic Cabinet, for example, met thirty-three times during the June 1985–June 1986 period, or once every eleven days. Sessions can be confrontational, however, and may result in the resignation of one (or more) of the participants. Since 1976 the president in turn has had to accept the resignation of three secretaries of the SHCP, three secretaries of the SPP and two directors of the Bank of Mexico with different degrees of regret.

All those coordinating instances had similar objectives but, up to now, full unity and consensus on the design and implementation of economic policy has not been achieved; since none of those bodies has disappeared, one can surmise that coordination entails more than simply adding institutional layers.

For example, the administration of the country's 500 para-state companies and entities is cumbersome when, as in present times, it is essential to alter the course of the development process. The management of public entities occurs through often-duplicated administrative mechanisms and controls that have operated on an *ex-post* basis and almost exclusively at the microeconomic level (Ibarra, 1976). Indeed, SEMIP's overall supervision is reproduced, on a sectoral basis, by other secretariats and by development banks, while budget allocations are determined in conjunction with the SPP and the SHCP. The negotiations and tensions between the dependencies that push to increase spending and those that want it to comply with financial restrictions or try to alter the criteria for the assignment of resources, reproduce themselves on another scale. Hence investment projects are not selected according to a rigorous economic process; the inertial forces of expansion by public enterprises prevail instead. Entities tend to increase their productive capacity to the detriment of projects aimed at innovation and change that do not enjoy the same institutional protection. The emergence of such resistances to alter significantly investment structures can only be overcome by disproportionately raising public spending.

The lobbying that occurs in Anglo-Saxon countries is not absent in Mexico; it simply assumes a different form. Convincing evidence of this phenomenon is provided by the development – almost without parallel in Latin America – of nationwide political mediation organizations with a broad-based membership, 'encompassing organizations' to use Olson's term, in both labor and business. The Labor Congress (CT) and the Workers' Confederation of Mexico (CTM), as well as the Business Coordinating Committee (CCE) and the organs that group businessmen by sector – CONCAMIN (Confederation of Industry) and CANACINTRA (Confederation of Small Business) – have created centers for economic research and have formed full-time panels of professionals and politicians dedicated to the extensive negotiation of economic regulations with government authorities.

Power in Mexico, at least as it influences economic policymaking, is not as monolithic or as biased as some academic studies and radical right- (or left-) wing critics would have it. There is significant and intense participation by interest groups, and there are also distinct divisions of varying magnitude, among the assorted public administration dependencies, between the states and the federal government, between the legislative and executive powers, and between the Revolutionary Institutional Party (PRI) and the state and federal governments.[4]

Real government power lies more in its capacity to mold the economic agenda, to recover and make acceptable the rhythm of change and the demands of the various social groups, than in imposing policies that lean in one direction or another. On the rare occasions in the postwar period that these political equilibrium imperatives were violated, the government has had to face the simultaneous risks of economic polarization and erosion of its political legitimacy. Hence, when faced with domestic and external constraints, the key question for the authorities becomes whether to preserve this delicate political balance or to accept the turmoil associated with the reconstruction of fundamental political understanding along new grounds.

THE CHANGING POLICY ENVIRONMENT

In Mexico, as in most parts of the western hemisphere, global economic management is a recent phenomenon whose origins can be traced to the confluence of several historical currents that converged in the 1950s to produce an impact that would be felt years later.

Since the 1920s, agrarian reform, investment basic infrastructure, the institution of social services, the reconstruction of the banking system, urbanization and industrial development had comprised the core of government activity whose bias was clearly developmentalist. At first, the economic aspirations of the Revolution dominated and determined the fundamental economic policy tasks, whose key objectives were rooted in a long-term vision in which the notion of macroeconomic equilibrium was either absent or occupied second place.

The influence of the doctrine of 'American progressivism' was also important: by upholding the dichotomy between politics and pragmatism, these ideas optimistically supported the possibility of social engineering. Keynesian thought, which emphasized the inadequacy of market mechanisms to ensure full employment and highlighted the possibility of manipulating aggregate demand, opened the door to the integration of development models into new macroeconomic formulas. Thus, Third World aspirations of growth resonated with the paradigm of full employment in developed economies.

The concept of planning, originally born of the experience of the socialist economies, acquired new vigor with the experimental programs of World War II and the methodologies actively espoused by the Economic Commission for Latin America (ECLA), the International Bank for Reconstruction and Development (IBRD), and the Organization of American States (OAS). Indeed, in the early 1960s, the Alliance for Progress promoted planning to achieve orderly development, and established mechanisms to provide for the periodic review of economic and social development in Latin America (Pan American Union, 1962).

Such diverse historical currents have several points of convergence: an optimistic view of the viability of deliberately attempting to close the development gap; a belief in the wisdom of combining market mechanisms with state intervention to guarantee sustained economic growth; and an alignment between the economic paradigms of the industrialized nations and the ideological models prevailing in less developed countries.

In Mexico, the concepts of macroeconomic administration and development planning emerged at the same time and occasionally reinforced one another, though they also created tensions in domestic economic policy management. In any case, the prevailing planning doctrine is not in opposition to the market economy; on the contrary, it maintains that the programming of public action complements static market information with signals to orient the action of the state. Hence, it sets priorities within the public sector and coordinates its programs with those of the private sector.

Methodological and administrative efforts to impose order on the economy and state activities had modest beginnings. In fact, in the 1950s, short-term macroeconomic management and the formulation of investment plans were not formally coordinated. This was neither an administratively nor politically happy solution since it perpetuated bureaucratic conflicts that have survived well into the 1980s.

The Secretariat of the Presidency attempted to solve long-term development problems in the old developmentalist tradition of the Revolution by giving public expenditure a key role. For its part, the Secretariat of the Treasury and the Bank of Mexico were concerned with price stability and equilibrium in the balance of payments. This dichotomy of functions gave rise to a divergence of economic viewpoints that reinforced the political fact that each was answerable to a different constituency. The Secretariat of the Presidency had to attend to the demands of state governments, para-state companies and other public entities always short of resources and whose portfolios were bursting with growth projects. The Secretariat of the Treasury, on the other hand, faced the taxpayers' resistance to finance a swelling budget. The argument that high taxes weaken the incentives to save and invest which are indispensable for sustained growth and stability (Ortiz Mena, 1969) had little empirical underpinnings but was hard to contradict since it was thought to be a well-established proposition in the case of developed countries. In a similar vein, the Bank of Mexico questioned the expansion of public expenditure because of the drain on foreign exchange with which they seemed to be associated and the subsequent risk of a devaluation.[5]

The confrontation between these two public-policy viewpoints recycled numerous arguments that were being hotly debated among academic economists. The lack of consensus on goals and the best means to achieve them divided professionals into at least two clearly differentiated camps: 'structuralists' who underlined the importance of accompanying development with distributional equity and with a long-term modernization of socioeconomic structures; and 'monetarists' who stressed growth with price stability as a precondition for a fairer distribution. The former voiced little confidence in market mechanisms, emphasizing state intervention both in economic management and direct production (Flores de la Peña and Ferrer, 1951;

Noyola, 1956; CEPAL, 1957; Carmona, 1963; Mújica, 1963; Kaldor, 1964), while the latter had greater confidence in the market and conditioned public spending and economic expansion on the supply of voluntary savings. Hence, while they did not reject state intervention out of hand, they emphasized the need to cover public-sector deficits with external funds or internal credit rationing through the legal framework (Navarrete, 1957; Siegel, 1957; Gomez, 1964; Solis and Brothers 1967; Ortiz Mena, 1969).

In the early 1960s, the Intersecretarial Commission prepared the Plan for Immediate Action, 1962–4, which has come to be recognized as the first modern attempt to create a coherent framework for short-term economic policy and represented the culmination of efforts to merge organically development planning with global economic management (see OAS, 1963). Henceforth, national, sectorial and regional plans would have, above all, the political-ceremonial function of revealing the government's intentions with respect to the direction in which the country's economy should be moving. In contrast, the development and daily application of policy would be accomplished separately, employing conventional methods of macroeconomic analysis.

Several factors – the least of which were the economists' powers of persuasion – inclined the debate in favor of short-term methods of economic management. In the first place, there were the well-known technical, administrative, informational, consensual and monitoring difficulties that are generally the downfall of attempts to incorporate planning methods into developing economies. Even more important was the fact that the economic transformation programs of the Mexican Revolution had ran out of political steam by the 1960s.[6]

At the same time, politicians began to be dislodged from higher public administrative posts by university graduates with a different outlook – not necessarily better but certainly more modern with respect to national problems. Revolutionary radicalism gave way to moderate ideological concepts. Among economists, there was a proliferation of models developed in the exterior or in new universities throughout the country that followed the Anglo-Saxon tradition, and slowly acquired pre-eminence among the middle and upper echelons of public administration (Solis, 1971, pp. 63–4). Finally, the increasing complexity of the productive system and its dependency on a dense network of institutions with their own dynamic and objectives made agreements on long-term national economic goals less obvious and more controversial.

Nevertheless, the 1960s typify a stage of fluid growth, in which a basic consensus on the national development strategy prevailed. Economic growth was high and inflation low; the international economic boom compensated to some degree for the disincentives to export associated with an import-substitution model; public-sector and balance-of-payments deficits were easily financed, either through domestic savings or the increased supply of external credit and capital; some in the vanguard began to call attention to the fact that exports were lagging, but the need to intensify the import-substitution process toward capital goods was generally acknowledged (Izquierdo, 1964; Balassa, 1970; and Ortiz Mena, 1969). With a few exceptions, unions adopted a policy of collaboration through implicit pacts where, in exchange for the systematic increase in employment opportunities in the modern sector, they agreed to hold wage demands to levels compatible with the growth in productivity and an intensive capital-formation process. Abundant investment opportunities opened up because of the import-substitution process and they were exploited by both Mexican entrepreneurs and a growing number of transnational consortia.

On the ideological plane, the polemic between 'structuralists' and 'monetarists' moved away from the public-administration arena and the political fora to find a haven in academics. Nevertheless, tensions between the government dependencies that were prone to spend and those that leaned toward moderate fiscal policies persisted and transformed themselves into a bureaucratic struggle. The necessity of promoting economic development was unanimously accepted, and the debate centered around two issues: first, the need to redistribute forcefully income on equity grounds and as a way to widen the internal market, with the danger that the supply of saving would dry up and the incentives to invest disappear; second, the wisdom of furthering external dependence by decreasing commercial protection, with the danger that domestic producers would become increasingly inefficient, thereby undermining the very foundations of growth (Aguilar, 1969; Cordera and Orive, 1970; Wionczek, 1970).

In sum, during the 1960s, Mexico adopted a developmentalist ideology consonant with the Keynesian paradigm prevalent in the industrialized world. The old reformist traditions of the Mexican Revolution slowly withered away when economic growth became the key objective of state action, instead of serving as the means to achieve goals of a higher order, as in times past. The practical advantages of this ideological development were many, for they permitted Mexican society to concentrate its energies on economic problems, thereby providing more for every social group and improving the population's standard of living. Calls for a change in the economic or political system were rare and had a minimal following. The fine-tuning of short-term economic policy held sway in the minds of policymakers. The issue of orienting development – and in particular investment – was largely left to the inertia of public and private institutions and to the forces of market stimuli.

The idyllic progress of the 1960s was abruptly reversed in the next decade. Growth was attained, but amidst increasing economic disequilibrium and political unrest. To the social turmoil of 1968 were soon added the effects of the obsolescence of the development model, evidenced in the loss of impetus in the import-substitution process, the stagnation of agricultural production, and the fiscal and balance-of-payments maladjustments that characterized the period 1970–6. There was a clear need to steer economic policy to correct the foreign trade and public deficit structural disequilibria in the short term, and to promote the reconstruction of the export sector, raise productive efficiency and provide the impetus for a new industrialization policy in the longer term.

Despite changes in the international monetary system, the government, under the advice of some economists, stubbornly persisted in maintaining the dollar parity, permitting the overvaluation of the currency and a growing misalignment of domestic and international prices. Historical and political factors were too strong in the early 1970s to make the devaluation of the peso acceptable as the basis for a new development strategy. Faced with social unrest, the government undertook an active policy of increasing wages and subsidies while controlling consumer goods prices. This had the double impact of increasing public expenditure and generating tensions with the manufacturing sector. The attempt to introduce fiscal reform, long deferred by the resistence of private-interest groups, was a failure. As a result the public deficit tripled as a percentage of the product, while prices increased and the external debt quadrupled from 1970 to 1976 (Solis, 1981). After more than a decade of stability and growth, the Mexican economy had entered a new phase of high and rapidly rising inflation, and greater fluctuations in the annual growth rate of production.

Other aspects of the economic policymaking process also changed. Up to 1970 there had been a neat division of labor and personnel between political and economic management. While the latter remained subordinate to the former, it was entrusted to groups of technicians who drew up the basic economic policy options for consideration by the executive powers and later, if need be, by the legislative chambers. From 1970 on, a dual phenomenom occurred: numerous economists and technicians became politicians, and in the face of the rising tensions that accompanied the failure of the development model and the broadening of state functions, heads of state themselves began to participate actively in designing basic economic policy.

A new fissure opened up among economists. On the one side were those who believed that the Mexican economy could recover its stability without jeopardizing growth by restoring confidence among business groups and making a few gradual adjustments in the import substitution process. At the opposite extreme were those who maintained that the old development path had come to an end and that economic policy strategies had to be radically modified to create new dynamic poles of growth based mainly on exports and an improvement in the standards of productive efficiency (Balassa, 1970; Ibarra, 1970).

Moreover, weakened economic stability and its sociopolitical consequence greatly intensified the process of negotiation of the economic strategy to be adopted between the government on the one hand and labor and business on the other. The success or failure of these exercises in social consensus exerted a powerful influence on the outcome of economic policy, as demonstrated by the contraction of private investment during the Echeverria administration and its expansion when President Lopez Portillo sponsored the Alliance for Production.

To put it in another way, when economic development was society's main goal, it became the relevant criterion to judge the legitimacy of public action. This simplified the range of political problems that had to be dealt with, but inexorably led to the politicization of economic strategy design and application. Furthermore, in the Mexican system, where presidential power is very strong, the only counterweights to its political power are economically independent businessmen and a well-organized and united working class, whose support is essential to the alliance that forms the basis of the PRI's strength. Through formal and informal contacts and negotiations, these two groups influence the economic decision-making process before legislative approval or direct policy implementation. Even beyond this stage, questions are commonly left open to the negotiation of amendments or measures to compensate groups adversely affected.

Thus, goal selection, the identification of alternatives, and the approval and implementation of economic policies are not distinct stages of a sequential process, where politicians, technicians, legislators and administrators intervene in that order. Rather, at all stages, political interaction takes place implying changes, reformulations and additions.

The government has a clear political need to preserve the equilibrium between the demands of the business sector, upon which depends the legitimacy associated with sustained economic growth, and those of workers, which provides the government with popular legitimacy. Such constraints explain why considerable wage hikes were decreed immediately after the traumatic devaluations of 1976 and 1982, even at the risk of exacerbating inflationary pressures and provoking new exchange-rate instability.

Despite the political and economic trauma that it caused after two decades of exchange-rate stability, the devaluation of 1976 started to correct the anti-export bias of traditional economic policy, although it also kept inflationary pressures alive. In 1977, an adjustment program aimed at dampening price increases and curbing the vertical rise of the public-sector deficit went into effect.[7] Initial results were encouraging: the economy grew, powered by a recovery of private investment and a strong increase in consumer spending fueled by salary adjustments in late 1976.

The petroleum boom temporarily alleviated the strangulation of the external sector and offered an alternative to the costs of moving from a strategy of import substitution to another based on greater competitiveness in international markets. The government thus opted for a policy that basically pursued higher levels of growth and employment, while relegating stability and nontraditional export promotion to second place.

The transfer of responsibility for budgetary matters from the Secretariat of the Treasury to the Secretariat of Programming and the Budget in 1977 tilted the bureaucratic balance in favor of the dependencies inclined toward spending, while intensifying disagreements by placing two economic policy-making centers with opposing, or at least differing, views in direct competition. Public expenditure rose from 33 per cent of GDP in 1976 to 52 per cent in 1984.

In its attempt to accelerate growth and increase employment, Mexico used its oil income and resorted to external credit, which ended up financing capital flight. Major changes on the supply side and in institutional organization were also implemented. Long-deferred tax and financial reforms were undertaken, and considerable investments in the country's industrial plant were made – particularly in petroleum and petrochemicals in the public sector and capital goods production in the private sector. Finally, a new effort to promote the modernization of the *campesino* economy was begun (NAFINSA-ONUDI, 1977; Sistema Alimentario Mexicano, 1980). Nevertheless, the debate over the need to modify the old pattern of development had yet to be resolved and remained in an unstable deadlock. Instead of assisting in the reconstruction of the export sector, external openness was used as an expedient to moderate inflationary pressures.

The creation of excessive effective demand partially frustrated structural change. The overvaluation of the exchange rate hampered the growth of non-oil exports and caused import coefficients to double between 1978 and 1981, aggravating balance of payments misalignments and the growth of the external debt. Public spending began to exceed income generation, causing a dramatic growth of the public deficit when oil prices began to fall. Thus, for a time, economic policy objectives were achieved, but at the cost of creating enormous domestic financial imbalances and increasing external vulnerability. When the world economy went into a recession in 1981–2, the resistance of the Mexican economy was extremely low, so it was unable to offset the simultaneous drop in export demand, increase in international interest rates and interruption in the flows of external financing.

The crisis of the 1980s does not simply consist of the decline in traditional export and the problem of the external debt. It is also an expression of cumulative lags in the Mexican economy, of the obsolescence of the import-substitution model, and of deepening social divisions. In the short term, it is essential to devote major efforts, as has been done, toward stabilizing prices and the balance of payments. In the longer term, the reconstruction of external economic relations, the modernization and integration of the productive apparatus, and the geographic decentralization of economic activity have been given high priority. In a political sense, the 1982 nationalization of the banking system exceeded the limits of the social consensus reached between the state and the economically relevant segments of the polity; similarly, the fact that the burden of the adjustment has had to fall primarily on salaried employees and workers has strained the political fabric of the country.

Without a doubt, economic policy, at the end of the 1980s, faces an extremely complex task bound by unprecedented restrictions. Hence, efforts have centered on fighting inflation and promoting structural changes in the redesign of the public sector and in external openness. There has also been a successful attempt to protect the private financial sector and the country's industrial plant through fiscal stimuli and the creation of a mechanism to cover the exchange-rate risks involving private foreign debt.

Progress has been mixed and action has not been taken in every field. Despite the emphasis on combating inflation and the acute economic recessions of 1983 and 1986, price increases have tended to accelerate. While the public-sector deficit has been considerably smaller than its pre-1982 level for several years, it is still too high. The foreign-exchange market has achieved stability through the undervaluation of the peso, the renegotiation of the external debt and the turnaround in traditional exports. The greater expectations derived from this latter fact tend to incline the debate towards those who favor an open economy and against those who favor protectionism. The process of capital formation – especially in the public sector – has been considerably weakened, as indicated by the nine-point drop in the investment coefficient between 1981 and 1986. Open unemployment in the cities has not exceeded the 7 per cent range in a paradoxically downward trend since 1983. In contrast, partial real-wage indicators show a deterioration of no less than 20 per cent during the 1981–6 period. It is not unlikely, therefore, that the distribution of the burdens of adjustment may create social divisions or require the reformulation of the prevailing consensus. The moment when the Mexican economy can begin another period of sustained development still appears to be far off.

ECONOMIC ADVICE AND MEXICO'S ECONOMIC PERFORMANCE

During the 1950s and 1960s, the Mexican economy grew at an average of 6 per cent annually, implying an almost 3 per cent increase in per capita income. It seems difficult to recall that today's debt-ridden economy grew so miraculously for twenty years. Economists in Mexico can hardly claim this performance is wholly attributable to their advice; society as a whole was responsible because it mobilized its energies behind an economic model that represented a way to give a programmatic content to the aspirations of the majority, as they had been forged during the Mexican Revolution of 1910. Hindsight suggests that the adoption of an import-substitution strategy was appropriate. Mexican economists collaborated with other Latin Americans in the creation of an integrated framework of analysis, so its features formed a consistent whole. These economists also became most outspoken defenders of that framework, forging an ideological and rhetorical understanding that facilitated the politician's task of arriving at a social consensus.

After World War II, significant changes in international trading patterns occurred, as developed countries turned their attention to reconstruction. Since exports could not be expected to provide the aggregate demand stimulus that they had during the 1940s, the development of an internal market became the overriding concern of many economists throughout Latin America. For this internal market to develop, however, several conditions had to be met. On the demand side, per capita income had to grow to guarantee sufficient effective demand. Thus, while real minimum wages grew only marginally during the 1950s and 1960s, the more than doubling of employment and the increase in per capita real income resulted in a sizeable increase in the wage fund that was spent on consumer goods.

On the supply side, an infrastructure had to be built and nascent industries had to be protected. As in many of the presently developed countries a century before, the creation of an infrastructure was not entrusted to market forces for three reasons: the difficulty of assuring property rights on the positive externalities it strives to create; the size of the investments that were required; and the difficulties private firms encountered to access sufficient financial resources. Hence the state invested heavily in transportation, communications, agriculture and industry, building roads, airports, hydraulic systems, and an industrial structure to facilitate import substitution and eliminate bottlenecks. This basic capital formation allowed gas and oil production to grow at an average annual rate of 6 per cent during the period, while the network of paved road's grew 8 per cent, irrigated land 9 per cent and electrical power capacity 10 per cent.

Private producers were shielded from foreign competitors by tariff protection on final goods (often higher than 100 per cent) but there were few restrictions on imports of raw materials and machinery to offer investors opportunities for profit on the generation of value added. Generous tax concessions on investment and preferential credit terms under the watchful eye of Nacional Financiera – the state investment bank – reinforced the incentives to create new firms. Finally, the devaluations of 1949 and 1954 undervalued the peso, thereby reinforcing effective protection. This last devaluation caused inflation to grow at 14 per cent in 1955 but became the harbinger of the 'Desarollo Estabilizador', a fifteen-year period during which growth was accompanied by relative price stability.

The praises of this development strategy need not be sung in detail to demonstrate that its basic elements confirmed a pattern of growth that reflected a social consensus whose political and administrative foundations had been built during the previous decades. Economists were certainly instrumental in the definition of that strategy, as well as in its implementation, but their clearest technical contribution may have been the design of the 1954 stabilization package and the decision to finance the public deficit with foreign debt, thus decreasing the need to levy an inflationary tax. This 'innovation' allowed the Mexican financial market to be more integrated into world centers than in the case of other Latin American countries, thus paving the way for the debt explosion of the 1973–83 decade.

In the best orthodox tradition, the 1954 stabilization program entailed a devaluation of the peso, a tightening up of monetary aggregates (M_2 decreased in nominal terms during the first part of the year) and a decrease in real government spending. As a result, imports fell, exports and government revenues grew, and surpluses appeared in both the balance of trade and government accounts. The price stability that ensued (inflation would hover around 3 per cent until the late 1960s) can be attributed both to conservative monetary and fiscal policies, and the numerous restrictions on the use of credit that were imposed afterwards.

The import-substitution growth model would not be without costs, however. Mainstream Mexican economists, both inside and outside the government, would not be the first to recognize the deleterious hidden effects of its disequilibria; an acknowledgement of the fact that the development strategy had to be altered did not occur until much later. The 1970s would end up being a decade of ungraceful change.

The foundations of social consensus were being eroded by the lack of any real progress in decreasing inequality and by a political structure that would not easily accommodate dissent. State finances were increasingly fragile (the public deficit, which had represented 2.5 per cent of gross domestic product from 1956 to 1972, grew to 8.0 per cent from 1973 to 1976 and 10.2 from 1977 to 1981), inflation was on the rise (16.7 per cent on average from 1973 to 1976 and 23.8 per cent in the next five years) and the balance of payments weakened (the current account deficit amounted to 2.5 of GDP during the 1956–72 period, 4.1 per cent from 1973 to 1976 and 3.4 per cent during the oil boom years of 1977–81, while the external debt service rose from 19.6 per cent of exports to 25.4 per cent and 44.5 per cent in the latter period).

It took a long time for Mexican economists to recognize that there was a problem, and even longer (if at all) to agree on a diagnosis. The number of unwise policy recommendations made during this confusing period can hardly be kept track of. Let us mention three:

1. Since unemployment and underemployment were widespread, it was thought that aggregate demand could be safely stimulated, leading to higher investment and growth with little or no inflation, since factors of production were available. This error was made during the early 1970s and then again about a decade later, under the advice of some economists whose graduate work had been done at Cambridge, England.
2. Inflation can be controlled by regulating prices and subsidizing production, if need be. This temptation still holds a powerful fascination over politicians.
3. Current-account deficits can be fought by limiting the value of 'non-

essential' imports with licenses; the ensuing anti-export bias is minor and easily counterbalanced by granting subsidies to specific industries.

The import-substitution model had created a new political clientele who insisted that it was the government's responsibility to lead the country back to the good old days when growth occurred without inflation. It was clear that market forces had led the country astray and it was the task of 'progressive economists' to use government policy to satisfy social demands. The oil revenues of the late 1970s, and the flow of fresh foreign credit that accompanied them, provided the funds for the implementation of such a program: massive public investment to dissolve bottlenecks, subsidies for energy, water and basic raw materials to control inflation, and a fixed exchange rate to reinforce deflationary tendencies. A program that shields the productive sector from international competition, while relying on external financial resources, is unlikely to be stable unless it provides the economy with a cushion to isolate it from external fluctuations; the Mexican oil boom was too short for that to happen. The vulnerability of the economy increased and the collapse of the oil market placed severe burdens on the weaker sectors of society which are directly traceable to these misjudged recommendations.

The oil shock of 1986, which entailed a loss of oil export revenues amounting to 6.7 per cent of the gross domestic product, provides another case study. If the shock were expected to be temporary, any model of intertemporal maximization of consumption would recommend additional external borrowing (or a drawdown in international reserves) to ease the drop in income. Nevertheless, the unwillingness of the international financial establishment to provide such funds voluntarily obliged Mexico to treat it as more permanent than it turned out to be. Since multilateral agencies (the IMF, the World Bank, and the BIS – Bank for International Settlements) did not move quickly, and the Mexican government would not resort to 'forced' borrowing in the form of unilateral actions for political reasons, a consistent economic strategy of containment had to be implemented to minimize the inflationary and recessionary impact of the collapse of oil prices.

The decrease in domestic absorption that had to occur could trigger a distributive battle in which each of the main economic factors would endeavor to transfer the cost of the crisis to another. The costs of such a process could be minimized if expenditure switching towards non-tradeables occurred (thereby freeing resources that could then be used to service the debt) and if the government was able to decrease real spending and/or find substitutes for the revenue it was losing. If, on the contrary, the shock had to be wholly accommodated through a decrease in private expenditure and the government had to resort to the inflationary tax to cover the additional deficit, the economy would be thrown into a dangerous adjustment path.

To shift expenditure towards non-tradeable goods and stimulate the production of tradeables, the devaluation of the peso was accelerated to achieve a significantly lower real exchange rate, while the liberalization process proceeded in earnest. Real government spending (net of interest payments which are endogenous to the inflation rate via nominal interest rates) decreased considerably, and revenues were increased by raising the real price of the goods and services produced by state enterprises. Domestic credit was tightened and private users crowded out by allowing real interest rates to rise. While this placed an extra burden on government finances because the internal debt had to be serviced at this higher rate, the ensuing credit shortage helped contain inflationary pressures and provided an incentive for repatriating some of the funds that had once been deposited in foreign banks.

This program could have been taken out of a textbook on modern open macroeconomic policy management, and it was very effective:

1. Gross domestic product fell by only one-half the amount of the shock.
2. Inflation was only 25 per cent higher than during the previous year.
3. Non-oil exports surged forward, reaching one billion dollars a month by the end of the year.
4. Imports and nominal tariff protection decreased, and international reserves, which had fallen during the first half of the year to partially accommodate the shock, grew in the second half of the year.
5. Contrary to conventional wisdom, private capital *did return* before the economy was totally stabilized, and, more than a year after it commenced, the flow has not been reversed.[8]

This package was put together by the government's economic team under heavy criticism from most quarters. Hindsight suggests that the fall in consumption went too far and that more international reserves should have been used to cushion the blow. As is often the case, however, it is easier to predict the course of events once they have occurred; in March of 1986 it was difficult to forecast with reasonable confidence the average value of oil revenues during that year and the recalcitrance of American banks substantially increased the costs of overconfidence.

From a short-term perspective, since the underlying structural problems can only be solved with longer-term programs, the stabilization gains are attributable to the advice given by some economists who went against large sectors of public opinion. In particular, the more the adjustment process is forced to rely on a continuing fall of the peso to improve the trade balance, the larger the deterioration in the terms of trade, that is to say, in the living standards of the Mexican population. By the same token, the more the external competitive edge is forced to rely on falling wages, the larger the erosion in the government's legitimacy. For these reasons, Mexico should rely on more rapid investment growth, productivity improvement and technological change rather than on peso and wage depreciation to stimulate larger exports. Without proper initiatives to enhance competitiveness from the supply side, the improvement in the trade balance could only by chance lead to a realignment of exports in high value-added areas, critical to the future growth of the country. However, high value-added industries are usually capital (and knowledge) intensive, and therefore constitute ventures not easily undertaken during periods of acute recession and credit restrictions. It remains to be seen whether the structural change effort will be redirected and maintained long enough to achieve meaningful results.

CONCLUSIONS

Based on the Mexican experience, three main conclusions seem to be in order. First, claims as to the scientific nature of economists' recommendations are somewhat unwarranted. Second, divergent economic paradigms and also divergent economic circumstances between developed and developing nations create havoc in the task of advising Third World governments on economic matters. Even when policy prescriptions are appropriate for the particular conditions of a country in a given time period, they might hinder growth or other social goals in the long run. A case in point was the inward-oriented industrial policies of Mexico that even today obstruct trade adjustments. Policy advice is not only value laden, its validity is also historically bound. Lastly, if economists are to regain prestige as policy advisers, there is a clear need to integrate economic and political criteria.

On the other hand, a few changes in the government's structure may enhance the role of economists in policy decision making. First, the economic cabinet should be presided by someone other than the president. Present arrangements seem to favor the instrumentation of programs that combine logically different proposals; these hybrids synergetically amalgamate the defects of their ancestors while minimizing their merits. A change in the chairmanship of the cabinet would favor the adoption of consistent programs under the responsibility of a single public official. That person would have to try to achieve consensus on what policy measures should be introduced but would be responsible for its ultimate outcome and hence could always be at liberty to follow his conscience more than his colleagues' advice. Consensus has recently been elusive in non-critical situations: during the debt emergency of 1981–2, the earthquakes in 1985, and the collapse of oil prices in 1986, both the origin of the problems and the immediate courses of action were easy to determine. At other times, however, discussions on what is happening and what has to be done seem to interfere with proper decision making.

The disrepute that economics and economists have fallen into reflects, in part, the increasing isolation in which economic policy discussions and decision making are carried out. Favoring open arguments and agreement-building in an explicit way in which participating social and political actors become jointly responsible for the outcomes would enhance the role of economists by clarifying their contribution and thereby facilitating its correct appreciation. Mutually concerted policymaking is effective because the first part of its instrumentation (explaining the purpose of a policy and the characteristics of its instruments to concerned parties) is carried out at the negotiation table before it actually goes into effect. Historical experience in several developed countries indicates this is an appropriate way to select economic programs that seems to bypass some of the trade-offs that are usually taken as a given when making proposals on inflation, unemployment, growth or distribution equity.

Finally, regulations have accumulated in Mexico for several decades with little but timid efforts in the last few years, to adapt them to current conditions. The result are layers of rules and institutions that obscure economic causal relationships and mediate the adoption of efficient policies. A systematic evaluation of the government's regulatory structure, strengthening some of its parts (for example in bringing environmental protection to international standards) while revoking numerous others would enhance economic logic in decision making by unfettering it from inefficient and unwarranted constraints.

NOTES

1. This is the case, for example, of the unequal effects of combating inflation with monetarist prescriptions which reduce aggregate demand or using incomes policy as recommended by the Keynesian school.
2. A development bank will unfailingly fight to broaden investment, independently of the phase of the economic cycle. In Mexico, or France, if the aim is to ration total credit rapidly without raising interest rates, it would be necessary to employ the well-developed administrative and institutional mechanisms for the assignment of bank funds.
3. From 1981 to 1986, measured per capita income in Mexico has fallen by between 10 and 15 per cent, without a definitive assignment of the corresponding adjustment in income distribution. Up to now, workers, salaried employees and some specific economic activities have carried that burden: the non-tradeables sector has been particularly hit (construction, some services, etc.).
4. Dissent may be manifested openly and publicly or be resolved in closed antechambers, but this does not mean that there is no room for processes of political interaction.
5. It should be noted that in Mexico, for twenty-two years (1954–76), the invariability of the exchange rate constituted a political taboo upon which the respectability of government economic policy rested.
6. This occurred with irrigation policies to open new lands, agrarian reform, electrification, highway construction and even import-substitution industrialization.
7. The deficit fell from 8 per cent of GDP in 1975–6 to an aveage of 5.5 per cent between 1977 and 1980.
8. See, for example, Dornbush (1987): 'Capital will wait until problems have been solved; it won't be part of the solution and even less serve as a bridge head.'

BIBLIOGRAPHY

Aguilar, A. M., *México: Riqueza y Miseria* (Mexico: Editorial Nuestro Tiempo, 1969).

Balassa, B., 'La política comercial de México: Análisis y proposiciones', *Revista Comercio Exterior*, vol. 20, no. 10 (October 1970, Mexico).

Berlin, I., *Four Essays on Liberty* (Oxford: Oxford University Press, 1969).

Carmona, F., 'Dependencia y subdesarrollo económico', *Investigación Económica*, vol. 23, no. 96 (Mexico, 1963).

CEPAL, *External Disequilibrium in the Economic Development of Latin America, the Case of Mexico* (New York: United Nations Economic and Social Council, 1957).

Cordera, R. and Orive, A., *México: Industrialización Subordinada* (Mexico: Taller de Asesoría Socio Económica, 1970).

Dornbush, R., 'The debt problem and some solutions', *Estudios Económicos de El Colegio de México*, vol. 2, no. 2 (1987).

Flores de la Peña, H., and Ferrer, A., 'Salarios reales y desarrollo económico', *El Trimestre Económico*, vol. 17, no. 72 (Mexico, 1951).

Gómez, R., 'Estabilidad y desarrollo: el caso de México', *Revista de Comercio Exterior*, vol. 14, no. 11 (November 1964, Mexico).

Ibarra, D., 'Mercados, desarrollo y política económica: perspectivas de la economía de México', in *El Perfil de México en 1980* (Mexico: Siglo XXI Ed., 1970).

Ibarra, D., 'Reflexiones sobre la empresa pública en México', *Foro Internacional*, vol. 17, no. 2 (Mexico, 1976).

Ibarra, D., 'Poilítica y economía en América Latina: El trasfondo de los programas heterodoxos de estabilización', in José Alberro y David Ibarra (eds), *Programas Heterodoxos de Estabilización*, Número Extraordinario de *Estudios Económicos de El Colegio de México* (Mexico, 1987).

Izquierdo, R., 'El proteccionismo en México', in R. Vernon (ed.), *Public Policy and Private Enterprise in Mexico* (Cambridge, MA: Harvard University Press, 1964).

Kaldor, N., 'Las reformas al sistema fiscal en México', *Revista Comercio Exterior*, vol. 14 no. 4 (April 1964, Mexico).

Lindblom, C. E., *Politics and Markets* (New York: Basic Books, 1977).

Mújica, E., 'Participación del sector público en el desarrollo económico de México', *Actividad Económica en Latinoamérica* (October 1963, Mexico).

NAFINSA-ONUDI', *México: Una Estrategia Para Desarrollar la Industria de Bienes de Capital* (Mexico, 1977).

NAFINSA-ONUDI, *México: Los Bienes de Capital en la Situación Económica Presente* (Mexico, 1985).

Navarrete, A., 'El sector público en el desarrollo económico de México', *Investigación Económica*, vol. 25, no. 100 (Mexico, 1957).

Nelson, R. H., 'The economics profession and the making of public policy', *Journal of Economic Literature*, vol. 25, no. 1 (March 1987).

Noyola, J., 'El desarrollo económico y la inflación en México y otros países latinoamericanos', *Investigación Económica*, vol. 16, no. 4 (Mexico, 1956).

Olson, M., *The Logic of Collective Action* (Cambridge, MA: Harvard University Press, 1965).

Organización de Estados Americanos (OAS), *Evaluación del Plan de Acción Inmediata*, Committee of 9 (Washington, DC, 1963).

Ortiz Mena, A., 'Economic development and stabilization', Paper presented on the occasion of the annual meeting of the International Bank for Reconstruction and Development and the International Monetary Fund (Washington, DC, September 1969).

Pan American Union, *Consultation on Economic and Social Development Planning* (Washington, March 1962).

Ros, J., 'Economía mexicana: evolución reciente y perspectivas', *Revista Economía Mexicana*, no. 1, Centro de Investigación y Docencia Económica, México (1979).

Shafer, R. J., *Mexico, Mutual Adjustment Planning* (Syracuse, NY: Syracuse University Press, 1966).

Siegel, B. N., *Inflación y Desarrollo: Las Experiencias de México* (Mexico: Centro de Estudios Monetarios Latinoamericanos, 1957).

Sistema Alimentario Mexicano, *Planteamientos Básicos y Primeras Medidas* (Mexico, 1980).

Solis, L., 'Mexican economic policy in the post-war period: the views of Mexican economists', *The American Economic Review*, Surveys of National Economic Policy Issues and Policy Research, Supplement, vol. 61, no. 3, part 2 (June 1971).

Solis, L., *Economic Policy in Mexico: A Case Study for Developing Countries* (New York: Pergamon, 1981).

Solis, L. and Brothers, D., *Evolución Financiera de México* (Mexico: Centro de Estudios Monetarios Latinoamericanos, 1967).

Spraos, J., 'IMF conditionality: ineffectual, inefficient, mistargeted', in *Essays in International Finance*, no. 166 (Princeton, NJ: International Finance Section, Princeton University, 1986).

Wionczek, M. S., 'La inversión extranjera privada en México', *Revista Comercio Exterior*, vol. 20, no. 10 (Mexico, October 1970).

THE FAR EAST

9 · JAPAN

Saburo Okita

In considering the role of the economist in the Japanese government, I have divided my analysis into four sections. The first section on economists in the Japanese government presents a brief explanation of the status and functions of economists within the government and how they are involved in policy formulation. The second section, drawing heavily upon my own personal experience, is a historical review of the role played by government economists in postwar Japan. Following that, the third section on government economists and economic planning and the fourth on the role of economists in formulating economic policies focus on specific economic plans and recent Japanese economic policies in an attempt to define the economist's function in the government through the case-study approach.

ECONOMISTS IN THE JAPANESE GOVERNMENT

Within the various ministries and agencies

Before any kind of meaningful analysis can be made, it is important to keep in mind that the term 'economist' carries very different connotations in Japan than in most other countries. Many of the career civil-service personnel working in Japanese government ministries and agencies have majored in economics. As Table 9.1 shows, the Economic Planning Agency (EPA), Ministry of Finance (MOF), and Ministry of International Trade and Industry (MITI), hire significant numbers of economics graduates every year.

Yet even though these people are economists by training and are hired by what are referred to in Japan as 'the three economics ministries', their careers differ from the careers of economists in other governments in a number of important ways. For one thing, virtually all of them have only bachelor's degrees. Although Japanese universities do have graduate-level programs in economics, most of the people who go on to graduate school are those who intend to study economics as an academic discipline and to teach it at university level later. These are not the people who go into government service.

The second distinguishing characteristic is that the person is likely to stay

Table 9.1 New employees at major economic ministries and agency

	Total for Japanese government		Economic Planning Agency (EPA)		Ministry of Finance (MOF)		Ministry of International Trade and Industry (MITI)	
	Total	Economics majors	Total	Economics majors	Total	Economics majors	Total	Economics majors
1971	729	57	10	9	23	6	37	6
1972	676	61	6	5	24	9	35	8
1973	632	55	6	4	17	9	36	7
1974	639	63	9	7	27	9	39	9
1975	661	64	7	5	27	7	44	13
1976	619	57	8	7	25	7	43	11
1977	567	48	8	6	23	7	37	8
1978	592	53	7	7	26	9	38	8
1979	645	61	5	4	28	8	42	10
1980	615	66	6	4	23	9	40	12
1981	614	55	5	4	24	8	41	11
1982	648	60	6	5	27	8	41	13
1983	618	58	7	6	25	7	42	12
1984	655	67	8	7	26	9	38	12
1985	688	63	7	6	24	8	43	8

Source: Compiled from *Annual Reports* issued by the National Personnel Authority

with the same ministry throughout his career. Just as it would be unusual for a government bureaucrat to move in mid-career to a position in academia or private business, so it would be unusual for someone to enter government service after a career in academia or private business.

Finally, the typical Japanese government bureaucrat is rotated from post to post on a two- or three-year cycle for broad on-the-job training. The fact that the person has majored in economics is no guarantee that he will be assigned to economic analysis or economic policymaking. Rather than training economic specialists, the aim is to mold generalists with a broad range of experience in all aspects of a particular ministry's operations. Both in private business and in government service, the new employee is hired not to fill a particular position but to become an integral part of the organization for the duration of his career.

The Japanese government economist

Still, there are certain people within the Japanese government who function as so-called 'government economists'. These are bureaucrats who, in their many years of government service, have acquired specialized expertise related to economic analysis, planning and policymaking and who have come to be regarded as economic authorities. These government economists often publish essays and books and give lectures on economic subjects, their activities closely mirroring those of university economists. Such government economists are especially numerous within the EPA, where I also served as a government economist for many years. I believe these Japanese 'government economists' have a greater impact on government economic policy decisions than do bureaucrats in similar positions in other countries.

The government economist in Japan enjoys certain advantages over the university economist. First of all, as a government bureaucrat, he is directly involved in the nation's economy in a way no university professor can be. In the day-to-day confrontation with a wide assortment of economic issues, the government economist becomes closely attuned to current economic problems and their practical ramifications. The university economist, on the other hand, has only limited practical experience and tends to concentrate on theoretical aspects.

The government economist has another advantage in his ready access to a wealth of statistical data. The Japanese government has a vast and well-organized mass of economic data, most of which has been collected and processed by government ministries and agencies. Finally, the government economist is backed by the organizational power of the government to implement policies based on his economic analyses. In recent years, this capability has been further strengthened as computerized information processing has greatly enhanced the process of economic analysis and policy formulation.

Policy formulation and the economist

Like any other civil service employee, the government economist has a hand in drafting economic policy proposals. This is particularly true in the EPA, which provides an excellent training by virtue of its function as coordinator among the various government economic policies. Of all the Japanese government's many ministries and agencies, the EPA probably provides the most economics-oriented input into the formulation of economic policy.

Some 500 people work in the EPA's five bureaus and one research institute. As already noted, the Agency's primary function is to coordinate national economic policies. Every year the Agency prepares an economic forecast which provides the basic guidelines for its coordination activities. Policy flexibility is maintained at all times to keep pace with changing circumstances.

Consistent with its position in implementing economic policy, the EPA also provides the secretariat for the Ministerial Conference for Economic Measures, a board consisting of those cabinet ministers most directly concerned with economic policy and the leaders of the ruling Liberal Democratic Party (LDP). Thus the EPA has played a central role in drafting, and the Ministerial Conference for Economics Measures a central role in approving, most of the Japanese government's policy measures, including the measures to balance Japan's international payments accounts and to enhance import market access since 1981; the measures announced since the autumn of 1985 to stimulate domestic demand; as well as the 6 trillion yen package of emergency economic measures announced at the end of May 1987.

A second function of the EPA is the drafting of long-term economic plans. As explained in more detail below, Japanese economic planning starts by formulating medium- and long-term outlooks for the Japanese economy and formulating policy responses for the various long-term issues that are anticipated. This ties in closely with the Agency's third function, analyzing economic trends. The Agency's annual *Economic White Paper* is generally considered the most authoritative report on the state of the Japanese economy. Agency personnel at the Economic Research Institute work together with guest researchers from the universities to develop, refine and apply a large-scale world economic model. One of the by-products of this kind of research is the compilation and publication of national income statistics. Finally, the fourth area of EPA concerns is to provide liaison and coordination for inter-ministry economic policy decisions such as those concerning consumer protection, price stabilization and other areas of Japanese life.

Economists are closely involved in all of these policymaking areas and the economic measures finally decided upon inevitably reflect these economists' thinking. Of course, the EPA's economists are not the only ones to participate in economic policy formulation. Beginning in the early 1980s, the MOF, the MITI and the Bank of Japan (though not strictly a government organ) have made a conscious effort to train their own economists. Indicative of these efforts has been the establishment of research institutions. The Bank of Japan set up its Institute for Monetary and Economic Studies in 1982, the MOF its Institute of Fiscal and Monetary Policy in 1985, and the MITI its MITI Research Institute in 1987. While these moves have yet to influence specific national economic policy measures to any discernible degree, they are bound to have an increasing effect over time.

Economic scholars and others from outside the government are given the opportunity to participate in policy formulation through a variety of advisory and deliberative councils. Nearly all Japanese government ministries and agencies have special councils that function as advisory bodies and provide formal channels for policy advice from former government officials, business representatives, labor representatives and academics. As might be expected, the councils dealing with economic policy issues make a special effort to include large numbers of economists.

In addition, the various ministries and agencies have informal and unofficial study groups to provide input from outside experts. Most recently, Prime Minister Nakasone has set up several such study groups to advise him on policy issues. The famed Maekawa Report announced in April 1986 was the product of one such unofficial group, and economists had a hand in its drafting.

Qualification requirements for a government economist

As may be seen, Japan's many government economists play a crucial role in economic policy formation. As a result, there are, I believe, certain characteristics required of the government economist. First of all he must have foresight. It is imperative that government economic policy not be swayed by short-term fluctuations and events. The government economist must be capable of predicting those changes that are likely to take place over the long term and suggesting measures to deal meaningfully with them.

Second, the government economist must have a firm grasp of the overall picture. In drafting economic policy proposals, the government economist must be sure that his proposals are in line with general government policy and are not biased to one side or another. This overall perspective is especially important both because government economists should be neutral and not partial to any special interests and because the Japanese government tends to be structured with a vertical arrangement in which each ministry and agency is more interested in protecting its own interests than with co-ordinating with rival ministries and agencies. A third characteristic is objectivity. The government economist must be objective in making his economic analyses and policy proposals.

HISTORY OF THE JAPANESE GOVERNMENT ECONOMIST

I was myself a government economist for many years, having joined the Economic Stabilization Board, predecessor to today's EPA, soon after the end of World War II. Although I retired from government service in 1963, I have continued to be involved in government economic policymaking, and it is based on my own years of experience that I would like now to review the history of the government economist in postwar Japan.

Recovery

I doubt if the term 'economist' would even have been understood in prewar Japan. It was not until after the war that the economist's function came to be recognized and understood. With the end of the war, the most pressing need for Japan was to rebuild the economy, and this meant that there was a need for economists. The Economic Stabilization Board played a major role in directing the nation's economic recovery in the immediate postwar years, and in the process it fostered the development of economists.

The first stimulus for the emergence of the postwar Japanese economist was the first Economic White Paper issued in 1947. This White Paper was written under the supervision of Shigeto Tsuru and issued by the Research

Division, which I headed at the time. Although this White Paper was the focus of considerable controversy, it was generally highly regarded for breaking with tradition and providing a starkly honest appraisal of the state of the Japanese economy. As a result, the Diet requested the Economic Stabilization Board to produce regular annual reports on the nation's economy, and this was a major impetus for the training of government economists.

A second factor encouraging the development of government economists was the need for economic planning. The Economic Stabilization Board had prepared a plan for economic recovery in 1949, but the incumbent Yoshida administration saw no need for planning in a free economy and the proposal was never adopted. In 1955, however, the Hatoyama administration recognized the need for planning even in a market economy, and the first postwar economic plan was drawn up – a five year plan to make the economy self-supporting. Ever since, economists have played a major role in deciding on the long-term goals and the measures to be implemented for their achievement.

Rapid economic growth

Government economists became increasingly important as the Japanese economy shifted from recovery to rapid growth and their input was seen to have a highly favorable impact upon the nation's economic performance. As explained in greater detail below, the 1960 Plan to Double National Income took an optimistic view of the economy's potential, stimulated business and consumers alike to think more positively about the future, and was thus a major impetus for growth. Again, economists were heavily involved in drawing up this ambitious plan, and the tools of their trade came to include national income statistics, industrial input–output analyses and econometric models.

By this time, it was generally recognized that economic policy was an important factor in preventing disruptive fluctuations in the business climate, and care was taken to provide economic and financial management responsive to changing economic trends. By the latter half of the 1960s government bonds were being issued and government economic policymaking had achieved considerable flexibility. Economists achieved greater status and came to play an increasingly vital role in the nation's economic policymaking in the period of transition from postwar recovery to rapid economic growth for a number of reasons. First, there was strong popular consensus on the primary need for economic growth. In the immediate postwar years, the Japanese people were banded together in the struggle to attain economic parity with the industrialized nations as rapidly as possible. Expectations were high, and the climate was ripe for the economist.

Second, the economic theories prevailing at the time substantiated the need for economists. In macroeconomic theory, for example, it was widely accepted that economic activity could be controlled by controlling effective demand. I remember Walter Heller, Chairman of President Kennedy's Council of Economic Advisers, telling me that the United States was capable of economic growth of 5 per cent or greater per annum and that he was confident this could be achieved with effective government policies. This kind of thinking also influenced the Japanese government and it became the accepted practice to formulate and implement economic policy measures in keeping with current economic trends. At the same time, macroeconomic models based on econometrics and computerized information processing came to be increasingly used in formulating economic policy.

In Japan, the EPA was among the first to set up and apply such models, finding them especially useful in preparing the macroeconomic frameworks for its economic plans. Thus new attitudes and the adoption of new tools gave the government economist enhanced standing and greater confidence that he could do his job.

Following the first oil crisis

The oil crisis of late 1973 was to mark the beginning of numerous trials and tribulations for the Japanese economy and hence for the government economist. Confronted by stagflation, a growing budget deficit, international balance of payments disequilibriums and other troubles, the government economist is no longer so confident of his ability to provide the correct solutions. More on this below.

THE ECONOMIST'S ROLE IN ECONOMIC PLANNING

I would like now to focus on economic planning in Japan, the role it has played in the postwar economy, the problems and issues that arose beginning in the late 1970s, and the ramifications for the Japanese economist.

The role of economic planning in Japan

Because Japan is a free-market economy, the basic allocation of resources is determined through the interaction of private-sector companies and consumers in the marketplace. While some foreign observers have said that there is heavy government involvement and intervention in the Japanese economy, it would be more telling to see the Japanese economy as one with very fierce corporate competition and the strong workings of market mechanisms. Japan's favorable performance in such areas as productivity and prices is basically because the private sector has been able to give full rein to its vitality with effective market mechanisms.

Given this, what role has economic planning played in Japan? The 1965 report of the Economic Council's Committee to Study Basic Issues in Economic Planning (chaired by Kazushi Ohkawa) pointed out three significant functions that economic planning fulfills. First is the educational and informative role centering on economic forecasting. With economic plans providing an overview of the outlook for the economy, private-sector companies are then able to formulate their own long-term plans with this in mind. Second is the statement of long-term commitments centering on practical planning. Every plan includes policy programs to be carried out by the government, including the distribution of investment in the major public sectors. As such, the plan is a statement of the administration's long-range policy directions. And third is its role in mediating among different interests. The Economic Council, which deliberates on these plans, includes industrialists, labor leaders, journalists, academic economists and other people representing a broad range of interests. As a result, the Council's deliberations serve to mold compromises among these conflicting interest and to forge popular consensuses on what kind of a society and economy Japan should strive to be.

Postwar economic plans

There have been ten economic plans in postwar Japan to date. These plans, including their main objectives and targets, are shown in Table 9.2. As seen, each plan was drawn up to meet the needs of the particular stage of development at the time of its adoption, and the need to meet changing conditions usually meant that plans were replaced by new plans before their terms were up.

The first set of economic plans were adopted in the mid-1950s to consolidate the immediate postwar gains and to put the economy on a solid footing, and the plans included resource mobilization as part of the effort to attain maximum-efficiency production and investment planning for industry. Next were those plans for the rapid growth of the late 1950s and 1960s. With the very favorable international climate that prevailed at the time, including strong expansion in international trade and the abundant availability of low-cost petroleum resources, plans were formulated for supergrowth.

In the late 1960s, plans were drawn up to rectify the various distortions and inequities that had developed in the rush to economic growth and to promote greater public welfare. Among the hidden problems lurking in the economy's closet were those of overcrowding in some areas and depopulation in others, increasingly serious pollution nationwide, and the inadequacy of welfare provisions, and there was a strong emphasis on social aspects to rectify these shortcomings. Thus it was that the plans came to include the word 'social' in their titles about this time. Finally, plans since 1975 have

Table 9.2 Selected features of main Japanese postwar economic plans

Name of plan	Date and incumbent prime minister	Period of plan (fiscal years)	Objectives	Projections in plan and actual performance: Average annual rate of real GNP growth (%)	Unemployment rate in final year (%)	Average annual consumer price increase (%)	External balance (current account) in final year (US$100 m.)
Five-year Plan for Economic Self-support	December 1955 (Hatoyama)	1956–60	Making the economy self-supporting Achieving full employment	5.0 8.7*	– 1.5	– 2.0	0 –0.1
New Long-range Economic Plan	December 1957 (Kishi)	1958–62	Maximising growth Improving the quality of Japanese life Achieving full employment	6.5 9.9*	– 1.3	– 3.5	1.5 –0.2
Doubling National Income Plan	December 1960 (Ikeda)	1961–70	Strengthening social overhead capital Modernizing Japanese industry Promoting export trade Advancing science and technology Securing social stability	7.2 10.7*	– 1.2	– 5.7	1.8 23.5
Medium-term Economic Plan	January 1965 (Sato)	1964–8	Rectifying imbalances	8.1 10.6*	– 1.1	Approx. 2.5 5.0	0 14.7
Economic and Social Development Plan	March 1967 (Sato)	1967–71	Achieving balanced and steady economic development	8.2 9.6 (10.9*)	– 1.3	Approx. 3 5.7	14.5 63.2
New Economic and Social Development Plan	April 1970 (Sato)	1970–5	Constructing an admirable society through balanced economic growth	10.6 4.9 (6.1*)	– 1.9	4.4 10.9	35 1.3
Basic Economic and Social Plan	Feburary 1973 (Tanaka)	1973–7	Promoting national welfare Promoting international cooperation	9.4 3.5 (4.1*)	– 2.1	4% level 12.8	59 140.0
Economic Plan for the Second Half of the 1970s	May 1976 (Miki)	1976–80	Attaining more affluent living and stable economic development	Slightly over 6 4.9	1.3–1.4% 2.1	6% level 6.4	Approx. 40 –70.1
New Economic and Social Seven-year Plan	August 1979 (Ohira)	1979–85	Shifting to stable growth Enriching the quality of life Contributing to the development of the international economic community	Approx. 5.7 4.1	Approx. 1.7 2.6	Approx. 5 3.6	Roughly balanced basic account
Outlook and Guidelines for the Economy and Society in the 1980s	August 1983 (Nakasone)	1983–90	Forging peaceful and stable international relations Forming an economy and society full of vitality Ensuring secure and affluent living	Approx. 4 4.3 (f.y. 1983–5)	Approx. 2 –	Approx. 3 2.0 (f.y. 1983–5)	Internationally harmonious balance

Note: Average annual real GNP growth rates are based on the SNA at calendar year 1980 prices (those marked with asterisks at calendar year 1970 prices). Top figures are projections and bottom figures actual performance.

emphasized the shift to slower but stable growth. The 1976 plan, for example, was an effort to chart a program for ensuring stable growth despite the economic turmoil in the wake of the 1973 oil crisis, and the 1979 plan was an attempt to create an economy led by domestic demand and to put government budgeting on a sounder footing.

Apart from economic plans, there have been a number of comprehensive land development plans dealing mainly with regional development in Japan. Issues such as urbanization, industrial siting and highway networks are covered in these plans. Preparation of these plans was originally done by the EPA, but the work has shifted to the National Land Agency (NLA) since that Agency was created in 1974, although economic planners rotate between the EPA and the NLA.

The economic planning process

Given this background, it is time to look at how these plans are actually drawn up and the role played by government and private-sector economists. The first step in the long process of drawing up an economic plan occurs when the administration sends a formal request to the Economic Council. This is simply a request for the Economic Council to draw up an economic plan, and it does not include details on the plan's priorities or other specifics. The most that it includes are a basic statement of the general objectives to be met and the period to be covered. The second step takes place when the Economic Council deliberates preparatory to drawing up its draft. The Economic Council itself includes former government bureaucrats, industrialists and businessmen, labor leaders, scholars, consumer and public-interest representatives, and because its deliberations are so wide-ranging, it typically empanels a total of 200–300 people on its subcommittees and subgroups to discuss specific areas of interest. Some of these people are economists. When the main points have been discussed and the directions clarified, the discussion is summarized and reported to the administration. This then leads to the third step, which is the writing of the administration's draft. Because the Economic Council is not formally part of the government, its report becomes an official government document only after it is approved by the cabinet. However, this cabinet approval is more or less a formality, and the Council's recommendations are usually adopted virtually intact as the administration's plan.

Government economists and other people play a number of important roles in this process. To begin with, they provide the Council with the materials it needs for its deliberations. Here, because government economists have ready access to a wide range of economic statistics and other data and can also use econometric models for economic analyses, they are able to meet the Council's expectations of them. These same people also play an important role in coordination and mediation between the Council and the various government bodies while the recommendations are being drafted. As a result of these efforts, the Council's recommendations have pretty much been approved by the important government offices by the time they are finally released, and thus it is that the Council's recommendations can be so easily adopted as the administration's plan.

The Plan to Double National Income

One of the most conspicuously successful postwar Japanese economic plans was the 1960 Plan to Double National Income. At the time, I was responsible for this income-doubling plan as Director-General of the EPA's Planning Bureau. In order to draw up the plan, the Economic Council supplemented its General Policy Committee with a statistical committee, public sector committee, private sector committee and seventeen subcommittees. A total of 250 experts from academia, business, the mass media and government were brought into this process, and they averaged a total of eight meetings each.

Under this plan, annual average real economic growth of 7.2 per cent was forecast which would double Japan's national income in approximately ten years. In fact, real economic growth averaged 10.7 per cent per annum during this period and the Japanese economy greatly exceeded the plan's target.

While most people looking back on this plan tend to emphasize the high growth rate that was achieved, the plan itself had five main planks: strengthening social overhead capital, modernizing Japanese industry, promoting exports and expanding cooperation with the developing countries, pushing back the frontiers of science and technology, and securing social stability by mitigating the dual structure of the economy. These are very progressive and ambitious goals even from today's perspective. As Professor Lester Thurow noted at the 1982 Effective Business Management symposium, 'the five elements in the Japanese . . . income-doubling (plan) . . . could easily serve as strategic objectives for the American economy by the year 2000.'

There are a number of reasons why I think this plan made the most efficient use of the abilities of Japanese government economists. First, it was a clear statement of the way the economists saw the future. The basic premise of the income-doubling plan was that it would be necessary, and that it was possible, to make fullest use of Japan's economic potential. When this was presented as an official government plan, it gave a major boost to private-sector confidence in the economy. And because it was a realistic reading of the economic future, the private sector was able to lead the way to the future. Second, this plan received strong political backing. While the Economic Council had been asked to formulate the plan by Prime Minister Kishi shortly before he left office, the new Prime Minister, Ikeda, adopted income-doubling as his prime political objective and gave it his full public support.

Recent economic plans

While there have been a number of economic plans since the one to double national income, they have gradually lost impact and influence. In 1973, a plan was drawn up for the second half of the 1970s, but it forecast a much lower growth rate than Japan had been used to and was primarily concerned with how to cure the stagflation that followed the first oil crisis. Yet the economy did not respond, and the next plan, the seven-year plan drawn up in 1979, was concerned mainly with the problems of dealing with Japan's current-account surplus and putting the government budget back on a sound footing. This plan was an effort to promote economic growth powered by domestic demand and to rectify the external imbalance by making aggressive use of public-works investment and other effective demand policies, and on fiscal restructuring it called for rationalizing government spending and instituting a broad-based consumption tax. However, the second oil crisis sent tremors throughout the economy in 1979, and the proposed consumption tax failed to gain public approval.

It was in this time of trial that the Outlook and Guidelines for the Economy and Society in the 1980s was drawn up in 1983. While it did postulate economic growth of approximately 4 per cent, it failed to spell out the specific economic paradigms and was satisfied on the issue of restoring budgetary soundness to simply call for an end to the dependence on deficit-financing government bond issues by the end of the plan's period (1990).

The Outline and Guidelines was inadequate in several ways when measured against the earlier criteria for economic planning. First, while an economic plan should present an overview of the future, the Outline and Guidelines failed to define the economic framework and simply postulated the growth rate, unemployment rate and rate of consumer price increases. This is clearly insufficient to take the lead in defining private-sector expectations about the future. Second, while earlier economic plans had included specific political commitments on both total public-works spending and its allocation, the Outline and Guidelines was devoid of any such commitment. It failed to specify what the government itself was prepared to do to attain the plan's goals.

Thus the Outline and Guidelines is little more than an empty rewording of campaign rhetoric. And as a result, it is impossible to conduct an effective review of the plan or to check it for consistency. While such an approach is admittedly easier on the administration, the same lack of rigor and discipline means that people have little faith in the plan or its pronouncements. The Outline and Guidelines is sorely lacking as an economic plan.

ECONOMIC POLICY AND THE ECONOMIST'S ROLE

Next, I would like to touch upon recent trends in Japanese economic policy and how they impinge upon the economist's role.

Two imbalances

The Japanese economy today must deal with imbalances in two important areas. The first of these is the government budget imbalance. The Japanese government fiscal balance has deteriorated sharply since the 1970s, both because of declining tax revenues in the face of slower growth and because of burgeoning expenditures for continued strong expansion in social welfare and public-works spending. This shortfall has been met with the issue of government bonds, and the government was dependent on bond issues for approximately 40 per cent of its funding in fiscal 1979. As a result, one of the most important issues for the government since 1980 has been that of putting its finances back on a sound footing.

The only way to restore budgetary balance is to increase revenues and hold down spending. However, because the general consumption tax proposed in 1979 failed to win public sanction on the revenue side, the government has been forced to make a major effort to control spending. General expenditures (meaning total expenditures minus debt service and transfers to local governments) have been held to very low growth rates since 1980, and they have actually been cut back from 1983 through 1987. The situation has been considerably improved as a result of these efforts. In fiscal 1987's initial budget, for example, the issue of government bonds was only 10.5 trillion yen (as opposed to 15.3 trillion yen in fiscal 1979) and the dependence on bond issues was down from 39.6 per cent in 1979 to 19.4 per cent.

The other imbalance is the external imbalance. From $6.9 billion in 1982, Japan's current account surplus jumped to $20.8 billion in 1983 and, after increasing steadily every year, was $86.0 billion in 1986. This massive external imbalance has in turn given rise to trade friction, currency appreciation and other problems, and has invited protectionist retaliation. While the government has embarked upon a series of market-opening measures,

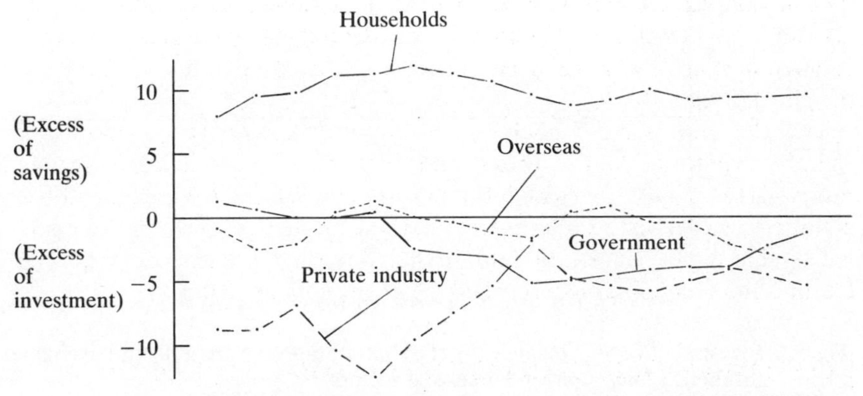

Fig. 9.1 Investment/savings balances for Japan

Source: Economic Planning Agency, *Annual Report on National Account*, 1987

Table 9.3 Investment/savings balances for Japan (%, in comparison to GNP)

	Households	Private industry	Government	Overseas
1970	7.7	−8.4	1.7	−1.0
1971	9.4	−8.4	0.9	−2.5
1972	9.8	−7.0	−0.1	−2.2
1973	11.4	−10.8	0.5	0.0
1974	11.5	−12.9	0.4	1.0
1975	11.8	−9.5	−2.8	0.1
1976	11.5	−7.0	−3.7	−0.6
1977	10.6	−5.6	−3.8	−1.5
1978	9.3	−2.4	−5.3	−1.7
1979	8.1	−4.3	−4.7	0.9
1980	9.0	−5.7	−4.4	1.1
1981	10.0	−6.3	−3.8	−0.4
1982	8.9	−5.0	−3.6	−0.7
1983	9.2	−4.2	−3.7	−1.8
1984	9.0	−4.6	−2.1	−2.8
1985	9.4	−5.4	−0.8	−3.6

action programs, domestic demand stimulation efforts, and more, the external imbalance shows no signs of any rapid abatement.

These two imbalances are clearly related in a trade-off relationship. As seen in Fig. 9.1 and Table 9.3, the budgetary imbalance has been steadily reduced since 1983, but the other side of this has been a steady increase in the external imbalance. The same is true of the United States (Fig. 9.2 and Table 9.4), where the external imbalance grew sharply after 1983 against a background of major budget deficits. If these two countries are really serious about reducing their external imbalance, Japan will slow down the pace at

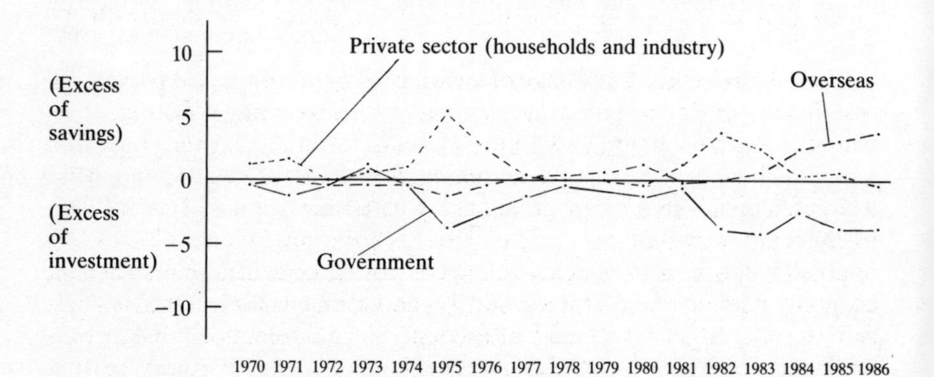

Fig. 9.2 Investment/savings balances for the United States (no breakdown is available for the US household and industrial sectors)

Source: Nihon Hyoron-sha, *America Keizai Hakusho 87* – 1987 White Paper on the American Economy

Table 9.4 Investment/savings balances for the United States (%, in comparison to GNP)

	Private sector	Government	Overseas
1970	1.5	−1.0	−0.5
1971	1.6	−1.7	−0.1
1972	0.1	−0.3	0.2
1973	0.4	0.6	−0.6
1974	0.9	−0.3	−0.4
1975	5.3	−4.1	−1.4
1976	2.5	−2.2	−0.5
1977	0.5	−1.0	0.4
1978	−0.3	0.0	0.4
1979	−0.4	0.5	−0.1
1980	1.5	−1.3	−0.5
1981	1.2	−1.0	−0.3
1982	3.5	−3.5	0.0
1983	2.6	−3.8	1.0
1984	0.3	−2.7	2.4
1985	0.7	−3.4	2.9
1986	−0.1	−3.6	3.6

which it is reducing its budgetary imbalance and the United States will have to work harder at reducing its own budget deficit.

The economist's role in policymaking

As an economist, I believe that Japan should respond to this troublesome situation by announcing that it intends to reduce its current-account surplus from today's level in excess of 4 per cent of GNP to something on the order of 2 per cent of GNP in about five years; and expanding its fiscal disbursements and adopting other macroeconomic measures consistent with this goal.

While I have taken advantage of a variety of opportunities to present the case for this policy response, the argument for expanding government expenditures has been opposed on the grounds that it goes against the effort to put the budget back on a sound footing. Likewise, the idea of announcing a target figure for the current account surplus has been opposed because: the figure could be cast in stone and end up tying the government's hands; it is impossible for the government itself to control the current account when the economy is left to market forces; and it is unreasonable for just the Japanese side to set a target for its current account, since international balances of payments are affected by the efforts by all major trading partners, particularly the United States.

Nevertheless, in view of today's external relations, I believe Japan has to work to reduce its external imbalance, even if this entails some sacrificing of the domestic goal of balancing the budget. Likewise, the workings of free trade may at times impede the attainment of a given government policy goal, but I feel that much of the overseas dissatisfaction with Japan stems from doubts about how serious Japan is in trying to achieve better external balance. As such, it is very important that the government announce policy programs in line with clearly stated goals. And if people are worried about the fact that the trading partners may not make concerted efforts to reduce trade imbalances, this goal might include a clear statement of what Japan expects of its trade partners, for example, that the United States will reduce its trade deficit by half in about five years.

How is one to evaluate this Japanese policy debate in terms of the economist's role? As noted above, the government economist has to have foresight, broad perspective and objectivity. In the Japanese government's case, non-economist bureaucrats such as those at the MOF often have overriding power on actual policy decision making. On the issue of foresight, some economists are predicting developments in the external balance. Given that Japan's exports are income-elastic and its imports income-inelastic, it is only natural that Japan should show a current-account surplus when commodity prices are stable and when the Japanese and overseas economies are dissynchronous.

There were also problems in the inability to view the larger picture. There are a number of economic factors that are in balance, and these balances are themselves interdependent. These include the macroeconomic balance between supply and demand, the external balances and the fiscal balance. In formulating economic policy, it is necessary to look at the total of all of these balances. However, economic policy in the 1980s seems to have been concerned mainly with the fiscal balance. Decision making did not sufficiently reflect international economic perspectives, and there was an over-attention to the bureaucratic brief for putting the budget back on a sound footing.

In sum, the history of Japan's recent economic policies is a history of economists' inability to fulfill the expectations held of them.

CONCLUSION

As seen, there were major changes in the working climate for Japanese government economists in the late 1970s and it became more difficult for them to play their proper role in the drafting and implementing of economic policy. There appear to be a number of factors responsible for this change. For one, as Japan succeeded in catching up with the western industrialized nations, there was a greater diversification of Japanese values and a greater dispersion of policy goals. As such, this was a new climate quite different from the era in which everyone was united in the quest for economic growth. Second is the fact that the traditional macroeconomic and econometric theories lost some of their credibility. Some would argue that the political pressures made it impossible for the government to fine-tune the economy and even out fluctuations effectively on the ground that discretionary fiscal policies invariably lead to deficits since it is much more difficult to reduce spending than to expand it. Third is the fact that the politicians have increasingly come to play a greater role in policy decisions, and the increasing diversification of policy goals, coupled with the slower growth rate which gives less 'new pie' to distribute, has made allocation of resources on purely economic criteria more difficult. Fourth is the increasing interdependence among the major economies of the world, particularly the rapid expansion in financial flows among countries.

Yet despite, or perhaps because of, these changes, it is imperative that Japanese government economists play an important role in policy formulation and implementation. While this may demand some systemic changes, it seems to me that the basic directions should be as follows.

First is the development of greater international perspective. As the Japanese economy has become more important internationally, so have Japan's international responsibilities increased. On economic policy issues, Japan must now play a vigorous role in assisting the developing countries, resolving the debt problem and dealing with other global issues. As a result, government economists need to exercise leadership not simply on domestic issues but also on international economic issues. However, they have yet to formulate policy from the global perspective and to speak in global terms. It is to be hoped that Japanese government economists will take a more active part in international exchanges and develop the ability to swim in international waters.

Second is the need to reconcile microeconomic market mechanisms and macroeconomic planning. There has recently been a strong shift to privatization, deregulation, and small government, and a worldwide tendency to prefer to leave the resolution of economic issues to the workings of market mechanisms. However, domestic macroeconomic management issues and global economic issues cannot be solved solely by the free workings of market mechanisms. Rather, there are a number of issues, such as the debt problem, that have been exacerbated by the lack of planning. It is imperative that there be some long-range planning, and economists must play a part in formulating such plans.

Third is the need for economists to become important actors in the effort to solve a wide range of problems. Economics is generally suited to dealing with issues scientifically, quantifying them as necessary and formulating consistent policies, and economists should not restrict themselves to economic issues alone but should be involved in the search for solutions to a wide range of social, environmental and other interdisciplinary issues. As such, the economists' role, far from becoming less important, is becoming increasingly important.

While economists themselves obviously have to work harder to ensure that they play a more effective role within the government, there may also be room for institutional improvements within the government so that these efforts can come to fruition. I would thus like to say a few words about these institutional arrangements.

Institutionally, a number of points need to be considered in formulating Japanese economic policy. First is the need for international-minded leadership and the introduction of new concepts in economic policy planning. If Japan is to enhance market access and to achieve economic growth powered by domestic demand, it is imperative that the conflicts of interests among different ministries and agencies be resolved. This in turn requires departing from the traditional bottom-up planning and finding the strong leadership needed to reconcile these conflicts and set priorities.

Second is the increasing importance of economic policy coordination. With the interwining and interaction among such problems as trade, exchange rates, international finance and industrial restructuring, there is an increasing need for an issue-oriented approach that cuts across the vertical delineations among ministries and agencies. A number of ideas have been advanced in response to this need, including strengthening the cabinet's coordinative functions, creating a special commission reporting directly to the prime minister, or creating a new bureaucracy that would be charged with liaison and coordination among the ministries. Personally, I think we already have the institutions – it is just a question of getting them to function properly. When the EPA was established, it was charged with coordinating views on economic policy. Rather than creating new structures, it would be better for the government to draw up meaningful economic plans with the EPA given the authority to do intra-governmental coordination. Likewise, the Economic Council was established with the idea of drawing upon the views of people from the private sector, and this is already reporting to the prime minister. If this functions the way it is supposed to, it should be possible for it to give direction to Japanese economic policy planning.

Until recently, the government of Japan has been able to work together to achieve the national goal of catching up with the industrialized West. Government economists played a role in leading the way to the rapid growth that made this possible. Today, the Japanese economy is again faced with major international economic issues and a need to act. Yet this time, the goal is not rapid growth but that of enabling Japan to fulfill its international responsibilities, and the question is whether or not the institutional arrangements that served so well in the past will be up to the present task.

BIBLIOGRAPHY

Economic Planning Agency, *Sengo Nihon Keizai no Tenkai: Keizai Kikaku-cho 30-nen Shi* (Japan's postwar economic development: a 30-year history of the Economic Planning Agency) (1976).

Economic Council, Report of the Committee to Study Basic Issues in Economic Planning (1965).

Komiya, R., and K. Yamada, 'Japan: the officer in charge of economic affairs', in *History of Political Economy* (Duke University Press, 1981).

Marris, R. L., 'The position of economics and economists in the government machine', *The Economic Journal* (December 1954).

Nelson, R. H., 'The economics profession and the making of public policy', *Journal of Economic Literature*, (March 1987).

Okita, Saburo, *Ekonomisuto no Yakuwari* (The role of the economist) (Nihon Keizai Shimbun-sha, 1973).

Okita, Saburo, *Tohon Seiso* (Hurried mission in East and West) (Nihon Keizai Shimbun-sha, 1981); translated as *Japan's Challenging Years* (Australian National University Press, 1983).

Okita, Saboro, H. Kanamori, Y. Kosai, I. Miyazaki, and K. Miyamoto, 'Seifu Ekonomisuto no Yakuwari' (The role of the government economist), *Nihon Keizai Kenkyu Center Kaiho*, Journal of Japan Center for Economic Research (May 1987).

Thurow, Lester, *The Management Challenge – Japanese Views* (Massachusetts Institute of Technology Press, 1985).

SOUTH AMERICA

10 · ARGENTINA

*José Maria Dagnino Pastore**

This chapter is devoted to the governmental activities of professional economists, a class of social scientists that has existed in Argentina for only a few decades. It will be useful, therefore, to begin with a review of the origins and development of professional economics in the country before describing the institutional arrangements in which economists operate within the government. Thereafter, an account is given of three major episodes in the recent economic history of Argentina and the performance of economists during these episodes is evaluated. The chapter concludes with proposals to enhance the effectiveness of economists in the Argentine government.

HUMAN RESOURCES AND TECHNOLOGY

Investments have been made in both labor and capital in the development of economics in Argentina. Economists have been trained primarily at universities abroad, although the Argentine universities have had an important role in attracting students to economics. Basic data for economic analysis and policymaking, such as national accounts, input–output tables and budget accounts, have been developed by the Central Bank and other government agencies, with the assistance of experts from abroad.

The growth of the economics profession

Until 1913 there were no economics faculties at Argentine universities. In that year a doctorate in economic science and a shorter course in accounting were created at the university of Buenos Aires.[1] Although economics was allegedly covered by the curriculum, in fact it was taught only in two courses, called Political Economy I and II, for almost half a century. However, the teaching of many other associated specialities permitted the faculty to host a group of scholars who taught or did research in economics from different backgrounds and experiences.[2] For example, the first course in mathematical

* Prepared in collaboration with Manuel Fernandez Lopez.

economics ever taught in South America was given by Gondra,[3] professor of the history of commerce, and H. Broggi, professor of mathematics, beginning in 1918. A. Bunge, an electrical engineer, taught statistics[4]; R. Prebisch, an economist, gave economic lectures that were usually attended by a large crowd of listeners, not all regular students[5]; and B. Souto, professor of biometrics who worked out the theory of comparative advantage.[6] Lacking a formal curriculum in economics, this faculty advanced the study of economics over four decades by performing four essential functions: transmission of economic knowledge, development of research,[7] publication of contributions[8] and communication with the world community of scientists.

Economists did not become prominent in government until the 1930s. Two eminent officials are distinguishable in this period, F. Pinedo[9] and R. Prebisch. The latter organized one of the most outstanding economic teams ever to serve the Argentine government. Prebisch also actively promoted economic research at the Central Bank's Department of Economic Research and encouraged Argentine graduate students to study at first-rate universities abroad.[10]

The academic and technical economic staffs were swept out by the Peronist government in 1946. Almost everyone, in one way or another, was forced to resign or dismissed from office. Some were hired by foreign central banks and other institutions, but the majority remained to carry out their profession in the private sector.

University chairs were occupied by less proficient personnel during the Peron era. Economic journals either ceased to exist (e.g. *Revista de Economía Argentina*, published by Bunge's institute) or were published sporadically (e.g. *Revista de Ciencias Económicas*) and their contents visibly deteriorated. Excepting perhaps for the work of B. Cornejo at the University of Cordoba,[11] and C. Dieulefait at the School of Statistics in Rosario,[12] the spectacle at every academic center was depressing. By the early and mid-1950s, it was apparent that there were no well-organized economic research groups using sophisticated techniques and modern equipment. Exceptional cases were those of J. Olivera[13] who raised the level of economic analysis, teaching and research at the University of Buenos Aires, and of O. Popescu[14] at the University of La Plata.

The Ministry of Economic Affairs was created in 1952. Its Secretariat of Economic Affairs began to employ talented young people, among them the national income group, who transferred from the Central Bank under the leadership of M. Balboa and A. Fracchia. The Faculty of Economic Sciences at the University of Buenos Aires sought to ameliorate the accountants' poor understanding of economics by creating a Master of Economics with the addition of several economic subjects to the accounting curriculum. However, recipients of this degree rarely chose economics as a distinct career.

In November 1957 an event of major significance was the formation of the Argentine Political Economy Association (AAEP).[15] Beginning with only fourteen members, this Association now has about 350 members and is the most representative institution of its kind in Argentina.

In 1956–57 a UNO mission worked in Argentina for a period of a year preparing a full study of the economy. A by-product of those activities was a course in economics sponsored by the Economic Commission for Latin America (ECLA), directed by J. Ahumada and shared by a great many Latin American professors, mainly from Chile. The course was attended by key officers of the government and university scholars. After that experience, the Faculty of Economic Science of the University of Buenos Aires offered similar courses for some time.

A strong drive for creating a formal curriculum in economics, distinctly splitting the training of accountants, economists and actuaries, developed in 1957 and 1958. In December 1958, the University of Buenos Aires authorized the teaching of sixteen new courses in economics. At about the same time, some private, mainly Catholic, universities were created (e.g. Argentine Catholic University – UCA – and the University of Salvador) which soon offered training in economics. UCA's influential department of economics was the work of Francisco Valsecchi.[16]

By the second half of the 1950s, the main American universities (Harvard, Chicago, Yale, MIT, Columbia, etc.) began to admit the first Argentine graduates as students for advanced degrees in economics. Upon their return, those scholars strengthened teaching and research in economics at several Argentine universities, such as A. C. Diz in Tucuman and A. Arnaudo in Cordoba.

Two important scholarly exchange programs were developed in the early 1960s. The first at the University of Buenos Aires, sponsored by the Ford Foundation, consisted of courses taught in Buenos Aires by professors from British universities.[17] The second at the University of Cuyo, sponsored by the University of Chicago, consisted of courses taught by professors from the University of Chicago and the Catholic University of Chile, with students from Mendoza and several neighboring provinces.[18]

Similar programs were not developed at other universities. However, the graduates from the University of La Plata and the Southern University managed to study abroad with the assistance of scholarships granted mainly by the Organization of American States (OAS) and the Fulbright Commission in the United States.

The decadence of the early 1950s was clearly reversed in the 1960s. Among others, the following factors led to this reversal: the high level reached in studies abroad by Olivera's students[19] and the steady inflow of graduates in economics from abroad, mainly at the PhD level. Most of these newcomers obtained new positions which were opened up by the creation of CONADE (National Development Council), CFI (Federal Council of Investments),[20] and five important economic research centers.[21] This process, which began in 1959–61, institutionalized economic research among organized groups.[22]

In 1963 the two new public offices and the research centers began to organize meetings to consider their common interests. This culminated in the first meeting of economic research centers at Cordoba in December 1964. A second meeting, which took place in the following year at Mendoza, provided the economic centers with an opportunity to reach an agreement with the AAEP to conduct annual meetings. Thereafter, scientific research in every field of economics attained an institutional framework and a continuity which has been preserved up to the present.

At that time several other private economic research centers were created, including FIEL (Latin American Foundation for Economic Research) supported by the main business association, OECE (Office of Studies for International Economic Cooperation) belonging to the firm of Fiat–Concord, the Office of Economic Studies at the CGE (General Economic Confederation), and study groups of the UIA (Argentine Industrial Union). Other smaller centers were organized at private banks, business chambers and trade unions. These research organizations increased the demand for economists and to some extent checked the propensity of Argentine economics graduates to emigrate (Guadagni, 1968).

The new courses in economics and the recently created economic centers sponsored visits by eminent foreign economists, including some future Nobel Prize Laureates. There is no doubt that the presence of these scholars in Argentina encouraged interest in the field and furthered economic research.[23]

A more detailed review of the activities of CFI and CONADE will be useful, since they were for some time the largest institutions employing economists within the government. CFI was created to promote the harmonious and integrated development of Argentina and fundamentally to direct investments on the basis of the economic potential of the various regions of the country. An early, remarkable project, undertaken by the CFI jointly with the Instituto Di Tella was *The Shaping of Regional Economic Structure*.[24] Although a great many provincial economic development projects were organized by CFI, only a small percentage (not more than 2 per cent) were actually completed. The CFI also produced regional statistics on a routine basis, but this was later interrupted.

During the 1960s CONADE filled a vacuum created by the absence of professional economic teams throughout the government. Under the direction of Carranza, CONADE assembled a good share of the young economists, from home as well as from abroad, to study various aspects of economics, including macroeconomics, agriculture, industry, the public sector, international trade, finance, transportation, public health, housing, energy and econometric models. In addition two teams were created by agreement with international institutions: the Income Distribution team – by agreement between CONADE and ECLA – and the Joint Program on Taxation of OAS, IDB (International Development Bank) and ECLA. Both teams, initially led by Argentines serving as international officers, eventually became integrated into CONADE. A team of the Harvard Advisory Group, led by R. D. Mallon with the collaboration of W. Van Rijckeghem and G. Maynard, was also active in 1963–6. Many team directors were later appointed ministers or state secretaries, which demonstates their high level of proficiency.[25]

After the overthrow of President Illia, many highly qualified officers and technicians scattered to other areas of government, went into private activity, or migrated abroad. In 1968–9 CONADE had a renaissance, which culminated with the publication of the National Development and Security Plan, 1971–5, approved in May 1971. But from then on it entered into a steep decline from which it never emerged, even under the statist government of 1973–6, due to lack of backing from the Minister of the Economy.

Also during the 1960s the presence of economists in business and in international trade was furthered by the creation of IDEA (Institute for Executive Development in Argentina), a graduate business school, and of INTAL (Institute for Latin American Integration).

The Peronist government of 1973 removed qualified professors from the universities and disbanded many teams in government. There were some exceptions: some teams remained, as in the Department of Commerce, and some new ones were formed, as in the Comptrollership of Public Enterprises. However, collaboration of the government with private institutes and foreign scholarships diminished and the brain-drain intensified.

The situation was reversed when Peron fell. Between the mid-1970s and the early 1980s three new economic research centers were created: CEMA (Center for Macroeconomic Studies in Argentina),[26] the Mediterranean Foundation in Cordoba[27] and CEDES (Center of Studies for Economic and Social Development).[28] Also ECLA opened an office in Buenos Aires.

The Central Bank began to take an active role in training economists, especially monetary economists, at home and abroad and in professionalizing its staff. The influence of the economics profession grew, as did employment opportunities. New private business schools and economic forums appeared, for example, ESEADE (Escuela Superiore de Estudios Argentinos de Empressa) at the University of Belgrano and CIIE (International Center of Information for Entrepreneurs). Two influential economic newspapers developed: *El Cronista Commercial* and *Ambito Financiero*, and economic sections were added to others. Professional economists also began to enter journalism,[29] industry[30] and finance.

Methodological improvements

Several technological advances improved the economist's performance within government.

National accounts

Except for balance-of-payments statistics, the calculation of national income is one of the oldest achievements among the Argentine economic tools.[31] The present stage dates back to the 1975 publication of *Product and Income of the Argentine Republic* by the Central Bank, which provided estimates of gross domestic product, national income, family income and expenditure, government income and expenditure, foreign transactions, and savings and investment. From then on, the Central Bank has routinely published quarterly estimates of aggregate supply and demand at constant prices. Estimates at current prices were discontinued around 1980.

Input–output

The first attempt to prepare an input–output table dates back to 1954 when a table was developed on the basis of 1946 census data. In 1956 at the request of ECLA, an input–output table was prepared at the Central Bank with 1950 data. Also at the request of the ECLA mission, M. Balboa wrote the study, *Use of the Input–Output Model in Projections of the Argentine Economy*. Later, the Central Bank developed a routine set of estimates for two tables of intersectoral transactions in the Argentine economy, one on the basis of data for 1953 (published in 1963) and the other on the basis of 1963 data (published in 1973).

Effective protection

During the economics ministry of Martinez de Hoz, an attempt was made to introduce an orderly scheme of effective protection. Foreign trading firms were required to present studies on effective protection in order to undertake foreign transactions and this inspired a considerable amount of empirical research. This requirement was later abandoned on the ground that it had little significance at the aggregate level and too much sensitivity at the commodity level. However, a regular flow of research papers on the theoretical and practical aspects of protection continued to appear.

Budget policy

The improvement of budget policy was linked to standby agreements between Argentina and the IMF during the early 1960s. In 1965, a financial statement was prepared for the government, including balance-of-payments and public-sector statistics and data for state enterprises. In the following years, especially since 1967, detailed financial accounts were developed under the guidance of E. Folcini and became a main tool of economic policy. In particular, for the first time accounts were developed for the social-security system and for public enterprises. New techniques of financial evaluation were adopted under the direction of R. Arriazu, and the analysis of the foreign and domestic monetary sectors was integrated as an outcome of the adoption of the monetary approach under Diz's Central Bank presidency.

Program budgeting
Since 1853 it has been the function of Congress to approve the expenditure budget and the investment account (Article 67 of the national constitution). However, the Argentine budget has had grave deficiencies. During the Illia government (1963–6), program budgeting was tried, but nothing was sent to Congress because of organizational problems in the Treasury. Under Minister Krieger-Vasena a set of basic goals was developed for public enterprises (investment, personnel and output) and by 1969 a complete budget was formulated. An inflation of 6–7 per cent annually encouraged the use of program budgeting, but the acceleration of inflation in the following years made it a vain hope. Most of the budget improvements were the work of C. Licciardo and his disciples.[32]

PERFORMANCE OF ECONOMISTS WITHIN GOVERNMENT

Economists began to be influential in the government in the 1930s. Since then, their influence has waxed and waned, depending on who controlled the government. They were least influential during the Peronist eras and most influential in democratic governments.

Institutional arrangements

Since 1853, Argentina has had a representative, republican and federal government. The central government is divided into three branches: executive, legislative, and judicial. The twenty-two provincial governments have also a tripartite division of powers.

Beginning in the 1930s, the central government has added a long list of economic functions. Professional economists have exercised an influence mainly within the executive branch; their role within the legislative and judicial branches has been irregular or transient. In the legislative branch, the economist works as adviser to individual legislators or to committees of the House of Representatives and the Senate. In the judiciary, the economist works as an *ad hoc* expert, and his labor usually results in the production of technical reports on specific cases.

In the executive branch, there is a more complicated set of relationships, which may be grouped into the following categories:

1. At the political level, there are economic authorities and key officials, such as the Minister of the Economy, who set economic policies.
2. At the bureaucratic level, there are economic technicians who produce technical reports and develop policy options.
3. At the advisory level, there are economic experts who are expected to design policies and strategies to solve specific economic problems.

Appointments at the political level are political decisions. Hence, in Argentina the distinctive feature of such appointments is instability. The average duration of tenure in office for ministers of the economy and presidents of the Central Bank is less than a year (only three ministers of the economy have held office for more than two years).[33] It is a prerogative of these higher-level officials to appoint technical teams and advisory staffs, so that their own instability is translated to their subordinates.

Public employees are subject to the wage scales fixed by the government. Sometimes a young graduate is attracted to enter the public service by the relatively high rate of pay; if he stays in office until he is about thirty years of age, he might reach the category of Director, which is the highest rank attainable, and therefore the end of his administrative career. In effect, the state trains an individual to reach full proficiency and then compels him to give up his position and to enter the private sector at a rather young age.

Another unavoidable feature of public employment is the loss of independence, which sometimes degenerates into ideological or political persecution. The arbitrary dismissal of public officers is an old evil which motivated the adoption in 1957 of an amendment to the constitution of the principle of stability of employment. However, as a consequence of the low wages at the top levels, the lack of independence, and potential instability of employment, it has been very difficult for the government to attract qualified economists. Every Minister of the Economy or Central Bank President has had to revitalize his staff. To attract highly qualified specialists, he often finds it necessary to offer considerably higher wages than those received elsewhere in the public sector, a situation which is sustainable only for the duration of his tenure.

Official advisers are recruited through contracts, which means that the quality of advisers, the programs they may serve and their impact on policy-making vary widely. The Argentine government has employed international as well as domestic advisers, depending on the rank of the office and the urgency of the assignment. The president has employed international advisers for specific purposes and definite terms.[34]

Within the central government, many offices employ professional economists. The main employers have been the ministries of economics, labor, and public works, the Treasury, and state secretaries of agriculture, industry, mining, domestic trade and foreign trade. A second category includes state enterprises (some of them very large, like YPF – Yacimiento Petroliferos Fiscales) and mixed enterprises (like SOMISA – Sociedad Mixta Siderugia Argentina). A third category are the national banks (the Central Bank, Bank of the Nation, the Development Bank and the Mortgage Bank). During various periods, there has also been a demand for economists on the part of CONADE, CFI, the eight sectoral development offices, and the ministries of defense and social welfare (Guadagni, 1968).

In the provincial governments, there also exist, but at a lesser scale, some offices that are like those of the central government: ministries of the economy, treasuries, provincial enterprises, provincial banks, and more recently provincial planning bureaus (Guadagni, 1968). All these agencies employ economists both at the staff level and as advisers.

Effectiveness of economists

'Let His Highness doeth good policy, and I shall do good economics.' The thought, ascribed to Colbert (quoted by Elizalde, 1980, p. 109), conveys the dependence of the economist's success within government on the overall political situation. In Argentina, political institutions have been highly volatile since 1930, transmitting instability to economic institutions and officers. Between 1958, when the Minstry of Economy was created, and 1985, there have been thirty-one ministers serving for an average of eleven months.

This average is influenced by the fact that three ministers lasted from thirty months to more than four years,[35] which means that many of them did not even serve as long as four or five months.[36] Only ministers who began their tenure in a new and strong government had the necessary political power to adopt new programs and last the minimum time necessary to see them carried out.

Another problem is the lack of economic data. How useful can a surgeon be without the help of a surgical knife? Similarly, it may be asked: How effective can an applied economist be without accurate data? In Argentina, there has been a steady deterioration in the quality of the statistical data and in the estimates derived from them, such as the system of national accounts. For example, the publication of GDP at current prices has been interrupted; the available estimates of fixed renewable capital, income distribution, and input–output are twenty to thirty years old; the figures produced by the Statistical Bureau are not consistent with those of the Central Bank; the sample used to calculate the index of industrial production is very old; the censuses are not taken according to internationally approved standards; etc. This poverty of data makes it impossible, for example, to compare the current GDP with its level ten or fifteen years ago. The available data provide a qualitative idea of the changes, but not precise measures.

The situation is even worse for short-term economic management, because the delays until data become available render many of them useless. For example, foreign trade data become available only after a delay of over four months; Treasury data lag by more than a month; and frequently the data are subject to substantial revision.

ECONOMIC SUCCESSES AND FAILURES

Given these preliminary observations, we are now in a position to identify some of the successes and failures of economists in the Argentine government.

Sectoral experience

Sharp differences may be found in the performance of sectors that have attained a clear picture of their problems and others that have not. The power sector is a case of successful intervention by economists. There have always been many engineers and a great deal of technical knowledge in this sector, but not many economists. However, since the early 1960s good planning with the aid of economists has been the norm, despite internal battles between supporters of hydroelectricity and defenders of atomic energy.

Economists have been less successful in the agricultural sector. There has been an inflow of forty PhDs trained abroad into agricultural economics. Even though the group is well trained, they have not been able to modify agricultural policies and many of them have returned to foreign assignments.

There is some degree of planning in the transport sector, but this is deemed unsatisfactory. There are intense internal battles in this sector, primarily because of the usual rivalry between railway and road transport. The best advice on transportation has been the Larkin Plan, which was prepared in the 1960s by foreign experts of the World Bank.

The financial sector is perhaps in the best position at present. The Central Bank is adequately supplied with economists and there are a great many economists in the private banks and the other financial institutions. This permits a useful dialogue among the economic teams of the Central Bank, the private banks and banking associations.

Macroeconomic experience

The experience of economists in macroeconomic policies has also varied greatly, from downright failure to considerable success. Here we discuss three cases in which the economist's performance has been at least partially successful. These cases illustrate the different ways in which the economist has influenced macro policies in Argentina.[37]

Economic policy of the Radical Party, 1963–6

In October 1963 the Argentine economy went into depression. GDP fell by 6.7 per cent in 1962–3. Manufacturing industry, accounting for some 45 per cent of GDP, declined 8 per cent over the same period. Unemployment in Buenos Aires was 8.8 per cent in July 1963. Idle capacity reached 70 per cent for the production of capital goods and semidurables, and 30 per cent for the production of consumption goods, averaging 45 per cent for all productive activites. Taxes and social-security contributions declined sharply. Many enterprises were not in a position to pay the duties for machinery and equipment which had been ordered during the investment boom of 1960–1 and had already entered the country, standing in the Buenos Aires customs house. Banking was sluggish and about 10 per cent of the loan portfolios were in default. The outcome for government finance was that, by 1964, 57 per cent of expenditure was financed by money issue and delays in payment. Foreign debt amounted to $3.4 billion, of which 56.2 per cent was due for 1964–6; the net foreign-exchange position was −$400 million at the end of 1963.

An economic policy was devised by government economists to improve the level of economic activity and employment, the monetary and fiscal situation and the balance of payments. The policy was intended to stimulate firms to produce more with modest increases in demand for inputs and capital goods from abroad. Employment was expected to increase – and with it taxes and social-security contributions – provoking an inflationary increase of aggregate demand. Money creation and the fiscal deficit were also to be checked in order to reduce inflationary pressures.

The following measures were implemented: firms were granted banking credit at easy terms and low interest to withdraw the machinery and equipment standing at the customs house and to put them to work; banks loans were made to firms employing a high proportion of domestic inputs and labor-intensive technologies; special bank loans were made to firms to settle their tax debts to the government; imports were regulated in order to reduce the demand for foreign exchange; securities were issued to foreigners to pay the foreign debt; the number of civil servants was frozen; and monetary policy was tightened.

The program was successful during 1964–5, when GDP grew at annual rates of 9–10 per cent in absolute terms, and 6–7 per cent in per capita terms. Manufacturing grew at annual rates of 12–15 per cent. Unemployment fell to 5–6 per cent of the labor force. The share of wages in GDP increased from 36.6 per cent in 1963 to 41 per cent in 1966. Foreign debt was reduced to $2.65 billion at the end of 1965, and by June 1966 the net foreign reserve position amounted to $100 million. Private investment in equipment rose 13 per cent in 1964 and 5 per cent in 1965.

The record on inflation was less successful. Measured by wholesale prices, inflation fell from an annual rate of 29 per cent to 24 per cent during 1963–5. Consumer prices fell from 26 per cent to 22 per cent in 1963–4, but then rose again to 29 per cent in 1965.

The 'Krieger-Vasena Plan', 1967–9

During 1966, GNP virtually stagnated, increasing only 0.7 per cent in absolute terms and decreasing 0.7 per cent on a per capita basis. Industrial production increased at an annual rate of only 1.6 per cent and agricultural production declined 0.4 per cent. On the other hand, inflation accelerated and the cost-of-living index rose 32 per cent.

A shock treatment was devised in December 1966 to freeze income shares and to reduce inflation without bringing about a recession. For the longer term, an attempt would be made to open the economy, thus abandoning the old model of growth based on import substitution and promoting economic integration with the other Latin American Free Trade Association (LAFTA) countries.

There were two main economic policy measures:

1. There was a large, sudden foreign-exchange devaluation, and a fixed-rate system was substituted for the crawling peg. The devaluation was allowed to produce its full financial effects. But its real effects on the agricultural sector were offset by establishing export duties on traditional exports and reducing import taxes, thus providing an incentive for nontraditional (i.e. industrial) exports.
2. Wages, which had been at a high level (the highest for a three-year period in real terms), were frozen for a year and a half (until December 1968) and collective bargaining was halted.

As a result of this policy, the rate of inflation fell persistently, whether measured by consumer prices (29 per cent in 1967, 16 per cent in 1968, and 7.6 per cent in 1969) or wholesale prices (25 per cent in 1967, 9 per cent in 1968 and 6 per cent in 1969). After the stagnation of 1966, GNP began to rise at the highest rate of growth since the end of World War II, an expansion which was to last until 1973. Since this program went into effect, about 20 per cent of Argentine exports have been industrial products.

The Austral Plan, 1985–6

This plan was put into effect because of the very high rate of inflation recorded during 1984 and a further acceleration during the first half of 1985. The average rate of price increase, measured by the cost-of-living index, was 18 per cent monthly during the last quarter of 1984 and 25 per cent in January 1985. When the price-stabilization plan was devised, prices were increasing at a rate of more than 20 per cent a month; in the month preceding the adoption of the plan, it was higher than 30 per cent. However, although high, the price increases did not yet give rise to a runaway hyperinflation, since contracts were still stated in money terms.

A shock strategy was adopted to stop inflation, while compensating for the financial effects on money contracts to avoid massive redistributions of wealth and income. Three types of policies were adopted:

1. Fiscal and monetary measures, including severe restraint on expenditure to reduce the fiscal deficit and the termination of the financing of the deficit by money issue.
2. Massive freezing of prices, wages, tariffs and exchange rates in order to halt the inertia of upward-spiralling prices.
3. A monetary reform to neutralize the distributive effect of a sudden and unexpected fall of the rate of inflation and to provide for constancy in real terms of the payments involved in money contracts. A new money was created, the austral, to replace the old peso at the rate of exchange

of 1:10,000. Forward contracts in pesos were converted into australs at a rate varying according to a predetermined time schedule.

The rate of inflation declined sharply – although it remained high by international standards – yet a severe recession was avoided. As an attack on inflation, the Austral program was undeniably successful at least until March 1986 (the so-called first stage of the plan). Later developments in the level of fiscal deficit, investment and prices should be attributed to subsequent policy errors and not to the design of the plan and its initial execution.[38]

Participation of economists

The Radical Party maintained a Committee of Economic Affairs, which included graduates of the old course in accounting. When Illia took over the presidency of the Republic in 1963, he appointed members of that committee to the economic posts of his administation.[39] Although these appointees were not all professional economists, their membership in the Radical Party made them a naturally cooperative team and their affinity to economic science enabled them to adopt the economist's language and policy orientation.

Economists contributed to the economic program of the Radical Party in the early 1960s through CONADE, which was directed by the engineer R. Carranza who was very influential in the government. He was very successful in supplying technical economic support to the governing party. As a by-product, the professional economist exerted more influence on economic policy than at any time since the early 1940s.

Krieger-Vasena designed his economic program between December 1966 and March 1967 with the help of Central Bank technicians under the direction of the vice-president of that institution and the directors of CONADE's financial, foreign and public-sector programs. After the program was announced on 13 March 1967, a remarkable economic team was formed, all the more so if it is recognized that, when Krieger-Vasena was appointed, there were no economists in the Ministry of the Economy. Technical support came from three independent teams:

1. An economic policy team, which was headed by the director of CONADE's financing sector who in turn drew several high-level technicians from CONADE.
2. A fiscal studies team that had been organized in the Treasury in 1965–6, with graduates of the University of La Plata, who specialized in fiscal policy.
3. A monetary policy team consisting of economists at the Central Bank, which had begun to attract young economists since 1965, who made monetary policy a major instrument of economic management.

The major difference between the experience under Krieger-Vasena and that of the Radical Party is that CONADE was not part of the Ministry of the Economy.

The Austral Plan was launched within the framework of an advanced professionalism among economists, supported by a strong Central Bank team with experience in economic analysis and techniques. The Minister of the Economy, himself a technocrat, managed to appoint first-rate economists to the key economy posts: Secretary of Economic Programming, the Treasury, and Secretary of Economic Policy. When the Austral Plan was being designed in the months before June 1985, many technicians inside and outside the government were called upon to evaluate specific aspects of the plan.

INSTITUTIONAL IMPROVEMENTS TO ENHANCE THE ECONOMIST'S ROLE

Three improvements can be made to enhance the role of economists in Argentina: improve the training of economists; create conditions which will encourage them to remain in Argentina; and promote more effective use of economists in government.

Development of economists

The economics curriculum in Argentina is of an acceptable intermediate level, but not higher. Students at Argentine universities are perhaps not too different from undergraduates at universities in the United States and other countries. Experience has shown that Argentine graduates can be successful at the graduate level abroad. It has also been observed with no significant exceptions that, whatever may be the level of Argentine students, studying economics at good universities abroad enhances their economics training and improves their effectiveness either as scholars or as government officials. Accordingly, arrangements should be made to encourage Argentine students to complete their economics training at first-rate foreign universities.

Retention within the country

Argentine economists exhibit a strong propensity to migrate abroad. However, forced retention within the country reduces morale and undermines the effectiveness of qualified people. It would be useful to develop study centers in the private sector where the economists may keep up to date and develop independent opinions. The government would then have pools or reserves of skilled economists capable of giving advice or filling government positions. To tap the available pool of economists, the government might enter into agreements or contracts with the private and university study centers for research in economic policy. Through the contracting device, the economist can earn more than he would earn as a government employee and in turn maintain an independent point of view while remaining in Argentina.

Effective use by the government

A major problem is that the government does not make effective use of the available economists. As a result of defective organization, there is a weakness of staff or advisory functions compared to line functions. This explains the most total absence of staffs within certain vital areas of government, like the Ministry of Foreign Affairs.

There is also a shortage of people to link economists with non-economic sectoral technicians (like engineers). To remedy this problem advisory teams might be set up in the main sectors of the government to plan, study and think through the economic problems of the sector. These teams would produce more efficient and rational economic analysis, especially in those sectors that suffer from internal battles about purely technical issues, like transportation, energy, health and education.

NOTES

1. In November 1823, the University of Buenos Aires created a chair in political economy. Eventually the course became compulsory for those seeking the economics degree. It has been taught every year since, except for the period 1831–53. These classes were attended, for example, by Carlos Pellegrini (1846–1906), who later became a lawyer, politician and President of the Republic (1890–2) and had to cope with the profound economic crisis of the 1890s. Pellegrini coped with the crisis and created a major institution of monetary control, the Bank of Argentina (1891). This is an instance of a non-economist who excelled as a successful economic policymaker.
2. Among others, mathematics, statistics, biometrics, actuarial mathematics, public finance, economic history, banking and transportation economics.
3. Luis Roque Gondra (1881–1947) was a lawyer and a politician. He was professor of history of commerce on the Faculty of Economics of the University of Buenos Aires in 1913–18 and professor of political economy in 1919–46. He published more than twenty books and numerous papers on economics.
4. Alejandro E. Bunge (1880–1943) was a graduate of the University of Saxony, Germany, professor of statistics on the Faculty of Economics of the University of Buenos Aires, and later General Director of the Statistics and Census Bureau. He published books on national income, labor statistics, foreign trade, unemployment, railways, regional industries, customs policy, the wine industry and provincial finance. He founded and directed the *Revista de Economía Argentina*, which was published from 1918 to the 1950s.
5. Raul Prebisch (1901–86) was professor of political economy at the University of Buenos Aires from 1925 to 1948. He held various posts in the Argentine government, including General Manager of the Central Bank from 1935 to 1943. He was executive secretary of ECLA from 1949 to 1963 and general secretary of UNCTAD from 1963 to 1969.
6. José Barral Souto (1903–76), born in Spain, was a public accountant and an

actuary (1929), as well as an economist. He was professor of statistics from 1933 to 1942, professor of economics in 1936–7, and professor of biometry beginning in 1942. His linear-programming solution to the Richardian theory of comparative advantage ranks among other noteworthy solutions, such as those discovered by Kantorovich and George Stigler. There is an English translation of his work (Souto, 1967).

7. For example, economic research was conducted by the Institutes of Banking and Biometry.
8. The faculty, graduates and students regularly published a journal of economic sciences, *Revista de Ciencias Económicas*, founded in 1913.
9. Federico Pinedo (1895–1971) was a lawyer and politician. He was Minister of the Treasury in 1933–5 and 1940–1. In 1931 he joined Prebisch and others in a project to develop a Central Bank, which was created in 1935.
10. In his inaugural lecture on economic dynamics in May 1945, Prebisch recalled that the Central Bank sent young graduates to Harvard for two years, where they obtained excellent training as well as the ability to think independently, and recommended procedures to create professors and researchers on economics. (*Revista de Ciencias Económicas*, 1945, p. 527.)
11. Benjamin Cornejo (1906–74), a lawyer, was vice-rector of the University of Cordoba from 1959 to 1963. He was a member of the Argentine Academy of Economic Sciences.
12. Carlos Eugenio Dieulefait (1901–82), a land surveyor, was vice-president of the Inter-American Institute of Statistics. He founded the School of Statistics in 1947–8, the University of Litoral in Rosario, and other centers of statistical research.
13. Julio H. G. Olivera, a lawyer, was professor of political economy and rector of the University of Buenos Aires from 1962 to 1965 and president of the Argentine Political Economy Association in 1957. He founded and directed the Institute of Economic Research at the university in 1961.
14. Oreste Popescu, a lawyer, was born in Romania in 1913 and received a doctorate in economics and political science from the University of Innsbruck in 1948. He was professor of economics and the history of economic thought at the University of La Plata. In 1952 he translated and edited *Biblioteca de Ciencias Económicas*, a series of foreign treatises on economics. He was the first director of the Institute of Economics and Finance at the University of La Plata and there began publishing the professional journal, *Económica*. He founded the Argentine Political Economy Association in 1956–7.
15. The founding members were Juan E. Alemann, Roberto T. Alemann, Julio Broide, Benjamin Cornejo, Aldo Ferrer, Juan José Guaresti, Carlos C. Helbling, Carlos Moyano Llerena, Julio H. G. Olivera, Federico Pinedo, Oreste Popescu, Ovidio Schiopetto, Francisco Valsecchi and Franciso Garcia Olano.
16. Francisco Valsecchi received his doctorate in economic science from the University of Bocconi, Italy, in 1929. He was director of the Economic and Social Secretariat of the Argentine Catholic Action from 1934 to 1958. As professor of the faculties of economics and medicine at the University of Buenos Aires, he taught sociology, economics and social legislation. He was the organizer and first dean of the Faculty of Economic and Social Sciences of the Catholic University of Argentina (1958–70) and was the Argentine Ambassador to the Netherlands from 1971 to 1972. He published the *Social Syllabus* (1939–43, 3 vols) and more than 100 books and articles.
17. Among the visiting professors in 1962–4 were Phyllis Deane, E. J. Mishan, W. Reddaway, L. Joy, Paul P. Streeten, Charles Clayton and Charles Prou.
18. At the University of Tucuman, the promotion of economics during the late 1950s was closely associated with Adolfo Cesar Diz, director of the economics depart-

ment and founder of the Institute of Economic Research. Diz was later appointed director of the Latin American Monetary Studies Center (CEMLA, Mexico) and president of the Central Bank in 1976.

19. Notably with Professors M. Sidrausky at the University of Chicago and MIT, R. Mandel at Yale and Harvard Universities, and G. Calvo at Columbia University.
20. The CFI, which was created on 29 August 1959, included all Argentine provinces except Buenos Aires which joined later. CONADE was created by Decrees 7290 and 7291/61, which have been in force since 30 August 1961.
21. These were the Center of Economic Research (CIE) of the Institute Torcuato Di Tella, formed by G. Di Tella; the Institute of Economic Research, Faculty of Economics, University of Buenos Aires, created by Olivera; the Institute of Economics Research, Faculty of Economics, University of Tucuman, created by A. C. Diz; the Institute of Economics and Finance, University of Cordoba; and the Center of Economic Research, University of Cuyo. The first is private, while the others belong to national public universities. All were created between the late 1950s and the early 1960s.
22. To the list may be added the Institute of Economic and Social Development (IDES), whose creation was inspired by A. Ferrery. IDES does not employ economists but promotes economic knowledge through teaching and the publication of the professional journal *Desarrollo Económico*, which began appearing in 1960.
23. Distinguished visitors during the 1960s included W. Leontief, W. Ropke, F. Hayek, W. Reddaway, R. Prebisch, O. Lange, J. R. Hicks, J. Kendrich, E. Schneider, W. W. Rostow, P. Baran, A. Smithies, A. Harberger, H. Johnson, D. Patinkin, R. Ferber, H. G. Johnson, H. Uzawa, and D. Jorgenson. There were also visiting scholars associated with the Ford Program at the University of Buenos Aires, the Cuyo Plan at the University of Cuyo, and members of the Harvard Advisory Group at CONADE.
24. *Relevamiento de la Estructura Económica Regional* (Buenos Aires: Instituto Di Tella, 1962, and CFI, 1965 in 5 vols), directed by H. J. C. Grupe, N. Gonzalez, A. Fracchia, and F. S. Tami.
25. The directors of special teams were O. Altimir, H. Nuñez Miñana, and J. V. Sourrouille. Gonzales is at present executive secretary of ECLA and formerly director of ILPES (Latin American Institute of Economic and Social Planning). Sourrouille has been Minister of Economy since 1985.
26. Where C. Rodriguez Areco, a University of Buenos Aires graduate, Chicago PhD and Columbia University professor, has a heavy influence.
27. Created and directed by D. Cavallo, a University of Cordoba graduate and Harvard PhD. He was president of the Central Bank.
28. Led by J. C. de Pablo, an Argentine Catholic University and Harvard graduate.
29. Inspired by A. Canitrot, an engineer and Stanford PhD. He has been number two in the Ministry of Economy since 1985.
30. Pioneered among others by the author of this paper.
31. The briefest account cannot omit: (a) Bunge's *Income and Wealth of Argentina* (1917), containing estimates based on the 1914 Census figures; (b) a team organized by Paul Prebisch and led by Manuel Balboa at the Office of Economic Research of the Central Bank, which operated from 1942 to 1946 and brought out a well-prepared unpublished estimate of national income for 1942, *National Income of the Argentine Republic* (1946) with estimates for 1935–45, and prepared other routine estimates; (c) the moving of the Central Bank team to the Secretary of Economic Affairs, culminating with *Product and Income of the Argentine Republic* for the period 1935–54 (1955); (d) after the national income

team was returned to the Central Bank, the operation in Argentina of a Joint Argentine Government–United Nations Group, from mid-1956 to mid-1957, appointed to prepare a report on the Argentine economy. This inspired other important research, including Alberto Fraccia's *Argentine Gross Investment and Capital by Economic Sectors and Type of Investment and Capital, 1900–55* and *Income Distribution by Earning Types and Activity Sector in Argentina*, Angel Monti's *Preliminary Estimate of Argentina's Gross Product, 1900–55, at 1950 Prices*, and Manuel Balboa's *Use of the Input–Output Model in Projections of the Argentine Economy*; (e) the development of the table of intersectoral transactions of the Argentine economy, by the Central Bank, with estimates for 1953; (f) the joint statistical work by CONADE–UNECLA, published as *Income Distribution and National Accounts of Argentina* in five volumes (1965).

32. The improvement of budget making is associated with Cayetano Antonio Licciardo, who was Director of the National Budget Bureau in 1966 and Minister of the Economy and Education in 1982–3. He has also been Dean of the Faculties of Economics of the University of La Plata, the Catholic University of Argentina and Buenos Aires University.
33. To wit, Adalbert Krieger-Vasena and José Alfredo Martinez de Hoz.
34. Raul Prebisch, 1955–6; Harvard Advisory Group, at CONADE, 1963–6; and Raul Prebisch again, 1983–6.
35. To Krieger-Vasena and Martinez de Hoz (see note 34), the Economics Ministry during the Radical Party administration may be added. This position was held by Eugenio A. Blanco from 1963 up to his death (ten months), succeeded by Juan Carlos Pugliese (twenty-two months).
36. To quote Elizalde (1980) again: 'What can one do in five months, but to go on carrying out what others did?'
37. For an account of postwar Argentine economic policies by those who made them, see Di Tella *et al.* (forthcoming).
38. For a detailed analysis of the plan and its implementation, see Dornbusch *et al.* (forthcoming).
39. The Economics Minister (Blanco), the Central Bank president (Elizalde), and the secretaries of the Treasury (Garcia Tudero), Industry and Mining (Concepción), and Commerce (Grinspun) were all PhDs in economic science or accounting; the vice-secretary of Labor (Lopez) was a chemist. Blanco had been a member of the faculty of economics (1945) and professor of accounting. Elizalde had taken a graduate course in finance and economics at Columbia (1950). Garcia Tudero was professor of statistics in the faculty of economics.

BIBLIOGRAPHY

Di Tella, Guido *et al.* (eds), *The Ministers Talk* (Oxford: Oxford University Press, forthcoming).

Dornbusch, Rudiger *et al.* (eds), *The Austral Plan* (Cambridge, MA: The MIT Press, forthcoming).

Elizalde, Felix, in Juan Carlos de Pablo (ed.), *La Economía que Yo Hice* (Buenos Aires, 1980).

Guadagni, Alieto Aldo, 'La investigación de la realidad argentina en la formación del economista, *Revista de Economía y Estadística* (Cordoba, 1968), 3–4, p. 72.

Souto, José Barral, The fundamental principles of the division of labor, *International Economic Papers*, vol. 12 (London, 1967).

11 · COLOMBIA*

Lauchlin Currie

INTRODUCTION

I must confess to some initial difficulty in discussing economic advice giving in Colombia. A discussion of the actual economic policies adopted and who gave what advice would doubtless be boring to a foreign reader. Whether the advice was 'good' or 'bad' is often a matter of personal judgement and would take me afield from the subject of this volume. Perhaps 'good' advice was ineffective either in the sense of not being acceptable or in being spoiled in its implementation. Presumably, advice played a role in the adoption of most policies but whether the persons advising qualify as economists is a matter of opinion. I have therefore decided to confine myself to a general treatment of the conditions under which economic advice by professional economists is offered and the administrative and organizational framework within which advice is offered and how it might be improved. Even the use of the term 'improved' implies judgement on the part of the writer on the 'goodness' of advice. I will try to minimize the element of judgement by adopting only the criterion of the impact of policy on growth. But even this is very ample and controversial. This criterion will be applied both to policy and the administrative organization for policy formulation.

A further cautionary word is in order. An element of judgement is involved in deciding the degree to which growth can be attributed to market forces – the 'invisible hand' – or to well-chosen economic policies. My personal view is that the considerable development of Colombia owes more to the former than to the latter, though on occasion policy and market forces have operated in harmony. But frequently mistaken policies have, I think, impeded growth. A further difficulty is that the credit (and blame) for a policy is generally

* In an attempt to substitute generalization for examples I have omitted some examples that can be found in *The Role of Economic Advisers in Developing Countries* (Currie, 1981).

This brief account can be usefully supplemented by an excellent review article by James Hanson of the World Bank on six recent books on Colombia, and which deals with more specific cases of advising (Hanson, 1987).

claimed by or meted out to a head of a ministry or department, and the adviser, if there is one, is unknown.[1]

Some words on the more recent economic development of Colombia is indispensable for what follows, but I will confine them to a bare minimum.

GROWTH IN COLOMBIA

It is helpful to divide growth since 1950 in two broad periods: 1950 to 1980 and 1980 to 1985. In the former, substantial economic progress was made. The average rate of growth was 4.7 per cent and it was fairly well sustained, the lowest annual figure being 1.1 per cent and the highest 8.5 per cent. The country passed from a predominantly peasant economy to a predominantly urban, non-agricultural economy. Despite the continuing importance of labor-intensive coffee growing, the ratio of rural to total population declined from 61 per cent to 34 per cent. The growth in per capita income was even more marked, rising from an average of 1.4 per cent in the 1950s to 2.7 per cent in the 1970s, owing to the fall in the birth rate that accompanied the urbanization–industrial process. Thus two of the necessary great transformations from being a lesser to a more developed country had been made by 1980. Development appeared to be well under way, attributable in good part to the operation of market forces aided by, or at least not nullified by, economic policies.

From 1980 to 1985 gross economic growth fell sharply and per capita growth was nearer zero – a dangerous condition in a 'growth-bound' economy, that is, an economy whose economic, social and political life depends on steadily rising employment and real incomes. In 1985 open unemployment was reported at around 13–15 per cent of the labor force. But this figure is misleading. With no employment insurance there was a marked growth in the 'informal' sector – small workshops and street merchants – people who would join the better-paid workforce if they could. In addition, there are too many rural people living on a bare subsistence income and a veritable army not only of soldiers but of lower-paid messengers, private guards, police and domestic servants. By early 1985 the gap between an extrapolation of the trend growth rate of the 1970s and the actual real GNP was some 17 percentage points – an accumulated loss of potential production of US$17 billion in 1975 dollars, or 86 per cent of the 1985 GNP itself. Economic policies that were adopted either contributed to the stoppage of growth or at least did not serve to reactivate the economy or counteract recessive forces. The situation improved in 1986 but this was probably due in large part to poor coffee weather in Brazil and hence increased receipts from coffee by Colombia – an exogenous market force.

ELEMENTS CONDITIONING ECONOMIC ADVICE GIVING

The cultural background

In explaining the handicaps under which the invisible hand works, which in turn influenced the type of economic advice adopted, it is first necessary to say a few words on the culture of the society in question, using the word 'culture' in the sense of the body of beliefs generally held. In this sense the culture has a profound influence on the type of policies adopted.

In Colombia, and I believe in most Latin American countries, there is little faith in the market. Everything must be controlled and regulated. The rise in prices is generally thought to be due to speculation, hoarding and monopoly. The economic system, by itself, is thought to make the rich richer and the poor poorer. This tendency, it is generally believed, must be resisted by direct intervention of the state. The minimum wage scale must be set as otherwise employers would, it is believed, exploit workers. In Colombia, the Labor Code governing relations between employers and the employed is a hefty volume. Fringe benefits, which often exceed the basic wage, are usually paid at the end of the year and create distortions and contribute to excessive monetary expansion at that time. This tends to spill over into the new year and to accelerate inflation.

It is true that many controls and regulations are ineffective in what is euphemistically called the 'informal' sector, but that is what enables the sector to exist. However, they do raise costs in the larger and more modern types of enterprise where the main hope for progress and competitiveness in world markets lies. Colombia must be one of the most legalistic and, at the same time, lawless countries in the world. Naturally the two characteristics are related as the more pervasive the controls, the more the evasion. All imports require permits in advance and customs duties are very high. Consequently, contraband is general and fairly open. Since there is a chronic 'shortage' of exchange, capital export and the possession of assets in foreign currencies are forbidden. As might be expected, all people with means possess unreported foreign assets. The society of builders recently stated that 500 legal requirements must be observed to build a house. Naturally many are evaded, particularly in what is called self-construction.

The list of examples could be extended almost indefinitely. The point I wish to make is that the culture which underlies this resort to controls, impedes and places obstacles to the functioning of a mixed market economy and reduces the competitiveness of the 'modern' sector in world markets.

The economics of the man in the street

There are a considerable number of economists in Colombia, many of whom have received advanced training abroad. But the economics of the people who make economic policy is usually that of the man in the street – what

Henderson (1986) calls 'do-it-yourself economics'. Regrettably, in this type of economics in all countries, what is sound is generally unpopular; what is popular is generally unsound.

An example might be the attitude towards rural poverty. This must, it is widely felt, be tackled directly in land-tenancy reforms, rural credit facilities and so on. The underlying theoretical basis, which even the World Bank on occasion has subscribed to, is that the productivity of all farmers must be raised and that there is insufficient work for country people in the cities. Explaining that the experience of all more developed countries suggests that the solution for rural poverty must be found outside of agriculture arouses violent opposition. Here, again, the complete lack of faith in the beneficent effects of the market, in this case in its mobility aspects, is shown. Every effort must be made to retain people in the countryside, and even in the localities they happen to be. The importance of rural life and of smaller cities is unquestioned, especially by writers living in large cities. The big transport program of the 1950s and 1960s was presented and accepted not as a means of extending competition and mobility, but on the more homely argument of giving smaller towns and rural areas access to the markets of larger cities.

The economics of the man in the street are specially dangerous in dealing with monetary policy. The emphasis is invariably placed on the beneficence of credit extension – the more, the better. Membership of the Monetary Authority is weighted with ministers who are concerned to obtain more credit for agriculture and industry and feel, despite all evidence to the contrary, that more credit tends to lower interest rates. It is a firm belief that low interest rates are a necessary ingredient of any economic program.

It may be objected that the economics of the man in the street are not confined to less developed countries but find expression in the more advanced as well. That is quite true. *Small Is Beautiful* (Schumacher, 1973) has sold nearly a million copies. The difference is one of degree. For one thing I suspect that the sheer number of well-trained economists in more developed countries tends to intimidate to some extent the non-economists who make policy. For another, the degree of populism is much higher in Latin America. Election campaigns are long drawn-out and supercharged with emotion and promises. In Colombia the president's term is short (four years) and he is not permitted to run for re-election until after another term has elapsed. The average term of ministers is close to two years. Hence the emphasis of policy is on the side of short-term, publicity-rich projects and programs.

Conflicting objectives of policies

Much has been written on whether there is a necessary conflict between the pursuit at one and the same time of the objectives of equity and efficiency, or on the one hand better distribution and on the other high and sustained growth. Particular examples of inequality have a great influence. Poverty is very real and widespread. In such an environment cases of conspicuous consumption are especially repugnant. Overcrowded and badly maintained buses travel side by side with Mercedes Benz and BMW cars with a single driver. Crowded neighborhoods lacking essential services are contrasted with luxurious enclaves of residences of well-to-do people with numerous private guards.

In these circumstances, it is difficult to maintain that there are forces in the economic system working toward a better distribution of the fruits of growth, at least as far as income from wages and salaries go, or that the share of the conspicuously wealthy in the national income is relatively small. Statements, even in academic courses, that the share of work is around 75 per cent of the national income in all more developed countries are dismissed as without relevance for developing countries. And it must be admitted that market forces are not particularly effective in moderating inequalities resulting from inheritance and property. Nor does the argument carry weight that it is better to improve distribution *after* income has been earned rather than to prevent initial income inequalities.

All this leads to direct 'attacks' on poverty and excessively punitive measures to redress inequality. One recent president campaigned openly against economic growth and the national four-year program of his administration was concerned with closing the gap between the rich and the poor and between regions. (However, at the close of his term he came out for a high rate of growth.) Another presidential candidate and later president stressed 'social' objectives and placed them far above 'economic' objectives, with somewhat disastrous results.

This subject is a difficult and a controversial one and I do not wish to pursue it further than to emphasize the point that the advice of national or foreign economists who tend to stress high and sustained growth is likely to be subordinated to direct 'attacks' on poverty. To advocate an open and competitive society has little popular appeal, especially in contrast to the emotionally charged indignation on the plight of the many poor. Hence for this reason much good advice is disregarded, at least in Colombia.

The resentment toward the rich and lack of any faith in the equity of the mixed economic system carries over to large companies. They are subject to a host of rules, controls and regulations that do not apply to small workshops and commercial establishments such as restaurants and domestic services. The larger companies, it is felt, should be subject to controls and pay higher salaries and larger fringe benefits just because they are larger and, presumably, have the ability to pay.

In such an environment, to talk of wage inflation and to argue that higher wage rates and employee pensions in larger establishments may increase the unemployed and swell the ranks of the very poor and the 'informal' sector would make one a public enemy. So, the attempt is rarely made. The belief that higher wage scales ensure a higher aggregate demand and larger real production is widely held. A consequence of such an environment is that the owners and executives of larger companies do not try to defend the system in academic terms but rather come to terms with the environment in more subtle ways. These take the form of evasion of all kinds, and the exertion of personal influence, and in some cases, bribery. After all, the owners belong to the same social class as those who are making and executing the economic policies of the country. It is understood that the latter must say popular things but also, it is felt, they need not be taken too seriously in the actual conduct of affairs. Such attitudes are widely known and add to resentment and to the feeling that the system itself is all wrong.

Practically all Latin American countries have suffered long and hard bouts of inflation and attempts to secure stability of prices have generally failed. Such attempts, as exemplified by the advice of the IMF, call for a reduction in public expenditure and an increase in taxes, slowing down of monetary expansion and the rate of wage increases – and are all most unpopular. Political administrations are faced with a hard dilemma: either to yield to popular sentiment which will surely make them unpopular in the long run and ultimately turn them out of office, or to accept advice for austerity, which will be immediately unpopular. All of this may explain the failure of so much advice to be accepted by (or even offered to) Latin American countries. Evidently, political and environmental conditions differ in some Far Eastern countries and this is the basic reason for the widely different type of economic policies adopted.

THE INSTITUTIONAL FRAMEWORK FOR ADVICE GIVING

The organizational framework for macro and micro advice differs. Colombia followed the British practice of placing a great deal of the authority for macro policy formulation in the hands of the Minister of Finance. He presides over the Monetary Authority, which also deals with exchange policy and advises the president on a national indexed savings–mortgage system. His ministry includes the Budget Office and is responsible for taxation and public credit (internal and external borrowing). Finally, he sets the salaries of government employees which, in turn, usually set the pattern for the private sector. There is a National Planning Department, which is supposed to formulate the overall objectives and strategy of government and to pass on the 'investment' part of the budget and on foreign borrowing. However, the status of the Minister of Finance is so dominant in the government hierarchy that few other ministers or heads of agencies take issue with him. Generally, therefore, insofar as macroeconomic policy is concerned, the economic advisers to the minister are the only ones that have much influence in this field. As he has a minimum economic staff of his own he relies, for technical matters, on the economists of the Central Bank and the economic advisers to the Monetary Board.

It can be seen that he is grossly overburdened. He can be summoned at any time to testify before congressional committees and at crucial times has had to devote most of his time to this onerous task. He has to do his thinking attending a host of meetings and has little time to read memos. He is the main channel to the president for both economic policy and the data on which it rests. As need hardly be said, the data presented and how they are presented exert a great deal of influence.

In the administration of 1982–6 there existed a Council of Economic Advisers to the President (of which I was a member). The work was part time and unpaid. The Council met at the call of the president and had a varying number of members, but usually six. At one point, it included an ex-president and two ex-ministers. Although generally attended by the president, the presiding officer was the Economic Secretary to the President. Unfortunately, most of the economic team of the government attended so that the attendance was usually from fifteen to twenty persons – much too large to permit an effective discussion. One had to talk into microphones to be heard at the end of an enormous table. When the Minister of Finance attended, he did most of the talking. The Council had little influence and quietly died with a change in administrations. I have dwelt on it in some detail as it was the only element in the economic team of the government where a case was made (unsuccessfully) for a massive devaluation and this, I think, is significant of the power of the Minister of Finance who, when it was urgent, strongly opposed devaluation and discouraged even any discussion of the possibility.[2]

There is a large Council of National Economic and Social Policies. Despite its impressive title, its activities in large part consist of approving large investment projects. Granting licenses of imports is the responsibility of a body called Incomex, attached to the Central Bank and whose head is a member of the Monetary Board. Customs tariffs are under the Minister of Finance. So, for macroeconomic policy formulation and for the approval of other policies, the influence of the Minister of Finance is overwhelming and much of the macro advice he receives originates with the technicians of the Central Bank.

The Central Bank is in a position to attract good local economists and to further their training abroad. Up until the present it has been strongly non-monetarist or perhaps I should say it has been skeptical of the influence of M_1 on prices, and rather has stressed the importance of interest rates and the provision of special credit lines to agriculture, industry and exports. On the other hand, it does not have a Keynesian inclination. The bias has been toward *ad hoc* measures to restrain monetary expansion (advance deposits by importers, delayed payments to some important exports, high average reserve requirements and higher requirements on incremental deposits on occasion) rather than on the more orthodox and effective open-market operations. Since 1972 monetary expansion has ranged between 20 and 30 per cent per annum and inflation has been chronic.

It is difficult to disentangle and weigh the influence of the large Monetary Board, heavily weighted with ministers and others interested in promoting credit extension, the personal views of the changing Ministers of Finance, the technical advisers (two) to the Board (who also are frequently changed) and the technical staff of the Bank, which is the strongest single continuing element. With the Central Bank engaging in so many and diverse activities, the number of transactions affecting reserves and reserve requirements is very large and, for the layman, difficult to understand. Finally there is a strong element of secrecy and the publication of vital information is unduly delayed so there is a lack of expert informed commentaries on current policy.

For micro advice, the institutional environment is also far from favorable. The inefficiency of the ministries has led to the proliferation of semi-independent agencies, often with their own sources of revenue or enjoying the receipts of earmarked taxes. A minister typically is a member of many boards but in reality possesses little authority to make changes or even to know what is occurring in his general field.

In certain technical fields, such as hydroelectric power facilities, the World Bank has been able to exert a certain degree of influence by virtue of its loans, but this has not prevented a large overcapacity of hydro facilities (and related foreign indebtedness), vulnerable to weather conditions, and with little reliance on the country's very large coal and natural gas reserves for domestic consumption.

In addition to the earmarking of specific sources of revenues (e.g. 2 per cent of salaries for apprenticeship training), large yearly transfers of funds from the national government to provincial and local authorities must be made for health, education and general 'investment ' purposes. So actually the Budget Division in the Ministry of Finance is more an accounting office than an agency responsible for the allocation of resources and the improvement of management in government.

Minimum wage scales are set by the government in December for the following year. After a great deal of negotiation with representatives of labor, the scale is generally set to offset the expected rate of inflation plus an optimistic allowance for increasing productivity. There appears to be little effort or scope for efforts to work out a coordinated program of reducing simultaneously the rates of monetary and wage inflation. Anywhere from a 20–30 per cent rate of increase in both is generally considered satisfactory, or if not satisfactory, unavoidable. In the generally populist environment, the government and its many agencies have proved to be poor bargainers *vis-à-vis* strong unions, as well as inefficient managers.

On foreign economic policy, with the exception of a few favorable periods, the country has not been a legally open society. Protection through tariffs has been high, but worse are the quantitative restraints. For a time in 1984–5, every import required an advance license which could only be obtained by submitting a mass of documents. This became necessary because of the overvaluation of the peso dating from the coffee boom of 1976–8 and foreign borrowing, which weakened the competitive position of non-coffee exports and gave an incentive to borrow still more. The heavy debt service and the consequent pressure from debtors was a leading factor in the delay from 1980 to 1985 in carrying out a massive devaluation, and then only in 1985 in the form of an accelerated mini-devaluation, maintaining convertibility throughout.

LESSONS THAT MAY BE DRAWN

Two lessons can be drawn from this perhaps excessively pessimistic account. I have already mentioned the strength of market forces. Up to 1980, growth was fairly high despite all the obstacles mentioned. The desire to secure higher profits or salaries or to secure a better position is indeed a powerful force. For example, in a short period of fifteen years, individuals surmounted all kinds of obstacles to develop a large market abroad for fresh flowers, especially roses and carnations. Colombia became the second largest exporter of flowers. In another case, houses and offices and commercial buildings are built despite the hundreds of legal requirements that must be surmounted (or evaded). New and faster-growing varieties of coffee were introduced by the federation of coffee growers. A foreign company recently discovered a very large oil field (though guerrilla activities made it difficult to keep the oil flowing in the pipeline). The Exxon Company made an enormous investment in a coal strip mining venture that required a new railroad and a port. And the country benefited from purely chance bad weather conditions for coffee in Brazil while possessing large stocks. Silently and opposed by official policy, the country became largely urbanized and the excessively high birth rate fell.[3] Even in the long and severe recession of the 1980s, with accompanying violence and insecurity, the rate of growth flattened but did not become negative. Probably the fiscal deficit helped but it was unplanned and every effort was made to reduce it.

However, there is a limit to the extent to which market forces and the self-perpetuating growth process[4] can make headway against questionable policies. The coffee boom of 1975–8 was accompanied by the all too familiar symptoms of 'the Dutch disease' – inflation, overvaluation of the currency for things other than the particular product of the boom, and excessive foreign borrowing. The growth in international reserves was only partially nullified and monetary expansion ranged from 24 per cent to 37 per cent per annum. Inflation ranged from 17 per cent to 29 per cent in the same period.

The general euphoria and high central bank reserves contributed to excessive borrowing in the latter years immediately following the boom, so that debt service rose from 14 per cent of exports in 1979 to nearly 40 per cent in 1983. By 1980 the country was in a vulnerable position and production began to fall and experienced its longest and most severe recession, until relieved by the second but minor and short-lived coffee boom in 1985–6 and by a greatly accelerated pace of exchange depreciation in 1985.

Surveying the period since 1950 it appears that many of the macroeconomic policies that were followed were ill advised. In the earlier part of the period the forces of the market were fairly vigorous. After 1974 exogenous developments and mistaken or inadequate policies shaped in large part the course of events. By the end of the period, the social and political conditions of the country had badly deteriorated. A correct diagnosis and a strong and persistent policy to counteract both recessionary and inflationary forces was urgently needed. The gap between possible and actual production had to be closed while at the same time inflation had to be reduced – somewhat the same problem confronting the United States in 1980–2.

THE ROLE OF ECONOMISTS IN ADVICE GIVING

Professional economic advice has originated from at least five principal sources: foreign economists (missions and advice from international agencies); the staff of the Central Bank and advisers to the Monetary Board; the staff of the National Planning Agency; economists attached to some trade associations; and private consulting firms and current economic publications.

Foreign advice

Foreign economic advice can be separated into two main types: 'untied' macroeconomic advice and advice tied to the financing of projects and programs. The first World Bank Mission of 1949 made a large number of both types of recommendations. Of those accepted and implemented, perhaps the most important was a complete transformation of the whole transport system – roads, air and rail. In a country which since its early days had suffered from a very difficult terrain and consequent lack of access to large markets, this transport program, with the exception of the rail part, had an enormous impact. Other advice of the same mission that was accepted included the establishment of a National Planning Agency, and the execution of a swift and unexpected devaluation that permitted, for some time, a much more open society.

Two other foreign economic missions had considerable impact: that of the IMF of 1966–7 and that of Richard Musgrave in 1968. The first recommended a massive devaluation, which is common, but in this case it was by the ingenious device of shifting transactions to an existing but much higher (lower in value) rate of exchange and, again in this case, not to a fixed but to a 'flexible' new rate. This latter advice led, almost inadvertently, not to a floating rate but to the 'creeping peg' system of small but continuous adjustments while maintaining convertibility.

The Musgrave Commission of 1968 advised the imposition of higher and more equitable tax rates. The advice, however, was not accepted until 1974 when, by chance, some younger national members of the Commission arrived at high office and a new president needed a 'reform' to fulfill campaign promises.

The last foreign overall economic mission was by Hollis Chenery whose report was made in the dying days of an administration and, naturally, was not acted upon. However, it was widely read and discussed and had an influence in this way. It was prepared mostly by Colombian economists.

Central Bank

The staff of the Central Bank and its role has already been mentioned. The Bank has provided secure positions for a considerable number of economists and they have exerted influence through the Bank's close and continuous relation to the successive ministers of finance. It is significant that IMF missions mostly deal directly with the staff of the Central Bank.

National Planning Agency

The National Planning Agency has been in existence since 1951 and its influence has varied. It has gone through various reorganizations and its present organization and functions have been spelled out in great detail by law. Although it has always had a strong macroeconomic or 'global' section, most of its work has been in studying programs and projects, especially those requiring or designed for foreign financing. In 1961 and again since 1969 it produced overall plans for new administrations. Mostly these are statements of objectives, but do indicate the basic orientation of the new administration toward growth and distribution.

Trade associations

An interesting recent development has been the infiltration of professional economists in the staff of the numerous trade associations (the Banking Association, the Agricultural Society, etc.). The economic quality of their publications and statements on current policies have improved markedly, though naturally the objectives of the particular associations continue to play a leading role.

Research organizations and periodicals

There are a number of research organizations either private or related to universities, and these have carried out a large number of studies under contract, mostly of a project-feasibility nature. However, some have been contracted for what might be called macroeconomic studies. The Commission on Public Expenditures of 1985–6 (of which I was a member) contracted a number of studies, including one on the macro aspects of fiscal policy. Economists have also found positions on the staff of a number of current periodicals concentrating on economic matters. Again, the quality of the commentaries has improved markedly.

Finally, a Colombian Economic Society has existed for a number of years and has secured legislation reserving various positions in the government to members of the Society.

CONCLUSIONS

The reader will probably be conscious of an apparent inconsistency between the earlier sections which tended to minimize the role of professional economists in the formulation of policy, and the previous section which lays stress on the growing number and training of economists in and outside the government. A part of the answer can be found in the section devoted to the organizational framework for policy formulation and especially macroeconomic policy. Given the dominant position of the Minister of Finance, the influence that economists can exert depends in good part on his use of economists. As emphasized earlier, he has little time for study or reading so that economic advice from any source other than the Central Bank influences neither the minister nor the president. The advice of the Planning Agency plays more of a role in decision making on individual investment projects.

Another explanation, and this involves elements of personal judgement on my part, can be found in the difference between macroeconomic theory, on which there is a considerable measure of agreement, and macro policy, in which wide differences may exist arising from differing personal values and the reliability and pertinence of the data used. Many economists feel that in Colombia the existence of elements of monopoly and oligopoly make regulations and price setting necessary. Others feel that widespread poverty justifies direct 'attacks' in the form of subsidies, price and wage fixing, reduced credit terms, rent controls, and so forth. For these reasons, the advice of economists has been divided, which is not unusual but which, perhaps, tends to minimize their influence. When, in 1972, I recommended the creation of a new savings and loan system in which the principal of both savings and mortgages were to be indexed, it was opposed by most economists as well as by others. This would have killed it if I had not had the ear of the head of the planning agency and of the president. In any case, despite the growing numbers and more advanced training of Colombian economists, many of the economic policies that are followed, presumably on somebody's advice, are open to question.

To repeat what was said earlier, the problem is not only to influence policy, but to influence it in a constructive way. Unfortunately there are still wide differences among macroeconomists on what is 'constructive'. The criteria here followed are those of the promotion of growth, with policies to secure better distribution to apply after income has increased rather than before.

SOME SUGGESTIONS

Developing countries in Latin America have all produced their own cadre of economists which is continually augmented by the incorporation of their own foreign-trained economists. However, one may offer some advice on possible improvements in the administrative or organizational framework for economic advice giving.

It will be recalled that Colombia followed the British practice of centralizing macroeconomic policy and economic advice in the Treasury. The American diffusion of macroeconomic policy advice giving by the Treasury, White House staff, Council of Economic Advisers and Federal Reserve Board and the various joint committees of the Congress appears messy in contrast with the British administrative centralization of advice. But it does have the merit of ensuring that the president is presented with differing points of view and alternative policies. The contrast between the divergences in economic advice giving in the Roosevelt administration and in the elimination of the dissidents on Vietnam in the Johnson administration may illustrate the point.

For another thing, the creation of such bodies as the Congressional Budget Office, the Joint Congressional Economic Committee and the Legislative Reference Bureau would serve two purposes: it would improve the content of legislation and open positions on their staffs for well-trained economists and lawyers. The present legislative process is chaotic, and there are no facilities to enable legislators to know the experience of other countries or even what can and cannot be done under existing laws. Actual laws range from giving the president in one sentence full power over personal savings to spelling out the organization and functions of each unit of the National Planning Office in twenty-seven single-spaced, legal-size pages!

Still another desirable institutional change would be the creation of a strong Budget and Management Office directly under the president, as was done in the United States in 1939, and whose head would carry as much or more political clout as have the ministers. Such an office, in conjunction with the ministries, could institute accounting systems appropriate for the different activities of the government and would be a force working against the constant proliferation of the functions of ministries among 'decentralized' agencies and other political entities and the accompanying earmarking of revenues for specific purposes and unconditional transfers of funds to local political entities.

The Monetary Authority badly needs to become a more professional full-time body with a sufficient degree of autonomy to enable it to resist the constant pressure from borrowers. Achieving stabilization without tears requires action on both the monetary and wage fronts, with an accompanying stimulus of a leading sector to offset the immediate recessive impact of more austere policies.

Consideration might be given to the re-establishment of a Council of Economic Advisers, limited in size and to people with professional qualifications, which could assume some of the macroeconomic advice-giving function of the National Planning Department and would in addition be required to make quarterly evaluations to the president of the economic situation and policies followed which, after a brief lapse, could be made public. To assure their autonomy and independence, it would be desirable to give the members fixed terms of office and a small but expert staff.

To dismantle the mass of regulations and controls that apply to all economic activity and to create a more open and competitive society is probably a requisite for the resumption of rapid and sustained growth. But undeniably it will be a most difficult task. The organizational changes suggested above would help to provide an atmosphere for change.

As mentioned earlier, advice which is tied to foreign financing is more likely to be accepted than 'pure' advice. This offers both a great opportunity and responsibility, especially for the World Bank. Most of its advice in the past has been of a microeconomic nature but there are encouraging indications that more attention will be paid in the future to macroeconomic advising and to sponsoring economic research in developing countries. However, this topic is treated in detail elsewhere in the volume.

Finally, leading economic graduate schools abroad might place less stress on mathematics and measurement in their economics courses, and more on the study of successful and unsuccessful economic policies in their own and other countries. There is a wealth of material to be analyzed and weighed but neither professors nor PhD candidates appear to have time to study the material. It is still not appreciated that policy formulation and implementation is much more difficult than theory. An analysis of what has been tried, what succeeded and what failed and why, should help improve the basis of judgement of students from developing countries and better the advice or the criticism they will offer when the opportunity offers.

NOTES

1. One of the qualifications for administrative assistants to the president in the United States Government Reorganization Act of 1939 was that they have a 'passion for anonymity'.
2. In the administration that assumed office in 1986 a small group of 'advisers' in the office of the president had, at the time of writing (1987) unusual influence, somewhat similar to that of the White House staff. They were persons in whom the president had confidence.
3. The government permitted the dissemination of family-planning information.
4. As set forth in a notable address by Allyn Young (1928).

BIBLIOGRAPHY

Currie, Lauchlin, *The Role of Economic Advisers in Developing Countries*, (Westport, Conn.: Greenwood Press, 1981).

Hanson, James, 'Growth and distribution in Colombia', *Latin American Research Review*, vol. 22, no. 1 (1987).

Henderson, P. D., *Innocence and Design, the Influence of Economic Ideas on Policy* (Oxford: Basil Blackwell, 1986).

Schumacher, E. F., *Small is Beautiful: Economics as if People Mattered* (New York: Harper & Row, 1973).

Young, Allyn, 'Increasing returns and economic progress', *Economic Journal* (December 1928).

INTERNATIONAL ORGANIZATIONS

12 · THE INTERNATIONAL MONETARY FUND AND THE WORLD BANK

*Richard Goode and Andrew M. Kamarck**

Among international organizations the International Monetary Fund (IMF) and the World Bank Group are generally considered unusually successful and influential. Since both are concerned with economic policies of member countries and employ large numbers of economists, an examination of the work of economic advisers in them can help in appraising the impact of the profession. In these international organizations, economists are free of some of the constraints that operate in national governments, but they face the difficulties – and the stimulus – of dealing with diverse groups of colleagues, officials and politicians and of applying their techniques in economies that often differ greatly from those of their native countries.

This chapter begins with a brief description of the two organizations and the position of economists in them. It then distinguishes between the 'inside' roles of economists in the management and policy formation of the institutions, and their 'outside' roles, that is, their work with and influence on member countries. Separate sections on the IMF and the World Bank follow. A short final section makes some comparisons and contrasts and states some conclusions.

THE ORGANIZATIONS AND THE PLACE OF ECONOMISTS IN THEM

The IMF and the World Bank (legal name: International Bank for Reconstruction and Development) were created according to plans approved at a conference of forty-five countries held at Bretton Woods, New Hampshire, in 1944. Their membership now includes nearly all independent states except

* While this paper is a joint product, Goode is primarily responsible for the section on the IMF and Kamarck for the section on the World Bank. Goode acknowledges with thanks helpful comments and suggestions from Margaret Garritsen de Vries. The section on the World Bank owes a great deal to the perceptive comments of Gerald Alter, Bernard Bell, W. David Hopper, and Benjamin B. King. The responsibility for any mistakes or misinterpretations rests with the authors, of course.

Switzerland, the USSR, Albania, Bulgaria, Czechoslovakia and East Germany. They are governed by Boards of Governors made up of a single representative of each member and resident boards of appointed or elected executive directors, now numbering twenty-two for each institution. Their chief executive officers, the Managing Director of the IMF and the President of the World Bank, are appointed by the executive directors.

The IMF is concerned with international trade and payments. Its purposes, as stated by its Articles of Agreement, are to promote international monetary cooperation, facilitate the growth of international trade, promote exchange stability and provide temporary financing for members with balance-of-payments difficulties. Originally members were expected to maintain par values of their currencies, which were to be changed only with the concurrence of the IMF. With the breakdown of that system in 1973 and the subsequent amendment of the Articles, members became free to choose floating or pegged exchange rates, subject to a general obligation to collaborate with the IMF and other members to promote orderly exchange arrangements and to avoid unfair practices. The Fund is enjoined to exercise surveillance over the system and to that end to collect information and conduct regular consultations with members. The activities that attract the most public attention are its credits to members and the conditions attached to them. In support of its main functions, the IMF carries on research, assembles and publishes statistics, and offers technical assistance and training.

Like the IMF, the World Bank is owned by its 151 member governments. The Bank is a complex organization consisting of the Bank proper, the International Development Association (IDA), the International Finance Corporation (IFC), the International Center for Settlement of Investment Disputes (ICSID) and the Multilateral Investment Guarantee Agency. All these have to greater or lesser degree the same government membership; all are responsible to the president of the Bank and the staffs wholly or partly overlap. The Bank's purpose is to help the economic development of its less developed member countries. It provides long-term capital to member countries for a wide spectrum of investments including schools, public health programs, farming, public utilities, manufacturing, etc. It provides technical assistance in the process of lending – emphasizing proper design, management, finance and economic justification of projects – and through training and economic research. The terms on which funds are made available vary widely depending on the economic and financial position of the borrower and its economic performance.

The Fund's business is primarily the preserve of economists. They make up the majority of the professional staff and hold most of the senior positions. Two of the seven managing directors, Per Jacobsson and H. J. Witteveen, have been professional economists, though Witteveen had moved into politics in the Netherlands several years before his appointment. A number of economists have served as executive directors. Because of the easy communication between professional economists at different levels, the IMF is less bureaucratic and hierarchical than many national and international agencies. Policy positions and relations with members, nevertheless, are firmly controlled from the top.

The Bank, in sharp contrast, requires the teamwork of a number of professions (engineers, financial analysts, agronomists, environmentalists, educators, etc.) in addition to economists. Initially, investment bankers were regarded as the key coordinating profession. Even when experience in the first decade taught top management that this did not work, it was not a foregone conclusion that people with economic training would assume this role. However, the economists recruited in the first decade had broad governmental experience in applied economics and so proved to have a comparative advantage over other professions in doing Bank work. By the end of the first decade, they had taken over most management positions and these have remained overwhelmingly held by individuals trained in economics. By 1987, all the senior vice presidents, even those responsible for raising money in international capital markets and for internal Bank administration, were economists. Although the presidency is still reserved for non-economists, economists as in the Fund are heavily involved in all major decisions.

Bank managers preserve less of the economist's professional attitude and mores than Fund officers do. Stemming from the mystique of working for a 'bank' and the initial banker orientation of the institution, when an economist becomes a loan officer or manager of a department or region he tends to abjure the name of 'economist' and often starts to classify himself as a 'banker'. This is not all adverse for economic policy: it frees the economics-trained managers (ETMs) to take a broader view of the process of economic development than many recently trained economists are able to take. On the other hand, the ETMs tend to pride themselves on their relevance to the real world and to feel that other economists may be tarred with the manifest unreality of much of present-day academic economics. This attitude kept the Bank for many years from encouraging and publishing economic research.

In every operational area or sector of the Bank dealing with Bank clients, other than in departments such as the legal or treasurer's, economists *qua* economists are present to discharge their special responsibilities. It is the economists who determine the classification of a country (too rich to be a Bank client, eligible for Bank loans, or poor enough to receive near-grants); who evaluate the country's economic policy performance; who recommend the country sector priorities the Bank should follow; who calculate whether the economic return on a project is acceptable.

Aside from these 'colonies of economists' spread throughout the Bank, there is also a central economist's organization, rather in the nature of a 'mother country' that is completely manned by professional economists. Whereas in the IMF the economists in the area departments were originally colonized from the mother Research Department, in the Bank the process proceeded in reverse. The ETMs and economists first won influence in the 'operational' departments. It was not until twenty years after the opening of the Bank that a new president, George Woods, decided in 1965 to establish a central economics department with a director recruited from an operational department and an economic adviser recruited from the IMF at the top management level. The central economics department had to battle for years to establish itself.

IMF and Bank recruitment standards have always been high. Generally, their economists hold a PhD from a leading university in the United States, Great Britain, or continental Europe or in a few cases from a Third World institution. Newly hired young economists go through an extensive training program, including assignments in different departments. Although no national quotas for staffing are observed, an effort is made to obtain a fairly wide distribution. Many of the nationals of less developed countries have studied abroad, however, and do not necessarily bring distinctive attitudes or methodology. In the early days, senior positions naturally were filled by persons who had held responsible positions in government, central banks or universities. While some senior and middle-level jobs are still filled from the outside, a large proportion of all positions have come to be held by persons who have spent most, or all, of their professional career with the Fund or Bank. These conditions facilitate communication and teamwork, but some executive directors and other spokesmen for developing countries have complained that the economics staff is insufficiently diverse and lacks appreciation for the special problems of their countries.

INSIDE AND OUTSIDE ROLES OF ECONOMISTS

Economists fill 'inside' roles at the Bank and Fund by participating in the formulation of operating policies and in management, and 'outside' roles by working with and influencing member governments. Like many other classifications, this one blurs at the margins. There is feedback from country work to the establishment and modification of general criteria for lending, for example. In the Bank, economists make a substantial, incalculable contribution to the area and project departments in educating and influencing the large number of non-economist professionals to give greater weight to economic methods and goals. Research is not easily classified; some of it is tied closely to operations with particular countries, some relates to institutional policies, and some is published to the world at large. Major examples of the outside roles of economists are their participation in discussions of loans; in technical assistance; and, in the Fund, in formal consultations with member governments.

The annual reports of the two organizations contain, in addition to routine information on their activities and finances, comments on economic conditions and policies of member governments. Although drafted by the staffs, the reports are legally the voice of the executive boards. Executive directors often spend many hours in detailed review and editing of the staff draft. These reports are the points of departure of many speeches at the annual meetings of governors. More technical and more clearly the work of staff economists are the annual *World Economic Outlook* of the IMF and *World Development Report* of the Bank. These documents are intended to influence public opinion and official policies, and they receive much attention in the financial press and quality newspapers of general circulation. How much effect they actually have is impossible to determine. The organizations turn out other publications intended mainly for users with specialized interests, including statistical bulletins and yearbooks, books, occasional papers and pamphlets. The Bank lagged far behind the Fund until 1965, when it initiated a systematic program of publication of Bank economic work. Publications of the two organizations are now invaluable sources of basic information on countries and of international financial and economic data that are otherwise not easily accessible. For many years, the Fund has published a scholarly journal, *Staff Papers*, containing mainly economic articles and some legal and technical papers. The Bank's corresponding periodical, the *World Bank Economic Review*, was launched only in 1986. These periodicals may indirectly influence government policies, and their authors no doubt share to some extent the attitudes prevailing in member countries. It is hard to believe with the present flood of economic periodicals in the world that any urgent unmet need demanded the creation of the new Bank review.

By their training programs, the two organizations hope to improve the skills and knowledge of member-government officials and to acquaint them with the sponsoring institution. The Bank's Economic Development Institute trains about 3,000 middle and higher-grade officials yearly from every sector of national economies involved in economic development. Its short, practical problem-oriented courses are held all over the world. In addition, the institute organizes senior policy seminars at which ministers, permanent secretaries and deputy secretaries exchange experiences among themselves and with Bank staff. The IMF Institute conducts a smaller program comprising longer courses at Fund headquarters, and seminars in Washington and other places for officials of ministries of finance, central banks and other financial agencies.

Certain forms of explicit technical assistance, formal consultations, and negotiation of Bank loans and Fund credits offer staff economists their most direct opportunities for advising member governments. The following separate sections on the IMF and the World Bank examine these outside roles.

INTERNATIONAL MONETARY FUND

The activities considered in this section involve extensive discussions with member-government officials in the field, sometimes supplemented by conversations at the IMF's headquarters in Washington. For formal consultations and negotiations concerning Fund credits, staff teams of three to six economists, assisted by a secretary, are normal. Technical assistance missions often follow the same pattern but may include only one or two staff members. Although staff teams convey preliminary views in the field, reports are prepared at headquarters and are not cleared with the member country before being finalized.

Influenced, no doubt, by ministries of finance and central banks, which supply most governors and executive directors and serve as the primary correspondents and contacts in the field, the IMF has a strong tradition of confidentiality. It never publishes consultation reports, papers relating to the use of Fund resources, or technical assistance reports, though some of them are widely circulated by member governments. Press releases about transactions are brief and bland. No public statements are issued when adjustment programs break down. Confidentiality is regarded as essential to prevent speculative abuses and to encourage members to supply information and carry on candid discussions. The practice affects the work of the staff and the ability of outsiders to evaluate it.

Consultations

Regular consultations are held annually with most member governments and less frequently with some others. In addition, special consultations may be conducted at the initiative of the Managing Director or to help in writing the *World Economic Outlook*. For the regular consultations, the process includes a staff visit of perhaps two weeks for discussions with officials followed by the preparation by the staff team of a paper on recent economic developments and a shorter report on the discussions and the staff's appraisal of the country's policies and prospects. The report is discussed by the Executive Board, and at the end of the meeting the Managing Director sums up the sense of the meeting. This summing up is immediately transmitted to the member, together with any formal decision that may be taken. Detailed minutes follow.

Consultations provide information for the Fund and offer an opportunity for an exchange of views between member-government officials and staff economists as well as comments by executive directors. They play a part in the surveillance over exchange-rate policies that the Fund is supposed to exercise. These are construed broadly to include macroeconomic policies as well as explicit exchange-rate and trade policies and practices.

The questions, preliminary oral comments and report of the staff team may influence the views and actions of officials and ministers. When the Fund economists can reinforce opinions held by some country representatives but not yet accepted by the government, their chances of affecting decisions are improved. A good staff report can stimulate a good Board discussion, and the report and Board minutes can influence the attitudes of governments.

The *World Economic Outlook*, which has been published annually since 1980, brings together information, analysis and projections for all member countries. This report and its discussion in the Executive Board and the Interim Committee of the Board of Governors are considered part of the surveillance process.

The surveillance process can elicit a defensive reaction. The term 'surveillance' implies oversight rather than joint consideration of problems and sympathetic professional advice. In the economic and political conditions of the past decade, surveillance seems to have been largely ineffective in influencing national policies and in promoting conditions favorable to exchange-rate stability at appropriate levels. A 1985 report by the deputies of the ministers and governors of the Group of Ten (the major industrial countries) stressed the importance of multilateral surveillance but concluded that it had been insufficiently effective. The deputies of the Intergovernmental Group of Twenty-Four (developing countries), in a report also issued in 1985, found surveillance largely ineffective in regard to major industrial countries but asymmetrically influential on developing countries using the IMF's financial resources. The IMF has taken steps to improve the process, but it is not yet clear whether they can succeed.

Use of resources

Negotiations concerning IMF credits offer staff economists their greatest opportunities for influencing government policies. This is because of the Fund's practice of conditionality. To obtain credit a member is required to adopt an adjustment program designed to enable it to eliminate an unsustainable balance-of-payments deficit and repay the Fund. Credit normally is extended under a stand-by arrangement covering one to two years, which allows a specific amount of drawings in installments, with repayments expected three to five years later. Some developing countries may obtain extended arrangements covering three years and a repayment period up to ten years; the poorest countries may qualify for low-interest structural adjustment loans with the same timing as extended arrangements. Both industrial countries and developing countries formerly had recourse to IMF credit, but in the past decade only the developing countries have borrowed.

A popular view is that the IMF imposes draconian programs on reluctant but necessitous borrowers. The Fund's position is that it helps member governments devise their own adjustment programs. No doubt, there are cases at both extremes; probably most fall somewhere in between. In all cases, Fund economists need analytical ability, knowledge of the country, diplomacy and forcefulness.

The conditions for a Fund credit are discussed with the national authorities in the field by a team of economists, who sometimes pay repeated visits but who in other cases are able to conclude the negotiations quickly because of their prior knowledge and the preparations of the member government. The terms of reference of the staff team are set out in a briefing paper prepared by them but subject to review by concerned Fund departments and approval by the Managing Director. In the field, there is a good deal of scope for filling in specifics and revising preliminary estimates. The adjustment program is outlined in a letter of intent signed by the minister of finance (or other senior person) and is described and analyzed in a staff report for the Executive Board, which usually approves the stand-by after a detailed discussion.

A typical IMF-supported adjustment program includes monetary and fiscal restraint, some liberalization of international trade and payments accompanied by a devaluation or the adoption of a flexible exchange rate, and certain ancillary provisions. These provisions and other government economic policies and practices are examined in some detail in the discussions between staff and officials and ministers of the member country and in the staff report. Special importance attaches, however, to a few provisions called 'performance criteria'. Failure to observe these criteria interrupts the member's right to further drawings under the arrangement. According to a formal decision of the Executive Board taken in 1979 and reviewed in early 1986, performance criteria are to be limited in number and normally confined to macroeconomic variables and those necessary to implement specific provisions of the IMF Articles and policies adopted under them. Other performance criteria are to be included only in exceptional cases when they are essential because of their macroeconomic impact.

The prime performance criterion is a ceiling on domestic bank credit, frequently accompanied by a subceiling on credit to the government. The economic rationale of the ceiling is a financial programming exercise based on a Fund model that may be regarded as an applied version of a monetarist theory of the balance of payments (Polak, 1957). The exercise involves projections of real output, the price level, the exchange rate, the money multiplier and the income velocity of circulation of money. Especially with a fixed exchange rate, for which the theory was developed and which is still found in most developing countries, the critical variable is credit expansion rather than the money stock because the money stock might be held down by a deficit in the current account of the balance of payments fed by an excessive credit expansion.

Although a staff team must conform to the IMF approach, it has considerable room for analysis, judgement and negotiation in estimating the critical parameters and variables and (more important) in agreeing with the member government on the specific measures to ensure observance of a credit ceiling. The most important actions in most cases are fiscal – revenue increases and expenditure reductions to reduce the fiscal deficit and the government's use of bank credit. Financial programming in practice is not inconsistent with the absorption approach to the balance of payments, which also originated at the IMF (Alexander, 1952). Also it allows scope for a pragmatic concern with political issues and administrative capabilities.

In addition to economic considerations, practical and political factors have commended reliance on credit ceilings as performance criteria. Information on bank credit usually is available more promptly and is subject to smaller statistical revisions than are figures on the budget deficit, the balance of payments or GNP. This allows quarterly monitoring of programs. A broad credit ceiling with a subceiling on credit to the government implies less detailed intervention in sensitive internal affairs than would microeconomic criteria or some alternative macroeconomic criteria.

IMF conditionality has been the subject of much controversy, technical and political. A review of the controversy cannot be undertaken here. Fund economists have contributed to the literature by general papers on related topics, and in recent years they have taken part in the institution's efforts to explain its policies in seminars and publications.

Fund economists have played an important part in elaborating and monitoring adjustment programs, although it is impossible (and would be politically counterproductive) to try to distinguish sharply between their contributions and the input of national officials. Programs in which the national input is large are most likely to be firmly supported by the member government.

We are unable to advance cogent generalizations on the successes and failures of adjustment programs on which Fund economists have advised or to evaluate definitively particular programs. This is due partly to the barriers of confidentiality and partly to methodological problems, including the usual difficulty of determining what would have happened in the absence of the program.

In the late 1960s and the 1970s Fund-supported programs appear to have effected quick turnarounds in the balance of payments of the United Kingdom, France and Italy. Current-account deficits were followed by surpluses, which together with capital inflows enabled prompt repayment to the IMF. Fund economists in extended discussions with British counterparts refuted the Radcliffe Committee's conclusion that monetary policy was powerless. They stimulated the production of a new statistical series on domestic credit expansion, which for a time was accepted as an important policy indicator in the United Kingdom.

Turkey, in response to a balance-of-payments crisis in 1980, adopted a stabilization and adjustment program with the support of a series of credits from the IMF and the World Bank and substantial concessional loans through the Organization for Economic Cooperation and Development (OECD) and from Saudi Arabia. It succeeded in increasing exports, improving the balance of payments, restoring economic growth and slowing inflation. Both the IMF and the Prime Minister of India pronounced as a success an extended arrangement for that country approved in November 1981 and voluntarily terminated by India in early 1984, leaving 1.1 billion special drawing rights (SDR) undrawn, after meeting the performance criteria for two annual segments of the three-year arrangement. However, the arrangement with India was controversial at its inception. Critics argued that the amount of finance was too large and the conditions too easy; the US executive director abstained from the vote on the arrangement.

Mexico, after encountering a severe financial crisis in late 1982, adopted a Fund-supported program that sharply reduced the fiscal deficit and obtained a large surplus in the current account of the balance of payments in 1983. The cost was almost a halving of the dollar value of imports and a 5 per cent fall in real output. By 1985 Mexico was again in trouble, owing partly to a relaxation of fiscal restraints, and was unable to continue drawings under its extended arrangement with the IMF because of failure to observe certain performance criteria.

In a number of other cases, programs intended to meet the external debt crisis that emerged in 1982 succeeded in improving the balance of payments mainly by compressing imports, and were accompanied by declining per capita incomes. Several programs, especially in low-income African countries, broke down. Some members became ineligible for IMF credits because of their failure to meet repayment commitments.

Technical assistance

In addition to advice and assistance in connection with consultations and the use of financial resources, the IMF offers explicit technical assistance to member countries. The purpose is to provide a general service and particularly to help governments form and carry out policies that will advance their national objectives and also the broad purposes of the Fund. The main fields covered are central banking, fiscal affairs and economic and financial statistics.

Technical assistance is rendered only in response to a request from the national authorities. While the need for assistance may be identified during discussions of a Fund credit, members are rarely, if ever, required to accept technical assistance to obtain credit. Staff economists giving technical assistance, hence, are in a position similar to that of national civil servants: they must rely on their own analysis and persuasiveness rather than the clout of the IMF. Sometimes, to be sure, they may gain prestige from their connection with the Fund, but in other cases it may inhibit frank exchanges of information and opinions.

The following comments address particularly technical assistance on fiscal matters, which is provided by the Fiscal Affairs Department in cooperation with other departments. Because of the political sensitivity of taxation and public expenditures, persons assigned by the IMF to assist on such matters serve only as advisers, never in executive positions. Although the IMF has no settled official views on most of the questions with which the advisers deal, the organization takes responsibility for the quality and content of their recommendations.

In response to a request, a staff member or a small team are sent to the member country to study the situation and prepare recommendations. The advisers are expected to assist the government in reaching the objectives of national policymakers. IMF advisers, like economists in national civil services, however, often find that the policymakers have not thought out their preferences on questions such as the appropriate degree of tax progressivity or the revenue goal, much less on details. The advisers have to seek to identify major national objectives and constraints, to identify inconsistencies and to present specific recommendations. The findings and recommendations are presented in a written report, which is finalized at IMF headquarters, though the principal points will have been discussed in the field. In accordance with IMF folkways, the circulation of the report is restricted. After the report has been transmitted a follow-up visit may be paid to discuss the authorities' reactions and to consider whether further assistance is required in putting into effect any of the recommendations that may be accepted. Staff members participating in consultations or use-of-resources missions may check on the status of action on the report. A long-term adviser may be assigned to assist in implementation of reforms.

In some cases, a clear connection can be traced between advice and government action on taxation or other fiscal matters. And in many cases it becomes fairly clear that no results can realistically be expected. Most often, however, the outcome is ambiguous: proposals may be accepted but carried out poorly or not at all, or reforms may be rescinded after a short time. A report that was ignored when submitted may be discovered and acted upon several years later when the problem that it addressed becomes more acute or a new minister of finance takes office. Proposals for incremental change seem to have affected government decisions more than sweeping recommendations for reform. When action occurs, it is nearly always the result of many influences, some obvious and some obscure.

Conclusions

The apparent ineffectiveness of surveillance over the international monetary system and exchange-rate policies reveals nothing about the quality of the staff analysis or the manner of presentation. National governments have been unwilling, or unable, to coordinate their economic policies in the way that would be required to maintain conditions favorable to more stable exchange rates at appropriate levels and to better international capital flows.

The 'firm surveillance' enjoined by the Articles of Agreement has been a soft substitute for the par-value system.

Fund economists undoubtedly have played an important part in shaping the adjustment programs that member governments have to adopt to qualify for financial assistance from the IMF and in many cases to obtain credit from commercial banks or to reschedule debts to official creditors. While adjustment programs supported by the Fund have worked as expected in the past in certain countries, notably in some large industrial countries, the record of programs with developing countries in recent years has been at best mixed. Staff economists have to advise within the framework of the Articles of Agreement, available resources and the attitudes of member governments. This compels the application of conditionality, limits the size of credits and dictates a fairly short maturity. It does not, however, closely circumscribe the choice of adjustment measures and performance criteria. Perhaps IMF economists should give renewed emphasis to the critical evaluation of past programs and the adaptation of their analytical models and policy prescriptions to the current economic environment and the special problems and circumstances of less developed countries.

Technical assistance is less subject to the constraints applying to the other outside roles of IMF economic advisers. Two observations may be added to earlier remarks. First, patience and avoidance of excessive standardization of advice are essential for a responsible program. Second, technical assistance is relatively so inexpensive and the results potentially so great, that the benefit–cost ratio can be very favorable if only a few efforts are successful.

Subject to the acquiescence of member countries, some careful relaxation of confidentiality could benefit the work of IMF economists by promoting broader understanding of it and exposing it to peer-group review.

THE WORLD BANK

World Bank economists interact with and influence member governments' economies in many ways. In half of the countries where the Bank is active there is a permanent Bank office and a practically continuous flow of Bank economists in and out, working with their counterparts across a wide spectrum of the economy. In the other countries, Bank economic missions are frequent visitors. It is impossible to identify the full impact of Bank economists on countries' policies. Only a small part of Bank economic work ever has resulted in a formal Bank–country agreement explicitly defining desired country policies. Normally, Bank economists make their contributions to country policy through a wide range of interactions with member government officials on many levels.

Because of the comparatively decentralized character of the Bank, the large variety of its activities, the recurrent major reorganizations as every new Bank president undertakes to reshape the Bank to his liking, and the varying weight that successive Bank presidents put on achieving lending targets as against securing improved country performance, practically every generalization about the impact of the Bank's economic work on the member countries is subject to important exceptions. Further, Bank economists from various departments may work with different parts of a government; consequently, Bank–government relationships may vary greatly across the government. Iraq, for example, for many years had cordial relationships with the Bank's Economic Development Institute (EDI) because it prized the training the EDI provided its officials; no one from the rest of the Bank was even allowed in. In recent years the growing strength of anti-modernization movements (such as Islamic fundamentalism) has drastically reduced the receptiveness of some governments (for example, Iran) to working with the Bank.

With these reservations, in the history of the Bank there has been a considerable variation in different eras in the direct influence of Bank economists on member countries' economic policies. In the first quarter-century to 1970 Bank economists had considerable influence and success; the 1970s were a low point; and the 1980s have shown a recovery and considerable promise. The indirect influence of Bank economists through a wide range of technical assistance and publications has not suffered the same wide fluctuations. As will be discussed in the final part of this section, there has been a continuous growth of Bank economic research. This growing volume has probably not had a directly proportional effect in influencing member countries' policies, but the trend has undoubtedly been upwards over the whole life of the Bank.

Policy influence through lending operations

Throughout the Bank's history it has emphasized a microeconomic approach in its operations. However, the Bank's principal objective of aiding economic development makes involvement in country macroeconomic policy inevitable. The degree and the manner of its involvement have varied over the years.

The Bank's emphasis on microeconomics was the direct result of the international financial débâcle following on the large-scale lending of the 1920s. The Bank's founders were convinced that international loans had to be directly related to specific investment projects if they were to make a real contribution to growth. Consequently, the Bank charter permits nonproject loans to be made only in exceptional circumstances.

In less developed countries, it is effective to begin with the micro level. By concentrating on a project, Bank experience, advice and guidance do secure better use of its investment funds and better management of resources. The close supervision of disbursements during the construction period gives the Bank a sanction to invoke if the agreements reached are not implemented.

Consequently, throughout the Bank's history, economic work in the Bank's member countries has always included improving microeconomic management and use of resources, project by project.

However, in many cases, to maximize the probability of securing a successful project, Bank officials insist on the creation of special project organizations outside of the existing permanent institutions. The project, consequently, is usually carried out effectively but the permanent administration is deprived of needed training and experience, and broader economic policy objectives are not attained.

In many countries with close collaboration between Bank staff and a borrower resulting from a succession of loans, the Bank's economic analysis of different sectors can be used to shape the composition of the Bank's lending program. Priority can be given to loans in sectors where modifications of price, interest-rate and foreign exchange-rate policies are desirable and can be influenced by the Bank. The Bank economists and other professionals thus can work together with the government in planning sector-wide investments, institution building, and policy improvements. At the same time, Bank staff may devote considerable effort to upgrading key personnel in their sector. The Bank's Economic Development Institute gives priority to accepting such personnel for training.

The sanctions behind such a sector-policy program approach are immediate and effective. The Bank can refuse to lend in a particular sector when the preliminary policy dialogue of the Bank economists with the government indicates that desired policy changes would not be forthcoming. When agreement is reached and for some reason the government fails to implement it, Bank disbursements are suspended or agreement is reached that the government will not submit disbursement requests. This method of securing sector-policy improvements was practiced by the Bank up to the 1970s, particularly in Latin America but also to varying degrees in other parts of the world, as will be indicated below.

In countries where the Bank is a major source of funds, sector-policy lending has considerable impact on national allocation and management of resources even without agreements on country-wide policy. However, in any country where the Bank's total lending is of significant size and includes projects in a number of sectors, Bank interest in the overall economic policies of the government is unavoidable. Consequently, Bank economists have been involved in member-government macroeconomic policy in varying degrees at different times in the Bank's history. With varying conditions in the different areas of the world and the considerable autonomy the regional departments have usually enjoyed in responding to their challenges, Bank practice in this regard over most of its history has varied from region to region and over time.

Before the 1980s, the Bank Board of Executive Directors was not actively involved in setting guidelines for Bank staff action in securing country policy changes, nor were sector or country agreements reached usually made public. In the case of Australia in 1952, the agreement was not even committed to paper but was confirmed by a telephone conversation between Bank Vice-President Garner and Australian Prime Minister Menzies.

Among the Bank's first set of borrowers were countries like Australia, Denmark, Iceland, Finland, Norway and Spain. All of these countries came out of World War II with highly controlled economies and maintained the controls well into the postwar period. The Bank had a major impact while lending for specific projects in persuading the governments to liberalize their macroeconomic policies. The case of Spain is especially interesting in this regard. When Spain joined the Fund and Bank in 1957, a Bank mission visited the country for an initial reconnaissance. Based on recommendations of the mission, the Bank president, Eugene Black, wrote to General Franco that the Bank could do nothing in Spain until the economy was freed from the over-centralizing direct controls, inflation halted, and the exchange rate adjusted. The Fund and OECD then joined in with similar recommendations. Spain took the advice and there followed its growth explosion of the 1960s.

The degree to which the Bank was responsible for the policy changes that were made during these early years is hard to assess. The Bank did not try to impose policies on the governments but to persuade them; and, even more important, its views were developed in cooperation with elements within the government who could give strong support in carrying out the desired policies. In the case of Spain, for instance, the Bank economists and the technocrats in the Spanish government were in agreement, and the Bank's intervention helped to ensure that Franco gave the latter the free hand they needed to carry out the desired policies.

Finally, the governments concerned in these cases were all reasonably competent and administratively and politically able to carry out major policy changes. This last point is especially important. In later years, in lending to countries where these conditions did not exist, the Bank found that success in macroeconomic policy conditionality was much more difficult to achieve. The tropical African countries are a good example.

While the Belgian Congo, Southern Rhodesia and the Federation of Rhodesia and Nyasaland were still colonies, the Bank secured agreement during loan negotiations on various macroeconomic policy improvements that Bank economic missions had worked out with their opposite numbers in these governments. And, both the governments and the Bank were satisfied with the implementation of the agreements. Later, after the African countries became independent, the Bank largely abandoned as futile any effort to reach similar agreements with their politically fragile, administratively weak governments. When the Bank, for instance, in making the Volta loan to Ghana secured an agreement on the size and composition of Ghana's investment program and on its investment policies, the government failed to implement it (as W. Arthur Lewis, whom the Bank persuaded the government to take as economic adviser, will testify). Consequently, until the 1980s, Bank economists in tropical Africa made little explicit attempt to secure macroeconomic policy improvements except through general discussion and persuasion in consultative group and other meetings. The Bank economists devoted most energy to trying to secure better policies and management in the wide spectrum of sectors in which the Bank financed projects.

With administratively stronger governments in Asia, more could be attempted. In the second half of the 1960s, the Bank tried to persuade India to carry out a number of macro and sector-policy reforms – liberalizing import policy, encouraging exports, freeing industry from internal controls, encouraging agriculture by raising domestic prices, etc. The attempt was only partially successful. The sector-policy changes, particularly in agriculture where a strong Minister of Agriculture was in full agreement with the Bank, were most successful: India became self-sufficient in food. The other policies, which the Government of India felt had been imposed on it and which it resented, were soon forgotten.

Indonesia, right through into the 1970s, was a happier story for Bank economists. At the end of the 1960s, a new government took the initiative in asking the Bank to help it formulate its macro policies and investment program. Bank economists and other professionals working in a permanent field mission made a major contribution in this regard, working closely with their Indonesian counterparts. This successful cooperative effort was realized through actions taken by the government rather than through 'conditions' laid down in loan agreements.

In the Latin American countries in the late 1960s, the Bank's Latin American department was headed by an economist who gave great weight to economic policy. Macro policy elements were largely integrated into country lending programs. Bank economists worked with countries to help prepare public investment programs and financing plans within a comprehensive economic framework. Discussions were held with governments on specific measures to mobilize more resources for financing their public-sector expenditures. The requirement of servicing external debt resulted in discussions, in cooperation with the IMF, on balance-of-payments problems and on measures to encourage increased exports of goods and services.

Policy in the 1970s

In the 1970s, Bank economists' ability to influence economic policy of member countries suffered severely from three major events: the 'recycling' of OPEC surpluses, the setting of Bank lending targets as an overriding priority, and the withering away of the interdepartmental Economic Committee.

During this period the commercial banks, flooded with funds from the enormous OPEC dollar surpluses, began large-scale lending to the less developed countries, particularly in Latin America. The World Bank contribution was swamped. Trying to act jointly with the Fund, the Bank had little success in urging moderation on the borrowers and on the commercial bank lenders.

Second, a new Bank president, Robert S. McNamara, introduced lending targets as a major policy objective of the Bank. Since then, achieving lending programs has remained a central activity of the institution. There resulted what some bitter Bank economists called a 'reversal of roles': a Bank official's career in some cases became dependent on the willingness of borrowers to accept loans, and Bank bargaining power suffered as a result. In general, the technical quality of loans remained high: no Bank engineer would pass an unsafe dam, for example. However, securing improvement in sector and national economic policy became much more dependent on the persuasive power of Bank economists. With little or no countervailing pressure to muster for change, politically difficult improvements in utility-rate policies or price policies in agriculture became in many cases practically impossible to attain. By the end of the decade, in many Bank borrowers there was a large accumulation of bad policy practices, that were economically costly and politically untouchable.

One of the prime macroeconomic responsibilities of Bank economists was also attenuated. Bank economists are relied on for the Bank judgement of the volume of international borrowing that a country can or should undertake. This is a complicated assessment that includes forecasts of the capability of a country to marshall the foreign-exchange resources necessary, its degree of willingness to make the sacrifices necessary to service loans, etc. With management pressure to achieve lending targets in the 1970s, creditworthiness judgements in some cases became purely formalistic. Loans were made to countries like Algeria where the flood of oil revenues had already pushed 'investment' spending to around half the GNP and was far beyond its capacity to absorb economically. In the earlier period, Algeria would have been advised to build reserves and to save its borrowing capacity for the lean years to come.

At the beginning of the 1970s, Bank economists also lost the one professional coordinating support-group mechanism they possessed. An Economic Committee consisting of the top economist from every department had been in existence from the early days of the Bank. The committee had been a forum of discussion on Bank-country economic policy and reviewed country economic analysis and judgements. With the creation of a strong central economics organization in 1965 the committee became the means to formalize and coordinate the Bank's approach to country macroeconomic policies. Fiercely resisted by some of the area and sector departments defending their autonomy, the Economic Adviser to the President insisted on having a thorough analysis and discussion of macroeconomic development problems and the Bank's policies relating to them for each of the Bank's borrowers as a prior condition for lending. The attendance was expanded to include the director of the loan operations department concerned and a representative of the Fund. During its short five years of active life, this effort did succeed in securing more attention to macroeconomic policy in the Bank and could be regarded as the precursor of the Bank's structural adjustment loans of the 1980s (discussed below).

The 1980s and present

With the end of large-scale commercial bank lending and the beginning of widespread member-country debt-repayment problems around 1980, Bank economists had the opportunity to re-enter the field of country macroeconomic policy. The Bank, with the leadership of the economist Senior Vice President, Operations, began a program of explicit country-wide, macroeconomic policy loans: the 'structural adjustment loans' (SALs). SALs are tied to government commitments to make changes in trade policy, mobilization of domestic and foreign resources, the use of domestic resources and institutional reform. Unlike the normal loans of the Bank, SALs are not directed to specific investments, they are purely 'economists' loans'. Tailoring a SAL to a particular country's needs requires a large input of economic analysis and study of the country's economy. Also, close collaboration with the Fund is required since the Fund-supported adjustment programs are complementary.

The ability to make major changes in macroeconomic policy in a country varies with the degree of political cohesion and the development and strength of the government administrative apparatus. The macroeconomic policies with which the Bank is concerned are especially dependent on the effectiveness of the administration. From the beginning of the SAL program it was clear that it would have to be limited to the small number of countries that would be willing to make such policy commitments to the Bank and could credibly propose the economy-wide comprehensive adjustment programs required. Consequently, the SALs are likely and have proven to be a relatively small part of the total Bank operation: the fiscal 1986 total of SALs was less than 0.5 per cent of total Bank lending.

While SALs have been made in all regions, most have been to Africa. In the first review of the results of SALs undertaken by the Bank's Operations Evaluation Department in 1986, it was concluded that of ten countries studied, four largely achieved their objectives, two failed, and in the remaining four results were mixed. It is still too early to make any final judgement, however, since it is still doubtful how permanent the structural reform measures put into effect are going to be.

For a wider group of countries, another program, narrower in scope, of 'sector-adjustment policy loans' (SAPLs) proved to be more applicable. Sector-adjustment policy lending began in 1979. SAPLs are related to the sector-policy investment loans that were discussed previously. The main difference between SAPLs and the older type of sector-policy loans is that the latter were always directed to specific investment accompanied by policy and institutional conditions for the sector. SAPLs, like the SALs, are 'economists' loans': they are primarily directed to policy and institutional changes and may not be related to any specific investment at all. They may simply provide quick-disbursing foreign exchange to finance general imports.

SAPLs are normally disbursed over two to six years with release of the later tranches linked to progress on the sector-adjustment program. The programs vary widely depending on the country and sector. The loans have a higher probability of success than the SALs: the objectives of the SAPLs are much narrower than those of the economy-wide SALs and are less demanding on government capability. They build on the deep sector experience and knowledge of the Bank and its capacity to provide sector technical assistance.

SAPLs grew fairly rapidly to around 14 per cent of total Bank lending in fiscal 1986. This is near or at its maximum. Stated Bank policy is that investment loans should remain dominant and SAPLs should not exceed 15 per cent. Together, then, SALs and SAPLs in total are likely to remain below a fifth of total Bank annual lending.

The major direct impact of Bank economists on country policies will continue to be, therefore, as it has in the past, exercised in the process of making project and sector-investment loans. If the Bank reverts to the best practice of the 1960s and uses the flow of project loans in a sector to help secure improvements in sector policies, institutions and management, then SAPLs will prove unnecessary. Further, in countries where the Bank financing is significant in total and in key sectors, the Bank–country dialogue can be used to help secure improvements in general economic policies. In short, the only purpose of continuing a program of SALs or SAPLs would be to handle those cases where a sudden, unexpected and large deterioration in a country's economic position requires quick international help.

In June 1987, the World Bank underwent its latest major reorganization. A large part of the motivation of the reorganization was to give greater priority to macroeconomic policy in Bank operations. The relative position of Bank economists was enhanced as a result. For the first time in the history of the Bank, the economist in charge of Policy, Planning and Research was made a senior vice-president on a par with the senior vice-presidents in charge of Operations, Finance and Administration. Further, for the first time this position was filled by promotion from within the Bank rather than from an outside organization or academia. Clearly, the opportunity exists for Bank economists to exercise more direct influence in shaping Bank policy and in influencing member-country economic policies than in any period since the beginning of the Bank. Whether this opportunity will be exploited is impossible to predict.

Technical assistance

As mentioned earlier, technical assistance to the member countries of the Bank is an important and continuing part of Bank economists' activity and is an integral part of the normal operations of the Bank. One of the most important components of this is the large continuing program of country economic and sector studies of the member countries in which the Bank is active as a lender. These countries include nearly all the less developed and Eastern European member countries. In the preparation of basic and updating reports, Bank economists visit the countries concerned on missions that last for weeks at a time and secure information and data on the economy and the forces that affect it from discussions with government officials, nongovernmental representatives, and actual observation and field work. In the process, the Bank economists help countries identify and evaluate their problems in the different sectors and the costs and benefits of alternative feasible means of addressing them. For many countries these highly detailed and comprehensive studies are the basic handbooks for the member-government agencies and everyone interested in the economy.

In a number of countries, the Bank takes responsibility for calling and chairing consultative group meetings of the donors interested in a country. Bank economists usually prepare the economic material that is the basis of the discussions on the economic policies and problems of the country and on the mobilization and coordination of assistance for it.

One of the most important contributions the Bank makes is in affecting and sometimes actually setting the agenda of economic development policy for the less developed countries and the donors. The president's speech to the Annual Meeting of Governors is most effective in this regard. At this meeting are finance ministers, central bank governors and many other world top decisionmakers in the fields of economic development. George Woods, during his tenure as president of the Bank, succeeded in changing the basic premise of the world development community. This had been that the amount of effective aid the less developed countries could absorb was strictly limited. Woods succeeded in securing acceptance that the absorptive capacity could be increased through aid and the limiting factor was instead the amount of aid that the industrialized world was willing to commit. The key to this change was an economic study based on the judgements of the experienced area and sector economists showing that the less developed countries could usefully absorb considerably more aid than was available.

Robert McNamara made the president's speech an even more important tool. It is no exaggeration to say that he was decisive in persuading most governments of less developed countries of the importance of the rate of population growth in economic development. Recognition of the need to target investment to help the people in 'absolute poverty' was also his innovation. In both of these cases, economists did the basic research to support his positions. However, the bulk of the credit goes to McNamara himself for focusing on these issues as important.

The Bank's orientation to the real world and the practical experience of most of the first generation of Bank economists led Bank policy to be guided by the analysis of the actual situation and the real problems confronting the member countries in their attempt to develop. In the first years, because of the run-down of capital equipment during the great depression and World War II, the less developed countries had trouble coping with the strong and growing demand of the postwar period. Consequently, the Bank economic doctrine emphasized investment in the conventional infrastructure. Once this period was ended and broader problems of development emerged, the Bank started lending for schools, agricultural development and small industries, and started to emphasize training and institution building.

In this broad, flexible approach of Bank economists, much of the then-conventional economic development theory was largely by-passed. Bank economists did profit over the years from the economic wisdom and experience of several notable non-Bank economists who came to the Bank as consultants or on short-term appointments. These included, for example, Alexander Cairncross, Albert Hirschman, Isaiah Frank, E. S. Mason, Paul Streeten, and Paul Rosenstein-Rodan. While economic development theorists were building elaborate capital/output growth models, Bank economists were fully aware that the amount of capital was only one factor in the complex economic development process. If the economists in the operational departments of the Bank emphasized any one factor, it was the overriding importance of good economic management. Most academic development economists still overlook the fact that the bulk of the less developed countries are in the tropics and face special problems arising from this climate. With the Bank borrowers concentrated in the tropics, the Bank became aware of and started to cope with their special problems. The dearth of applicable knowledge on tropical agriculture led the Bank to organize and sponsor a global network of tropical agricultural research institutes and to finance adaptive research in its member countries. Tropical diseases became manifest as a vital problem in many projects and the Bank sponsored special anti-disease programs and a new network of tropical disease research.

In recent years, while the major economic work in the Bank has continued as in the past with its concern with real problems, the build-up of the central economics organization has led to a flowering of economic research. This is directed to help member countries improve development policy and practice from project design and implementation to macroeconomic policy. The emphasis has been on applied research, although some work of purely academic interest has been included. One feature has been the outreach of the Bank to collaborative research with institutions and individuals throughout the world – both to help develop research capacity in less developed countries and to influence development theory and policy.

CONCLUDING REMARKS

A combination of advice and finance, both provided by the IMF and World Bank, is more potent than either alone. This fact has shaped the roles of economists in the two organizations. Except for a short time at the beginning of its operations, most Bank loans have gone to developing countries; hence, the work of Bank economists has related mainly to those countries. In the past, the Fund extended credit to industrial countries as well as developing countries, but for a decade only the developing countries have drawn on IMF credit. The influence of Fund economists with governments of industrial countries accordingly has diminished.

Economists in the Fund work in fewer fields and devote a larger proportion of their time to work that the profession would recognize as economic analysis and advice than do much of the Bank staff with economics training. Bank economists cover a wide spectrum: they work in almost every field of applied economics (agriculture, education, health, power, transport, etc.). Fund economists are subject to closer control from member governments, exercised mainly through the Executive Board. Member governments feel less need for such control for Bank economists who tend to have a symbiotic relationship with their government opposite numbers.

The Fund's simple organization and its staffing practices have always allowed economists ample scope for performing both inside and outside roles. There are now five area departments and several economics-oriented functional departments and bureaus whose heads report direct to the Managing Director and Deputy Managing Director. As described earlier, Bank economists have experienced ups and downs in the past. Their relative position is now high, owing to a movement to give greater priority to macroeconomic policy in Bank operations and the creation in 1987 of a post of senior vice-president for Policy, Planning and Research. However, as long as Bank presidents continue the policy of the last quarter-century of giving priority to achieving lending goals, no matter how high Bank economists rise in the hierarchy their ability to induce improved economic management in member countries will be severely restricted. Bank staff will feel pressured to make loans and the sanction of a refusal to lend if a reform is not undertaken will rarely be exercised.

The Bank and its staff generally enjoy more friendly relations with developing countries than do the Fund and its staff. In particular, conditions for Bank loans have provoked less criticism than has the Fund's conditionality. The Bank is helped by its practice of working with counterparts in many sectors and of maintaining many resident missions in member countries. The Fund may suffer from its emphasis on confidentiality and an image of aloofness. More fundamental are differences between project loans and conventional sector loans on the one hand and balance-of-payments credits on the other hand. The former leave tangible evidence of benefits to the country; the latter appear to leave only a repayment burden. In the past, Bank loans to individual countries have been numerous, each relatively small in most cases. Denial of such a loan does not imply a negative judgement on the government's policies as a whole, as does denial of a Fund credit. The movement of the Bank into structural adjustment lending and sector adjustment policy lending, however, is likely to involve the Bank and its staff in difficulties similar to those faced by the Fund and its economists.

With the changes in Bank lending and the increased concern of the IMF with structural adjustment and in response to prodding by member governments, the Bretton Woods institutions have been collaborating more closely. This trend may broaden and strengthen the functions of their economists, with beneficial results for them and for member countries.

BIBLIOGRAPHY

International Monetary Fund

Alexander, Sidney S., 'Effects of a devaluation on a trade balance', *IMF Staff Papers*, vol. 2 (1952), pp. 263–78.

de Vries, Margaret Garritsen, 'The International Monetary Fund: economists in key roles', in A. W. Coats (ed.), *Economists in International Agencies, an Exploratory Study* (New York, Westport, Conn., London: Praeger Special Studies, Praeger Scientific, 1986), pp. 53–66.

Group of Ten, Report of the Deputies to the Ministers and Governors, 'The functioning of the international monetary system', 1 June 1985, *IMF Survey*, Supplement (July 1985).

Intergovernmental Group of Twenty-Four, Report of the Deputies to the Ministers and Governors, 'The functioning and improvement of the international monetary system', 23 August 1985, *IMF Survey*, Supplement (September 1985).

Polak, J. J., 'Monetary analysis of income formation and payments problems', *IMF Staff Papers*, vol. 6 (1957), pp. 1–50.

World Bank

Baldwin, George B., 'Economics and economists in the World Bank', in A. W. Coats (ed.), *Economists in International Agencies* (New York: Praeger Scientific, 1986), pp. 67–90.

Helleiner, Gerald K., 'Policy-based program lending: a look at the Bank's new role', in Richard E. Feinberg *et al.* (eds), *Between Two Worlds: The World Bank's Next Decade* (Washington, DC: Transaction Books, 1986), pp. 47–66.

Kamarck, Andrew M., 'McNamara's Bank', *Foreign Affairs*, vol. 60 (Spring 1982) (2), pp. 951–3.

Kamarck, Andrew M., 'The World Bank and development: a personal perspective', *Bretton Woods at Forty: 1944–84* (Washington, DC: International Monetary Fund and World Bank Finance and Development, 1984), pp. 18–20.

Kamarck, Andrew M., *The Tropics and Economic Development* (Baltimore, London: The Johns Hopkins University Press for the World Bank, 1976).

Oliver, Robert, *International Economic Cooperation and the World Bank* (London: Macmillan, 1975).

World Bank, 'Structural-adjustment lending', *The World Bank Annual Report 1985* (Washington, DC, 1985), pp. 52–4.
World Bank, 'Sector-adjustment lending', *The World Bank Annual Report 1986* (Washington, DC, 1986), pp. 47–9.

13 · THE ORGANIZATION FOR ECONOMIC COOPERATION AND DEVELOPMENT

*J. C. R. Dow**

In this account of the work of economists at the Organization for Economic Cooperation and Development (OECD), I will concentrate on work connected with macroeconomic policy: though far from the whole of OECD's work, this has usually been regarded as the most important element.

The role of an economist at the OECD differs from that of an adviser to a national government in that he works in a unit which provides only economic assessment and advice – since the OECD has practically no operational responsibilities. The work nevertheless remains political. The institutional background to this work is described in the first section.

One question that people ask is not just what such an economist who works there does, but how much difference his work makes. Since his work is to assist international economic cooperation, that is a large question. Fashions in economic policy have changed greatly in the nearly thirty years of the OECD's existence. In the last decade or so, policies have been unadaptive; the scope for coordinating them has therefore been restricted; and – though this phase may be passing – international organizations have had less of a role. These changes have affected what OECD economists do, as I try to describe.

Their work can, I think, claim a degree of intellectual interest; and in the second section I note what seem to me some of their intellectual contributions. Seen as a contribution to international policymaking, the OECD's influence is one strand among many; and international policy coordination is

* This account rests in part on my experience: I was Assistant Secretary General at the Organization for Economic Cooperation and Development (OECS) and in charge of the Department of Economics and Statistics in the years 1963–73; and when at the Bank of England attended all meetings of the Economic Policy Committee in the years 1973–83. It also draws heavily on the book by three who are, or were, senior members of the Department, Llewellyn, Potter and Samuelson (1985), refered to in the text below as Llewellyn *et al.* It draws too on Artis and Ostry (1985); Sylvia Ostry was later my successor in charge of the Department. I am much indebted to Stephen Potter for his comments; to John Fay, who spent most of a lifetime in the Department, and was latterly most deservedly its Director; to Stephen Marris; and to David Henderson, its present Director.

often a matter of unremarkable piecemeal adjustment rather than explicit joint bargains. But in the third section I point to occasions when, I believe, the work of OECD economists has been specially effective and useful for governments' policies. There is a short recapitulation at the end.

THE INSTITUTIONAL SETTING OF OECD'S ECONOMIC WORK

The work economists do at OECD is influenced by the nature of the institution, which is best explained in terms of its history. Its methods of working stem directly from those established by its predecessor, the Organization for European Economic Cooperation (OEEC). OEEC was set up in Paris in 1947 in the days of Marshall Aid, as a grouping of most European countries west of the Iron Curtain[1], with three functions: collectively to agree on the allocation of Marshall Aid; collectively to scrutinize recovery programs submitted by each; and to encourage cooperation among them in achieving recovery. The sort of multilateral discussion among a peer group thus instituted has characterized the work of OEEC and OECD ever since. The initiative which led to OEEC came from the United States, then confronted with the prospect of a divided and impoverished Europe, in danger of turning towards communism, and unlikely to recover quickly without massive external aid. The political motive for US support of the Organization, though changing with changing times, has remained important. The United States and Canada took part in OEEC's work only as 'associates'.

In 1960 OEEC was transformed into the OECD, consisting of the what were then eighteen European members together with the United States and Canada (now as full members). This step again owed much to the United ',12States: such a group appeared a means to counter a potentially autarchistic development of the European Economic Community, established with six members in 1957. The objects of OECD were declared to be 'to achieve the highest sustainable economic growth and employment . . . while maintaining financial stability . . . and to contribute to the expansion of world trade on a multilateral non-discriminatory basis. Other countries have subsequently joined: Japan in 1964; Finland in 1969; Australia in 1971; and New Zealand in 1973.

There remains a select list of further countries who may become members later; but at the moment OECD's members thus number twenty-four. This is a fairly small and manageable group, between them account for the greater part of world GNP, and whose policies do much to determine what happens in the rest of the world. The heyday of the Organization was probably its first dozen years, when, among other things, US interest was greatest: since then there has been a tailing off.

The Organization is legally a Council of Permanent Representatives at ambassadorial level who represent its member countries. In fact it is an untidy collection of specialized committees consisting mostly of officials responsible at home for a particular branch of policy, and coming to Paris for odd days.[2] The fields covered were alway diverse, and have multiplied: not only economic policy, but trade, payments, industry, steel, infrastructure, fisheries, aid to developing countries, science policy, nuclear energy, and many more (see Secretary-General's annual report, *Activities of OECD*).

Each group of committees has its own secretariat, so that the OECD secretariat is a collection of many groups, of which the Department of Economics and Statistics which serves the economic committees is the largest. It now numbers some 170, of whom half are professional grades, all either economists (about 75) or statisticians (about a dozen). There are as many more economists (perhaps 100) in other parts of the secretariat, which not totals 1,800.

The economic committees are the Economic Policy Committee (EPC); its working parties (now two); and also the Economic and Development Review Committee (EDRC) which examines the situation of each country annually, and discusses a secretariat survey of the country concerned before publication. The members of the EPC (which now meets twice a year) are the senior official (or his immediate deputy) in finance ministries or departments of economics, and similarly senior officials from central banks. The Chairman is now usually the Chairman of the Council of Economic Advisers in Washington. The EPC is large: more serious discussion takes place in a smaller committee, Working Party No. 3 (WP3), which meets more frequently (in the 1960s five or six times a year; now quarterly).[3] This useful committee structure was largely the work of Walter Heller and Bob Roosa who held the senior economic posts in the Kennedy administration.[4]

The role of the economic staff serving these committees is not merely to carry out the committee's wishes and to prepare papers that are asked for. To be effective, the work of the Department has to be purposive and organized. What topics the committee should discuss in future may be as much for the head of the department as for the chairman to decide. Some topics are so contentious that discussion is sterile: subjects have to be those likely to produce profitable discussion. The quality of discussion depends in part on the quality of the papers provided for the committees: they need to be not only intellectually rigorous, up-to-date and accurate, and clear and simple: but also diplomatically well judged. To stimulate an exchange of view, the papers need to single out questions for discussion. These are not abstract questions, but relate to one or more countries' policies, and the countries concerned are likely to be sensitive to criticism by others. Papers for committees have to be produced to a rigorous timetable, allowing time for translation[5] and transmission.[6]

At the meetings senior members of the Department normally intervene in discussion along with national delegates, though since, like the Pope, they command no battalions, the points they make need to be good ones. Though geographically detached from national capitals, the work cannot be politically detached, but has to be done with close awareness of what member governments are thinking and what is happening in each country. For an economist working there, OECD is an unsurpassed vantage point from which to observe the world economy.

For an international and neutral secretariat, there are limits to what subjects can be raised, and how bluntly. There are thus constraints that a head of department has to impose on himself. The same considerations may lead the Secretary-General as head of the Organization to require to see major economic papers before they are circulated; practice in this respect has varied. But to be well done the work has to be carried out primarily by the Economics Department acting on its own judgement and on the strength of its own reputation. The Department has in fact largely been in a position to run its own house. There are, for instance, no rigid nationality quotas for the staff: though a good mix is desirable, and though national authorities may seek to exert pressure, it can still be said that those appointed are those thought best for the job. Generally speaking, then, the nature of the Organization is inherently congenial to the economist as a policy adviser.

OECD's work on economic policy is in much the same field as that of the International Monetary Fund (IMF). But there are these three differences: OECD's membership is far smaller; discussions in IMF potentially relate to financial operations; and most discussions are conducted in its Executive Committee of national representatives permanently stationed in Washington. These factors dictate a less intimate style of debate than in OECD. Discussions of economic policy in the European Economic Community (EEC) in practice also cover much the same field as OECD, confined however to its narrower membership (now twelve). But procedures are more cumbrous because the EEC sees itself *en route* to economic union, and its commission as a government in embryo. OECD's lack of operational responsibility and of aspiration to supranationality means that its committees have no decisions to take, and procedures can be informal.[7] In the absence of these trappings of grandeur, OECD has to survive on the basis of the quality of discussion for which it provides a forum

OECD ECONOMISTS' ANALYTICAL CONTRIBUTIONS

OECD is not a research body, but one intended to assist member countries' policy. Its work nonetheless can claim a degree of intellectual interest. To illustrate this, I will comment first on some of its published work; second, I will describe its work in economic forecasting – in both these cases covering the whole span of OECD's existence; and, third, I will discuss the work leading to the Smithsonian Agreement in 1971. How far OECD's work has influenced countries' policies is left for consideration in a later section.

OECD macroeconomic publications

Many of OECD's publications start life as papers for committees; and the character of the work of economists in OECD may be illustrated by the kind of papers produced for them.[8] These papers are designed for a specific purpose and a specialized audience. They are meant to inform members of a committee of developments in countries other than their own (with which they may otherwise be only vaguely familiar), thus enabling them to take part more confidently in discussion of others' affairs. They provide coherent assessments of each country's prospects, which members of the committee may compare with what representatives of the country tell them (these, being spoken, may be difficult to grasp fully without a tabulated presentation). They analyze cross-country effects, which are often complex – and which officials coming from national capitals, preoccupied with their national concerns, may not have fully grasped. The papers presented to the committees also seek to single out questions about countries' policies likely to be of concern to other countries, and to raise them in a form which observes the diplomatic civilities of discussion between representatives of sovereign states.

Since 1967 the secretariat papers given to the EPC have (with minor amendment) been published twice a year as the *OECD Economic Outlook*. The *Outlook* makes available to the general public a mine of up-to-date information, and remains afterwards a valuable source of reference and research. It is particularly useful for the processed aggregated data (for instance on trade between OECD countries as a group and the rest of the world; or data on budget positions distinguishing discretionary policy changes from other effects).

There are a number of areas where the analysis is inevitably more superficial or where the claimed attribution of causality appears insecure. Given the emphasis until recently on monetary targets, OECD was bound to follow national authorities in documenting rates of change of monetary aggregates – even though the figures here are more clear cut than anything that can be deduced from them.[9] After the first oil crisis (for reasons not really understood), there was a significant shift from profits to labour incomes (Llewellyn *et al.*, p. 37). The rise of wage costs in terms of total factor prices has widely been interpreted as a cause of (so-called classical) unemployment (Malinvaud, 1977, 1982; Bruno and Sachs, 1985), a fashion which OECD has followed – but since the starting point is unexplained, that may be dubious. Attempts at forecasting international capital flows and/or exchange rates have everywhere met with little success; and OECD documentation, while providing considerable past information, makes little attempt to do so – a reticence no doubt well justified.[10]

In addition to the world surveys provided by the *Economic Outlook*, OECD also produces surveys, usually once a year, of each member country.

These discuss short-term macroeconomic developments, with assessments of past policies and recommendations about what each country should do in future. These, too, start as committee documents; and the recommendations may be said to represent the view of the secretariat in so far as these are endorsed by the Committee – or, where the country involved objects, as insisted on by the Committee. In some smaller countries, these country surveys play a central role in domestic discussion of economic policy. From year to year, this staple diet has been varied by discussion of longer-term trends or policies; by accounts of particular sectors (e.g. the labor market or the financial sector); or by discussion of 'micro' measures designed to improve macroeconomic performance, with exhortation to countries to pursue such an approach. In recent years when discussion of macroeconomic policies has seemed less profitable, 'structural' questions of this sort have had more emphasis.

The Department has also put out a succession of independent studies of various sorts. As an example, there have been retrospective studies covering a decade or more of experience, generally produced by the economic staff working alone. Thus in the period when growth rates were more stable than now, detailed projections were made for a quinquennium or so ahead (e.g. *The Growth of Output 1960–80*; OECD, 1970).

At the other extreme is the report produced by Working Party No. 3 in 1966 on *The Balance of Payments Adjustment Process* (OECD, 1966). This was a text discussed and agreed in committee, which was an agreement among the ten countries represented about how they would proceed in cases of payments imbalance, and what they would expect of each other. In effect it was a practical rule book for the operation of the Bretton Woods system as it was then understood – a question which (as will be argued in the section on the influence of OECD economists) may not be utterly irrevelant to present-day concerns. Senior committees cannot as a rule spare time for the exhausting business of drafting in committee, and few other reports were produced in this way.

The study on *Fiscal Policy in Seven Countries* (Hansen, 1969) by Bent Hansen (acting as full-time consultant) was a considerable research study. The question he examined was whether fiscal policy had mitigated short-term fluctuations in output – on which he concluded that, to some degree, it had, except in the United Kingdom. Reliance on fiscal policy, having for a time been thoroughly out of fashion, may now be reviving; and the work by Hansen and others on this subject may retain some interest.[11] But questions of short-term instability have certainly been dwarfed by the much worse instability that hit OECD economies after 1973.

After the early 1970s inflation in all OECD countries became faster, and economic growth slower. A rather early and ambitious attempt to diagnose what had gone wrong and to map the escape route was made in *Towards Full Employment and Price Stability* (McCracken *et al.*, 1977), usually known as the McCracken Report. In form, this was a report produced by a group of former policymakers and senior academics, meeting under the chairmanship of Paul McCracken (formerly chairman of the US Council of Economic Advisers).[12] In practice, there was a heavy input from the OECD economists (notably Stephen Marris); nor were the group completely agreed. Even at the time, the conclusions seemed optimistic: that there was a 'narrow path' back to prosperity, by keeping demand growing rather fast but not so fast as to reawaken inflation. In fact, renascent recovery was again to be knocked off course by the second oil crisis.

Slower growth has lately been accompanied by the erection of significant barriers to trade. A report more microeconomic in character should perhaps be mentioned as noteworthy: *The Costs and Benefits of Protection* (OECD, 1985). Since 1983, *OECD Economic Studies* has published in more academic form some of the background work underlying the current analyses produced for working parties and committees.

Economic forecasting at OECD

The OECD pioneered the production of world economic forecasts; from the beginning in 1963 it has made its own country forecasts, which are then discussed twice yearly at meetings of national forecasters, and modified in the light of that discussion. This procedure ensures that OECD is well informed, but also is an efficient way of transmitting information to national forecasters, and is thus valuable to them.

OECD's work on forecasting has become progressively more sophisticated; and though the IMF has followed and the EEC also produces forecasts for its more restricted group of countries, OECD's exercise probably remains the most elaborate. Development has been in three broad phases. The country experts, whose work had previously been to review past trends in each country and comment on their policies, began in the early 1960s to produce forecasts for each country, initially based only in small part on econometric models. It was frequently the case that the sum of what the country experts predicted for the exports of their countries was inconsistent with the sum of what they collectively predicted for their countries' imports; and rough attempts would be made to adjust for such inconsistencies.

In the late 1960s and early 1970s, models of international trade were developed to permit consistent prediction of trade volumes and prices (Adams *et al.*, 1969; Meyer-Zu-Schlochtern and Yajima, 1970; Samuelson, 1973, 1976). These were used to provide a check on the forecasts by the country experts of their countries' balance of payments. Confrontation of this sort would indicate need for revision of the country forecasts, which would then in turn require reworking of the trade model. These feedback effects were thus taken care of 'by hand' by successive iteration.

In 1969, work began on an integrated forecasting model (called Interlink) for the OECD area (Llewellyn *et al.*, pp. 161–86), which consists essentially of three elements.

1. A set of medium-sized (150 equations) econometric models, one for each OECD country, which broadly reproduce the simulation properties of the larger models used by national administrations.
2. To capture the response of the rest of the world to events within OECD, reduced-form models for eight non-OECD regions.
3. To model the links both between OECD countries, and between the OECD and other areas, additional models for the volume and price of international trade in foods and services; and also models which attempt, though with much less success, to predict international capital flows and/or exchange-rate movements.

In a model in which events external to the area are treated as a response to OECD behavior, OECD policy variables in principle determine the pace of the whole system; and, given information on these, forecasts could be made 'centrally' without assistance from country experts. In practice, country experts are responsible for inputs and inspect initial results, and there are further rounds of the process, so that the procedure remains one of successive iteration. The Interlink model provides efficient handling of a large volume of data, and ensures international consistency at each stage.

Forecasts are made twice yearly, and are for three or four half-years ahead. (The forecasts made in July of year n extend to the end of year $n+1$: those made in December to the end of year $n+2$.) In assessing the results, there are a number of questions, some relatively straightforward, some of greater complexity: OECD forecasting must be seen as assisting member countries' separate efforts at forecasting and in effect part of that forecasting, and similar questions arise about the whole enterprise. Econometric forecasting is capable of endless refinement, and the natural urge to do better has everywhere produced increasing elaboration. This, however, has not brought the improvement originally hoped, and major errors continue to be made.

A first question is how accurate have OECD forecasts been. Though full post-mortems are not available, some surveys have been made (Llewellyn *et al.*, ch. 6). The collective national output of OECD has on average been forecast only within ± 1 per cent: errors in predicting individual countries' output were somewhat greater. Since 1977 the rate of inflation has also been forecast only to within ± 1 per cent. The way in which forecasts have to be made gives them a bias towards predicting normality. An economy normally grows: rising national output normally generates rising real factor incomes, which are normally most spent. This process may be accelerated or retarded by 'abnormal' events, many of which for OECD countries come – on a first analysis – from outside the area. In modeling this process, these abnormal factors have to be identified and quantified; and that tends to be done only incompletely. What rate of growth can be taken as 'normal' has varied over the period; but taking account of that, it seems that almost all the errors lay in predicting a more 'normal' growth rate than in fact occurred. The effects of the first big oil-price rise (1973–4) were not well foreseen; those of the second (1979–80) were better predicted. Underestimation of the cumulative collective effect of a major shift towards expansion in several countries' fiscal policies might account for underprediction in 1968 and 1976.

A second question is whether OECD forecasts were better than those made by the member countries themselves. There were cases when OECD's were clearly better, or clearly worse, but on average there is probably little to choose. This is not surprising: each was trying to do the same thing (countries as well as OECD tried as best they could to allow for the international transmission of demand influences); and each had access to the other's forecasts.

A third question is whether countries' forecasts benefited by participation in OECD forecasting meetings – a hypothetical question to which there can be no clear answer. The OECD procedure certainly provides a quick way of transmitting the information each country needs to assess the likely trends and policies of its neighbors – a service for which the smaller countries in particular are grateful. It is probably also true that an international organization is better placed to assess international transmission effects. To do this effectively requires a fairly large econometric apparatus, the cost of which is shared if done at OECD rather than in each national capital.

The final test of forecasting is not its absolute accuracy (which is not attainable); but whether forecasts pointed policy in the right direction, or their errors misled it. That answer depends on the sort of policy being followed. Up to about 1973 the main aim of policy was to secure adequate, and restrain excessive, demand growth. Policy of that sort has to be based on forecasts. The forecasting record in that period was somewhat mixed. Though both the 1968 boom and the subsequent slowdown were significantly underpredicted, the build-up to the boom in 1972–3 seems to have been well forecast (Llewellyn *et al.*, Table 6.1), and OECD predictions may have been somewhat better than the sum of the countries' own predictions (ibid., Table 6.2).

Faster inflation after 1973 made restraint of inflation a main aim of policy. The history of the period can be summarized as two external inflationary shocks (in 1974 and 1980), each producing an absolute decline in output; and each followed by a waning of inflation, and an incomplete recovery of output. In the first phase, policy was two-faced; at first restrictive, it became expansionary in 1975 (Llewellyn *et al.*, Table 3.1). When the second wave of inflation struck, restraint of inflation was much more clearly the dominating aim. Fiscal and monetary policy largely ceased to be seen as a means of demand management. After 1973, therefore, there is hardly a question of forecasts having misled policy: within broad limits, policy was little dependent on the precise course of the economy.

It may seem paradoxical that countries, nonetheless, continued to devote as much effort as ever to economic forecasting and to attend, as before, discussions of prospects at OECD. The truth may be that while policy in appearance became largely passive, its impact on demand in fact remained a consideration in the formulation of policy, even though not one highlighted in its presentation. The shift in countries' policy approach after 1973 will be discussed in the third section, along with some episodes in collective policy-making; and some further points about OECD forecasting are best deferred for discussion in that context.

Staff work for the Smithsonian Agreement

OECD's role in the devaluation of the US dollar in 1971 will be discussed in the next section; here the technical aspects of OECD staff work will be discussed. The Smithsonian Agreement, it has been said, was based on the most elaborately quantified macroeconomic analysis ever to underpin an international agreement. Without that preparatory work, in which the IMF and OECD collaborated closely, agreement might hardly have been possible. The preparatory work – though a workable model of the world economy then barely existed – was essentially a simulation exercise, not without complications in practice.

Though the US current account did not move into deficit until 1971, its current surplus had for several years been increasingly inadequate to match the regular outflow of private and official capital; and other countries had been adding, increasingly reluctantly, to their holdings of dollars. The possibility of an exchange-rate realignment was too sensitive a question to be openly discussed in WP3. But as a way of focusing attention on the underlying imbalance, the papers for the working party had for some time been collating what came to be called countries' 'current-account aims' – thus pointing to the discrepancy between what countries would like to see and what was likely to occur on the basis of current exchange rates. These 'aims', as set out by the secretariat, were in some cases drawn from national statements, or planning documents; in others, based on what countries said in the working party; and in a few, merely propositions intended as a basis for discussion. These exercises always showed that countries' aims, as first stated, were mutually incompatible (out of a mercantilist bias, countries in effect hankered after a larger surplus or smaller deficit than, collectively, was possible). The secretariat would therefore suggest how they might be scaled down and a compromise reached.

Two further complications had to be taken into account. Activity in the United States was then cyclically low, and in some other major countries cyclically high. The US current account was accordingly less unfavorable than it would have been if activity everywhere had been at the average level experienced in the past, and expected in the future. OECD had therefore developed the concept of cyclically adjusted current balances. To provide estimates of them was a less difficult task then than it would be now since all countries had relatively high employment, so that the question of what level should be taken as normal did not raise great dispute. For the purposes of the exercise, major countries also made estimates of cyclical adjustment factors. In principle the factors for OECD countries should sum about to zero; but again it was always found that national estimates tended to be incompatible – in a direction that added to the mercantilist bias of countries' statements of their aims and prospects. Since the estimates were intended to form the basis for a lasting pattern of exchange rates, it was also necessary to estimate the cyclically adjusted pattern of payments balances some years ahead. That involved extrapolating the trend, where any was perceptible, in cyclically adjusted balances; and allowing also for any foreseeable special factors.

These were the main elements in OECD's estimate of the US payments imbalance and its counterparts in other countries – an estimate translated into terms of required exchange-rate changes by the IMF staff.[13] The estimate was of course subject to a wide margin of error. But in any case it served only as the starting point for a process of political compromise. For while the United States wished for a larger devaluation, its partners wished to limit the appreciation of their currencies. The negotiations are discussed further in the next section.

THE INFLUENCE OF OECD ECONOMISTS

How far has the work of OECD economists affected countries' policies? Although the question may be naive in a complex world where the number of actors is legion, it is perhaps helpful to see what can be answered.

OECD is not the only body engaged in multinational economic cooperation. Its work is part of the fabric of cooperation that has grown up since World War II; and, while the Bretton Woods consensus lasted, it functioned as part of that. The breakdown of that consensus may have been due in part to economies getting less well-behaved, and the problems of policy more intractable. But it also reflected a shift of opinion to market solutions; and, since the felt need for active macroeconomic policy was less, the need and scope for international coordination of such policies also declined. These changes in the world policy regime profoundly affected OECD's role; and I will deal separately with the time before and after the break, which can be dated roughly at about 1973. Evidence of a direct effect on countries' policies is not the only test to apply: OECD's influence (like that of anybody) was for much of the time indirect, general and not easily picked out. I will, however, point to a number of cases where its influence was, perhaps, more overt.

The Bretton Woods era

Theory points to clear gains from joint action by several countries. For instance, a balance-of-payments constraint on each country's policies may be removed if all act together. Recent literature has examined in some detail the possibilities of international cooperation in this high sense (see for instance Johansen, 1982; Hamada 1974, 1976; Oudiz and Sachs, 1984; Miller and Salmon, 1985). But in practice the scope for such deals has been limited, for reasons to be noted below.

The gains of concerted action may be obtained not only by plans of action devised to meet particular occasions, but by adherence to general agreed rules of behavior. One example is mutual agreement to reduce tariff barriers, as under the General Agreement on Tariffs and Trade (GATT) (whose rules, however, have been honored more in the letter than the spirit). The operation of the Bretton Woods exchange-rate regime involved general agreement about the conduct of macroeconomic policy; and general adherence to these rules, in effect, also provided the benefits of coordinated action.

The system embodied in the IMF Articles of Agreement provided a well-balanced framework for countries' policies, and therefore also for the work of OECD. Its main components were that exchange rates in the short term were fixed within narrow limits, but in the longer term were variable. Macroeconomic policies were, up to a point, to aim to maintain the fixed rates. But if the fixed exchange rate could be maintained only by domestic policies that led to unacceptable deflation or inflation (i.e. in case of 'fundamental', rather than transitory, disequilibrium) the central fixed exchange rate could be adjusted, on a scale to be agreed with the IMF. To avoid premature adjustments of the rate, reserves could be supplemented by drawings on the IMF, on a scale, however, which was limited, and subject to an increasing degree of conditionality – the conditions being that macroeconomic policies were changed in a way likely to support either the old rate, or a new one if adjustment had become necessary.

The system encouraged countries to maintain high, non-inflationary levels of employment; and, as applied to industrial countries, worked well in conditions where high levels of activity were already well established and inflation was moderate. Exchange rates were managed; and since rates in general were fairly well aligned, adjustments could usually be confined to a single currency that had got out of line. The IMF was the policeman: its power to grant conditional finance gave it considerable influence (though far from dominance) over countries' policies, more especially in the case of deficit countries.

The first dozen years of OECD's existence were the heyday of the Bretton Woods era; and OECD's role was essentially an adjunct to that of the IMF. Like any international body, the IMF is an association of sovereign states, whose power as a body rests on agreement among its members. OECD, representing its more important members, provided a useful forum for unscripted discussion of the issues. The fact that OECD had no responsibility for decisions may be thought to have put OECD at a disadvantage. But as already noted, this meant also that its proceedings could be less formal or legalistic, which was a major convenience. The work of economists in OECD helped to promote understanding of the world economic situation, and agreement on what should be done about it, among the most powerful members of the IMF. This was also the heyday of the Keynesian consensus; and the IMF Articles of Agreement both provided a framework for the aims of demand management, and focused attention on its use.

The British problem in the mid-1960s

During the years 1964–8 the main problem case was the United Kingdom. Its situation figured prominently on Working Party No. 3's agenda and was perhaps the case where OECD discussion had most influence in this period. A Labour government had come to power determined to replace the 'stop–go' cycle – which was seen as having undermined previous British performance – by a period of steady expansion (Blackaby, 1978, pp. 28–51). That was not achieved. If it had been, it would have further weakened a balance of payments already weak; and, from the beginning, the policy appeared to many observers to be incompatible with an unchanged exchange rate. The government, however, resisted devaluation for three years, and resorted to various alternative expedients; and when finally accepted in 1967, devaluation took time to improve the balance of payments. Throughout the period, therefore, there were repeated runs on sterling; repeated resort to borrowing through swap facilities with other central banks; and on two occasions (1965 and at the time of devaluation) drawings on the IMF.

The influence of OECD discussions was the greater because at this time the IMF was short of usable currencies, and, in order to lend to a country in need, had itself to borrow. To meet this need, the General Agreement to Borrow (GAB) had been negotiated between the IMF and the Group of Ten, the countries constituting which were almost identical to those represented in WP3 (and the same people were their official representatives). These countries' assent was required each time the GAB was activated. Exceptionally at this time, the working party thus had a financial sanction similar to that of the IMF. Minutes were not normally kept of discussions in the working party; but in the case of the discussions on the United Kingdom's position, the conclusions of the working party were summarized in the form of a letter by the chairman[14] to the chief UK representative. In my view, this pressure probably made UK policy somewhat more restrictive than it would otherwise have been.

It is worth considering how such international influence may be thought to work. In the stylized mode of theoretical discussion, each country is credited with a clearly defined internally consistent set of aims. In reality, any government is a coalition of factions: its collective aims are not fully articulate; and the predilections of powerful ministers, who may be swayed by their chief advisers, count for a good deal. It is probably always the case that an international organization can exert an influence only by strengthening the arguments of one side or other in an internal debate. Since an international secretariat in effect is an additional adviser, the direct influence of its view must usually be small. More important are the views of other governments, more especially if there is agreement among them – which it may be the job of the international secretariat to articulate. Outside views are likely to count for more if there is a financial sanction – as there often is for deficit countries in a fixed-rate regime. Participation in discussion of national policies gives an international economist a sensation of power. But there are usually many people involved in any important act of policy, and the work of international economists, such as those at OECD, can only be one strand among many.

The Smithsonian Agreement

This was a later case where OECD played an important role. At the end of 1971, the nominal external value of the US dollar was changed for the first time since World War II – a more momentous step than may now appear. A depreciation of the dollar had long been thought to be legally impossible under the Bretton Woods rules; and though, when it came to it, ways round legal obstacles were found, it was bound to be a complex operation whose necessity the United States accepted only after long reluctance. A fall in the effective rate of the United States involved a rise in that of other countries, and the counterpart to the US imbalance was distributed unevenly among other countries. A uniform appreciation of their currencies would therefore have been inappropriate in theory and unacceptable in practice. Because the parity of the US dollar as declared to the IMF had been taken to be stable, the dollar was the fixed point in the system: other countries, in declaring their own parities, had determined their exchange rates in terms of the dollar. If the fixed point were removed, a multilateral negotiation would be required to establish a new pattern of exchange rates.

At the IMF/IBRD (International Bank for Reconstruction and Development) meetings in Washington in September 1971 the major countries decided to undertake such a negotiation. In view of Working Party No. 3's previous discussion of balance-of-payments aims, OECD was asked for an assessment of the extent of world payments imbalances (see the preceding section). The exchange-rate changes required to correct their payments imbalances were then estimated by the IMF staff. This formed the starting point for negotiations among the ministers of the Group of Ten; and was in fact to be fairly close to what was agreed after negotiation between them. The US dollar was devalued by varying amounts relative to the other currencies, and by 9 per cent on average. The effective exchange rate of Japan appreciated by some 11 per cent, and that of Germany by 6 per cent. For other countries the changes were mostly small.

Much of the credit for this considerable achievement in economic co-operation must go to Paul Volcker, then Under-Secretary for Monetary Affairs at the US Treasury (and, as such, his country's representative on WP3). In the event the agreement did not prove a lasting settlement. Rightly or wrongly, the belief gained ground that the Smithsonian realignment had been insufficient. A second depreciation of the dollar was negotiated by Volcker in the course of a hasty tour of foreign capitals in early 1973. The new pattern of rates lasted only weeks, being superseded in March by the general adoption of floating rates. The idea of fixing rates by agreement went into a long period of eclipse. Even though soon to be superseded, the Smithsonian Agreement should still be seen as one of the rare successful cases of concerted joint action. The subsequent adoption of floating rates was in effect a decision to avoid decisions by handing over to the market. The Smithsonian was thus to be the last throw of the Bretton Woods era.

The post-Bretton Woods era

In the decade after 1973, various shifts in opinion combined to make a profound change in the philosophy of policymaking.[15] The adoption by major countries of floating rates took out a whole dimension of policy, and largely removed countries' needs both for reserves and for official finance to supplement them. The IMF thus lost much of its role, especially in relation to industrial countries; it was practically in cold store until, in the early 1980s, it found a new role in dealing with the debt problems of developing countries.

There was also progressive erosion of belief in neo-Keynesian policies. The first inflationary surge in the early 1970s meant that policy had two aims which were irreconcilable; and, in the event, pursuit of high and stable employment was inevitably blunted. By the mid-1970s, belief had waned even in fiscal policy's influence on demand. It was still credited with power to influence inflation, though perhaps less power than monetary targets; and since inflation was slow to subside, both fiscal and monetary policy became inactive and not concerned with the short-term behavior of the economy.

The world economy has also been in a much more disturbed state; events have perhaps become less easily predictable and harder to make sense of; and international demand and cost linkages have become more dominant. OECD's purely informational function has perhaps acquired greater value.

Despite a working agreement on the principles in the IMF charter, there had always been differences in countries' priorities. Some countries (West Germany and others) were dominated by fear of inflation; others (the Scandinavians and at that date the United Kingdom) were more concerned with employment and growth; and the majority were somewhere in between. The task of an international secretariat is to seek a compromise; but by the

1980s the split between countries' priorities had hardened, and the role of a neutral secretariat accordingly became less easy and, some have felt, less rewarding.

The response to the first oil crisis

The new era opened with the first great rise in the price of oil in 1973–4. This had unprecedented effects on the economies of OECD countries, which were at first difficult for them to disentangle; and created dilemmas for policy of a new order of magnitude (Llewellyn *et al.*, pp. 32–6, 243–4). OECD analysis was prompt, perceptive and useful.

The oil-price rise had three main effects on OECD countries. First, it had a large and abrupt inflationary impact. The quadrupling of the price of internationally traded oil probably directly raised the OECD price level by two percentage points above what it would otherwise have been. Over the next few years the indirect effect of the induced wage/price spiral was to multiply this figure severalfold. Second, it had a demand effect. The oil-price rise represented a transfer of income to the Organization of Petroleum Exporting Countries (OPEC) – from the OECD area and from developing countries which did not produce oil. The transfer was huge – about 2 per cent of the combined GNP of OECD countries; and since it was much more than the oil producers could quickly spend, total demand in OECD countries must have been cut by something like this amount. (The price of coal, oil and gas produced in the OECD area also rose in sympathy. This internal transfer of income was also spent only with a lag and thus resulted in a further reduction of total demand. The additional effect, though not noticed at the time either by OECD or others, was perhaps half the size of that resulting from the transfer to OPEC.) OECD countries thus faced a very large and abrupt deflationary impact on their economies.

Third, there was a major balance-of-payments effect. Since OPEC now earned much more, but did not spend it, it suddenly had a large current-account surplus of some $80 billion in 1974. Other countries in total inevitably had an equivalent deficit. OECD countries went into deficit to the tune of about $25 billion – a major contrast with the $5–10 billion surplus which they had had over the preceding decade – and had previously sought hard to retain.[16] This economic turnaround in their position was something which OECD countries were now going to have to accept. Given OPEC's behavior, an individual country could improve its position only by worsening that of other non-OPEC countries.

The situation at the time appeared even more complex. For the main fear at first was not any of these three effects, but of a serious physical insufficiency of world oil supplies.[17] OPEC had indeed suddenly discovered that it had a stranglehold over the industrial world. Countries, naturally enough, were at sea in their reactions. Many people disputed any inflationary impact: few in the immediate aftermath had quantified the demand and balance-of-payments impact. The outcome was not perfectly forecast by OECD – nor could it have been, since the price of oil was notched up only gradually.[18] But the qualitative assessment presented to the Economic Policy Committee in November 1973 and May 1974 provided an essentially correct analysis; and by the end of 1974 the figuring had become fairly firm.[19]

The policy response to the oil crisis was a compromise. In 1974 policy in most countries was mildly restrictive, though less so in the small countries.[20] Then in 1975, after a sharp fall in output in the early part of the year – and despite inflation still at about 10 per cent a year – policy became expansionary. In 1976 output grew at nearly 5 per cent, so recovering briefly its pre-1973 growth rate.

The 1978 Bonn Summit[21]

After this recovery, however, the pace of growth was not sustained, and became markedly uneven. In 1977 the United States was recovering relatively rapidly, and its external position was deteriorating. West Germany and Japan were expanding relatively slowly, and they had strong current-account positions and also lower than average inflation rates. The US authorities argued that Germany and Japan should do more to maintain world growth. Other countries felt that a more expansionary policy on their part was ruled out by their weak payments positions – a constraint that would be loosened by faster growth in Japan and Germany.

OECD was therefore led to propose a graduated policy of fiscal expansion, on a scale depending on the situation of each country, after allowance for the effects on each of other countries' action (the 'locomotive' or 'convoy' approach). Such an approach was considered by the OECD Economic Policy Committee in the middle of 1978,[22] and became a main ingredient in the summit agreement at Bonn in July – the only such meeting where OECD was closely involved. Achievement of an international policy package was as always a highly political process dependent both on the characters and position of the heads of state involved, and on complex negotiations within and between national administrations; and the circumstances which made agreement politically possible are evidently rare (Putnam and Bayne, 1984, Ch. 6).

Under the agreement Germany undertook to take fiscal action equivalent (on an impact basis) to 1 per cent of GNP; Japan pledged itself to achieve growth 1.5 per cent higher than in the previous year, and took action shortly after equivalent to 1 per cent; Canada, France and Italy agreed to modest additional stimulus (but not the United Kingdom which had already enacted a fiscal stimulus). Up to this date, the United States had kept domestic fuel prices down, so failing to economize on energy consumption; it now agreed to decontrol domestic oil prices.

The Bonn Summit seemed a textbook example of cooperation. As was said by Anthony Solomon,[23] one of those closely involved, it 'was unique because it meant that countries were willing to make commitments that they had not necessarily planned on purely domestic grounds, but they were willing to take as part of an overall deal'. How far it was successful is difficult to assess. It is not clear how far the expansionary measures taken were due to the agreement, or might have been taken in any case. Expansion got under way in 1978 and 1979, and for the first time since 1973, unemployment in Europe started to fall. The Iranian revolution, and the resulting cut in oil supplies, then produced the second major rise in oil prices, in 1979–80. The resulting renewed surge in inflation later made some countries (particularly West Germany, where inflation moved above 5 per cent) bitterly critical of the Bonn package.

The eclipse of economic management, 1980–8

The second oil-price shock had an impact on OECD demand, and on the OECD price level, as large as on the first occasion. Much more clearly than on that previous occasion, the response was to give priority to containing inflation. Chief reliance was placed on a monetarist policy of progressively slowing the growth of monetary aggregates. Fiscal policy was restrictive for the next three years – though in many countries this represented not explicit demand management so much as a long-term aim of reducing 'structural' budget deficits. The pace of inflation fell off rather more rapidly than after the first oil shock (for OECD as a whole, from nearly 13 per cent in 1980 to 5.5 per cent in 1983). Judged by this standard, policy was successful – at a cost in lost output and rising unemployment.

Some have described the post-Bretton Woods regime as a 'non-system'; and the period after 1980 can similarly almost be described as a 'no-policy' era. It became the standard argument that governments were incapable of controlling exchange rates directly; or that if they tried, it would make things worse. Inflation could be 'squeezed out' by steady monetary pressure. Provided that were done, market forces left to themselves would produce both stable and appropriate exchange rates, and satisfactory economic growth. A large part of unemployment was thought to be 'structural'. Governments would be happy if it fell, but could not do much to reduce it; if they tried, they would reactivate inflation, and negate beneficent market adjustment.

Such a strategy was essentially medium term, leaving no room for purposive short-term adaptations of policy; it consisted too of essentially separate *national* policies. That left little place for international coordination. It may seem surprising that, whereas in the 1960s international organizations found it difficult to attract ministers to meetings, the habit of summit meetings of heads of state, which sidestepped the established organizations, now took root and flourished. Starting as secret gatherings, they became public shows with worldwide press and television coverage. Meetings of heads of state may, like meetings of senior officials, be useful as such. Aside from this, after 1978 the results of summits have been thin; and their communiques have contained little more than mutual admonition to persevere – as can also be said of ministerial meetings at OECD.[24]

The years 1980–5 were the low point of international cooperation. Since then there has been the beginning of a recovery. An early sign was perhaps the resurrection at the 1982 summit of the idea of multilateral surveillance – a term dating back to OECD and Group of Ten discussions in the 1960s; chosen to sound something, but to mean conveniently little; sounding French but not part of the French language: now formally devolved upon the IMF. As since developed by the Fund, it includes the establishment of 'performance indicators' (such as the rate of inflation, growth rates or unemployment) by which countries agree to have their performance judged. That, however, does not go far, since countries have their own ideas of which is important.

By 1985 the international stance of different economies had become rather similar to that which prompted the 1978 Bonn Summit, without this time prompting much movement towards agreed policy response. Fiscal policy in the United States had been expansionary (less for Keynesian reasons than as a result of the defense program and a belief in the virtues of low taxation); growth there had been much faster than elsewhere; and the US current account had moved into large deficit. This situation, and its relation to exchange rates, has dominated international discussions, in OECD and elsewhere, since 1985. Countries' attitudes have, however, remained wide apart. The United States has been pressed by other countries to reduce its fiscal deficits. This was not so much because the US economy was overheating, but rather because the size of the deficit, large in absolute terms (though not in fact especially large in relation to GNP) was itself thought to be an imbalance. The United States, on its side, has pressed fiscal reflation on other countries, in particular Japan and Germany. After the eclipse of fiscal policy in the previous quinquennium, belief that it had a role in demand management has thus begun to re-emerge – though in a form which has appeared to be for export only.

There has been more agreement that by 1985 the dollar had become seriously overvalued; and, by then, the old orthodoxy of benign neglect seems suddenly to have melted. Since then, it has been possible once again to have proper discussions in groups like WP3. The declaration in September 1985 by finance ministers and governors (at the Plaza meeting) was a successful attempt to depreciate the dollar. That having been done, all countries wanted to limit the dollar's fall, but disagreed only too publicly about the means. The United States saw stronger growth in Japan and Germany as a way of reducing the required scale of its devaluation. Other countries saw stabilization as impossible without a reduction in the US fiscal deficit. The old disagreement was thus deepened and embittered; and the outcome hangs unsure.

It seems difficult at this time to predict the future for international cooperation. In recent years OECD has played an informational role; and in a world of great uncertainty it is, I believe, important that there should be opportunity for countries to discuss the situation together. How far OECD (or the IMF) can do more than this is not so clear; but one can list a number of factors that will affect it.

On the theoretical plane there remain major disagreements among economists; and this theoretical disarray is bound to be reflected in disagreement about what policy can and should do. It also appears that our understanding as economists has not fully caught up with the rather major upheavals of economies in the last fifteen years. The great disputes among economists have not been directed very much to this aspect of reality; and I doubt if it can be said that we understand why most countries for most of the time up to about 1973 had high employment and rapid growth, and have since lost it.

Nevertheless, the climate of opinion continues to evolve. There is a constant interplay between events, which are often surprising, the effort to make sense of them, and the half-blind evolution of policies under the pressure of events. As if fashions in policymaking went in cycles, there are signs of revival of belief both in exchange-rate management and (less clearly) in demand management. It is perhaps possible to see practical agreement emerging of the sort needed to provide orderly exchange rates. It is less easy to see general acceptance of a set of ground rules that might produce coordinated policies for world growth.

International economic cooperation since the war has seemed to depend on clear leadership by the United States as a dominant country; and effective policy coordination in OECD seems unlikely unless the United States plays a guiding role. In the past, however, outward-looking policies in the United States have been intermittent.

A BRIEF RECAPITULATION

The OECD grew out of its predecessor organization, the OEEC – formed to foster mutual assistance in the days of Marshall Aid. It consists basically of a series of committees of senior or very senior officials coming to Paris for odd days from national capitals, dealing with a large variety of subjects. Of these the general economic committees (particularly the Economic Policy Committee and Working Party No. 3, backed by the Economics and Statistics Department) are usually recognized as the most important; and the present chapter has concentrated on this aspect of OECD's work.

The strengths of OECD, I have suggested, are that it has inherited from its predecessor (OEEC) a tradition of multilateral discussion, in which countries can put pressure on each other; that, having few administrative responsibilities, discussion is informal and flexible; and that it possesses an energetic and effective secretariat. The heyday of OECD was also the heyday of the Bretton Woods system. That contained a well-balanced set of rules which provided countries with the theoretical benefits of cooperation without having to arrange, *ad hoc*, specific deals between them; and up to about 1973, OECD's macroeconomic role was essentially to serve as an adjunct to the IMF. It provided a place for unscripted discussion of current issues; and, being a fairly compact and manageable group of twenty-four countries, it helped to promote understanding among IMF's major members, and agreement on how issues should be handled.

Since then there has been a sea-change in the fashion of policymaking. Inflation accelerated, and emphasis shifted to the containment of inflation, which, it was believed, could be handled by a policy of continued monetary attrition. Demand management fell out of fashion, so that fiscal policy, also, got locked on long-term goals. Exchange rates came to be thought to be either best left to markets, or inevitably determined by them, not governments. In that world, which now seems, in its turn, to be passing out of fashion, international organizations lost much of their *raison d'être*: the IMF, for instance, was without a role until the debt crisis gave it a new one. The scope for international cooperation seemed to shrink to little more than the exchange of information. But since events in that unordered world became less certain, OECD's purely informational role became, if anything, more important and useful.

I have described how OECD pioneered international economic forecasting and, though the IMF has followed, its six-monthly exercises are probably still the most elaborate. They were always intended as a means of facilitating exchange of information among member countries and helping to improve their own forecasts.

The influence of any organization is for the most part of a general sort, and its specific impact not easily identified. But I have tried to pick out a number of cases where OECD's influence was most marked, and its contribution most visible. I have cited by way of illustration discussion of the UK position in the 1960s – the main debtor position at that time; of the realignment of the US dollar in the Smithsonian Agreement of 1971; of the impact of the first oil-price shock in 1973–4; and, finally, of the situation which led up to the agreement at the Bonn Summit in 1978. For the five years or so after that, there was rather little of substance in international cooperation. But latterly renewed concern with exchange-rate stability may be a sign that the pendulum of fashion is swinging back.

In many organizations an economic adviser may be allotted a subordinate role. That is not true of the macroeconomic side of OECD: lacking administrative responsibilities, it deals only in economic analysis and advice, and the role of the economist is central. Whether OECD has itself a major or only a marginal role has depended in part on the intellectual climate among nations – as well as on OECD's success in exploiting its comparative advantages as against the international organizations with which it is in competition.

I have tried to show how at its best OECD has offered an economist working there scope as great as anywhere, even though in more recent years it may have been less rewarding. Greater international cooperation in future – and a greater role for an economist engaged in helping that process – will, I believe, depend chiefly on the three countries who are now dominant recovering an ability not to quarrel and to talk constructively about policy.

NOTES

1. Not Finland nor Spain. West Germany was at first represented by the occupying powers. For a full account see Hogan (1987).
2. On less important committees countries may also be represented by a member of their permanent delegation in Paris.
3. Nominally a subcommittee of the EPC, it in fact meets independently; nominally concerned with balance of payments questions, it in fact discusses policy generally. Its membership is restricted to ten countries: the United States, Japan, France, Germany, Italy, the United Kingdom, Sweden, Canada, the Netherlands and Switzerland.
4. Mention should also be made of Working Party No. 1 (Working Party No. 2 was abolished in 1980). This discusses the analytical underpinnings of the move presented to EPC, and new areas of work – nowadays as much microeconomic and structural as macroeconomic.
5. The official languages of the Organization are French and English; though in economic discussions English is most used, all papers have to be available in both.
6. Papers need to reach national capitals two weeks before a meeting, to allow time for discussion there and for the preparation of briefs by each bureaucracy for the representatives who will represent the country at the OECD meeting.
7. No formal records, for instance, need be kept nor for many years were kept of discussions in EPC or WP3.
8. For a personal account of what it is like to work as an economist at OECD, see Marris (1986).
9. There is no generally agreed analysis of how and how far central banks are able to affect the behavior of the financial system: see Dow and Saville (1988).
10. Forecasts of exchange-rate change may indeed be inherently contradictory. If changes could be forecast with high probability, market forces would produce change instantaneously and forecasts of further change would be erroneous. Within a range, exchange rates may be indeterminate and unpredictable (see Dow and Saville, 1988).
11. The debate on the subject perhaps started with my conclusion (Dow, 1964) that fiscal policy in the United Kingdom had in the short term been destabilizing. Some have read that as discrediting any reliance on fiscal policy; the moral intended was that policy should be improved. Hansen's conclusions have been challenged in later studies, some by former OECD economists (see discussion in Llewellyn *et al.*). Hansen has also himself partially disowned his study, on the grounds that it neglected the monetary effects of fiscal changes. Such crowding-out effects can, however, be regarded as due not to fiscal, but to monetary, policy (see Dow and Saville, 1988).
12. The other members of the group were G. Carli (formerly Governor, Bank of Italy), H. Giersch (Kiel Weltwirtschaft Institute), A. Lindbeck (Stockholm

University), R. Marjolin (formerly Vice-President of EEC Commission), R. Matthews (Cambridge University), A. Karaosmanoglu (formerly Deputy Prime Minister of Turkey), and R. Komiya (Tokyo University). As in other organizations, similar groups of independent experts have been appointed for other inquiries.

13. It has long seemed to me that it would be valuable if OECD and IMF working papers relating to the Smithsonian Agreement could be made the subject of an expert monograph. It would be natural for such a study to assess also the effects and adequacy of the 1971 realignment.
14. Then Emile Van Lennep, later Secretary General of OECD.
15. The changes in conventional economic wisdom are well described in Marris (1984).
16. See discussion of countries' balance of payments aims in the previous section.
17. Thus the OECD *Economic Outlook*, December 1973, said: 'The most serious immediate problem is, of course, the impact of the shortage of oil on the level of economic activity.' The fear of fuel shortage led to the establishment of the International Energy Authority as an independent body linked to OECD.
18. The end-1973 forecast for 1974 predicted a halving of the rate of OECD growth, while in fact there was no growth. Llewellyn *et al.* (Table 6.1) treat this as a large forecasting error. That judgement is too harsh. The price of oil rose in steps; and when the first forecast was made, only a third of the ultimate rise on the oil price had appeared. Policies, also, were tightened after the forecast was made.
19. See OECD *Economic Outlook* for December and June of these years. The end-1974 figuring was not published in full but is given in unpublished documents.
20. These judgements are based chiefly on the estimate of discretionary budget changes in Llewellyn *et al.*, Table 6.1.
21. This account follows Llewellyn *et al.*, pp. 244–9.
22. See OECD *Economic Outlook* for July 1978.
23. Then Under Secretary for Monetary Affairs at the US Treasury: the quotation is from Mesnil and Solomon (1983).
24. See tabulation of conclusions of summit meetings between 1975 and 1984 in Artis and Ostry (1985). The Council of OECD meets yearly at ministerial level and there are meetings of ministers concerned with particular branches of policy (agriculture, education, etc.).

BIBLIOGRAPHY

Adams, F. G., Eguchi, H. and Meyer-zu-Schlochtern, F., *An Econometric Analysis of World Trade* (Paris, OECD, 1969).

Artis, M. and Ostry, Sylvia, *International Economic Policy Coordination* (London, Routledge, and Kegan Paul for Royal Institute of International Affairs, 1985).

Blackaby, F. (ed.), *British Economic Policy 1960–74* (Cambridge, Cambridge University Press, 1978).

Bruno, M. and Sachs, J. D., *Economics of Worldwide Stagflation* (Oxford, Basil Blackwell, 1985).

Buiter, W. H., and Marston, R. C. (eds), *International Economic Policy Coordination* (Cambridge, Cambridge University Press, 1985).

Dow, J. C. R., *The Management of the British Economy 1955–60* (Cambridge, Cambridge University Press, 1964).

Dow, J. C. R. and Saville, I. D., *A Critique of Monetary Policy: Theory and British Experience* (Oxford, Oxford University Press, 1988).

Hamada, K., 'Alternative exchange rate systems and the interdependence of monetary policies', in R. Z. Aliber (ed.), *National Monetary Policies and the International Financial System* (Chicago, University of Chicago Press, 1974).

Hamada, K., 'A strategic analysis of monetary interdependence', *Journal of Political Economy*, vol. 84 (1976), pp. 677–700.

Hansen, B., *Fiscal Policy in Seven Countries 1958–1965* (Paris, OECD, 1969).

Hogan, M. J., *The Marshall Plan* (Cambridge, Cambridge University Press, 1987).

Johansen, L., 'A note on the possibility of an international equilibrium with low levels of activity', *Journal of International Economics*, vol. 12 (1982), pp. 257–76.

Llewellyn, J., Potter, S., and Samuelson, L., *Economic Forecasting and Policy; the International Dimension* (London, Routledge and Kegan Paul, 1985).

Malinvaud, E., *The Theory of Unemployment Reconsidered* (Oxford: Basil Blackwell, 1977).

Malinvaud, E., 'Wages and unemployment', *Economic Journal*, vol. 92 (1982), pp. 1–12.

Marris, S. N., 'Managing the world economy: will we ever learn?', Princeton University Financial Section, *Essays in International Finance*, No. 155 (Princeton, NJ: Princeton University, 1984).

Marris, S. N., 'The role of economists in the OECD', in A. W. Coats (ed.), *Economists in International Agencies* (New York: Praeger, 1986).

McCracken *et al.*, *Towards Full Employment and Price Stability* (Paris: OECD, 1977).

Mesnil, G. de, and Solomon, A. M., 'Economic summitry' (United States Council on Foreign Relations, 1983).

Meyer-zu-Schlochtern, F., and Yajima, A., 'OECD trade model, 1970 version', *OECD Economic Outlook, Occasional Studies* (Paris: OECD, 1970).

Miller, M. H., and Salmon, M., 'Policy coordination and dynamic games', in Buiter and Marston (1985).

OECD, *The Balance of Payments Adjustments Process* (Paris: OECD, 1966).

OECD, *The Growth of Output, 1960–80* (Paris: OECD, 1970).

OECD, *The Costs and Benefits of Protection* (Paris: OECD, 1985).

Oudiz, G. and Sachs, J., 'Macroeconomic policy coordination among the industrial economies', *Brookings Papers on Economic Activity* (1984).

Putman, R. D., and Bayne, N., *Hanging Together: The Seven-Power Summits* (London: Heinemann for Royal Institute of International Affairs, 1984).

Samuelson, L., 'A new model of world trade', *OECD Economic Outlook, Occasional Studies* (Paris: OECD, 1973).

Samuelson, L., 'The OECD world trade model: some recent extensions', in R. Courbis (ed.), *Commerce International et Modèles Nationaux* (Economica, 1976).

14 · THE EUROPEAN ECONOMIC COMMUNITY

Manfred Wegner

INTRODUCTION

The European Community (EC) represents a unique endeavor and has no historical precedents. The initiatives for European integration reflect an old vision of creating a unified Europe which can be traced back to Rousseau, Napoleon, Briand, Naumann and Churchill. The primary aim of the European Community was 'to lay the foundations of an ever closer union among the people of Europe and by pooling resources to preserve and strengthen peace and liberty' (Preamble to the Treaty of Rome). The process of European integration was envisaged to proceed from an extended customs union to an economic and monetary union and finally to a political union. Most of the actual problems suggest that the Community is still in its transitional stage.

The institutions of the European Community are now over thirty years old and have passed through many serious crises. Some observers have even remarked 'that the single greatest achievement of the European Common Market has been that it has survived' (Balassa, 1975). Through these years the Community has been enlarged from six to twelve members[1] and has changed its priorities, working methods and sometimes even its primary objectives. The initial goals of the Treaty of Rome, the establishment of a common market and the adoption of common agricultural and commercial policies, have largely been achieved notwithstanding their shortcomings. The Community has also made some progress in other areas and has attempted to define an employment and social policy, an industrial and technological policy, an energy policy, a regional policy, an environmental and consumer protection policy, and a policy for developing countries. But one can doubt whether the degree and intensity of economic cohesion within the Community in 1985 was higher and stronger than at the beginning of the 1970s if we neglect the impact of the enlargements. The completion of the internal European market is envisaged only for 1992 and the monetary integration remains incomplete based on the fragile arrangements of the European Monetary System (EMS).

The EC has weathered many shocks and heavy storms. There have been several moments where the Community was threatened by disintegration or even an imminent breakdown: for instance, after July 1965, when de Gaulle practiced the policy of the 'empty chair' and damaged one fundamental pillar of the Treaty of Rome, majority voting; or in 1979, when the British government under Thatcher insisted on the 'juste retour' of budgetary payments. The history of the EC reads sometimes like the management of permanent institutional, budgetary, monetary and economic crises.

The life of the Community has been fraught with astonishing contrasts: rapid progress in dismantling trade obstacles and quotas and deadlocks in some important policy fields such as transport, technology and capital markets; ambitious plans for economic and monetary unification and manifold disappointments in implementing efficient cooperation of economic and monetary policies; unprecedented increase in economic and social welfare in the 1960s and slow growth and a rapid rise of unemployment rates in the late 1970s and the 1980s; ardent promoters of the process of European integration in the early years and reluctant politicians and skeptical economists haggling over diverse solutions to national and international difficulties.

It is a challenging and difficult task to assess the role and the effectiveness of economists working within the Commission which is, besides the Council, the main Community institution. The professional life of the Euro-economist is squeezed not only by institutional and political constraints but also by the contradictions between plans and reality. First, there is the outside world and the changing economic and political environment of member and non-member countries. Second, there is the tight information network of European institutions and advisory committees, the daily surveillance of rules embodied in the Treaty of Rome, the management of the established mechanisms and funds and the initiation of new proposals extending the activities of the Community. Finally, there are the grand designs and ambitious summit communiques often hiding divergent views behind pompous phrases. Can we really blame the European economists for failing to realize the many glorious intentions, for the incomplete Common Market and the stagnation in the process towards European integration?

The following observations are by no means exhaustive. They are a selection of some important macroeconomic issues impressed by the biased experience of the author.[2] They may reflect an overcritical and disappointed attitude produced by the difficulties which have faced the economist in the European policy debate. But they are based on the conviction that European integration is necessary and worthwhile, and that resignation is not justified.

After a brief reference to the external factors which have promoted the European integration in the 1950s, the institutional and organizational framework is described in which economists operate within the EC Commission. The following sections analyze their role and effectiveness in two main areas of economic policy: the coordination of short- and medium-term macroeconomic policies and the attempts to initiate and intensify the monetary integration. The final section presents some modest proposals on how the efficiency of economic advice within the existing EC machinery could be improved. In summing up the limitations, failures and partial success, reference is made also to the plan to complete the internal European market in 1992, reviving the hope for new progress towards a united Europe.

ECONOMICS AND THE EUROPEAN COMMUNITY

Economic arguments have never been the main motive for establishing the EEC. The various plans and proposals for European integration and institutions were all seen as instruments for further political unification. Hallstein, the first President of the EC Commission, once said: 'We are not in business at all, we are in politics.' The ideas of European integration have been taken up enthusiastically by the Schuman Plan (1950) seeking to make a war between France and Germany not only 'unthinkable but materially impossible'. This political emphasis lost impetus when the grand designs of creating a European Defence Community and a European Political Community were rejected by France and Britain in 1954.

A new Benelux initiative launched the idea to circumvent the political difficulties by creating a common market which would initiate the process of economic cooperation and pave the way for the achievement of the primary political goal. The vision of the Spaak Report (1956) laying the base for the Treaty of Rome stressed the economic benefits from economic integration: comparative advantage, reduced costs by realizing economies of scale and increased competition by opening up national markets. The drive for economic integration in Europe was strongly promoted both by favorable conditions in the postwar reconstruction period and by theoretical thinking.

The ground for accepting the ideas on economic integration was prepared by the writings of academic economists who transformed the time-honored issues of international trade theory into the arguments defending the formation of regional customs or economic unions. Already in the pioneering work of Meade (1953, 1955) and Scitovsky (1958) the crucial problems are spelled out how members of an economic union can reconcile national balance-of-payments equilibrium (external balance) with full employment at stable prices (internal balance) when the autonomy of using national policy instruments is gradually reduced. The most instructive survey of the 'thought on economic integration' by Machlup (1977) reveals the fact that the basic theoretical thinking on economic integration has been dominated by Anglo-Americans (Viner, Meade, Lipsey, Kindleberger).

Among professional economists in continental Europe there was less agreement both on the desirability of economic integration on a regional basis and even more on the means and methods to achieve the integration of national economies and markets. Neoliberalists like Röpke and Allais warned against the dangers of the Common Market which would encourage trade diversion, the transmission of inflationary tendencies and the spreading of 'dirigist' and interventionist policies in the Community. The free traders and 'universalists', led by the British government and supported also by the former German Minister of Economic Affairs, Ludwig Erhard, defended the creation of a free-trade area in Europe.[3] The dichotomy of 'integration by governments' versus 'integration by markets' has since accompanied the debate on economic integration. The earlier efforts to coordinate governmental actions has progressively been replaced by a more microeconomic market-oriented approach.

The move towards economic integration in Europe was eased by the favorable international climate and by lucky circumstances. The removal of trade restrictions and exchange controls started early in the 1950s on a multilateral basis. The United States, which initiated the Marshall Aid program for the reconstruction of Western Europe, encouraged European economic integration through the Organization for European Economic Cooperation (the forerunner of the OECD) (1948), reinforcing the European Payments Union.

The worldwide reduction of the general level of tariffs negotiated in the Dillon and the Kennedy Rounds in the GATT proceeded hand in hand with the establishment of the European customs union. The dismantling of tariffs and other trade barriers among the EEC members progressed more rapidly than initially planned. The Community appeared to be swimming strongly with the international tide but its existence contributed to the success of the trade negotiations. More generally, because of the difficulties in imagining what would have happened otherwise it is hard to measure the impact of the formation of the Common Market on growth and trade. But there are few doubts that the foundation of the Common Market was a radical departure from traditional coalitions, protectionist policies and segmented markets and therefore an important source for the dynamic impetus behind the rapid growth in the 1960s (Olson, 1982).

The Treaty of Rome is long on fixing rules to achieve an extended customs union but short on defining the means and ends of economic policy. The neglect of general economic policy and a lack of policy guidance reveal the incomplete and permissive character of the Treaty. Only a few sketchy provisions are concerned with economic and monetary affairs which remain exclusively the primary responsibility of the member states. Member countries 'shall consider their policy relating to economic trends as a matter of common interest' (Art. 103) and their exchange-rate policy as 'a matter of common concern' (Art. 107). In order to facilitate the attainment of the economic objectives of the Treaty – equilibrium in the overall balance of payments, maintaining confidence in the currencies of the member countries, high level of employment and price stability (Art. 104) – member states 'shall coordinate their economic policies' (Art. 105). Besides some cautious provisions in case of balance-of-payment difficulties (Art. 108) nothing is said about the obligations, rules and instruments to define or to implement such a coordination or a common policy within the Community. The Treaty does not give guidance on which policies should be handled at the EC level in the transitional stage.

In 1962 the EC Commission presented an ambitious 'Action Programme of the Community for the second stage'. It was based on the concept of consolidating the integration process of the customs union (sometimes called 'negative integration') by coordinating the national economic policies to pave the way for the transition to an economic and monetary union with a common economic policy. 'A customs union that was not geared to a broader economic union would scarcely be viable' (EC Commission, 1962). Another proposal for a full-fledged economic and monetary union (EMU) evolved from the first European summit in The Hague in December 1969 and the Werner Report. It has been the last of the grandiose plans laying down the process of economic and monetary integration. The reasons for the failure of the EMU plan are considered later.

Economists and the EC

The institutional framework of the Community forms today a hybrid mixture of supranational elements and intergovernmental structure. Decisions and other formal acts are made by the Council of Ministers based only on proposals by the Commission. The decision-making mechanism of the Community was much damaged by the French refusal to accept qualified majority voting, thus investing veto powers in all matters vital to national interests. Since the disaccord of Luxembourg in 1966 the Council was often reduced to an intergovernmental body and the Commission to a technical secretariat. The Single European Act (adopted in 1987) attempts to strengthen the decision-making mechanism of the Community by introducing again qualified majority voting.

The Commission has many responsibilities: some are executive in nature, but the main functions are guarding the treaties to protect Community interests, initiating new policies and mediating between national interests. For operating its several functions the Commission has established an administrative structure. The Commission staff is organized into general directorates; originally nine large units which have been enlarged today into twenty-two units corresponding to the main areas of Community policy.[4] In total there were more than about 10,000 civil servants in the Commission in 1986. After excluding the administrative and secretarial staff and the large number of translators and interpreters (about 1,200) the staff of higher civil servants (top levels with university or similar training) is relatively small and increased from almost 2,000 in 1973 to about 3,200 in 1986, of which perhaps 30 per cent may have a training as professional economists.[5] Only the General Directorate of Economic and Financial Affairs, responsible for the horizontal economic and monetary policies in the Community, is manned exclusively with (120 top level) economists. Almost all other departments employ economists together with lawyers, technical specialists and administrators who monitor, manage and execute the responsibilities laid down in the Treaty of Rome and work out new proposals to advance the economic cohesion of the Community.

It is nearly impossible to summarize their complex activities, ranging from agricultural, industrial, regional and social affairs to the areas of development aid, external trade, competition and R&D policies. Are there domains where the Euro-economist has been most successful or where he failed? The details and intricacies of Community affairs do not allow a general answer. It may be fair to say that economists have had, to put it mildly, little success in shaping a more efficient agricultural policy due to the dominance of special interests. A positive example of the microeconomic influence of economists is the EC competition policy, framing and safeguarding the principles of the free and undistorted access to the common market. The rules of competition laid down in the Treaty of Rome have established strong supranational powers in the hands of the EC Commission and the Court of Justice and have spread a competitive order to all EC countries.

There are many sources by which the policymaking in the Community has been influenced and by which new ideas and concepts have been introduced. At least three channels have been of importance:

1. The many *ad hoc* groups of independent academics and high national civil servants which presented important reports[6] on a wide array of fiscal, public finance, economic and monetary issues, or the more permanent European lobby groups such as the Action Committee for Europe.
2. The tight network of official advisory bodies and committees operating within the EC machinery and bridging the need for information and consultation between the national governments and the Commission.
3. The debate in and between the Community institutions: Commission, Council of Ministers, European Parliament and European Economic and Social Committee.

According to the general philosophy of the Community, the coordination and progressive alignment of national economic policies should proceed in the Council of Finance and Economic Ministers based on proposals and recommendations of the Commission. To organize a 'soft' form of policy coordination between the member states a web of advisory bodies has been set up. The most influential institution was and is still the Monetary Committee, already provided for in the Treaty of Rome (Art. 105), followed by the Economic Policy Committee established in 1974 and comprising the former Short-term Economic Policy Committee (1960), the Budgetary and the Medium-term Economic Policy Committee (1964). Of similar importance are the Committee of the Governors of the Central Banks (1964) and the Coordinating Group for short-term economic and financial policies (1972).

Thus advisory committees abound. They all consist of high officials from national ministries, central banks and the Commission. They have no decision-making powers but are the regular meeting places for the continuous and reciprocal exchange of information and for consultation on economic trends and forecasts, on the possible impact of policy decisions and national policy intentions.

Very often the 'Eurocrats' in Brussels are blamed for all the unsolved problems, unrealistic plans and verbose window-dressing activities of the Community – the much abused scapegoat of the European debate. At first sight the professional life of an economist in the EC Commission is not very different from that of his counterpart in national and international departments: analyzing economic trends and policy measures, preparing forecasts, writing memos and attending long meetings. His special job is made difficult by the fact that he should understand the details of the situation of each member and spill-over effects, and develop and defend an optimal policy course of the Community, whose identity and preference function is vaguely defined and whose political and economic environment is changing all the time. His efficiency has suffered also from the radical changes in the conventional wisdom about the effects of domestic instruments, the role of exchange rates and the usefulness of policy coordination at the European and international level (Marris, 1984). For most of the 1970s and still in the early 1980s the larger member countries followed diverging policy mixes based on markedly different economic priorities and perceptions about how their respective economies work. At the same time the role of rules vs. discretion has undergone opposing trends: more rules in domestic policies and more discretion in the management of international affairs (Padoa-Schioppa, 1985). The collective learning process of finding a better mixture of rules and discretionary actions in Community policies has been long and painful.

In general, the European macroeconomist, unlike his microeconomist colleague, is neither much supported by a legal framework (such as rules on trade and competition) nor is he able to manage a large arsenal of instruments or huge financial funds (such as in agriculture policies). His main weapons are economic arguments and his persuasive power. His opposites are skeptical civil servants coming from well-established institutions of the member states with divergent traditions, priorities and prejudices. Unlike in the Secretariat of the OECD in the 1960s there was no mainstream (Keynesian) economic concept nor the prevalence of Anglo-Saxon pragmatism. German thinking in the framework of economic order (*Ordnungspolitik*) contrasted with the interventionist attitudes of French economists and the adaptability of Italian and Belgian policy traditions. The collective learning process of an independent European civil service had to evolve in the context of vague European loyalties and in an environment of profound structural transformations in the world economy, international disturbances and many political changes in the Community.

ECONOMIC POLICY COORDINATION: INSTRUMENTS AND LIMITS

Coordination of economic policies and convergence of economic performance are fundamental to the integration of national economics in the Community. It is here where the European economists have to execute most of their skills and efforts, but also where they have to accept the limits of their competence when divergent national interests prevail and (large) member states shrink back from surrendering any national sovereignity, be it real or apparent. Are there also lessons to be learned from the Community experience for international coordination? The issues dealt with here are limited to some macroeconomic examples; the manifold attempts at coordinating structural (agricultural, industrial, regional, energy and trade) policies are neglected.

There was little pressure at the beginning of the Community to coordinate the short-term policies of the member states. The member states enjoyed high and sustained growth and low and convergent inflation rates. The emergence of (important) balance-of-payments disequilibria could be avoided mainly due to the discipline of the Bretton Woods system but also because the United States tolerated large and protracted payments deficits. Although the intra-trade expanded very rapidly, the degree of interdependence remained low and the non-convertibility between the currencies of the Six allowed considerable freedom of national action. There were a few exchange-rate changes after 1958 (a revaluation of the Deutsche Mark and the Dutch guilder by 5 per cent in 1961, a delayed French devaluation by 11.1 per cent in 1969 and a German revaluation by 8.5 per cent in the same year) caused mainly by rising balance-of-payments imbalances and price differentials in the second half of the 1960s.

In the early years of the EEC, policy coordination activities were limited to procedural arrangements, the regular surveillance of short-term developments in the member countries and to some non-binding recommendations encouraging the fight against inflation. For example, proposals to create a short-term policy board and a stabilization fund were not taken up seriously.

First debate: planning vs. markets

Unfortunately but perhaps inevitably the Community started the policy coordination debate on the wrong foot. The Action Programme of the Commission in 1962 gave rise to a heated public argument between the French planners and the German neoliberals. Whereas in France, Belgium and Italy some soft form of indicative medium-term planning had been used in guiding public policymaking and private industry, no such concepts or sectoral planning instruments existed in West Germany. The proposals of the Commission to establish a Community program as 'a necessary guide for the plans or programmes being drawn up by a growing number of member countries' based on growth projections were vehemently opposed by Ludwig Erhard, who not only objected to industry-level targets but considered also medium-term forecasts to be useless or even harmful.

After a dramatic debate in the European Parliament between Erhard and Hallstein (1962) and an extensive discussion, the EEC Council adopted procedures for establishing a Community medium-term program related to overall quantitative projections covering five years. The draft programs, elaborated in the following years at regular intervals by the Medium-term Committee and adopted by the Council, were regarded as an outline for the coordination of national and Community policies laying 'the foundation for a better management of the member countries' economies and for a more realistic and more ambitious programming of structural change'. In looking back to this first fundamental policy controversy in the Community, the ensuing medium-term programming work and the voluminous literature on the subject at that time (Colloque de Rome, 1962; List-Gesellschaft, 1964; Denton, 1969; Balassa, 1975), it is surprising how rapidly the efforts have been forgotten which absorbed large intellectual and technical resources within the Commission and a large number of advisory bodies.

There are many reasons explaining the frustrations of these efforts. The four medium-term programs (the draft Fifth Programme has never been adopted as such) have rarely been taken seriously by the member states. Contrary to expectations, greater consistency in national targets and economic policies was not realized. The underlying quantitative macroeconomic projections often have proved to be wide from the mark of the actual development due to external shocks or radical policy changes. And, even more disappointing, the various EC programs did not prevent the disastrous development of the Common Agricultural Policy which led to huge surpluses, inefficient resource allocation, exploding budgetary expenditures and to a deterioration of external relations between the EEC and other industrial and developing countries alike. The EC medium-term programming was neither able to cope with the structural adjustment or declining sectors such as steel, shipbuilding and textiles, nor to stop the sectoral interventions of the member states running wild after 1973.

Yet, the medium-term debate has perhaps contributed to a greater consensus among the French and German policymakers on the economic order of the Community and improved the understanding of market forces and of the benefits of competition. More and more the French planners have abandoned the instruments of sectoral planning which became obsolete with the opening of French markets. The German policymakers have accepted more active macroeconomic and budgetary management, the medium-term programming of public expenditure and even the forecasting of important macroeconomic variables. The medium-term debate and programming exercise was probably a necessary and collective learning process with very long-term rewards. The Community had to go through the errors and misconceptions of medium-term target fixing and short-term fine-tuning, to come back, finally, to the desirability of more stable and long-term oriented policies.

1974 convergence decision

Pressure for more efficient policy coordination emerged with the acceleration of inflation rates in Europe and elsewhere in the late 1960s. After a series of international monetary crises, policymakers in the Community became aware again of the need to strengthen monetary integration and to establish an Economic and Monetary Union (EMU).

The philosophy on the 'coordination of economic policies and monetary cooperation within the Community' was first set forth by a Commission Memorandum in February 1969 recognizing the risks and ineffectiveness of isolated measures at the national level, and their spillover effects for the members of a highly integrated area. The memorandum urged for more realistic and compatible medium-term objectives and for more effective concertation of economic policies.

Following the EMU debate and the first steps towards monetary integration, the Council adopted in 1974 a wide array of procedural arrangements aimed at improving the network of prior information and consultation and strengthening the convergence of the economic policies in the Community, namely:

1. Three regular meetings yearly of the Council responsible for economic and financial affairs to examine the economic situation, to adopt and adjust the economic policy guidelines to be followed by each member state.
2. The transmission of quantitative budgetary guidelines limited to the growth rate of public expenditure and revenue, the size of the budget surplus or deficit and the way the latter are to be financed or used.
3. The establishment of periodic reports on the regional situation of the Community and a draft medium-term economic policy program (at least once every five years).

4. The presentation of an annual report on the economic situation which became the most substantial reference document for economic policy in the Community, containing not only consistent economic forecasts and an integrated view of economic policy at national and Community level but also a common strategy in relation to common policy.[7]

The '1974 convergence decision' can be seen as the most systematic attempt to coordinate budgetary policy, which again heavily involved the economists of the Commission in providing the technical support for the many meetings and reports. Already the Werner Report had argued that an effort to coordinate the budgets of member governments was one of the first steps to be taken on the way to monetary union, reflecting the then prevailing Keynesian thinking. The main argument for this budgetary dominance in the coordination efforts is the fact that public expenditure amounts today to 50 per cent of GDP (1960: 30 per cent) and that discretionary fiscal policies were seen as central instruments for demand management and stabilization policies in the 1960s and 1970s.

The experience with the extensive machinery of policy coordination has been unsatisfactory, especially in the second half of the 1970s. The efforts did not lead to cooperative solutions responding to the collapse of the international monetary system, the inflationary impacts and balance-of-payments imbalances unleashed by the first oil shock. The Commission complained that even the obligations to mutual information and prior consultations were met only in a formal way. The spirit of '*sauve qui peut*' among the member states eroded the solidarity of the Community members and the basic achievements of the Common Market.

It has been argued that the Community and its institutions were not prepared to face such drastic external disturbances which have changed the whole course of economic policy in the western industrial world. In a troubled world abounding with risks and conflicts, countries return to the well-established protective reflexes of the nation state. It may also be that the weak performance of policy coordination was due to the constitutional constraints of budgetary policies. Budget policy is an inherent part of internal national policy bargaining and is not easily changed even when there is the political will and mutual trust. Control of revenue and expenditure is the essence of parliamentary sovereignty. Examples of the inflexibility of budgetary policies can be found in the obstinacy of deficit problems in Italy and the more recent stalemate in reducing the budget deficit of the United States. Changing the course of public finance appears to take somewhere between five and ten years (Emerson, 1983).

Finally, the insufficiencies of policy coordination in the 1970s were due to fundamental differences in the priorities given to price stability, the diverging capacity of member states in keeping inflation under control and the different degree of exposure to balance-of-payments constraints (Wegner, 1985).

From the 'locomotive' approach to the cooperative growth strategy

The 'locomotive' or 'convoy' approach, developed originally by the OECD Secretariat (Llewellyn *et al.*, 1985) but vigorously supported by a mandate from the EC Council, presents a much debated example for the hardest and most difficult form of policy coordination: a concerted action as agreed at the Bonn Summit in 1978. With the benefit of hindsight this concerted budgetary action can be criticized as neglecting monetary constraints, the impact of expectations and the commitment to implement the original promises. The full story of this ambitious program has still to be written (Emerson 1983). The majority of German economists saw in this episode a grave policy error, a verdict which explains also why German policymakers today are vehemently opposed to a similar concerted effort, this time to ease the adjustment burden of the United States.

The Commission has recently stressed not only the arguments in favor of a new effort of policy concertation but also the fundamental differences in relation to the Bonn Summit experience: the serious risks of instability in the world economy, the slow growth performance of the EC and the unsolved unemployment problem[8], and, finally, the more stable exchange-rate environment of the EMS and the considerable convergence in economic priorities and policies (Wegner, 1987).

The highly expansionary fiscal stance of the 1970s was replaced by policies giving priority to the fight against inflation and the reduction of excessive public deficits. Even France returned – after an isolated attempt at demand expansion under Mitterand (1981) – to the '*politique de rigueur*'. The average inflation rate in the Community came down from 12 per cent in 1981 to almost 3 per cent in 1987. It is perhaps the first time since the early 1970s that there exists a basic consensus both on the priority of price stability and the instruments to reverse the structural problems and rigidities accumulated in the last twenty years. A joint and concerted policy effort by the Community is urgent and possible now, contributing also to the unwinding of large international imbalances. The framework for this European coordination effort is the current commitment to a 'cooperative growth strategy' which has found in principle the broad support of the social partners within the Community.

In line with the 'two-handed approach' of the Macroeconomic Policy Group of the Centre for European Policy Studies (Blanchard *et al*, 1985), the Commission presented in 1985 conditions for an employment-oriented growth strategy. The Commission proposed a sustained moderation of real wage incomes and supportive demand measures in form of tax cuts and higher public investments accompanied by supply-side reforms to improve further the adaptability of markets. According to model simulations an annual growth rate of 3 to 3.5 per cent over the next few years (instead of 2 to 2.5 per cent baseline growth) could bring down the unemployment rate to around 7 per cent by 1990 without a surge in inflation (EC Commission 1985 and 1986). The proposal – implying differentiated reflationary actions – still waits to be translated into practice in order to push the Community towards a path of sustained, employment-creating growth.

EUROPEAN MONETARY INTEGRATION: BLUEPRINTS AND REALITY

The framework of the EEC was based implicitly on a smoothly functioning monetary system as embodied in the Bretton Woods agreement. This assumption was taken for granted and explains the long years of complacency and indifference. At the end of the 1960s, stimulated by the failures in coordinating economic and monetary policies and the growing threat of exchange-rate crises, the first ideas and blueprints for European monetary integration were sketched out.

Economic and Monetary Union and the 'snake'

Endorsed by the Hague Summit in 1969 a committee[9] under Pierre Werner, the Prime Minister of Luxembourg, presented an ambitious plan to establish an Economic and Monetary Union (EMU) by stages. The Werner Report (1970), produced by high-level civil servants from the six member states and the Commission, was either praised as the most important document of the European integration since the Treaty of Rome or criticized as a technician's scheme without regard for the political environment. The report envisaged progress in parallel towards economic policy coordination and towards the reduction of the margins of exchange-rate fluctuations. Assuming the permanent political support of the member governments, the final goal of a unified currency was expected to be reached by 1980.

The first steps were taken in narrowing the exchange-rate margins (1972) although many professional economists remained doubtful about the feasibility of the EMU and the chosen approach. The next steps such as the progressive pooling of reserves and growing competence for an embryonic monetary fund were blocked by the upheavals of the international monetary system and the repercussions of the oil price shock. For a while the Community defended the 'snake in the tunnel' arrangement and a common float *vis-à-vis* the US dollar. Different policy reactions and the resulting balance-of-payments imbalances and price differentials forced the French franc and the Italian lira to opt out of the 'snake' and to float independently. The rump of a Deutsche Mark zone survived but was fragile and of little importance.

The failure of the first monetary endeavor can be explained by three main sources: the unfavorable and unpredictable events in the world economy, the lack of will to master the crisis jointly and finally the insufficient perception among the member countries of the preconditions for a viable economic and monetary union (Marjolin Report, 1975).

The widespread mood in 1976 was best described by a former chairman of the EC Monetary Committee and high Dutch Treasury official:

> We know now, wiser and sadder after many years of frustration about Economic and Monetary Union, that at any rate the timing of the Werner Report was not realistic. Personally, I have very little hope that we can achieve full monetary union even by 1990, for I believe that we shall need the escape hatch of exchange rate adjustment for a very long time to come. For all sorts of well-known political and economic reasons, our economies will not be locked on a parallel course until we are very much further advanced along the road of economic policy co-ordination, economic and social solidarity, and real interdependence in economic development and the growth of income. A premature locking of exchange rates, before our economies are definitely on a parallel course, would only end in disaster.
>
> (Oort, 1976)

The step-by-step approach via the 'snake' was not the only proposal available. The recommendations differed on how to tackle the most difficult problem, the transition to complete European monetary union. Several academic economists (Magnifico and Williamson, 1972, Giersch *et al.*, 1975) presented plans based on the issue of a parallel currency (the 'Europa') slowly to replace the national currencies. The most radical version suggested an 'inflation-proof' European currency with constant purchasing power, thus using the competitive market pressure to introduce the 'Europa'. Some praised this 'highly attractive monetary reform which should be implemented as early as possible' (Parkin, 1976); others qualified the idea as 'a brilliant non-starter' (Corden, 1977).

To sum up the royal battles fought in the 1970s, economists in and outside the Community had to learn the hard lesson that the EMU could not be introduced by the back door and implemented like the formation of the customs union. The process of monetary integration has to recognize the large differences which still exist between the Community members in preferences, wage behavior, adjustment capacities and the institutional setup of monetary management, and to come to terms with insufficient political commitment towards a unified Europe.

The disaster feared in the 1970s was avoided. But in the second half of the 1970s a split developed between 'snake' members and floaters which tended to increase the divergence between nationally oriented policies. The mechanism of policy coordination established in 1974 deteriorated rapidly as mentioned above. The process of economic integration became regressive.

European Monetary System

Dissatisfaction with the floating regime and the concern over the steep decline of the US dollar and the cohesion of the Community were the main reasons for the latest attempt to create 'a closer monetary cooperation leading to a zone of monetary stability' in Europe. Preceded by a forceful plea made by Roy Jenkins, the President of the EC Commission, in 1977 the initiative taken by President Valery Giscard d'Estaing and Chancellor Helmut Schmidt led to the establishment of the European Monetary System (EMS) in March 1979. Again, many economists remained skeptical, seeing the EMS as at best a superfluous and at worst a dangerous experiment.

The founding fathers of the EMS borrowed many features from the old 'snake' arrangement, expanded heavily the credit facilities to improve the credibility of the intervention commitments and added some new characteristics such as the official instrument of settlement and reserve asset, the ECU, a composite monetary unit, and the divergence indicator. The EMS is based on stable but adjustable exchange rates and has developed into a system *sui generis* functioning on a regional base (EC Commission, 1982; Van Ypersele and Koeune, 1984). The smooth functioning of the EMS has been secured by a pragmatic balance between the use of simple rules and flexible discretionary policy decisions (as described elsewhere – Wegner, 1989). Some of the institutional innovations have played a much smaller role than originally expected. The planned transition to a more definite institutional framework (European Monetary Fund) was set aside.

In the ten years of its existence the EMS has shown a surprising resilience notwithstanding the many unexpected external shocks and internal policy changes. The EMS has survived the period of dollar strength in the early years as well as the recent period of dollar decline. It has achieved its immediate objective, creating a zone of monetary stability, by reducing substantially the intra-EMS exchange-rate variability compared to the dollar, the yen, the pound sterling and to the pre-EMS period. The eleven currency realignments since 1979 have been in line with the direction of inflation differentials between EMS members. Parity changes have become more and more truly collective decisions within a multilateral framework with the Commission not merely providing technical services to these negotiations but also acting as honest broker.

Compared to earlier experiences, the quality and intensity of policy coordination has increased significantly since the inception of the EMS. The improved cooperation efforts are manifested in the efficient mixture of concerted interventions, exchange-rate changes and macroeconomic policy adjustments.

Competitive devaluations or overshooting of real exchange rates could be avoided. Yet there is less agreement on whether the EMS has contributed to a greater degree of economic policy convergence. Most observers would argue that the monetary discipline of the EMS has 'induced several countries to disinflate more than they otherwise would have done' (Melitz, 1987) and that the EMS 'provided a framework in which anti-inflationary policies could be pursued more efficiently' (Ungerer *et al.*, 1986). There is growing convergence of growth rates for monetary aggregates accompanied by a corresponding moderation of wage incomes and the abolishment of widespread wage indexation systems; only the fiscal policies are lagging behind the progress in the monetary field.

Often the EMS has been regarded as an extended Deutsche Mark zone in which the Bundesbank became the monetary center of gravity and the anchor for weaker currencies because of the superior stability of the West German economy. At the same time, the existence of the EMS has not undermined the Bundesbank's monetary control and strict anti-inflationary policy, thus contradicting the earlier fears of German policymakers.

The actual EMS is still a voluntary and fragile arrangement based on the mutual benefits recognized by its members. It suffers from many insufficiencies: the United Kingdom has not yet joined; capital controls have been used in the past in some countries to shield them against the need to raise their interest rates. The risks of a prolonged undershooting of the dollar and the planned full liberalization of capital markets in the EC will be a serious test for the system in the years ahead. The danger of destabilizing capital movements may lead to more frequent parity changes, or strengthen the disciplinary forces of the exchange-rate constraint and the degree of monetary coordination.

The EC Commission has always championed a European monetary system in order to provide a credible base for the trade and investment decisions within the Common Market. The economists of the Commission have generated a continuous stream of ideas and proposals for strengthening the EMS and the official and private use of the ECU (EC Commission, 1982, 1987; Padoa-Schioppa, 1984; Van den Bempt, 1987) supported by some academic economists (Triffin, 1983, 1985). But the move towards a more complete monetary union will be a slow one and probably interrupted by international disturbances. The member states are still reluctant to take decisive steps to transfer national monetary power to an independent European institution. There is still fear of premature locking of exchange rates and of inflationary risks. The call for more independent central banks in France and Great Britain, similar to the Bundesbank, is gaining only slow support. Notwithstanding the many unsolved issues and the painful experience in the past, the realization of a European monetary union remains a clear and long-term objective of the Community.

EURO-ECONOMISTS AND THE FUTURE: THE IMPOSSIBLE JOB

Although the thirty years of the Community are remembered as a history of crises, the EC has survived the many bitter disputes. The enlargement from six to twelve members since 1973 has shown its continuing appeal. The Community has become a major influential actor in the political landscape of Europe and the world and seems even to have entered a new stage in the process of a more profound economic integration.

It may be that 'in public discussion of European integration economists have played only a limited role' (Cairncross *et al.*, 1974). And even the question 'who runs the Commission?' could well be answered in favor of the Euro-lawyers as they have a comparative advantage over the economists. From the beginning the Community was seen as a 'creation of law, a source of law and legal order' (Hallstein, 1973). In general, lawyers in the Commission seem to be favored in mastering the intricate details of thousands of decisions and directives of Community law which now fill libraries and data banks. Euro-economists tend to shrink back from this legalistic and interventionist attitude and now prefer a more functional and market-oriented approach to advancing the cause of European integration. But the macroeconomist has learned from painful experience that forceful decision making requires powerful European institutions and that policy coordination is only feasible and efficient when based on institutionalized cooperation in contrast to *ad hoc* arrangements.

Unlike other international organizations the Community disposes of an extensive framework of institutions and advisory bodies. The member states are linked closely by trade and financial relations and share common economic and social values and basic political convictions. In spite of these advantages the results of the various coordination efforts have been limited, whereas the expected gains remain difficult to prove. The obstacles are, above all, of a political nature, for the member states are unwilling to renounce any domain of national sovereignty or to accept an enforcement rule. Further, the design and implementation of coordinated policies poses a host of economic and technical difficulties, for example, in understanding the economic feedback mechanisms and adjustment costs of demand- and supply-oriented policies, in evaluating the distribution of gains from coordination, or in controlling consistent national target variables in an environment of deregulated financial markets. The coordination problems inside the Community are as serious as in relation to the outside world.

After the golden years of the first decade (1958–68) the EC entered unchartered waters and failed to cope with both the adjustment shocks and the rigidities of the 1970s. The grand designs for Europe of the early 1970s dwindled away amidst the successions of external shocks and uncoordinated policy responses. But the main achievements of the Community survived.

The tide of pessimism started to reverse in the early 1980s. The extended Community moved slowly back towards its basic concepts and origins. The EMS arrangement, having outlived the gloomy forecast of many observers, achieved unexpected success in managing a quasi-fixed but adjustable exchange-rate system and contributed to an effective policy coordination and to converging economic performance of the member states. Inflation rates fell to a record low, although the unemployment problem remains unsolved and the growth rate was sluggish until 1988. In 1985–6 the Commission presented a medium-term strategy offering a cooperative attempt at an employment-oriented growth policy.

The final part of the emerging overall concept is based on the EC resolution to complete the internal market in 1992, creating a 'Community without frontiers'. The program of the White Paper (EC Commission, 1985a), described as 'a milestone in the development of the Community' and as 'a positive supply shock' (Giersch, 1987), could increase the rate of growth of potential outputs in the medium term by around 4¼ to 6½ percentage points of GDP by speeding up structural adjustments and ensuring higher efficiency in many areas (EC Commission, 1988).

The future of the Community may lie in this three-pronged approach generating synergies and forceful dynamics: a strengthened exchange-rate system including the United Kingdom, coordinated employment-growth efforts in the member states and a Community-wide liberalization program abolishing all barriers and internal borders for goods, services and capital markets.

Improving the effectiveness of large bureaucracies such as the EC Commission is an heroic task. A serious risk for the Commission and its staff lies in the tendency to defend sectional interests and to concentrate on 'single-handed' solutions to the immediate problems. There is a widespread bias built into specialized departments to focus on isolated issues and to neglect wider repercussions and longer-term spillover effects of sectoral policies. There should be a general economic department within the Commission structure which defends the overall economic approach, draws attention to medium- and long-term effects and to interlinkages, and warns against open and hidden inconsistencies of policy at the Community level. Such a powerful economic department should act – like the 'Legal Service' – as the economic conscience of the Commission. It has to be seen if the Commission is willing to reverse the tendencies of compartmentalization in order to improve economic efficiency and coherence of Community proposals.

The arguments of the economists inside the Community institutions and even more in the wider public may gain weight by establishing a European Council of Economic Advisers. The German Council of Economic Experts can serve as a model for a small independent body, whose members would be appointed by the Commission and serve for several years. The practice of using *ad hoc* committees does not allow a build-up of know-how, continuity and familiarity necessary for understanding the complex and interlinked issues, like trade and money, agriculture and finance, taxes and the liberalization of markets.

Torn between plan and reality, frustration and hope, the Euro-economist will, as in the past, have to shoulder a Herculean labor. More than anybody else he will suffer from the delays, deadlocks and failures and be blamed for the imperfections and policy errors. To do the job properly, the ideal Euro-economist must have many virtues and talents: an unrivalled knowledge in economic theory and policymaking, an unflagging optimism and patience, the stubbornness and courage to oppose national prejudices, the wiliness of a politician, flowing eloquence when proving the wisdom of his proposals, and a large part of humility.

NOTES

1. The original European Economic Community (EEC) (1958), consisting of France, Italy, the Federal Republic of Germany and the three Benelux countries, was enlarged by the United Kingdom, Ireland and Denmark in 1973. The accession of Greece followed in 1981 and of Spain and Portugal in 1986.
2. The author spent twenty years, from 1963 to 1983, in the Commission of the EC in Brussels, mainly in the General Directorate for Economic and Financial Affairs.
3. The European Free Trade Area (EFTA) was created in 1960 by seven countries (Austria, Denmark, Norway, Portugal, Sweden, Switzerland and the United Kingdom).
4. The basic units are (besides the Secretariat General, the Legal Service, Information, Budgets, the Interpreting and Conference Service and the Statistical Office) the following General Directorates: External Relations, Economic and Financial Affairs, Internal Market and Industrial Affairs, Competition, Employment and Social Affairs, Agriculture, Transport, Development, Personnel and Administration, Regional Policy, Energy, Science/R&D, Telecommunication and Information Industry.
5. The number of higher civil servants from the original six countries increased between 1973 and 1986 from almost 2,000 to 2,500. (*Source*: answers of the EC Commission to written questions of the European Parliament, August 1986.)
6. To name only a few of the *ad hoc* reports: Neumark Report (1963) on fiscal and financial questions, Werner Report (1970), Marjolin Report (1975) on the EMU, McDougall Report (1977) on the role of public finance in European integration, Padoa-Schioppa Report (1987) on the economic system of the EC.
7. *European Economy* regularly publishes the Commission's proposal for the annual report containing the economic policy guidelines to be followed by the member states in the year ahead, a detailed background analysis (the annual economic review) and reports and studies on the Community's financial instruments and activities, the EMS, employment, budgetary, investment and tax issues.
8. Since 1979 the unemployment rate of the EC has more than doubled to 12 per cent in 1987.
9. The Werner group was composed of the chairmen of the important EC advisory committees and the Commission.

BIBLIOGRAPHY

Balassa, Bela (ed.), *European Economic Integration* (Amsterdam: North-Holland Publishing Press, 1975).
Blanchard, Olivier *et al.* 'Employment and growth in Europe: a two-handed approach', *CEPS Papers*, no. 21 (Brussels, 1985).
Cairncross, Alec *et al.*, *Economic Policy for the European Community: The Way Forward* (London: Macmillan Press, 1974).
Colloque de Rome, *La Progammation Economique Européenne et la Programmation Economique Nationale dans le Pays de la CEE* (Florence, 1962).
Commission of the EC, Memorandum of the Commission on the action programme of the Community for the second stage (Brussels, October 1962).
Commission of the EC, Memorandum to the Council on the Coordination of Economic Policies and Monetary Cooperation within the Community (Brussels, February 1969).
Commission of the EC, Report of the Council and the Commission on the realization by stages of the economic and monetary union in the Community (The Werner Report) (Brussels, 1970).
Commission of the EC, GD II, Documents relating to the European Monetary System, *European Economy*, no. 12 (Brussels, July 1982).
Commission of the EC, *Completing the Internal Market*. White Paper from the Commission to the European Council, COM (85) 310 final (Brussels, 14 June 1985a).
Commission of the EC, GD II, Annual Report 1985/86, *European Economy*, no. 26 (Brussels, November 1985b).
Commission of the EC, GD II, Annual Report 1986/87, *European Economy*, no. 30 (Brussels, November 1986).
Commission of the EC, *Efficiency, Stability and Equity. A Strategy for the Evolution of the Economic System of the EC* (Report of a study group appointed by the EC Commission and presided by T. Padoa-Schioppa) (Brussels, April 1987).
Commission of the EC, The economics of 1992, an assessment of the potential economic effects of completing the internal market of the EC, *European Economy*, no. 35 (Brussels, March 1988).
Corden, Max M., *Inflation, Exchange Rates and the World Economy* (Chicago: The University of Chicago Press, 1977).
Denton, Geoffrey R., 'Planning and integration: medium-term policy as an instrument of integration, in G. R. Denton (ed.), *Economic Integration in Europe* (London: Weidenfeld and Nicolson, 1969).
Emerson, Michael, 'Western Europe's capacity for sustained growth', *CEPS Papers*, no. 2 (Brussels, 1983).
Giersch, Herbert, 'Internal and external liberalisation for faster growth', Commission of the EC, *Economic Papers*, no. 54 (Brussels, February 1987).
Giersch, Herbert *et al.*, 'A currency for Europe', *The Economist* (1 November 1975).
Hallstein, Walter, *Europe in the Making* (London: Allen and Unwin, 1973).
List-Gesellschaft, Plitzko, A. (ed.;, *Planung ohne Planwirtschaft, Frankfurter Gespräch* (Tübingen: J. C. B. Mohr, 1964).
Llewellyn, John *et al.*, *Economic Forecasting and Policy: The International Dimension* (London: Routledge and Kegan Paul, 1985).
Machlup, Fritz, *A History of Thought on Economic Integration* (London: Macmillan Press, 1977).
Magnifico, Giovanni, and Williamson, John, *European Monetary Integration* (London: Federal Trust, 1972).

Marjolin, Robert *et al.*, Report of the Study Group 'Economic and Monetary Union 1980' (EC Commission, Brussels, March 1975).
Marris, Stephen, 'Managing the world economy: will we ever learn?', *Essays in International Finance*, no. 155 (Princeton, 1984).
McDougall, Donald *et al.*, *Report of the Study Group on the Role of Public Finance in European Integration* (vols 1 and 2) (EC Commission, Brussels, April 1977).
Meade, James E., *Problems of Economic Union* (London: Allen and Unwin, 1953).
Meade, James E., *The Theory of Customs Union* (Amsterdam: North-Holland, 1955).
Melitz, Jacques, 'Monetary discipline, Germany, and the European monetary system', *CEPR Discussion Paper*, no. 178 (April 1987).
Neumark, Fritz, *Report of the Fiscal and Financial Committee on Tax Harmonization in the Common Market* (European Economic Community, 1963).
Olson, Mancur, *The Rise and Decline of Nations* (New Haven and London: Yale University Press, 1982).
Oort, Conrad J., Lecture delivered at the Royal Institute of International Affairs, London, 18 June 1976.
Padoa-Schioppa, Tommaso, *Money, Economic Policy and Europe*, Commission of the EC, European Perspectives Series (Brussels, 1984).
Padoa-Schioppa, Tommaso, 'Rules and institutions in the management of multi-country economies', in L. Tsoukalis (ed.), *The Political Economy of International Money* (London: Sage Publications, 1985).
Parkin, Michael, 'Monetary union and stabilization policy in the European Community', *Banca Nazionale del Lavoro Review* (September 1976).
Scitovsky, Tibor, *Economic Theory and Western European Integration* (London: Allen and Unwin, 1958).
Triffin, Robert, 'The future of the European monetary system and the ECU', *CEPS Papers*, no. 3 (Brussels, 1983).
Triffin, Robert, 'Proposals for the strengthening of the European monetary system', *IfO-Digest*, vol. 8 (Munich, September 1985).
Ungerer, Horst *et al.*, 'The European monetary system: recent developments', *IMF Occasional Paper*, no. 48 (Washington DC, December 1986).
Van den Bempt, Paul (ed.), *The European Monetary System: Towards More Convergence and Closer Integration* (Acco/Leuven: European Policy Study-Group, 1987).
Van Ypersele, Jacques, and Koeunen, Jean-Claude, *The European Monetary System*, Commission of the EC, European Perspectives Series (Brussels, 1984).
Wegner, Manfred, 'External adjustment in a world of floating: different national experiences in Europe', in L. Tsoukalis (ed.), *The Political Economy of International Money* (London: Sage Publications, 1985).
Wegner, Manfred, 'Scope and limits of international economic policy coordination', in *The World Economy*, vol. 10, no. 3 (London, 1987).
Wegner, Manfred, 'The European monetary system', in H.-J. Vosgerau (ed.), *New Institutional Arrangements for the World Economy* (Berlin: Springer-Verlag, 1989).

15 · THE GENERAL AGREEMENT ON TARIFFS AND TRADE

William B. Kelly

What is the role that economists have had and are having in the General Agreement on Tariffs and Trade (GATT), its operation, and its influence on governments' policies and actions? Keynes might have replied, 'a large role', as he believed that 'the ideas of economists and political philosophers . . . are more powerful than is commonly understood' and that, 'indeed the world is ruled by little else' (Keynes, 1949, p. 383). Conventional wisdom, however, regards economists as having a minimal effect on international trade issues. Cited in this connection, for instance, is the failure of the petition of 1,000 economists (actually 1,028) urging President Hoover to veto the exceedingly protectionist US Hawley–Smoot tariff legislation after its passage by Congress in 1930. But the subsequent persistent and successful efforts of economists in the following decades to reverse the protectionist trade policies of the 1930s, which culminated in the establishment of GATT, often go unsung. Thus, George Stigler's view that 'the influence of an economist's work and the popular (non-professional) esteem in which he is held are most likely to be *negatively* correlated' (Stigler, 1976, p. 354) could be said to apply to economists and their role in the GATT.

In examining the question of what role have economists had in the GATT, it is necessary first to define who is an 'economist'. There appears to be no widely shared agreement on the required credentials. An academic background? Yes, but what kind of background? Kenneth Boulding received BA and MA degrees from Oxford but never received a PhD degree in any subject, much less economics. Yet, he has been a distinguished professor of economics at several US universities and is a former President of the American Economic Association. There are many more examples of 'economists' in governments and international institutions who do not have advanced degrees in economics. Consequently, an 'economist' in the context of this paper is someone who approaches problems with an analytical framework that is concerned with such concepts as comparative advantage; optimum allocation of resources; opportunity costs; supply, demand, and prices; costs versus benefits of particular economic measures; and similar questions. In other words, economists have a special 'way of thinking' and those who think this way are 'economists'.[1] Many involved in the creation of GATT and subsequently in its working were and are such individuals, whether representing a particular country or serving GATT directly as members of its Secretariat.

Although the GATT is primarily concerned with economic issues, it is the result of an essentially political process – when it was negotiated in 1947, in its day-to-day implementation, and in the subsequent six rounds of multilateral trade negotiations, culminating in the Tokyo Round of 1974–9 and the Uruguay Round initiated in 1986. Domestic and foreign political considerations have always been a significant factor. Therefore, it is not surprising that from both an economic and even a legal point of view, GATT is an imperfect document, and its operation and the negotiations that it has sponsored are marred by various political compromises. Consequently, there is a widely shared view that the economist's influence on the GATT is nil or almost nil. Some of GATT's most extreme critics are 'purist' economists and lawyers.

GATT is not an academically pure 'free-trade' agreement. In fact, it was never intended to be such nor is this its objective today. But, despite its imperfections, GATT is *the* international contract and organization of trading countries that has maintained reasonable order in the world trading system. This relative stability has been an essential condition for the investment and other decisions that have stimulated overall growth and prosperity since World War II.

The GATT has sponsored the program of trade liberalization that has been under way for the past forty years and that has made possible the remarkable expansion of world trade. US tariffs, for example, have been reduced from the Hawley–Smoot average of around 50 per cent to less than 5 per cent. Since 1950 the volume of world trade has increased more than sixfold (more than twenty-five times in value). If the beggar-thy-neighbor policies of the 1930s were to have continued after World War II, what would world trade, growth, income and resource allocation be like today?

The GATT is the product of much economic thought, planning and action. The influence of economists has been substantial. They have provided the economic parameters within which domestic political decisions were made and international trade negotiations took place. Also, they have made decisions themselves or prodded others to do so on questions of trade policy. This chapter will examine the role of economists in the origins of the GATT, in the provisions of the General Agreement itself, and in its administration by the GATT Secretariat.

ORIGINS OF THE GATT

The GATT did not emerge willy-nilly at the end of World War II. The formation of an international trade organization, along with the International Monetary Fund and the International Bank for Reconstruction and Development, was part of the wartime planning for the postwar world economy. In fact, the origins of the GATT are deeply embedded in US commercial policy that was formulated in the interwar period. Since 1934, this policy has been based on three economic principles: nondiscriminatory or unconditional most-favored-nation (MFN) treatment; opposition to quantitative restrictions or quotas as protective measures against imported products; and negotiated reductions of tariffs. All of these principles are reflected in the provisions of the GATT.

The United States formally adopted a policy of unconditional MFN treatment in 1923. In large part, this policy adoption was based on a report and recommendation of the US Tariff Commission (1919) which at that time was chaired by Frank W. Taussig, a Harvard Professor of Economics who later served as President of the American Economic Association. US policy opposing the use of quantitative restrictions was crystallized in 1927 with signature and ratification of a League of Nations sponsored International Convention on the Abolition of Import and Export Prohibitions and Restrictions. Although from time to time the United States has deviated from this policy, particularly in connection with domestic agricultural programs, textiles and clothing, and the more recent negotiation of so-called voluntary-restraint arrangements, this policy has nevertheless remained a guiding principle. The Trade Agreements Act of 1934 reversed the previous high, untouchable tariff policy and granted the president authority for the negotiated reduction of tariffs. This legislation also required that reduced duties be extended to all foreign countries, thereby making unconditional MFN treatment a statutory provision.[2]

The Trade Agreements Act of 1934 launched the United States and much of the trading world on a program of negotiated bilateral agreements in which US tariffs were reduced in exchange for reductions of foreign tariffs on US exports. Although the stated objective of the trade-agreements program, the promotion of US exports, was mercantilistic in nature, the agreements lowered trade barriers on a reciprocal basis and moved the world toward an economy based on comparative advantage. There was (and still is) a very long way to go, but at least a start was made in this direction. Under successive renewals of the trade-agreements legislation, twenty-eight agreements were negotiated during the 1930s and early 1940s. The negotiation of the GATT in 1947 was a multilateral extension of these bilateral agreements, and many of GATT's provisions were based on provisions contained in these agreements. For example, a reading of the US–Mexican Agreement of 1942 is in some respects almost indistinguishable from sections of the GATT. The subsequent series of major multilateral trade negotiations, including the present Uruguay Round, are a continuation of the US trade-agreements program.

Cordell Hull, Secretary of State under Franklin Roosevelt, is regarded as the father of the US trade-agreements program. Even though he was not an academic economist, he took a disproportionate interest in economic matters, particularly trade policy, which he believed had critical importance for harmonious relations among nations. A relatively small number of dedicated government officials did most of the planning for and execution of the trade-agreements program. The focal point for this activity was the interagency Trade Agreements Committee, which was chaired by the State Department. Its membership of economists and neo-economists varied over the years, but the Departments of Agriculture, Commerce, and Treasury, as well as the Tariff Commission (now the International Trade Commission), were always represented.

In 1943, when the White and Keynes plans for postwar financial collaboration were published, trade officials in both the United States and the United Kingdom were discussing and drafting plans for a postwar trade organization. In fact, in informal 'seminars', officials exchanged ideas and discussed the proposed UK Commercial Union, which was drafted primarily by James Meade, and the proposed multilateral convention on commercial policy that emerged from the US interagency trade structure. These and other wartime developments leading up to the Havana Charter for an International Trade Organization (ITO) have been well documented (see e.g. Brown, 1950). It need only be noted here that economists played an important role in these developments, *inter alia*, the Atlantic Charter, Article VII of the Lend-Lease Agreements, the Preparatory Committee meetings for the Havana Conference in London and Geneva, and the concurrent tariff negotiations in Geneva that resulted in the GATT. This role continued when many of the officials who had participated in the GATT and ITO negotiations went on to represent their governments in GATT affairs or to join its secretariat.

THE GENERAL AGREEMENT ON TARIFFS AND TRADE

When the GATT was originally negotiated, it was essentially an agreement on tariffs and other trade barriers, pending the coming into effect of the ITO. The GATT incorporated the results of the multilateral tariff negotiation conducted in Geneva in 1947, and it contained provisions that were designed to safeguard the benefits of negotiated tariff concessions. When the ITO failed to be ratified, the GATT, in effect, became the postwar international trade organization, and it has been functioning as such for forty years.

As indicated above, the GATT is based upon three economic principles of US commercial policy: unconditional MFN treatment, opposition to quantitative restrictions for protective purposes, and the negotiated reduction of tariffs.

Most-favored-nation treatment

Nondiscrimination or MFN treatment has long been favored by economists. In the same way that tariffs or other import restrictions displace low-cost imports with higher-cost domestic products, discriminatory restrictions cause imports to be diverted from low-cost to higher-cost sources. Conditional MFN treatment requires third countries to pay for the benefits of negotiated trade concessions and, therefore, does not ensure nondiscriminatory treatment. Unconditional MFN treatment automatically extends negotiated trade concessions freely to third countries. The unconditional form of the MFN clause is the first article and one of the key provisions of the GATT.

As a practical matter, the GATT negotiators of 1947 excepted a number of existing tariff preferences from the unconditional MFN clause. However, no new preferences were permitted, and existing preferences were to be reduced or eliminated in subsequent negotiations. But customs unions and free-trade areas were excepted, provided that they eliminated duties and other trade barriers on substantially all trade among the member countries and, on the whole, imposed no higher or more restrictive trade barriers than those previously in force *vis-à-vis* third countries. Despite the 100 per cent discrimination against the trade of third countries inherent in such customs unions, they can be of net benefit to world trade and to the better economic use of resources if the trade created between the members outweighs the trade diversion from non-members. As James Meade and other economists have pointed out, customs unions are more likely to have such a positive result if, *inter alia*, the economies of the partner countries are very competitive or similar but potentially very complementary or dissimilar. Furthermore, a partial reduction may be preferable to a complete elimination of duties (Meade, 1955).

The GATT, however, has no reference to trade creation versus trade diversion, competitive versus complementary economies, or partial versus complete customs unions. But it is difficult to fault the economic planners and negotiators, who may have assumed that if the criteria in the GATT customs union exception were met, net trade creation would likely result. The writings of Meade and the pioneering work of Jacob Viner were not published until several years later (Meade, 1955; Viner, 1950). Furthermore, there was no reason for particular concern about such preferential arrangements, as they were virtually nonexistent. The formation of the European Economic Community was a decade or so in the future.

In any event, the economic founders of the GATT cannot be held responsible for the gross violations of the MFN principle that have followed. The European Economic Community, as originally conceived, may have resulted in net trade creation. It is much more problematical whether the free-trade-area agreements negotiated between the European Community and the member countries of the European Free Trade Association (EFTA), or the EFTA agreement itself, have had such a positive result. Furthermore, the so-called free-trade-area agreements that the European Community has negotiated with African countries in the Lomé Convention and with the Magreb and other Mediterranean countries are nothing more than discriminatory arrangements against the trade of other countries, both developed and developing. Other developments, particularly the Common Agricultural Policy (CAP), have resulted in diversion of third-country trade on a massive scale. The CAP, coupled, *inter alia*, with huge export and domestic subsidies, has transformed the European Community from a net importer to a net exporter of grains, sugar, beef and butter.

The Generalized System of Preferences (GSP), under which developed countries unilaterally grant varying degrees of preferential tariff treatment to developing countries, necessitated a formal waiver from the GATT MFN clause. Many developing countries regard GSP as fostering their economic development. They appear to have closed their eyes to the weakened negotiating position that beneficiary status has bestowed on them in dealing with various protectionist measures of developed countries, which may far outweigh the presumed benefits of GSP.

As a result of these and other aberrations from unconditional MFN treatment, it is estimated that only about half of the trade conducted by GATT member countries is on an MFN basis.

The principle of nondiscrimination is also reflected in the GATT provision for national treatment of internal taxes and regulations, i.e. imported products, once they have entered the country, are to be treated the same as domestic products. From an economist's viewpoint, this is a very important provision. However, it is flawed by two economically indefensible exceptions. Government procurement laws and regulations, such as the many 'buy-national' policies of countries, are specifically exempted from the national-treatment requirement. Also, governments may grant domestic subsidies exclusively to national production.

Opposition to quantitative restrictions

In instances where domestic industries are to be protected from the competition of imported products, economists have long favored the use of tariffs rather than of quantitative restrictions or quotas. Tariffs interfere with but do not eliminate competition between domestic and foreign producers. Quotas, on the other hand, eliminate all competition; once the permitted amount is imported, neither price nor other forms of competition can increase the quantity of imports. Furthermore, under a tariff system, MFN treatment can be ensured, but a quota system is inherently discriminatory. The GATT reflects this economic preference – it permits tariffs but subjects them to negotiated reductions, and it outlaws quotas.

Although a fundamental principle of the GATT prohibits quantitative restrictions as a form of import protection, an important exception to this prohibition permits the imposition of import restrictions on agricultural products *if* the like domestic product is equally subject to restrictive production limitations. In order for a country to implement an agricultural program that maintains domestic prices at a level higher than world prices, import restrictions become necessary. The GATT exception is an attempt to ensure that these restrictions do not alter the relationship between imports and domestic production that might be expected to exist in the absence of restrictions. If imports are cut back by 10 per cent, domestic production must also be cut back by 10 per cent. From an economist's viewpoint, such domestic agricultural programs may not themselves be economically defensible, but the conditions for imposing the import restrictions to implement them are. Because import restrictions imposed by the United States under Section 22 of its Agricultural Adjustment Act could not meet these conditions, the United States had to obtain a GATT waiver from this obligation.

A second exception to the prohibition of quotas permits quantitative restrictions for balance-of-payments reasons. Under the fixed exchange-rate system emanating from Bretton Woods, such restrictions were necessary for many countries in the immediate postwar period, so as to allocate the use of scarce foreign exchange to essential food, raw materials and industrial equipment. However, the MFN principle is to be applied to their administration, i.e. restrictions are to be administered in a nondiscriminatory manner with the objective of a distribution of trade approximating the share of imports that exporting countries might have obtained in the absence of restrictions.

Negotiated reduction of tariffs

Theoretically, global free trade is the optimum condition for capitalizing on countries' comparative advantages and for maximizing the utilization of the world's resources. Domestic political considerations effectively rule out such an ideal world. In the absence of global free trade, unilateral elimination of a country's trade barriers would eliminate the domestic economic distortions inherent in protection against the competition of imported products. Again, for political reasons, a unilateral policy of free trade is practiced in only a few entrepôt centers like Hong Kong and Singapore. A negotiated reduction of a country's trade barriers in exchange for a reduction of foreign barriers on a country's exports has had greater political acceptability. This is the GATT concept of reciprocity, which has been criticized by economic purists.[3]

Apart from political acceptability, the negotiated reduction of trade barriers under the principle of reciprocity, if carried to its logical conclusion, should lead in time to the optimum world of free trade. Unilateral reduction is much less likely to do so, because some countries would not lower their trade barriers in response to the reductions of others. Practical economists and the GATT have recognized this distinction. But these economists would also agree with Harry Johnson's mercantilistic characterization of tariff negotiations in which:

> . . . the reduction of one's own tariffs is regarded as a loss, to be carefully weighed against the gain obtained from reduction of the other fellow's tariffs; in fact, the primary national gain from tariff reductions is the increased efficiency that results from being able to use low-cost foreign products instead of high-cost domestic products. In this respect, the mythology of tariff negotiation is very similar to that of seduction: in each case the benefit to be received is treated as a loss for purposes of negotiation; and in each case the consequence of this fiction is continual frustration and frequent non-consummation.
>
> (Johnson, 1962, p. 25)

Like skinning a cat, there are many ways to negotiate on tariffs. In the 1930s, a horizontal or linear approach to tariff negotiations was considered within the US government in connection with the Trade Agreements Act of 1934. This approach would reduce all duties by some uniform percentage or formula or down to some uniform *ad valorem* equivalent. Also considered was a selective or item-by-item approach that would require separate consideration of each and every tariff rate with varying or no reductions, depending on the competitive strength of the domestic producers and the probable effect on them of a duty reduction. The merit of the horizontal approach is that it is more likely to result in deeper tariff cuts and thereby lead to a greater expansion of trade, because it gives less attention to domestic protected interests. For political reasons, the United States opted for the selective approach in the bilateral negotiations under the trade-agreements program.

Prior to the GATT negotiations of 1947, consideration was again given to the horizontal reduction of tariffs, but again for political reasons, these negotiations were based on the selective approach. Some 123 bilateral negotiations involving some 50,000 items were concluded among the twenty-three participating countries. The final results of these negotiations were incorporated in a single document, the General Agreement on Tariffs and Trade, and they were extended to all signatories. The simultaneous negotiation of these bilateral tariff agreements and the generalization of their results overcame some of the disadvantages of the selective approach. The more ambitious horizontal approach had to wait until the Kennedy and Tokyo Round negotiations of the late 1960s and 1970s.

Negotiated tariff reductions that are extended freely to other countries under unconditional MFN obligations undermine a country's negotiating leverage *vis-à-vis* the MFN beneficiaries. If third countries obtain the benefits of others' tariff reductions without paying for them, what inducement is there for them to participate in such negotiations? The answer, devised by ingenious US economic officials in the 1930s, is found in the chief-source rule under which concessions are negotiated only on products of which a country is the chief or an important source of imports. This principal-supplier rule, as it is now known, has been the basis of the original and subsequent bilateral GATT negotiations. It has enabled the MFN principle to apply to them.

In addition to the fundamental provisions of the GATT discussed above, there are other substantive issues of interest to economists. These include the application of antidumping and countervailing duties and the protection of 'infant' industries.

Antidumping and countervailing duties

The GATT does not outlaw the practice of dumping or differential pricing in international trade. Dumping, like fire sales and some forms of discount pricing, can be a useful marketing device. (Good examples are the bargains that can be purchased in Filene's basement in Boston.) However, the GATT permits the imposition of antidumping duties if the dumped imports cause material injury to domestic producers. Viner and other economists have considered predatory dumping, whereby the purpose is to eliminate competitors, as the most objectionable form of dumping (Viner, 1923). In principle, at least, the GATT standard of 'material injury' is closely related to Viner's standard of 'predatory dumping'.

The GATT treatment of countervailing duties parallels that of antidumping duties, i.e. export subsidization is not subject to offsetting measures unless it causes material injury to domestic producers. Consequently, the GATT makes no distinction between the ability of private entrepreneurs to resort to dumping and the ability of governments to subsidize exports. But there are financial limits to an entrepreneur's ability to dump; a government's ability, on the other hand, is limited only by its taxing powers. It has always been an anomaly to this writer why the GATT prohibits the government of an importing country from exercising the option of taking countermeasures against the export subsidies of another government, whether or not injury to domestic producers is involved. In purely economic terms, what is the difference between a government-imposed tariff that replaces lower-cost imports with higher-cost domestic products and a government export subsidy that replaces lower-cost foreign production with higher-cost domestic products? Both distort resource allocation. From a purely national point of view, non-injurious subsidized imports have an economic benefit for the importing country. Nevertheless, the principle of reciprocity should permit the imposition of countervailing duties, particularly since the concept of material injury is somewhat nebulous and in some instances very difficult to determine.

For many years, US legislation differentiated between the treatment of antidumping and countervailing duties, requiring injury determinations in dumping cases but not in cases of export subsidization. Under pressure from its trading partners, the United States agreed to include an injury requirement in its countervailing-duty legislation as part of the Tokyo Round negotiating package.

Infant industries

The GATT recognizes the importance of economic development, particularly for developing countries. Consequently, it reflects the infant-industry argument of economists by permitting the imposition of import restrictions in developing countries for purposes of their economic development. Unfortunately, as in the argument itself, the protected industries seldom grow up and shed their protection, and there has been no vigorous review to encourage the diminution or elimination of import restrictions.

As indicated above, the principal substantive provisions of the GATT reflect for the most part economic principles that most economists support. This is a tribute to the considerable influence of economists in the planning and negotiation of the GATT and to their role in the formulation of US commercial policy during the interwar period upon which many of GATT's trade rules are based. Criticism of GATT is better directed at its implementation by government officials subject to national and international political pressures than at its provisions worked out by the economic thinkers and practitioners who gave it birth and who continue to work for its growth.

THE GATT SECRETARIAT

The GATT Secretariat is unique among the other organizations in the United Nations System. When the GATT came into force at the beginning of 1948, it was essentially a tariff agreement, and for this reason it did not contain and still does not contain provisions for an organization, much less a secretariat. However, the Havana Conference of 1948, when agreeing on the text of the ITO Charter, established an Interim Commission for the International Trade Organization (ICITO). ICITO, which was given a staff headed by an Executive Secretary, had responsibilities relating to the coming into force of the ITO; it also provided secretariat functions for the GATT. When the ITO failed to come into force, the GATT and its secretariat remained the only function of ICITO. As its name implies, ICITO was to be temporary, but it remains the legal status of the GATT Secretariat today. Few know it and fewer understand it, but the ICITO Executive Committee, which includes China (a non-GATT country) in its membership, still meets to approve formally the appointment of its Executive Secretary, who since 1965 also wears the hat of GATT Director-General.

Given the key role of the GATT in the world economy, its secretariat is very small. In round numbers, the GATT Secretariat has 300 permanent and 50 temporary employees as compared with that of the International Monetary Fund's 1,700 and more than 5,000 at the World Bank. This GATT figure of 350 includes all personnel – professional, support staff and maintenance. Professionals constitute about 40 per cent of this total, of which around 70 work on substantive trade issues that require at least some advanced training in economics.

As a general rule, only the personnel of GATT member countries are employed in the Secretariat, but there are no national quotas. Furthermore, there are no secondments where government officials are deputed to the GATT for a few years before returning to government service. This does not mean that some government officials do not spend a part of their careers in the GATT Secretariat, but there are no formal arrangements. Consequently, hiring is based upon professional qualifications and at least a general understanding and appreciation of the basic principles of GATT.[4] Only three officials, the Director-General and his two Deputies, can be regarded as having political appointments, but they must have the approval of the contracting parties.

The economists of the GATT Secretariat work in essentially two areas, the Operating Divisions and the Economic Research and Analysis Unit (Research Unit). The Operating Divisions deal, *inter alia*, with tariffs, non-tariff measures, agriculture, safeguards, balance-of-payments restrictions, antidumping and countervailing duties, government procurement practices, product standards, import licensing, customs valuation, civil aircraft, services, intellectual property, investment, developing countries and textiles. The economists in the Operating Divisions have diverse backgrounds, some of which have not focused primarily on economic matters in the usual professional sense.

The Operating Divisions service the various GATT bodies and negotiating groups. They prepare papers in advance of meetings and report on the results. Although their work is subject to the pressures of national delegations, the Secretariat has a well-deserved reputation for producing even-handed papers and reports. This does not mean that the Operating Divisions assume the role of a football kicked back and forth by aggressive delegations. On the contrary, they have a nuanced but direct influence on the course and outcome of GATT operations and negotiations by pushing liberal economic principles to the maximum possible within the parameters of very real political constraints. The successful conclusion of seven major multilateral trade negotiations and of dozens of bilateral negotiations bear witness to the Secretariat's influence.

The Operating Divisions also service the panels established to settle disputes among the contracting parties. They sit in on panel procedures, give oral and written advice and opinions when requested to do so, and draft the reports of panels that are transmitted to the GATT Council. In these and other subtle, and not always so subtle ways, they 'keep the faith' by explaining and standing up for GATT's trade rules.

The Research Unit deals with all economic aspects of the GATT. It is staffed with around ten economists, primarily of an academic bent. Jan Tumlir was the Director for many years and Richard Blackhurst has now succeeded him. Blackhurst also teaches at the University of Geneva's Graduate Institute of International Studies, as did Tumlir. The Research Unit prepares *International Trade*, GATT's annual report, and periodically it prepares papers for publication in *Studies in International Trade*. It also produces economic analyses and statistics for use by the Secretariat, for various meetings of the contracting parties, and for delegations. To a considerable extent, the Research Unit operates on its own, independently of the Operating Divisions. In this role, it serves as an economic conscience, not only for the Secretariat and for the contracting parties, but also for resident national delegations, who often consult with its members.

The influence of the Research Unit is less direct and less nuanced than that of the Operating Divisions. The annual reports of the GATT contain much statistical and analytical material on world trade, but they also contain policy chapters that are written from an economist's point of view. Unlike publications of many other organizations, these policy chapters, as well as all other GATT publications, are not subject to prior review or approval by the contracting parties. The annual report and other publications are subject to review by the Director-General and his Deputies, but there are no fundamental economic policy differences within the Secretariat. The old saw that 'if all the economists were laid end to end, they would not reach a conclusion' does not apply to the GATT Secretariat. Even a cursory reading of GATT reports clearly indicates that they reflect the economists' free-trade philosophy and often even its verbiage. These reports receive considerable press attention and quotation.

Since 1971, usually on its own initiative, the Research Unit has drafted and published several economic studies (GATT, *Studies in International Trade*, 1971–80). The most recent dealt with trade relations under flexible exchange rates. This publication preceded a similar IMF study (IMF, 1984) that was mandated by the 1982 GATT Ministerial Meeting and prepared in consultation with the GATT Secretariat. Not surprisingly, neither the GATT nor the IMF studies found any statistically significant link between exchange-rate mariability and trade or that the economic value of trade liberalization is negated by fluctuations of exchange rates.

At the request of the GATT contracting parties, the Research Unit prepared in 1984 an extensive report on textiles and clothing prior to consideration of renewal of the trade-restrictive Multifiber Arrangement (MFA). This report, which was highly regarded, particularly by developing countries, analyzed trends in production and trade in these industries and the possible effects on importing and exporting countries of renewal or non-renewal of the MFA. Although recommendations were not requested by the contracting parties on this politically sensitive issue, the report concluded that there is no economic justification for treating the trade-related problems of the textile and clothing industries differently from those of other tradeable-goods industries and that the fundamental issue is structural adjustment (GATT, 1984). Although the MFA was renewed in July 1986, the Ministerial Declaration on the Uruguay Round prescribed that 'negotiations in the area of textiles and clothing shall aim to formulate modalities that would permit the eventual integration of this sector into GATT on the basis of strengthened GATT rules and disciplines, thereby also contributing to the objective of further liberalization of trade' (GATT, 1986, p. 5).

It is difficult to evaluate the extent to which GATT economic publications have influenced the trade policies of national governments. How many higher-level policy officials have time to read, much less evaluate and apply, the increasing flow of ideas, analyses and recommendations in printed form? But GATT publications are read and respected, and in some cases they have provoked debate on important economic issues. A good example is the international controversy on the cause of inflation in industrial countries during the 1970s. As economists in international institutions meet regularly and exchange thoughts on current problems, there is often a consensus of views among them. However, the OECD and the GATT had very different explanations for the inflationary surges of 1973–4 and 1978–80. The OECD opted for the oil-push hypothesis; the GATT, for the monetary hypothesis. It appears that the GATT was on target. As one commentator observed, 'the empirical evidence allows one to dismiss this hypothesis [oil-push] as a serious explanation of the acceleration of inflation' and 'inflation rates are, more than in the past, nationally determined and must be explained by national monetary policies' (de Grauwe, 1981, pp. 178, 185). Another interesting contrast of views involved the GATT, the OECD and the UNCTAD on the problem of adjustment to economic change, particularly trade-induced change (Wolf, 1980). Also, the GATT was one of the first to put forward the 'structural-rigidity' or 'reluctance-to-adjust' explanation for the slower growth and rising unemployment in industrial countries that began to appear in the late 1960s and early 1970s (GATT, 1977, pp. 18–24).

The influence of the Director-General and his deputies both on Secretariat policy and on GATT operations and negotiations is considerable. Internally, review of policy-oriented publications has been mentioned. Articles and other manuscripts by Secretariat personnel for non-GATT publication are encouraged but are also subject to review, which is usually of a pro-forma nature, particularly because the views contained in them are attributed to the authors. Externally, influence is exercised in public speeches and public and private meetings with government and nongovernment officials. Many of the agreements reached among the contracting parties are first worked out on an informal basis in the offices of and at the initiatives of the Deputy Directors-General or of the Director-General himself. This was especially true in the early days of the GATT during the tenure of Eric Wyndham-White, the first Director-General. He was not a professional economist but was extraordinarily creative and effective in negotiating agreements on contentious issues. Office deals are more difficult to negotiate today with more than ninety contracting parties, many of whom want to be in the room at the same time as all the others. Nevertheless, these frequent occasions present additional opportunities for Secretariat influence on economic issues.

It has not been the practice of the GATT to employ outside economic consultants. Mention must be made, however, of two reports prepared by prominent economists with the drafting and other assistance of the Secretariat. In 1957, the contracting parties established a Panel of Experts, composed of Roberto de Oliveira Campos, Gottfried Haberler, James Meade and Jan Tinbergen, to prepare a report on agricultural protectionism, extreme fluctuations in the prices of primary products, and the failure of developing countries to expand exports at a rate commensurate with their import needs (GATT, 1958). The panel was chaired by Haberler, and its report led in 1958 to the initiation by the contracting parties of the three-pronged 'Program for Expansion of International Trade', whose three committees dealt with tariff reductions, agricultural protection and other obstacles to trade, particularly trade of developing countries. The work of these committees was the focal point of much of GATT activity during subsequent years and led, *inter alia*, to the 1960–2 Dillon Round of tariff negotiations. Whatever the impact of the Haberler Report, it was requested by and submitted to the governments of the contracting parties, and therefore it should have influenced their policy considerations.

In 1983, Arthur Dunkel, the Director-General of GATT, commissioned seven eminent persons, Bill Bradley, Pehr Gyllenhammar, Guy Ladreit de Lacharrière, Fritz Leutwiler, I. G. Patel, Mario Henrique Simonsen and Sumitro Djojohadikusumo, to study and report on problems facing the international trading system. Again, the GATT Secretariat assisted the panel in the drafting of its report. Although not all members of the group, which was chaired by Leutwiler, consider themselves to be economists, their unanimous recommendations are soundly based on economic principles. For example, they proposed that the costs and benefits of countries' trade-policy actions should be analyzed in a 'protection' balance sheet; that no special treatment for particular countries or commodities should be included in rules for agricultural trade; that trade in textiles and clothing should be fully subject to the ordinary rules of the GATT; that the rules permitting customs unions and free-trade areas need to be clarified and tightened up, so as to prevent further erosion of the multilateral trading system; that safeguard measures for particular industries should not discriminate between different suppliers, should be time-limited, and should be linked to adjustment assistance, and should be subject to continuing surveillance; that developing countries should be integrated more fully into the trading system; that ways and means of expanding trade in services should be explored; and that a new round of multilateral GATT negotiations should be launched (GATT, 1985). Not surprisingly, this report did not receive the universal acclamation of the contracting parties, because it recommended politically difficult actions by most of them. Nevertheless, the Uruguay Round was launched in 1986, and its agenda for negotiations closely resembles the substance of the Leutwiler Report.

CONCLUSIONS

The extent of the influence of economists on the GATT probably falls short of Keynes's omnipotent characterization of the power of their ideas, but it is clear that economists have been an important force – in the liberal origins of the GATT in US trade policy, in the text of the agreement itself, and in subsequent rounds of trade negotiations. It is also evident that economists have not had a free hand, reflecting the fact that GATT is very much a political as well as an economic animal.

It is generally recognized that the remarkable and highly favorable contrast between the world economy of the past forty years as compared with the interwar period would not have been possible without the guiding economic principles of the GATT. Eric Wyndham-White (1956) may have put it best:

> . . . It can, I think, be confidently asserted that the GATT has come to have a continuous and powerful influence on national policies. In some respects this has come to be almost embarrassing. One of the continuing influences of the GATT lies in its use by national administrations as a basis for resisting undesirable developments. It is used by the national administrations in many countries to oppose tendencies in their own countries which they themselves do not agree with. Very often it proves politically easier to oppose sectional interests by citing clear and specific international obligations rather than by more sophisticated and complicated arguments of the national interest. This of course has the unwelcome effect of attracting powerful animosities and resentments to the GATT. In a large number of countries the GATT has become widely known both to public opinion and to private interests as something which interferes with the freedom of national policies. It all too rarely occurs to these same observers that the restraint works to their advantage, when the GATT rules operate to restrain harmful actions in other countries. Moreover, the principal beneficiary of the activities of the GATT is the

consumer, the least organized of all the social classes. The GATT, then, is influential but tends to pay a high price in terms of general unpopularity. At the same time there is a much wider acceptance today of the basic philosophy of the General Agreement. The General Agreement is, therefore, less widely regarded as an expression of theory and doctrine, and increasingly accepted as a practical and useful institution based on experience and realism.

What might be done to enhance the role of the economist in the GATT? The question presumes that such enhancement would be desirable. But the Director-General and his Deputies, the officials ultimately responsible for economic policy in the Secretariat, should not be, or at least should not act like, academic economists. The result would be the alienation of the economic and political realists who represent their governments and whose cooperation is essential to achieve practical results. It would also label the GATT as an ideological free-trade organization, to be written off in the serious consideration of politically acceptable, alternative policy decisions. Much better is for the Secretariat to keep pointing in the liberal trade direction and in a low-key manner, over time, to move a little bit more forward than backward. It's the net that counts! This is what effective, liberally oriented economists, both in and outside the Secretariat, have been doing for years. That is why the GATT with all of its defects has been the most successful trade organization in the history of the world economy.

The future of GATT and of the world trading system is now in jeopardy. Economists have a role, indeed an obligation, to explain and demonstrate at every opportunity the economic benefits of a liberal trade regime and the economic costs of protectionist measures and of a world without trade rules. The beggar-thy-neighbor world of the 1930s had drastic results for all concerned. But the promulgation and communication of this vital message should not require any fundamental institutional change in the role of economists. It is to be hoped, however, that they will be more successful than the 1,000 petitioners of 1930.

NOTES

1. Sir Alec Cairncross has said that this 'way of thinking' is the economist's biggest single advantage (Cairncross, 1985, p. 4).
2. For a detailed discussion of the origins of US commercial policy see Kelly (1963).
3. The term 'reciprocity' has been reinterpreted in recent US legislative proposals to mean a unilateral determination of whether access to a foreign market is substantially equivalent to the access provided by the US market and unilateral retaliatory measures to correct any imbalance. This concept is unique and at variance with the GATT.
4. In commenting on the recruitment of personnel, Charles Kindleberger (1955, p. 349) has said that an international organization can 'succeed in getting the best talent available; it can permit discards from the national civil service to be foisted

off on it; or it can, in the course of hiring, acquire an average level of national talent'. In this respect, the GATT does not have a perfect score, but by and large it meets Kindleberger's first criterion.

BIBLIOGRAPHY

Brown, William Adams Jr., *The United States and the Restoration of World Trade*, an analysis and appraisal of the ITO Charter and the General Agreement on Tariffs and Trade (Washington, DC: The Brookings Institution, 1950).

Cairncross, Sir Alec, 'Economics in theory and practice', *The American Economic Review*, vol. 75, no. 2 (May, 1985).

de Grauwe, Paul, 'OECD versus the GATT on the source of inflation', *The World Economy*, vol. 4, no. 2 (June 1981).

GATT, *Studies in International Trade*: No. 1 – Industrial Pollution Control and International Trade (July 1971); No. 2 – Japan's Economic Expansion and Foreign Trade, 1955 to 1970 (July 1971); No. 3 – Trends in United States Merchandise Trade, 1953–1970 (July 1972); No. 4 – Specific Duties, Inflation, and Floating Currencies (November 1977); No. 5 – Trade Liberalization, Protectionism, and Interdependence (November 1977); No. 6 – Adjustment, Trade, and Growth in Developed and Developing Countries (September 1978); No. 7 – Networks of World Trade, by Areas and Commodity Classes, 1955–1976 (1978); No. 8 – Trade Relations under Flexible Exchange Rates (September 1980).

GATT, *Trends in International Trade*, a report by a panel of experts (Geneva, October 1958).

GATT, *International Trade, 1976/77* (Geneva, 1977).

GATT, *Textiles and Clothing in the World Economy* (Geneva, July 1984).

GATT, *Trade Policies for a Better Future*, proposals for action (Geneva, March 1985).

GATT, Ministerial Declaration (20 September 1986).

IMF, *Exchange Rate Volatility and World Trade*, Occasional Paper No. 28 (Washington, DC, July 1984).

Johnson, Harry G. 'Canada in a changing world', *International Journal* (Toronto, Winter 1962–3).

Kelly, William B. Jr. (ed.), *Studies in United States Commercial Policy* (Chapel Hill: University of North Carolina Press, 1963).

Keynes, John Maynard, *The General Theory of Employment, Interest and Money* (London: Macmillan, 1949).

Kindleberger, Charles P., 'Economists in international organizations', *International Organization*, vol. 9 (1955).

Meade, James E., *The Theory of Customs Unions* (Amsterdam: North-Holland Publishing Company, 1955).

Stigler, George J., 'Do economists matter?', *Southern Economic Journal*, vol. 42, no. 3 (January 1976).

US Tariff Commission, *Reciprocity and Commercial Treaties* (Washington, DC, 1919).

Viner, Jacob, *Dumping: A Problem in International Trade* (Chicago: University of Chicago Press, 1923).

Viner, Jacob, *The Customs Union Issue* (New York: Carnegie Endowment for International Peace, 1950).

Wolf, Martin, 'Tower of Babel: conflicting ideologies of adjustment', *The World Economy*, vol. 2, no. 4 (February 1980).

Wyndham-White, Eric, 'The achievements of the GATT', address at the Graduate Institute of International Studies, University of Geneva (December 1956).

INDEX

academic economists and government
  Argentina, 195–9
  Austria, 94, 95
  Canada, 144
  Colombia, 226
  France, 74–7
  Germany, 48–9
  Japan, 173
  UK, 35
Adams, F. G., 261
Adenauer, Konrad, 55
administration and economists
  Austria, 97–102
  Canada, 126–7, 144–5
  France, 75–7
  Germany, 55–8
  Japan, 174–5
  UK, 36–7
Aguilar, A. M., 158
Ahumada, J., 197
Alberro, José-Luis, vii, 12, 147–68
Albert, Michel, vii, 73–88
Alexander, Sidney S., 239
Allais, Maurice, 75, 282
Anderson, Sir John, 28
Androsch, Hannes, 106
Argentina, 195–212
  academic economists and government, 195–9
  Austral Plan, 206–7
  effectiveness of economic advisers, 203–7
  Federal Council of Investments (CFI), 197, 198
  influence of economic advisers, 207–9
  Krieger–Vasena plan, 205–6
  Ministry of the Economy, 12, 196, 207–8
  National Development Council (CONADE), 197, 198–9, 207
  organization of economic advisers, 199–203
  policy formulation, 204–7
  Political Economy Association (AAEP), 196–7
  politics and economic advice, 12
Arnaudo, A., 197
Arriazu, R., 200
Atlantic Charter, 304
Austria, 6, 89–106
  academic economists and government, 94, 95
  administration and economists, 97–102
  Council of Social and Economic Affairs, 9, 102–5
  government, 89–90
  influence of economic advisers, 95
  Institute of Advanced Studies (IHS), 94
  Institute of Economic Research (WIFO), 101–2
  Keynesianism, 6, 90–2
  organization of economic advisers, 95–106
  politics and economic advice, 93

Balassa, Bela, 158–9, 279, 287
Balboa, Manuel, 196, 200
Balogh, Thomas, Lord, 33, 42
Barre, Raymond, 75, 84
Bayne, N., 271
Beckerath, Erwin von, 48
Benassy, J. P., 83
Berlin, Sir Isaiah, 149
Beveridge, William, 26
Black, Eugene, 245
Blackaby, F., 267
Blackhurst, Richard, 312
Blanchard, Olivier, 290
Böhm, Franz, 48, 59
Böhm-Bawerk, Eugen von, 96
Boiteux, Marcel, 75
Boulding, Kenneth, 301
Bradley, Bill, 314
Brandt, Willi, 54
Bretton Woods agreement, 6, 16, 231, 260, 265–7, 275, 307
Bridges, Edward, 29
Broggi, H., 196
Brothers, D., 157
Brown, William Adams, Jr, 304
Bruno, M., 259
Bunge, Alejandro E., 196

Cairncross, Sir Alec, vii, 3, 13–14, 25–45, 251, 295
Campion, Harry, 27
Campos, Roberto de Oliveira, 314
Canada, 9, 14–15, 125–45

Canada (*continued*)
academic economists and government, 144
administration and economists, 126–7, 144–5
Bank of Canada, 130, 137–8
Department of Finance, 130, 138–9
Economic Council, 5–6, 128–9, 141–2
effectiveness of economic advisers, 131–2, 137
energy policy, 132–6
inflation, 14–15, 137–8
influence of economic advisers, 131, 137
macroeconomic policy, 136–9
organization of economic advisers, 126–9
politics and economic advice, 143
program and expenditure management, 139–41
Royal Commissions, 128
Candessus, M., 85
Carmona, F., 156
Carranza, R., 207
Carter, Jimmy, 113, 121
Catto, Sir Thomas, 29
Chapman, Sir Sydney, 26
Chenery, Hollis, 223
Cherwell, Lord, 42
China, People's Republic of, 19
Clay, Henry, 27–8
Clerk, Colin, 26
Coats, A. W., 1
Colombia, 11–12, 213–27
academic economists and government, 226
Budget Office, 218
Central Bank, 219–20, 223
Commission on Public Expenditure, 224
Council of Economic Advisers to the President, 219, 226
Council of National Economic and Social Politics, 219
effectiveness of economic advisers, 222–4
Finance Ministry, 218
growth, 214
influence of economic advisers, 217, 222–4
Monetary Authority, 216, 218, 220
National Planning Agency, 218, 223
organization of economic advisers, 218–21
policy formulation, 216–18
politics and economic advice, 12, 215–18
Corden, Max M., 292
Cordera, R., 158
Cornejo, Benjamin, 196
Cournot, A., 75
Cripps, Stafford, 30
Currie, Lauchlin, vii, 11, 213–27

Daley, Sean, 73
Dalton, Hugh, 29–30
de Gaulle, Charles, 280
de Grauwe, Paul, 313
Delors, Jacques, 77, 84, 87
Denton, Geoffrey R., 287
deregulation, 18–19
Devons, Ely, 28, 44
Dieulefait, Carlos Eugenio, 196
Diz, Adolfo Cesar, 197, 200
Djojohadikusomo, Sumitro, 314
Dow, J. C. R., vii, 16, 255–77
Dunkel, Arthur, 314
Dupuit, J., 75

Economic Commission for Latin America, 155, 197–8
economists in government, 1–22
1930s and 1940s, 3–7
1960s, 7–10
1970s and 1980s, 10–15
today, 17–19
Argentina, 195–212
Austria, 89–106
Canada, 125–45
Colombia, 213–27
EEC, 279–97
France, 73–88
GATT, 301–17
Germany, 47–65
IMF, 231–53
influence (*q.v.*) of, 20–2
international organizations, 15–17
Japan, 173–90
Mexico, 147–68
OECD, 255–77
organization (*q.v.*) of, 2–6
and politics (*q.v.*), 13, 18
UK, 25–45
USA, 109–24
World Bank, 231–53
see also academic economists; administration; effectiveness; policy formulation
effectiveness of economic advisers
Argentina, 203–7
Canada, 131–2, 137
Colombia, 222–4
France, 81–8
Germany, 58–63
Mexico, 162–7
UK, 37–40
USA, 117–22
Elizalde, Felix, 203
Emerson, Michael, 289–90

Erhard, Ludwig, 4, 47–51, 54–5, 59, 282, 287
Eucken, Walter, 48
European Economic Community (EEC), 16, 258, 279–97
  Action Programme, 283, 287
  aims, 258, 279
  Economic and Monetary Union (EMU), 283, 288–94
  economists in, 283–6
  European Monetary System (EMS), 279, 293–4
  forecasting, 51
  and France, 16, 290
  future, 295–7
  and Germany, 16, 290
  'locomotive' to cooperative strategy, 290–1
  origins, 5, 281, 286
  planning *vs.* markets, 287–8
  policy coordination, 281–3, 286–91
  Schuman Plan, 281
  Spaak Report, 281
  trade, 305–6
  Treaty of Rome, 279, 282, 284
  and UK, 39, 294, 296
  Werner Report, 283, 289, 291–2
European Free Trade Association (EFTA), 305–6

Ferrer, Aldo, 156
Flores de la Peña, H., 156
Folcini, E., 200
Ford, Gerald, 113
forecasting
  EEC, 51
  France, 77
  OECD, 261–4
Fourastié, J., 85
Fracchia, Alberto, 196
France, 73–88
  academic economists and government, 74–7
  administration and economists, 75–7
  Bank of France, 79
  budget preparation, 81–3
  Commission on Competition, 79
  Commission of Planning, 80
  Economic and Social Council (CES), 77–8
  and EEC, 16
  effectiveness of economic advisers, 81–8
  forecasting, 77
  government, 78–80
  income distribution, 83–5
  influence of economic advisers, 73–7, 87
  National Institute of Statistics and Economic Studies (INSEE), 75, 76–7
  National School of Administration (ENA), 5, 75–6, 79
  organization of economic advisers, 77–80
  working time reduction, 85–6
Franco, General Francisco, 245
Frank, Isaiah, 251
Freiburg School, 4, 48
Friedman, Milton, 3

Gaitskell, Hugh, 38
Garner, Robert L., 245
General Agreement on Tariffs and Trade (GATT), 6, 15, 266, 301–17
  antidumping and countervailing duties, 309–10
  basis, 304
  Dillon Round, 282
  infant industries, 310
  and inflation, 313
  influence, 315–16
  influence of economic advisers, 301–2
  Kennedy Round, 282, 308
  most-favored-nation (MFN) treatment, 303, 305–6, 307
  negotiated tariff reduction, 307–9
  Operating Divisions, 311–12
  organization, 310–15
  origins, 302–4
  and politics, 302
  and quantitative restrictions, 306–7
  Research Unit, 312
  Secretariat, 310–15
  subversion of, 15, 266
  Tokyo Round, 302, 308
  Uruguay Round, 302, 313, 315
Generalized System of Preferences (GSP), 306
Germany, Federal Republic of, 47–65
  academic economists and government, 48–9
  administration and economists, 55–8
  Agricultural Advisory Council, 50
  Chancellors, 53–4, 64–5
  Commission on Economic and Social Change, 50
  Council of Economic Experts, 8–9, 50–3, 55–62, 69
  Council of Experts for Environmental Issues, 52–3, 69
  Economic Advisory Council, 4, 58–9, 69
  and EEC, 16
  effectiveness of economic advisers, 58–63
  Finance Advisory Council, 4, 49, 58, 59, 69
  German Institute for Economic Research (DIW), 49, 71

Germany, Federal Republic of (*continued*)
  government, 47
  HWWA-Institute for Economic Research, 49, 71
  IFO-Institute for Economic Research, 49, 72
  influence of economic advisers, 53, 62–5
  Institute of World Economics, Kiel University (IfW), 49, 71
  Monopolies Commission, 52, 62, 70
  organization of economic advisers, 49–53
  politics and economic advice, 53
  postwar, 47–9
  Rhine-Westphalia Institute for Economic Research, 49–50, 72
  Social Security Advisory Council, 50, 62, 70
  Stability and Growth Act, 52, 58
  trade unions, 56–7, 72
Giersch, Herbert, 55, 292, 296
Giscard d'Estaing, Valery, 293
Gomez, R., 157
Gondra, Luis Roque, 196
Goode, Richard, vii, 6, 15, 231–53
Goodman, John C., 19
Griffiths, Brian, 42–3
Guadagni, Alieto Aldo, 198, 202–3
Guitton, Professor H., 74
Gyllenhammar, Pehr, 314

Haberler, Gottfried, 314
Hague, Sir Douglas, 43
Hall, Robert, 30, 38
Hallstein, Walter, 281, 287, 295
Hamada, K., 266
Hansen, Bent, 260
Hanson, James, 213n
Harding, Harry, 19
Hawtrey, R. G., 26
Hayek, Friedrich von, 101
Heath, Edward, 41
Heller, Walter W., 8, 118, 179, 257
Hemming, Francis, 27
Henderson, David, 44, 73, 216
Henderson, Hubert, 26–9
Hirschman, Albert, 145, 251
Hull, Cordell, 304

Ibarra, David, vii, 12, 147–68
Ikeda, Prime Minister Hayato, 183
Illia, President Arturo, 207
inflation, 11–15
  Canada, 137–8
  GATT and OECD, 313
  Mexico, 164–6
  UK, 40
  USA, 11, 14, 119–21
influence of economic advisers, 20–2
  Argentina, 207–9
  Austria, 95
  Canada, 131, 137
  Colombia, 217, 222–4
  France, 73–7, 87
  GATT, 301–2, 315–16
  Germany, 53, 62–5
  Japan, 178–9, 187–8
  Mexico, 167–8
  UK, 44
  USA, 101–17, 122–4
  World Bank and IMF, 243–8, 252, 266
International Bank for Reconstruction and Development *see* World Bank
International Monetary Fund (IMF), 6, 16, 231–53
  and Argentina, 222–3
  and Austria, 92
  consultations, 236–7
  and economists, 231–5
  and India, 240
  influence on policy, 252, 266
  and Mexico, 151, 165, 250
  technical assistance, 240–1
  and Turkey, 239–40
  use of resources, 237–40
Izquierdo, R., 158

Jacobsson, Per, 232
Japan, 13, 173–90
  academic economists and government, 173
  administration and economists, 174–5
  Bank of Japan, 176
  Economic Council, 180, 182–3, 190
  Economic Planning Agency (EPA), 5, 173–6, 179, 182, 190
  economic plans, 7–8, 178, 179–84, 189
  Economic Stabilization Board, 177–8
  government economists, 174–5
  imbalances, 185–7
  influence of economic advisers, 178–9, 187–8
  Ministry of Finance (MOF), 5, 173, 176
  Ministry of International Trade and Industry (MITI), 5, 173, 176
  organization of economic advisers, 173–7, 190
  policy formulation, 175–6, 184–8
Jeanneney, Jean-Marcel, 75
Jenkins, Roy, 293
Jewkes, John, 27–8
Johansen, L., 266
Johnson, Harry G., 308
Johnson, Lyndon B., 113, 118–19

Kaldor, Nicholas, Lord, 33, 38–9, 157
Kamarck, Andrew M., vii, 6, 15, 231–53

Kamitz, Reinhardt, 96, 105–6
Kelly, William B., vii, 15, 301–17
Kennedy, John F., 8, 110, 113, 118–19
Keynes, John Maynard, ix, 1, 6, 26, 29, 301, 315
Keynesianism, 3–4, 11
  Austria, 6, 90–2
  Mexico, 9, 155, 158
Kiesinger, Kurt Georg, 54
Kishi, Prime Minister Nobusuke, 183
Klaus, Josef, 106
Kloten, Norbert, vii, 4, 47–65
Koeunen, Jean-Claude, 293
Koren, Stephan, 96
Kreisky, Bruno, 106
Krieger-Vasena, Adalbert, 201, 207

Lacharrière, Guy Ladreit de, 314
Lacina, Ferdinand, 105
Layton, Walter, 26
Lazarsfeld, Paul, 94
Leith-Ross, Sir Frederick, 27, 29
Lesourne, Jacques, 75
Leutwiler, Fritz, 314
Lewis, Sir Arthur, 246
Licciardo, Cayetano Antonio, 201
Lindblom, C. E., 149
Llewellyn, John, 259, 262–3, 270, 290
Lopez Portillo, President José, 160

McCracken, Paul, 260–1
Machlup, Fritz, 281
Macmahon, Kit, 37
McNamara, Robert S., 247, 250–1
Magnifico, Giovanni, 292
Malinvaud, Edmond, 75, 76, 83, 259
Mallon, R. D., 199
Marjolin, Robert, 75
market mechanism, 19
Marris, Stephen N., 261, 285
Marshall Plan, 6
Martinez de Hoz, José Alfredo, 200
Mason, E. S., 251
Masse, Pierre, 75, 87–8
Mauroy, Pierre, 84, 85
Maynard, G., 199
Meade, James E., 4, 29–31, 281, 304–5, 314
Melitz, Jacques, 294
Mendes-France, Pierre, 81
Menzies, Sir Robert, 245
Mexico, 9, 12–13, 147–68
  Bank of Mexico, 152, 156
  Commerce and Industrial Promotion Secretariat (SECOFI), 152
  Economic Cabinet, 153
  effectiveness of economic advisers, 162–7
  Energy, Mines and Parastate Industry Secretariat (SEMIP), 152, 154
  ideology, 150–1
  inflation, 164–6
  influence of economic advisers, 167–8
  Intersecretariat Commission, 9, 153, 157
  Keynesianism, 9, 155, 158
  organization of economic advisers, 151–5
  policy formulation, 155–62, 167–8
  politics and economic advice, 12, 148–51, 154–5, 160
  President's Council of Economic Advisers, 153
  Programming and Budget Secretariat (SPP), 152, 154, 161
  Spending and Finance Commission, 153
  Treasury Secretariat (SHCP), 152, 154, 156
Meyer, Fritz, W., 59
Meyer-zu-Schlochtern, F., 261
Miller, M. H., 266
Mises, Ludwig von, 101, 105
Mitterrand, François, 290
Monnet, Jean, 5, 77, 87
Morgenstern, Oskar, 94, 101
Morrison, Herbert, 29–30
most-favored-nation (MFN) treatment, 303, 305–6, 307
Mújica, E., 157
Müller-Armack, Alfred, 48
Multifiber Arrangement (MFA), 312–13
Musgrave, Richard, 222–3

Nakasone, Prime Minister Yashuhiro, 176
Navarrete, A., 157
Neild, Robert, 33
Nelson, Robert H., vii, 1–22
Nemschak, Franz, 101
Nixon, Richard M., 113, 120–2
Nourse, Edwin, 109
Noyola, J., 157
Nußbaumer, Adolf, 96

Ohkawa, Kazushi, 180
Okita, Saburo, viii, 5, 7, 13, 173–90
Olivera, Julio H. G., 196
Olson, Mancur, 154, 282
Oort, Conrad J., 292
Organization of American States (OAS), 155, 157
organization of economic advisers, 2–6
  Argentina, 199–203
  Austria, 95–106
  Canada, 126–9
  Colombia, 218–21
  France, 77–80
  Germany, 49–53
  Japan, 173–7, 190
  Mexico, 151–5

organization of economic advisers (*continued*)
UK, 35–6, 41–2
USA, 111–17
Organization for Economic Cooperation and Development (OECD), 6, 16, 255–77
and Austria, 92,
Bonn Summit, 271–2
Economic and Development Review Committee, 257
Economic Policy Committee, 257
forecasting, 261–4
influences on policy, 265–74
and oil crisis, 270–2
organization, 256–8
publications, 259–61
Smithsonian Agreement, 264–5, 268–9
and UK, 267–8
Orive, A., 158
Oritz Mena, A., 156–8
Oudiz, G., 266

Padoa-Schioppa, Tommaso, 285, 294
Pani, Alberto J., 152
Parkin, Michael, 292
Pastore, José Maria Dagnino, viii, 12, 195–212
Patel, I. G., 314
Pechman, Joseph A., viii, ix–xi, 14, 109–24
Pinedo, Federico, 196
Plowden, Sir Edwin, 30
Polak, J. J., 238
policy formulation
Argentina, 204–7
Canada, 132–41
Colombia, 216–18
EEC influence, 281–3, 286–91
Japan, 175–6, 184–8
Mexico, 155–62, 167–8
OECD influence, 265–74
UK, 29–30, 32, 40–3
USA, 112–17
World Bank and IMF influence, 243–8, 252
politics and economic advice, 13, 18
Argentina, 12
Austria, 93
Canada, 143
Colombia, 12, 215–18
GATT, 302
Germany, 53
Mexico, 12, 148–51, 154–5, 160
UK, 43
USA, 114
Popescu, Oreste, 196
Prebisch, Raul, 196
Putnam, R. D., 271
Pütz, Theodor, 94

Radcliffe Committee, 239
Reagan, Ronald, 113, 121–3
Robbins, Lionel, 3–4, 28
Robertson, Dennis, 26
Robinson, Austin, 28
Roosa, Bob, 257
Röpke, Wilhelm, 48, 282
Rosenstein-Rodan, Paul, 38, 251
Roth, Gabriel, 19
Rothschild, Kurt, 94
Rothschild, Lord, 41
Rüstow, Alexander, 48

Sachs, J. D., 259, 266
Salcher, Herbert, 105
Salmon, M., 266
Salter, Arthur, 26
Samuelson, L., 261
Samuelson, Paul, 3
Schiller, Karl, 52, 56
Schmidt, Helmut, 53, 55–7
Schumacher, E. F., 216
Schumpeter, Joseph, 96
Scitovsky, Tibor, 281
sector-adjustment policy loans (SAPLs), 248–9
Seidel, Hans, viii, 9, 89–106
Siegel, B. N., 157
Simon, Sir John, 28
Simonsen, Mario Henrique, 314
Smith, Sir Hubert Llewellyn, 26
Smithsonian Agreement, 264–5, 268–9
Solis, L., 157, 159
Solomon, Anthony, 271–2
Souto, José Barral, 196
Spraos, J., 151
Stamp, Lord, 26–8
Steindl, Josef, 94
Stewart, Ian, viii, 15, 125–45
Stigler, George J., 301
Strauss, Franz-Josef, 56
Streeten, Paul, 251
structural adjustment loans (SALs), 248

Taucher, Wilhelm, 96
Taussig, Frank W., 303
Thatcher, Margaret, 39, 41, 280
Thurow, Lester, 183
Tinbergen, Jan, 314
trade *see* General Agreement on Tariffs and Trade
Triffin, Robert, 294
Tsuru, Shigeto, 177
Tumlir, Jan, 312

Ungerer, Horst, 294
Union of Soviet Socialist Republics (USSR), 19

United Kingdom (UK), 3–4, 13–14, 25–45
academic economists and government, 35
administration and economists, 36–7
Budget Committee, 30, 38
Central Economic Information Service, 27–8
Chief Economic Adviser, 26–7, 37
Department of Economic Affairs, 8, 32
Economic Advisory Council, 26
Economic Section, 4, 28–32, 33, 38
effectiveness of economic advisers, 37–40
financial policy *vs*. economic policy, 29–30, 32
Government Economic Service, 33–5, 40
inflation, 40
influence of economic advisers, 44
monetary policy, 39
National Economic Development Organization, 32
and OECD, 267–8
organization of economic advisers, 35–6, 41–2
policy formulation, 40–2
politics and economic advisers, 40–3
prime ministers, 41–2
publications, 44
taxation, 39
Treasury, 25, 29–30, 32, 41
World War II, 3–4
United States of America (USA), 109–25
Congressional Budget Office (CBO), 110–12, 114, 122
Council of Economic Advisers (CEA), 4, 8, 109, 111–14, 119, 122
deregulation, 18–19
effectiveness of economic advisers, 117–22
Federal Reserve System, 110, 111, 114–15, 122
and GATT, 303–4
inflation, 11, 14, 119–21
influence of economic advisers, 110–17, 122–4
investment/savings balances, 186–7
Joint Economic Committee, 110, 122
new economics, 118–19
Office of Management and Budget (OMB), 110, 111, 113, 116
organization of economic advisers, 111–17
Planning, Programming and Budgeting System (PPBS), 8
policy formulation, 112–17
politics and economic advice, 114
progressive movement, 19
Smithsonian Agreement, 264–5, 268–9
supply-side economics, 121–2
tariffs, 301, 302
Treasury, 111, 113, 122

Valsecchi, Francisco, 197
van den Bempt, Paul, 294
van Rijckeghem, W., 199
van Ypersele, Jacques, 293
Viner, Jacob, 305, 309
Volcker, Paul, 269
Vranitzky, Franz, 98

Walters, Sir Alan, 39, 42–3
Weber, Max, 53
Weber, Wilhelm, 94
Wegner, Manfred, viii, 16, 279–97
Werner, Pierre, 283, 289, 291–2
Williamson, John, 292
Wionczek, M. S., 158
Witteveen, H. J., 232
Wolf, Martin, 313
Woods, George, 250
World Bank (International Bank for Reconstruction and Development), 6, 15–16, 231–53
and Africa, 245–6
and Argentina, 220, 222, 226
and economists, 231–5
and India, 246
influences on policy, 243–8
and Mexico, 165
and planning, 155
and Spain, 245
technical assistance, 250–1
World War II, 3, 10
Wyndham-White, Eric, 314–16

Yajima, A., 261
Younés, Y., 83